Project
Management

Project Management

Editor

PAUL C. TINNIRELLO

CRC Press
Taylor & Francis Group
Boca Raton London New York

CRC Press is an imprint of the
Taylor & Francis Group, an **informa** business

First published 1999 by Auerbach Publications
Taylor & Francis Group
6000 Broken Sound Parkway NW, Suite 300
Boca Raton, FL 33487-2742

Reissued 2018 by CRC Press

© 1999 by Taylor & Francis
CRC Press is an imprint of Taylor & Francis Group, an Informa business

No claim to original U.S. Government works

A Library of Congress record exists under LC control number: 99024921

Publisher's Note
The publisher has gone to great lengths to ensure the quality of this reprint but points out that some imperfections in the original copies may be apparent.

Disclaimer
The publisher has made every effort to trace copyright holders and welcomes correspondence from those they have been unable to contact.

ISBN 13: 978-1-138-10562-1 (hbk)
ISBN 13: 978-0-203-71073-9 (ebk)

Visit the Taylor & Francis Web site at http://www.taylorandfrancis.com and the
CRC Press Web site at http://www.crcpress.com

Contributors

Kwasi Amoako-Gyampah, *Assistant Professor, Information Systems and Operations Management, University of North Carolina, Greensboro, NC*

Thomas B. Clark, *Executive Vice President, Young, Clark & Associates, Inc., Atlanta, GA*

James R. Coleman, *President, Yazoo Enterprises, Lawrenceville, GA*

Richard H. Deane, *Professor of Management, Georgia State University, Atlanta, GA*

Robert DeMichiell, *Chair, Department of Information Systems, Fairfield University, Fairfield, CT.*

Dana T., Edberg, *Assistant Professor, Computer Information Systems, University of Nevada, Reno, Reno, NV*

Raoul J. Freeman, *Professor and Chair, Computer Information Systems, California State University–Dominguez Hills, Dominguez Hills, CA*

Frederick Gallegos, *MSBA-IS Audit Advisor and Faculty Member, Computer Information Systems Department, California State Polytechnic University, Pomona, Pomona, CA*

Michael L. Gibson, *Professor of Management, Auburn University, Auburn, AL*

Fritz H. Grupe, *Associate Professor, Computer Information Systems, University of Nevada, Reno, NV*

Carl Stephen Guynes, *Professor, College of Business Administration, University of North Texas, Denton, TX*

Pamela Hager, *Principal Instructor and Consultant, Russell Martin and Associates, St. Louis, MO*

Richard D. Hays, *President, Hays Consulting, Sarasota, FL*

Abbas Heiat, *Associate Professor, Information Systems, Montana State University, Billings, MT*

Joseph Judenberg, *Manager of Outsourcing, Coopers & Lybrand Consulting, New York, NY*

Leon A. Kappelman, *Department of Business Computer Information Systems, University of North Texas, Denton, TX*

Naomi Karten, *President, Karten Associates, Randolph, MA*

Mark M. Klein, *Senior Vice President and Managing Director, Management Consulting Services, Gateway*

Ralph L. Kliem, *Co-Founder, Practical Creative Solutions, Inc., Redmond, WA*

ROBERT F. KNIESTEDT, *Independent Consultant, St. Louis, MO*

RICHARD W. KOONTZ, *President, Object Technologies Group, Eagan, MN*

WILLIAM N. LEDBETTER, *Professor of Management, Tuskegee University, Tuskegee, AL*

ALBERT L. LEDERER, *Professor, MIS and Ashland Oil Fellow, College of Business and Economics, University of Kentucky, Lexington, KY*

CLINTON O. LONGENECKER, *Stranahan Distinguished Professor of Management, University of Toledo, Toledo, OH*

IRWIN S. LUDIN, *Co-Founder, Practical Creative Solutions, Inc., Redmond, WA*

STEVE MAR, *Manager, KPMG Peat Marwick, San Francisco, CA*

ERWIN MARTINEZ, *Partner, CSC Consulting, San Francisco, CA*

DAVID M. MASSEY, *Director of Business Development, ISERV Co., Grand Rapids, MI*

HOWARD W. MILLER, *Managing Director, Information Technology Institute, Byfield, MA*

NANCY BLUMENSTALK MINGUS, *President, Mingus Associates, Inc., Buffalo, NY*

MARK MULIAS, *Vice President, Information Technology, Aeroquip Corp., Maumee, OH*

NATHAN J. MULLER, *Independent Consultant, Oxford, CT*

RAGHU NATH, *Professor, Graduate School of Business, University of Pittsburgh, Pittsburgh, PA*

POLLY PERRYMAN KUVER, *Independent Consultant, Stoughton, MA*

ROGER S. PRESSMAN, *President, R.S. Pressman & Associates, Inc., Orange, CT*

TOM L. ROBERTS, JR., *Assistant Professor, Middle Tennessee State University, Murfreesboro, TN*

LARRY D. RUNGE, *Chief Information Officer, Wheels, Inc., Des Plaines, IL*

CRAIG A. SCHILLER, *Senior Analyst, PARANET, Inc., Houston, TX*

S. YVONNE SCOTT, *IS Audit Manager, GATX Corp, Chicago, IL*

JACK L. SIMONETTI, *Professor, Management, University of Toledo, Toledo, OH*

STANLEY H. STAHL, *Managing Partner, Solution Dynamics, Los Angeles, CA*

CHRISTINE B. TAYNTOR, *Manager of Corporate Staff Applications, AlliedSignal, Inc., Morristown, NJ*

LOIDA TISON-DUALAN, *IS Audit Analyst, Price Waterhouse, Pomona, CA*

JON WILLIAM TOIGO, *Independent Writer and Consultant, Dunedin, FL*

ROBERT E. UMBAUGH, *Principal, Carlisle Consulting, Carslisle, PA*

JAMES A. WARD, *Independent Consultant, Hoboken, NJ*

KATHY B. WHITE, *Director of Information Management, AlliedSignal, Inc., Morristown, NJ*

JOHN WINDSOR, *Interim Chairman, Information Systems Department, College of Business Administration, University of North Texas, Denton, TX*

DUNCAN M. WITTE, *President, D.M. Witte and Associates, Inc., Plano, TX*

A.P. (DENNIS) YOUNG, *President, Young, Clark & Associates, Inc., Atlanta, GA*

Contents

Introduction

Business globalization, combined with the relentless change of new technology, continues to challenge our ability to adequately manage enterprise computing activities. Past efforts used to control the various aspects of system integration are no longer effective in today's diverse and complex information environments. The need for more competent project management techniques is paramount to the survival of those organizations who rely heavily on the benefits of computing technology. Thus, this book was developed to meet the requirements of those individuals who are responsible for managing the delivery of multifarious technical projects.

Effective project management is a formidable effort, and in comparison to other IS related tasks, it is frequently shrouded with perceptions rather than viewed as set of adjacent management principles. It is still surprising to find that many IS professionals often ignore basic concepts in an attempt to formalize a single approach that can handle the various facets associated with technical projects. In recognition of such perceptions, this book has been organized into five sections that cover a large spectrum of issues that traditionally exist within the project management framework.

Successful delivery of most IS applications requires a solid understanding of principles which are germane to the project management process. Section 1, 'Essentials of Project Management' provides the important background information to establish the necessary link between concepts and practice. Experienced IS professionals have learned how to apply the basic concepts regardless of the project. At the same time, it is equally important to acknowledge differences in project scope without blind adherence to the rules. The cost of ignoring sound management principles is typically disastrous, and in many cases occurs well into the schedule of a given project. Many professionals who fail at project management are either victims of rigid discipline or reckless experimentation. It is recommended that this section of the book be read initially, and then read again after completing the other sections.

A crucial component of project management is the ability to utilize human resources in meeting application goals. Section II, 'Establishing and

Strengthening Business Relationships,' offers numerous insights that can leverage the knowledge held by business experts and technical professionals. Historically, acquiring the skills needed to manage people had been less emphasized than having the skills to handle technical details. Although this may explain why IS professionals struggled with human relationships, it is no longer acceptable to remain as merely the technical agent. Clearly, the most successful project managers have mastered the art of working with diverse organizational types, including vendors, contractors and consultants. These important skills are not easily acquired and often need years of experience to cultivate. However, the information in this section of the book, can provide good insight and lessen the traditional time required to become proficient.

The shortages of skilled professionals, as well as the need to focus on core competencies, has prompted many, if not all, organizations to seek expertise beyond traditional boundaries. Section III, 'Effectively Managing Outsourced Projects', describes the unique challenges when using external resources to fulfill project objectives. While the promises of outsourcing have been well identified, there are many issues that still require the experience of project management. Merely outsourcing technical tasks does not guarantee successful completion, nor does it automatically ensure that the best interests of the project will be accomplished. Unfortunately some IS professionals abdicate their responsibilities when using external resources. This has caused numerous organizations to re-evaluate procedures when engaging in outsourcing activities. However, outsourcing will likely remain as a strong complement to internal resources needed in applications development. Understanding the appropriate risks and rewards for using outsourcing is now a mandatory part of any project management strategy.

Some projects are the function of unusual circumstances or occur less frequently than most other computing activities. These type of applications are described in Section IV, 'Planning and Controlling Special Projects,' and include various discussions on topics such as: system integration due to mergers or acquisitions, application reengineering, and the well-known Year 2000 conversion. Managing these unique types of projects can challenge even the most experienced and seasoned professional. Sometimes, there is a tendency to administer similar procedures as with more conventional projects and the results can be less favorable than expected. The most important aspect to remember in these situations is that project management should not be exercised with such regulation that it ignores the peculiar attributes of such one time projects. Examining the different projects described in this section can improve those project management skills required for future projects that may have less definable characteristics.

Project management cannot be viewed as a solitary management activity but rather a set of dynamic principles that can be cultivated and improved through practical experience. Ignoring the need for continuous improvement would be as detrimental as ignoring the basic principles for applying project management itself Section V. 'Measuring and Improving Project Management Success,' is offered as the last segment in the book. In some respects it could be considered the most significant portion of the book. On the other hand, it is yet another facet of the intricate process that defines the overall manner of project management. Despite the obvious need for managing projects and the necessity to improve the process, many organizations continue to fail in the consistent and repeatable application of project management principles. This may be due, in part, to the overwhelming difficulties of technical projects, partial success, or misunderstanding the evolution of the project management life cycle. Nevertheless, without a commitment to measurement, further improvements to project management efforts will stagnate and organizations will rely on ineffective techniques to manage computing activities. This section does not constitute the only recommendations for management growth, but it does focus on the specifics that apply to the development of hardware and software systems.

To use this book effectively, it is recommended that the reader complete Section I before proceeding to other areas. Several sections may examine the same topic, but from a different perspective. Some concepts can also be applied differently depending on the circumstances, so the reader is advised to evaluate the situation from various viewpoints, including those provided in the book. It is also suggested to reread several of the chapters in Section I in order to fully absorb the content of the underlying basic principles.

Planning the project management activities for the challenges of tomorrow's business environment will remain difficult, but not impossible. Opinions and predications about future computing technology or shifts in economic direction should be viewed cautiously, especially since many predications tend to confuse rather than aid in project management endeavors. For those of us who have earnestly pursued the rigors of managing projects, it has demanded the best of our skills, including the dedication to succeed. From my own experiences as a senior IS executive, I appreciate the challenges that project management poses in a time of rapid, yet exciting technical change. I hope this book provides you with many important concepts that add knowledge to your existing expertise, as well as provide you with the tenacity to improve your management skills.

Paul C. Tinnirello
Editor

Section I
Project Management Essentials

Chapter 1
Seven Steps for Highly Effective Project Management

Nancy Blumenstalk Mingus

IS departments are constantly being downsized or outsourced, therefore, well-run projects are vital to an IS professional's career. Carefully managing project details, including time and materials, is essential now that IS is being asked to deliver more using fewer resources. There are several effective, relatively inexpensive project management scheduling and tracking packages available for PCs. These types of packages have been around on mainframes since the early 1970s, though they cost hundreds of thousands of dollars. Today shareware packages start at under $100.

Many of these products assume a knowledge of project management that many technical managers do not have. Without an understanding of the basic concepts of project management, managers may find the software is sometimes confusing and hard to use.

PROJECT MANAGEMENT STEPS

All projects can be managed by following these seven basic steps:

- Break the project down into measurable tasks.
- Determine the inter-task dependencies.
- Assign lengths to each task.
- Assign resources (i.e., staff and equipment) to each task.
- Refine the plan.
- Communicate, revise, and update the project status regularly. Perform a post-implementation review.

Although these steps sound simple, the technical and interpersonal dynamics in most IS projects keep project managers on their toes. Resources change, project scope changes, and deadlines change. The following sections explain the key tasks in each step to keep projects on track.

0-8493-9998-X/00/$0.00+$.50
© 2000 by CRC Press LLC

Breaking Projects Down Into Measurable Tasks

The first step is to break the project down into a series of tasks and organize them into a hierarchy called the work breakdown structure (WBS). Different companies have different terms for the various levels in a WBS. Some levels include stages, steps, and tasks, or phases, activities, and tasks.

Regardless of terminology a company uses, the purpose of the WBS is to organize the project into various deliverable or summary reporting levels. Some of the traditional stage (or phase) levels in IS projects include:

- Project definition.
- Analysis.
- Design.
- Development.
- Testing.
- Implementing.
- Project review.

Whether a project has standard levels or not, the main purpose of these higher levels is to group the detail tasks, allowing project administrators to more easily track the project's progress.

Determining Inter-task Dependencies

Once the tasks have been listed and organized into a WBS, inter-task relationships need to be established. These relationships, also called dependencies or links, exist when the start or completion of one task is somehow related to the start or completion of another task.

There are three types of inter-task dependencies: finish–start, start–start, and finish-finish. The tasks that must be performed first are called the "predecessor tasks" and those that follow are "successor tasks."

Finish–Start. The finish–start relationship is the most common dependency relationship. In the finish–start relationship, the predecessor task must finish before the successor task can start. Some examples of this type of relationship include situations in which:

- Project definition must be done before analysis can start.
- Systems design must be done before coding can start.

Start-Start. The start–start relationship is a less common dependency relationship. In the start–start relationship, the predecessor task must start before the successor task can start.

This relationship is often erroneously interpreted as meaning that both tasks start at the same time, but that is not always true. An example of this type of relationship is a situation in which setting up interviews must have started before the interviews themselves can start.

Finish-Finish. The finish–finish relationship is also a less common dependency relationship. In the finish–finish relationship, the predecessor task must finish before the successor task can finish.

This relationship is often erroneously interpreted as meaning that both tasks finish at the same time. This type of relationship occurs when, for example, coding must finish before testing can finish or when systems testing must finish before implementation can be completed.

Assigning Task Lengths

There are two major ways to estimate the lengths (i.e., durations) of tasks. The simplest way is to estimate the elapsed time of a task.

If someone says it will take him a week to do a particular task, he is probably offering an elapsed-time estimate. They generally mean that it will take him one work week to get a task done, not that it will take them 40 hours. When estimating elapsed time, people generally account for not working on the project tasks full-time, and for working on other, higher-priority tasks first.

In most projects, however, lengths should be estimated based on the amount of work, not the amount of time. That way, adding resources will shorten a task, and using resources only part-time will lengthen a task. Tasks that fluctuate like this depending on the resources assigned are called resource-constrained tasks.

There are several ways to estimate the resource time for a task. One is to let the project manager calculate the estimates based on an employee's performance on similar tasks. Another is to let the employees performing the tasks calculate their estimates, generally based on how they performed on similar tasks. A third way to estimate is to use standard metrics for generic tasks.

Although many project managers like to follow the standards established by these generic metrics, their plans are generally more accurate when they and their employees do their own estimating. It usually takes three to five projects to become proficient, but the eventual accuracy is worth the delay. Sometimes tasks will not be resource-constrained and can be estimated based on the elapsed times. Examples would be training classes or project meetings. Even though two or more people may attend a class or meeting, the length of the task does not shorten. These types of tasks are called time-constrained.

Assigning Resources

If estimates are being provided from standard metrics or project managers, then resources (i.e., employees) should be assigned after task lengths are determined. If estimates are coming from the employees performing the tasks, obviously these steps will be reversed. Regardless of the order of these two steps, one or more employees should be picked for each task that is resource-constrained.

Employees assigned to multiple tasks are often scheduled for too much work while there are simultaneous tasks to complete and not enough work when there are no task assignments. To maintain a consistent workload, resources need to be "leveled." There are only two main ways to level resource allocations: by adjusting the task schedule or adjusting the resource assignments. Project management packages generally adjust the schedule to increase the amount of time it takes to finish the project.

Refining the Project Plan

Once the major portions of the project plan have been laid out, project administrators might want to refine it by adjusting the delay or overlap on task dependencies, or changing the scheduling type on noncritical tasks. Lower-end project management software is generally not capable of performing some or all of the refining techniques. If a particular technique is important to the project plans in an organization, project administrators must ensure that the software supports it.

Lead Time. A technique called lead time is used to represent partial dependencies. By using lead time, certain tasks can overlap by a fixed amount or by a percentage of the predecessor task. For example, a project plan might stipulate that testing can start when 30 percent of coding is finished. It can be thought of as the predecessor task getting a head start, or lead, before the successor task starts. Because the term is easy to confuse with lag time, lead time is also referred to as overlap or negative lag.

Lag Time. Lag time indicates time spent waiting for something to happen, such as waiting 30 days for a new computer or software to be delivered. Lag time is also referred to as gap.

Scheduling ASAP. ASAP means that a task will be scheduled to start as soon as possible based on dependencies and resource availability. Even if a task has a lot of slack, it is scheduled to start when the predecessors are all finished and when the resources are available. This is the way tasks should be scheduled. That way, if any of the tasks run late, there is still time to make up the delay.

Scheduling ALAP. Using ALAP, a task is scheduled to start as late as possible in the task's slack time. This sometimes helps reduce resource over-allocation. Project managers using this technique must be careful, however. Noncritical tasks that slip may become critical and affect the outcome of the project.

The most appropriate use for this type of scheduling is when a task might suffer if scheduled too early in the plan. For example, if project administrators are planning on baking a cake for the post-implementation celebration, this task would have no predecessors other than the go-ahead for production, but the cake would get a bit stale if it were baked a month or even a week in advance.

Baselines. A baseline is a static view of the plan at a given point. This view is used to help project administrators compare the actual times and costs of a project to the original estimates for the times and costs.

Baselines are taken once the plan has been finalized and before any actual figures are added. Baselines may also be taken when the scope of a project changes so drastically that the original estimates are irrelevant.

Communicating, Revising, and Updating Project Status

The only way to keep projects on time and on budget, and to better plan the next project, is to communicate the plan, revise the plan, and track the actual progress of the tasks in the plan. These are critical yet commonly neglected steps in project planning.

PERT Charts. In the late 1950s, project managers came up with a management tool they called the Program Evaluation and Review Technique (PERT). By creating PERT charts (also called network diagrams), project managers could determine how each task related to others in the plan, and they could calculate a target completion date. When used in combination with another method called Critical Path Method (CPM), PERT charts help a manager determine which tasks are likely to extend or shorten the plan and what financial risk is associated with extending or shortening the plan. Today, most people use this combined method and still call it PERT.

The basic premise of a PERT chart is that the completion of each detail task is represented by a circle or box, called a node. There are also nodes for the project start and the project finish. From the start node, arrows representing the task activities are drawn to the nodes, designating the task dependencies. Once all these dependency arrows are created, a variety of paths through the network can be seen leading to the finish.

Critical Path. A string of tasks representing the longest distance through the project is called the critical path. They are called critical tasks because any changes in the duration of any of these tasks will change the project duration. If a task lengthens, then the project lengthens. If a task shortens, the project shortens.

Slack Time. Tasks that have room for them to take longer than scheduled without affecting the plan deadline are said to have slack. There are two types of slack in any plan. "Free slack" is the amount of time a task can slip without delaying another task. "Total slack" is the amount of time a task can slip without delaying the project. Slack time is calculated from the PERT chart durations.

Gantt Charts. Henry Gantt invented his floating bar chart as a way to compare planned information to actual information. Even during the planning stage, though, the Gantt chart can be a useful tool because it is much easier to see task durations.

To create a Gantt chart, all tasks must be listed down the left side of a chart and a time scale should run across the top. The time scale can represent minutes, hours, days, weeks, months, even years, depending on the relative time frames in the project, although most Gantt charts use daily, weekly, or monthly time scales.

Once the project tasks and time scale have been entered, a line or bar should be drawn from the start date to the end date on each task. The first start date is determined from the project start, and subsequent start dates from the start of the first task and depend on the length of each task and any inter-task dependencies.

Many project management packages display task dependencies and the critical path on the Gantt chart, but traditional Gantt charts did not contain this information. Because this information is now available on Gantt charts, many project managers have stopped using PERT charts.

Monitoring Dates, Hours, and Costs. Once the original plan has been saved, either in hard copy if planning manually or stored as a baseline in an automated planning package, actual figures can now be tracked. Although the actual start and end dates are important, what is most important in terms of improving projects next time are the actual durations. Elapsed durations should be tracked for some of the tasks, but for most, actual hours should be tracked.

The temptation at this point, especially for harried project managers and team members, is to say that tasks started and ended as scheduled and took only as many hours as scheduled. In fact, tasks rarely go according to estimates, and unless project administrators track the actual hours correctly, they will never improve at planning subsequent projects.

Time Sheets. Status reports are good for recognizing potential problems caused by project scope shift and resource conflict, but to gather the fundamental details of times spent on tasks, some type of time sheet is needed. The most useful time sheet lists the tasks to be worked on, then leaves spaces for the actual hours per time period. The time period is usually daily, with a final column in which to put weekly totals.

Because project team members fill out these time sheets, they must understand how important it is to enter the actual times regardless of whether they are significantly over or under estimate. Again, if they do not provide accurate data, the current project may go fine, but the next one could be a disaster.

Post-Implementation Review

Of all the steps in the project planning process, the post-implementation review is the most often ignored. However, performing this step is the only way to improve project management skills.

Calculating Variances. Once the project is complete, project variances should be calculated. Although start date and end date variances may show when and how projects got off track, the real value is in calculating duration variances.

To do so, the baseline duration should be subtracted from the actual duration for each task. A negative number indicates that the project did better than estimated, whereas a positive number indicates that it was over its estimate.

In addition to calculating duration variances, project administrators may want to calculate budget variances. This works the same way — the baseline costs should be subtracted from the actual costs to arrive at the cost variance.

Evaluating Variances. There are several possible reasons for task variances, so once they have been calculated, project administrators need to determine what might have caused them. Looking for patterns in the numbers can help in evaluating the variances. If most of the overages are in one or two summary levels, the estimates are probably at fault. If most of the variances result from a specific employee's performance, then the person either needs help estimating or might need additional training on the assigned jobs.

Regardless of the reason for the variance, when the variances are significant, adjustments should be made to subsequent projects. In addition to performing these variance calculations, some type of final project meeting should be held to let the team rehash what went well and what went poorly in the project. Such a meeting allows the whole team to have a say in what should be fixed the next time around.

CONCLUSION

This chapter introduced the basic steps of project management and some of the common and more esoteric terms associated with project management software packages on the market today. It also pointed out some potential weaknesses in some of these packages. Once a project management team understands the basics of project management, its chances of finishing projects on time and on budget are greatly improved.

Chapter 2
Effective Systems Development Management: The Experts' Advise

Tom L. Roberts, Jr.
Michael L. Gibson
William N. Ledbetter

The effective management of systems development projects is an elusive goal for all systems development professionals. The industry has a poor track record in bringing projects in on schedule, within budget, and with full performance characteristics and capabilities. Many factors contribute to the success or failure of a systems development project. A systems development project is often a complex interplay of project management tools, systems development methodology, and CASE tools.

Every systems development project has individual characteristics and priorities that make the management of the project unique. For every project, systems development managers must adapt their management skills to the unique aspects of the project to maintain quality and the project schedule. Because this task is complex, it is no surprise that effective systems development can be so elusive.

To help systems development mangers better understand the complexities of systems development project management, twelve leading systems development experts were interviewed to give insight to systems development management. They were interviewed to help systems development managers identify the project management skills and areas needed to bring a project to a successful conclusion. Among the topics discussed in these interviews were: roles and responsibilities, the development process, and the use of automated tools.

0-8493-9998-X/00/$0.00+$.50
© 2000 by CRC Press LLC

THE INTERVIEWS

The authors selected the twelve experts by using citation lists, leading consultants mentioned in IS literature, and consultants who were members of a large non-profit organization of system professionals. All the individuals selected are very knowledgeable in systems development methodologies. The mix of experts includes external consultants and practicing system professionals, who may not be as well-known but have extensive experience in practical IS projects. The experts interviewed are:

- *Ed Yourdon,* Yourdon & Associates; consultant, author, methodologist
- *Garland Favorito,* consultant
- *Ken Orr,* Ken Orr & Associates; consultant, author, methodologist
- *Vaughan Merlyn,* Ernst & Young; consulting partner, author
- *Dr. Sami Albanna,* Yourdon & Associates; consulting manager
- *Donna Wicks,* consultant
- *Mike Rice,* Coopers & Lybrand; managing associate
- *Dennis Minnium,* Texas Instruments; IEF developer
- *John Riley,* Texas Instruments; national consulting practices manager, IEF
- *Rick Bastidas,* consultant
- *Susan Ball,* IDE Director, Educational and Consulting Services
- *Mariann Manzi,* Dun & Bradstreet Software; software development manager

The structured interview given to each expert was developed on the basis of reviewing systems development methodologies, CASE, and IS projects in existing MIS and computer science literature concerning systems development methodologies. The structured interview questions were open-ended and intended to prompt the experts to freely and more completely offer insight on their perspectives and experience in developing and using methodologies, using CASE, and participating in IS projects.

The interviews were either conducted in person or by telephone and lasted one to two hours. Each interviewer followed the same structured interview guide with little variation. All interviews were taped and transcribed to assure complete reconstruction of answers to each question.

The content of each interview was analyzed. The interviewers separately identified and extracted items of importance from each expert's interview. They then combined the set of extracted items from each interview into a single set for that interview. A second content analysis was performed across the twelve different combined sets of extracted items to derive the final set of combined items across all expert interviews. The results of the second content analysis were compiled and collectively evaluated.

The rest of this chapter examines the most important points from the interviews.

THE IMPORTANCE OF UNDERSTANDING LIFE CYCLE PHASES

Valuable Points from Experts

- One must understand the phases to use a methodology.
- The methodology will guide you through the life cycle phases.
- Preceding phases build products for succeeding phases.
- Knowing the deliverables of each phase is crucial.
- You must understand the phases to assure proper utilization of the methodology not in terms of fixed deliverables.

Discussion

A vital point of the experts is that a methodology cannot be used unless its life cycle phases are defined and understood. The organization should have some individuals who understand all of the phases. However, many specialists involved in the process may not necessarily need to know all of the details. Many of these specialists may only need to know methodology phase deliverables (i.e., the output of each phase). Understanding a methodology's deliverables is crucial to its use.

Knowledge of the life cycle phases should be a major focus in training of personnel using the process. Training programs should possess segments that provide explanations of each life cycle phase to personnel involved with the phase. The use of experienced personnel and expert consultants can also help in making sure that the individuals involved in the process understand the methodology.

UNDERSTANDING WHEN SOME LIFE CYCLE PHASES MAY BE SHORTENED

Valuable Points from Experts

- Laying out the project plan at the beginning of the project.
- Recognizing that there are a variety of different factors for particular projects.
- Realizing that alternative life cycles enable one to customize the life cycle to a particular project.
- Training everyone on the overall life cycle and life cycle phases.
- Understanding what happens if certain activities are deleted.
- Knowing the dangers of making everything optional.
- Realizing that typically the entire universal set of a methodology is not used on every project.
- Making the life cycle phases flexible.

Discussion

The project plan should be laid out at the beginning. This plan should put together the schedule and identify and allocate the resources necessary to complete the project. The methodology provides the basis for carrying out a project. It can be customized to an environment for new system development, enhancements, maintenance, or packaged software acquisition. Adaptability of any life cycle-based methodology is critical at the project level. In training, everyone involved needs to know the overall life cycle and individual life cycle phases, as well as pay particular attention to what happens if certain activities are deleted. An inherent danger exists in making too many of these activities optional.

For efficient use of a methodology, a systems development manager plans each individual project and customizes the portions of the methodology to be used for the project. The realization that every project has its own characteristics should be taken into account. The key is coordination between methodology and project specifics.

UNDERSTANDING WHO SHOULD BE INVOLVED IN CERTAIN PHASES

Valuable Points from Experts
- Key players are needed for required activities.
- Roles and responsibilities are keys to phases.
- Specialists with particular skills are needed for each phase.
- Understanding who is involved in changes over the life cycle of a project.
- Identifying who should be involved in specific phases provides ownership of a particular deliverable, and identifies roles and accountability.
- Not having the right people reduces system quality.

Discussion
Roles and responsibilities should be clearly defined for the project. Project success is based on having the right people with the proper skills at the appropriate time and place in the life cycle. Projects lacking people with the proper expertise are vulnerable to mistakes.

Coordination and efficient use of personnel by systems development managers is vital to successful project management. IS managers must decide upon the exact personnel needed to complete each phase of the project. These personnel decisions must be made before the start of the project during the project planning phase. Matching knowledge and expertise with methodology phases is essential to every project.

UNDERSTANDING THE REUSABILITY BETWEEN LIFE CYCLE PHASES

Valuable Points from Experts
- Realizing that the basis for any phase needs to be the deliverables from the previous phase.

- Making sure that one phase's deliverable is a clear communication document to the next phase.
- Understanding the transition between phases.
- Identifying reusable components.
- Making sure the life cycle used has full integration from phase to phase.
- Understanding that a full life cycle methodology is cumulative.
- Realizing that it is difficult to implement and control reusability.
- Having requirements traceability throughout the project to make sure original requirements are met.

Discussion

A full life cycle methodology should be integrated from stage to stage. The results of one stage should be used to start the next stage; without such integration, some type of bridge must be built. The only real reason to have a full life cycle methodology is its cumulative nature.

The successful IS project manager will realize the capabilities of a methodology and use them as adeptly as possible. Virtually every methodology contains components that may be reused from one life cycle phase to the next. It is the challenge of systems development managers to reuse as many components as possible to streamline a project. However, systems development managers should exhibit some measure of caution to control reusability to ensure quality. Requirements traceability is a must for satisfying this need.

MANAGEMENT INVOLVEMENT IN LIFE CYCLE PHASES

Valuable Points from Experts

- Having project champions from the business.
- Project management and management involvement all the way through project and methodology implementation.
- Each management level understanding their project roles.
- Upper management understanding that their role is to force the use of the methodology.
- Management keeping track of the deliverables.
- Management knowing what types of people from their organization are needed in the project.
- Creating an overall plan, a schedule, and a resource plan for the project.
- Management knowing what resources are needed from phase to phase.
- Management training on the methodology.
- Feedback to managers on projects.

Discussion

Project management is the critical role. Project management and management involvement must begin at the outset and stay current all the way through the project. Management's role is to force the use of the methodology. Management must believe in the life cycle-based methodology; otherwise, people will abandon it.

Additionally, the project will need a champion from the business user group to sell the project to end users. The champion should know what types of people from their organization are needed as the project progresses through the life cycle.

Management must realize the importance of its role for successful projects. The only way for a manager to guarantee project success is to get directly involved with the project. IS managers should make an effort to understand the technology involved with the methodology being used and an effort to sell the benefits of this technology to IS personnel.

MANAGEMENT'S TIME COMMITMENT FOR IMPLEMENTING THE METHODOLOGY

Valuable Points from Experts
- Management allowing enough time to implement the methodology.
- Management providing enough financial funding to implement the methodology.
- Management understanding the learning curve, decreased productivity, and limited benefits before a methodology takes hold.
- Management commitment of time, resources, and money as well as the process changes.
- Realizing that short-cuts will lead to lower quality.
- IS personnel realizing that management cannot wait too long.
- Management commitment to retraining personnel for the new methodology.

Discussion

Management must understand that they are tooling and re-tooling an IS factory. Commitment of learning curve time and resources is essential to implementing the methodology. Management must realize that the first few projects may increase in overall project completion time by several months. Adequate time to complete the project must be allowed, or short-cuts will be taken that cause problems for the whole process. The flip side is for management to not have to wait too long for project completion. If the methodology adds too much time to the process, then the project will probably never be started. As a result, it is best to have the first projects that are completed with the new methodology to be important projects that have a relatively short duration time.

Patience is the key to using new technology and methodologies. Systems development managers must focus on the project process. They must understand that the benefits from using the new methodology will be realized once the learning curve concerning the technology has been reached by IS personnel.

DEVOTING ENOUGH TIME TO PERFORMING THE MODELING ACTIVITIES

Valuable Points from Experts

- Understanding that enough time must be allocated or it is not worth attempting.
- Realizing that modeling takes a lot of time.
- Knowing enough time must be devoted to analyzing the area of study to determine what is necessary.
- Understanding that methodologies emphasize where to spend time.

Discussion

A methodology should place emphasis on where system personnel should spend time as opposed to where they would naturally spend the time. The process is going to take a lot of time, especially if staff members are going through classroom training. The learning curve on using the methodology for modeling will take a considerable amount of time.

Systems development managers should recognize that very few projects offer short-cuts to the system development process. Business and system modeling are vital components to system project success and performance. Many times, project schedules attempt to circumvent modeling activities to simply get a system completed. Every effort should be made by systems development managers to resist any attempts to take short-cuts to just simply get the system out of the door.

MANAGEMENT'S RESOURCE COMMITMENT TO IMPLEMENTING THE METHODOLOGY

Valuable Points from Experts

- Having a methodology coordinator to develop in-house training.
- Having a champion for the methodology.
- Management planning for the methodology implementation.
- Management bringing in consultants to help with the paradigm shift.
- Management understanding what resources are necessary.

Discussion

If IS does not commit time, people, and dollars, then it really does not have a commitment to the methodology. There must be a methodology coordinator who, among other activities, will develop in-house training. If there is no champion in an organization, methodology implementation will not be successful.

Systems development managers should focus their efforts on getting resources for the IS project. They should have an understanding of what resources are necessary for each particular project from the initial project planning phase. Once project specifics are known, managers should act as project champions in attempt to sell it to senior management. This championing of a project is an essential part of getting the resources needed for a successful project.

MANAGEMENT FOLLOWS THROUGH WITH THE PROCESSES

Valuable Points from Experts

- Upper management requiring that the methodology be followed.
- Management providing a method of measurement to show some measurable observable benefits to the developers.
- Management commitment to the methodology.
- Management following through with the implementation process.
- Management creating an implementation plan.
- Management understanding the need for investing in retraining and modernization.
- Project managers and IS personnel taking operational responsibility.
- Management realizing that a cultural change is not completed unless it is mandated, enforced, watched, and measured.

Discussion

False starts kill business; if management does not assume the responsibility for the process of implementing the methodology, then it will not be done. A cultural change is not completed unless it is mandated, enforced, watched, and measured. It is important that managers measure across the implementation process just as they do elsewhere. One does not just take a methodology and dump it into an organization and expect it to grow by itself; one needs an implementation plan. If management forgets about it, then people will also forget about it. Management must show commitment throughout the implementation and use of the methodology, not just at the beginning.

Following through with new technology is important. The key is involvement with the processes. Systems development managers must continually illustrate to their staff how important the process is to each project.

THE VALUE OF USING LIFE CYCLE SUPPORT TOOLS

Valuable Points from Experts

- Integration between different life cycle phases.
- Realizing if the tools are poorly integrated, the gains made during one phase may be dissipated in another phase.
- Tools to implement techniques.
- Integrating code with models.
- Maintaining diagrams from which the code gets generated.
- Automating the system development process.

Discussion

In the paper-based methodologies of the 1970s, problems were fixed directly in the code and not the specifications. Today, it is critical that a methodology be supported by automation and that the coding is eliminated. Diagrams from which the code is generated are maintained rather than the code itself.

Systems development managers should understand that automation supporting most information system development techniques exists in today's computing environment. Managers should make every effort to take advantage of these automated tools to assist with the development process.

THE VALUE OF SHARING FRONT AND BACK END CASE SPECIFICATIONS

Valuable Points from Experts

- Ensuring specifications.
- Making sure application systems reflect the business requirements.
- Allowing models to help generate code.
- Creating traceability.
- Reducing the need for documenting code and speeding up the maintenance process.

Discussion

Specifications should waterfall. The bottom line is that one should be able to take an attribute and not have to enter it in again later in the physical design. Models should help generate the code. They should be tied together; otherwise, the whole reason for doing the modeling is lost.

THE VALUE OF USING OTHER WORKSTATION TOOLS

Valuable Points from Experts

- Measuring a project's progress.
- Providing automated means for documenting work.

- Supporting presentations.
- Producing high-quality, better-looking documents.
- Providing error-checking capabilities.
- Helping to control the software development process.

Discussion

Online methodologies of the future will tie together workstation tools (project management, estimating tools, and CASE). The organization should have a project management-based methodology and graphics support. It is clear that some automated means of documenting the results of work is needed. Graphics on one life cycle phase should feed the next phase.

ACTUALLY USING TOOLS THE WAY THEY ARE DESIGNED TO BE USED

Valuable Points from Experts

- Understanding which tools are flexible.
- Using tools the way your goals and objectives are set up.
- Finding innovative ways to use tools within the process.
- Realizing when innovations can impact the next phase of the life cycle.
- Realizing that tools assist the methodology.
- Standards to follow when using tools.

Discussion

In today's environment, the use of automated tools is essential. Many of the processes cannot be done by hand. Tools must be used the way they are designed in order to gain the greatest benefit from them. Some tools can be used to make the end deliverable look different than the original intent. These changes are not necessarily bad as long as they do not affect the next life cycle stage. Tools should be used consistently with the goals and objectives, and every organization is going to be different. However, one should not get carried away with using the tools for special purposes for which they are not designed.

OTHER POINTS ABOUT PROJECT MANAGEMENT

The experts made supplementary statements that were not prompted by specific questions, but are additional points of importance to project management.

Valuable Points from Experts

- Using estimating tools to estimate throughout the project.
- Providing greater productivity.
- Ensuring quality and information integrity.
- Realizing that initially there will not be productivity gains.

- Keeping people on track with the methodology.
- Eliminating redundant activities.
- Realizing the tools do not solve the problem.
- Guiding the process.

Discussion

Project management tools are essential to successful projects. In general, project management tools keep people on track and guide the process. Estimating tools are important in producing guidelines for the life cycle. The combination of these tools provides a more complete set of workstation tools in support of using a methodology and completing IS projects on time, within budgets, and with a satisfactory final product.

CONCLUSION

The experts leave little doubt as to the need of managing the life cycle phases of the methodology. Knowing the phases and what goes into each phase is vital to successful projects. However, this knowledge does not guarantee success. The use of automated life cycle support tools is a necessary extension to the methodology in successfully completing IS projects. These tools should span the project management activities, project estimation, and actual performance of system development tasks. Their integration is a prerequisite of a reliable project completion process.

The most important issues about systems development according to the panel of experts are:

- The importance of understanding life cycle phases.
- Understanding when some life cycle phases may be shortened.
- Understanding who should be involved in certain phases.
- Understanding the reusability between life cycle phases.
- Management's involvement in life cycle phases.
- Management's time commitment for implementing the methodology.
- Devoting enough time to performing the modeling activities.
- Management's resource commitment to implementing the methodology.
- Management's follow-through with the process.
- The value of using life cycle support tools.
- The value of sharing front- and back-end CASE specifications.
- The value of using other workstation tools.
- Actually using tools the way they are designed to be used.

Recommended Reading

Cash, C. H. and Fox, R., "Elements of Successful Project Management," *Journal of Systems Management,* Vol. 43, No. 9, September 1992, pp. 10–12.

Davis, D.B., "Develop Applications on Time, Every Time," *Datamation,* Vol 38, No. 22, November 1, 1992, pp. 85–89.

Franch, J., "CASE for the AS/400," *Systems/3X & AS World,* Vol. 17, No. 11, November 1989, pp. 46–64.

Fried, L.,"The Rules of Project Management," *Information Systems Management,* Vol. 9, No. 3., Summer 1992, pp. 71–74.

Henderson, J.C. and Lee, S., "Managing I/S Design Teams: A Control Theories Perspective," *Management Science,* Vol. 38, No. 6, June 1992, pp. 757–777.

Howard, G.S. and Rai, A., "Making it Work: Tips for Implementing IS Innovations," *Information Strategy: The Executive's Journal,* Vol. 9, No. 2, Winter, 1993, pp. 5–12.

Lederer, A.L. and Gardiner, V., "Meeting Tomorrow's Business Demands Through Strategic Information Systems Planning," *Information Strategy: The Executive's Journal,* Vol. 8, No. 4., Summer 1992, pp. 20–27.

Lejderman, J., "CASE: The Technology Transfer Issue," *Datamation,* Vol. 13, No. 15, July 23, 1987 pp. 18–19.

McClure, C., "CASE: Full Life Cycle Tools — Methodology in Path from Art to Science," *Software Magazine,* Vol. 9, No. 7, June 1989, pp. 33–42.

McClure, C., "Don't Wait for Perfection, Try Corporate CASE," *Computing Canada,* Vol. 18, No. 13, June 22, 1992, p. 35.

McCusker, T., "Tools to Manage Big Projects," *Datamation,* Vol. 37., No. 2, January 15, 1991, pp. 71–75.

Raghavan, V. and Webster, J., "Strategic Traps in System Development," *Journal of Systems Management,* Vol. 43, No. 12, December 1992, pp. 8–11.

Roberts, T., "Factors Impacting the Implementation of a System Development Methodology," unpublished dissertation, Auburn University, 1993.

Ryan, H.W., "The Management Cycle: The Key to Control," *Journal of Information Systems Management,* Vol. 7, No. 2, Spring 1990, pp. 62–65.

Saarinen, T., "System Development Methodology and Project Success: An Assessment of Situational Approaches," *Information & Management,* Vol. 19, No. 3., October 1990, pp. 183–193.

Simon, L., "Making CASE Pay Means More than a Purchase," *Computing Canada,* Vol. 18, No. 13, June 22, 1992, p. 31.

Ware, R., "Project Management Software: Project Panacea," *Journal of Information Systems Management,* Vol. 8, No. 1, Winter 1991, pp. 79–83.

Chapter 3
Project Management: A Structured Framework

Howard W. Miller

Most systems development managers view project management as such a basic management technique that they feel they already understand it and do not have to learn it. Yet, systems development managers need to relearn effective project management techniques many times during their careers. Not only do they have to relearn project management, they must train their employees in project management techniques.

Furthermore, in the last 30 years, the primary focus of the project work environment has shifted from development projects to maintenance projects. Most organizations have automated their major business functions, and it is not uncommon for a systems development department to invest 60 percent or more of its productive time on maintenance or enhancement activities.

The nature of the demands on the systems development department has also changed. Users who previously required support are now conducting their own queries, developing reports, and their own small systems. Instead of requesting support for these functions, they are requesting data downloads to microcomputers, decision support databases, and system enhancements to make data more accessible. It is not uncommon for a systems development department to field 3,000 to 5,000 requests each year. The demand on the systems development department has become request driven.

This chapter describes a simplified project management procedure that satisfies this request-driven environment. This procedure consists of four steps:

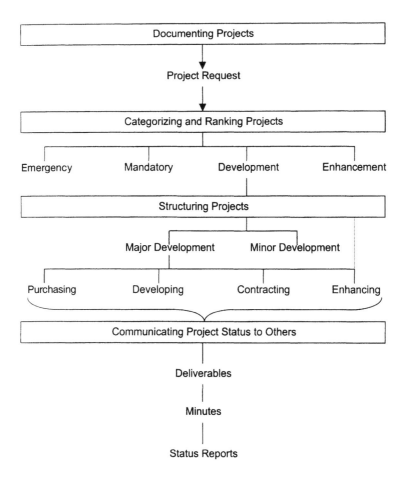

Exhibit 3.1. Framework of the Project Management Process

---

1. documenting projects
2. Categorizing projects and ranking them according to priority.
3. Structuring projects.
4. Communicating project status to senior management and users.

Exhibit 1 illustrates the structure of the procedure outlined in this chapter.

The goal of this procedure is to:

- Separate the large projects from the smaller support projects.
- Provide a less labor-intensive structure for managing the smaller support projects.
- Provide a method to test a large volume of requests and to verify that the changes are consistent with the organization's Information Technology Architecture.

- Maintain an inventory of valid requests.
- Provide a structure for large systems development projects.

DOCUMENTING PROJECTS

Project management starts with the request for service. Documentation of all support requests is essential to the project management process. It is impossible to direct technology, meet schedules, rank requirements according to priority, and produce a quality product when there is a large number of phantom, undocumented projects in process. For the purpose of this discussion, the request for IS support is called a service request. Service requests are typically forms — paper documents that could just as easily be electronic documents where electronic mail facilities are available. Documentation of a service request consists of three basic steps, which are outlined in the following sections.

Determining What Requires Documentation. Not all support activities require a service request. One rule for systems development managers to follow is that activities that require less than one half an hour per day and no more than four hours per week do not need to be documented. Activities that relate to requests for information, rather than actions, do not require documentation (e.g., requesting information on how to solve a particular problem). In a time management system, such activities can be charged to miscellaneous support.

The documentation procedures must not be so rigid that the staff is burdened with documenting insignificant activities. Systems development managers must limit this activity so the staff can focus on its mission.

Documenting the Service Request. The systems development department should document service requests in the simplest way. If possible, users should complete the service request in their own words. It is far more important, however, that the request be documented than that the user do it personally. Although some users resist this kind of bureaucracy, most have become accustomed to written requests for service. If there is resistance, the systems development manager should simplify the procedure by putting the form on electronic mail or taking the initiative and having a systems analyst complete the form.

Typically, a service request contains the following information:

- A unique project control number.
- A project title that should be short, descriptive, and meaningful — the title is a shorthand name that the systems development staff uses when discussing the project.
- A priority designation of emergency, mandatory, or enhancement — high and low are not valid designations because users view everything as high priority.

- A realistic target date for when the service should be completed — requests with no target date are low priority. In addition, requests with target dates of yesterday indicate that some alternative is already in place, and these also are frequently low priority.
- A detailed description of the request should be attached when available or applicable.
- The date of origin for the request and the identity of the requestor.
- The date the request was received by the systems development department.

Evaluating the Request. A request should be evaluated if the service request is valid or if it benefits the organization. Some requests can be satisfied through procedural changes. The systems development manager should establish a dialogue with the requestor and find out the reason for the request. Frequently, simple procedural changes can simplify or eliminate the need for a software change. In other instances, it will be apparent that the solution is different from the request, and a different project will develop.

A solution may already be available through existing online queries or reports. It is not uncommon for one department to be struggling to compile information that someone else is already receiving.

Because a feature is not working correctly or that it can be improved may not be valid requests to start a project. Frequently, such requests are time-consuming to implement, a way already exists to circumvent the problem, and there is no appreciable benefit.

A request should be viewed as an opportunity to evaluate surrounding systems. The request may be the symptom of a larger problem, or an opportunity might exist to gain larger benefits by expanding the scope of the project.

Acknowledging Receipt and Identifying Disposition. The systems development department should identify the disposition of each request within a reasonable time frame. Five working days is an appropriate amount of time. The disposition can be as simple as stating that the request is an emergency and is being addressed, that it will be started on a specific date, or that it is being held pending a priority assignment or further evaluation.

Again, the intent is to communicate. It is crucial to communicate the status and give the user the opportunity to appeal the disposition. It is best to avoid misunderstandings at all cost. Nothing destroys credibility faster than having the user think the department is working on the request when it is not.

CATEGORIZING AND RANKING PROJECTS ACCORDING TO PRIORITY

After the appropriate service requests have been properly documented, systems development managers must organize them into a meaningful structure. Projects labeled emergency require immediate attention. Mandatory projects must be addressed because of changes in the law or the direction of the business. Projects labeled enhancement are optional, have no target date, and do not require immediate attention. Those labeled development projects require additional analysis before they can be addressed.

Other categories could be proposed. For example, projects that enhance the systems development staff's abilities by enhancing existing technology or introducing new technology could be labeled housekeeping. Projects that account for such ancillary activities as education, sickness, vacations, holidays, and meetings could be labeled overhead.

Project classifications vary according to the procedures used by the organization. This chapter discusses only emergency, mandatory, enhancement, and development projects because they are the classifications applicable to most organizations. The following sections describe these classifications in detail.

Emergency Requests. This type of request requires a correction to a system when one of the following error conditions occurs:

- Production application software supporting a business function fails completely or produces erroneous results.
- A computer failure occurs, and support from IS is required to reestablish computer processing.
- An interruption in service occurs because of human error.

Because they represent an interruption in computer service, emergency requests receive the highest priority regardless of the project duration or the amount of labor required. To ensure that there are no repeat occurrences, emergency requests are only considered satisfied when a permanent solution to the problem is installed.

Mandatory Requests. In most cases, a mandatory request is a minor enhancement that adjusts for changes in the law, strategic direction, accounting conventions, or other similar conditions. Mandatory support requests are necessary to support the business or to comply with legal requirements. These requests require change to a system by a specific date, and priority for these services is driven by that date.

Systems development managers need to be cautious of mandatory requests. When the scope exceeds 10 days of labor or takes more than one calendar month to complete, mandatory requests need to be scrutinized closely. It is common for most software development groups to have more work queued than they have staff to address it. Requestors therefore attempt to take the engineering staff hostage by attaching discretionary enhancements to mandatory requests, thereby expanding the scope of the mandatory requests. However, if the scope of these larger requests is valid, they need to be managed as if they were major or minor development.

Enhancement Requests. Enhancement requests address some minor modification to an existing information system. One rule for systems development managers to follow is to define enhancements as projects that require less than 10 days of labor and that can be completed within one calendar month.

Systems development managers should take an opportunistic posture toward enhancements. An enhancement project is an opportunity and it makes smart business sense to address as many enhancement projects as possible with a minimum amount of bureaucracy. For example, a project could have high financial return with a minimal labor investment, labor could be available at that time, the timing might be right to implement such a change, or it might be a favor to some especially supportive individual or department.

Enhancements should be grouped according to the application system that is being enhanced, thereby creating an enhancement project that can be addressed by each task or as an entire development project. The enhancement requests could be evaluated, ranked according to priority, and scheduled on a monthly basis by a committee consisting of representatives of the user community.

Typically, the number of systems enhancement projects increases over time. Usually, more enhancement requests are received than there is staff available. The speed with which the number of enhancement projects increases is a barometer of the health of the system. If the number of requests is low, it can be assumed that the system is in good health. If, however, the number of requests is high, the system may need an overhaul.

An effective way for systems development managers to determine if a system needs an overhaul is to perform an operational analysis. By investing a small amount of time and money, the operational analysis process can resolve the problems and extended the life of the system. This is discussed in more depth later in the chapter.

Development Requests. Development projects require major investments in labor and money. Examples of such projects would be the development of an entirely new system to replace an existing system or to extend the life of an existing system. Development projects are divided into two categories: major development and minor development.

Before a major development project is undertaken, the users and the systems development department jointly conduct a feasibility study. Major development projects obviously require substantial commitments of labor and money and result in the purchase, development, or major enhancement of an information system. Because of this large commitment, the results of such feasibility studies should be presented to a steering committee before the projects are scheduled. Major development projects require more than 60 worker-days and may extend over several years. In addition, the staff should produce a major deliverable every six months.

A minor development project frequently consists of an improvement to an existing information system. It is more complex and labor-intensive than an enhancement, less involved than a major development project, and does not have the rigid target dates of a mandatory request. A minor development project requires the completion of multiple, interdependent phases to accomplish a goal, whereas an enhancement does not. Typically, a minor development project is approved and given its priority by a steering committee. A minor development project should take more than 10 but less than 60 worker-days and no more than six calendar months to complete.

STRUCTURING PROJECTS

Managing the Small Project

Systems reengineering for emergency, mandatory, and enhancement requests is both an opportunity and a major resource drain. It is common for an organization to receive 3,000 to 5,000 requests per year, and emergency, mandatory, and enhancement projects can consume from 20 percent to 60 percent or more of the labor of an IS department. However, a well-managed emergency project results in a permanent solution to an emergency condition, ensuring that the interruption does not recur. This is an easy way to improve productivity and creditability.

Mandatory and enhancement projects also provide an opportunity to change the software systems and make them better conform to the strategic direction of the IS department while satisfying the user's immediate need. Mandatory and enhancement projects also present the systems development department with an opportunity to introduce change in small, painless increments. These small increments demonstrate the positive effect of new technology and inspire creativity. Over time, the system evolves, frequently extending the life of the original investment.

However, emergency, mandatory, and enhancement projects usually do not require a great deal of formal structure. None of them should ever consume a large amount of resources. Therefore, the consequences of an error are never severe.

If the emergency, mandatory, and enhancement service requests are consistently late or the quality of the product is poor, additional structure can be added. As a general rule, extensive formal structure could unnecessarily increase the amount of resources required to accomplish the project while adding little or no value. It is more important to accomplish as many of these projects as possible while improving quality and increasing the system's strategic usefulness. The one exception to this rule is the mandatory service request. As noted earlier, these requests could be large enough to require the same structure as a minor or major development project.

Redirecting System Design

For one of many reasons, a computer-based system may experience a crisis. A system crisis is manifested by an increase in the frequency of requests for change or enhancement and by the accumulation of large numbers of unsatisfied requests. A large backlog of unsatisfied requests may result from the system's failure to meet the changing needs of the business, a simple lack of priority for the system, inadequate systems development staff levels, or a combination of all of these.

A systems crisis often causes the user to discard the existing software system and purchase or develop a completely new one. The most common pitfall, however, is for the user to assume that there is no alternative to replacing the system. Replacement of a system is rarely the only solution or the best solution for satisfying a system crisis. If the system is replaced, even the specifications of the replacement system are eventually undermined enough by change and enhancement to render it ineffective, and the cycle is repeated. This could be a never-ending process.

The problem is usually that the architecture of the software system does not have sufficient flexibility to accommodate change and enhancement. The design of the software system assumes a fixed architecture, and as the organization and computer technology evolve, the only solution might seem to be replacement of the software system.

To alter this cycle of replacement, the systems development manager must define the systems change process in terms of evolution, not replacement. This evolutionary perspective is achieved by establishing a direction for the system. The systems development department must determine what the user wants the system to do in one year, five years, and 10 years. The systems direction is established by evaluating the operation of the system and identifying the changes required to make it conform with the organization's strategic direction and the direction of computer technology in general (e.g., using online processing or supporting the use of microcomputers for end-user computing).

An effective way to redirect the systems design is to cluster unsatisfied requests for change and enhancement. One way of achieving this goal is to use a project tracking system. Systems development managers can first cluster requests for change or enhancement on the project tracking system by application (e.g., general ledger, payroll, accounts payable) and then, within that group, cluster them by logical processing unit (e.g., job, program, subroutine). This makes it possible for systems development managers to assess the magnitude and severity of the required changes. By comparing these clusters to the system's technical and strategic directions, it is usually easy for managers to determine the changes that will further the direction and those that will not.

Most organizations find that 80 percent of the functional capability of a system, even one in crisis, works correctly. The source of the unsatisfied requests for change or enhancement is almost always in the remaining 20 percent. The new perspective created by clustering small projects makes it easier for systems development managers to identify high-return changes or enhancements. By making the high-return areas the department's highest priority, the organization usually can obtain an 80 percent improvement by attacking only 20 percent of the problems. In addition, some cosmetic (i.e., low-return) changes can also be accomplished.

Therefore, clustering allows the systems development department to address high-return changes with a very small commitment of staff, and it reduces a disproportionate amount of request backlog for the amount of labor invested. In addition, accomplishing cosmetic changes results in an improved relationship with the change requestor.

The clustering of mandatory and enhancement requests modifies the development cycle and extends the life of a software system. Through the exertion of a small effort (e.g., less than 20 percent of the replacement cost), the evolution of a software system is altered to correlate with the direction of the organization. Rather than making random changes to the system, the changes are directed at correcting problems that can extend the life of the system through selective maintenance, renovation, or augmentation. Every organization has a choice: It can make random changes to its systems, or it can direct the changes. Clustering is a tool that assists the direction of change.

Conducting an Operational Analysis

Although clustering can be used to extend the life of the system, this approach has limits. Clustering only addresses the documented requests for changes or enhancement. It does not address benefits derived by introducing such new technology as imaging, telephone voice technology, or personal computing. One way to extend the effectiveness of clustering is to look for hidden changes, to seek out new technologies, or to identify the reason for a requested change. This process is called operational analysis.

An operational analysis identifies and defines the functions of a software system, isolates the requested changes, and recommends a series of changes that customizes the system to conform with the system architecture and the direction of the organization. The objectives of an operational analysis are to:

- Identify and analyze the objectives of the major functions involved in processing data.
- Identify undocumented improvements that cause unnecessary effort or result in the loss of data integrity.
- Identify new technology or procedures that would improve performance.
- Formulate remedial actions or suggested improvements.
- Identify mandatory changes needed to resolve data security or data integrity problems.
- Calculate financial or other benefits derived from remedial actions.

To implement an operational analysis the systems development manager has to:

- Identify the current status of the system, including:
  - Source of the data and documents
  - People who physically handle the documents.
  - Recipients of the output.
- Review open enhancement service requests and requests for change.
- Interview personnel who use the system for undocumented changes and improvements.
- Define how the system works, including:
  - Paperwork flow.
  - Processing steps.
- Segment processing into its logical steps, as follows:
  - Data receipt and preparation.
  - Data input and validation.
  - Automated processing.
  - Management and administrative activities.
- Document input, including:
  - Type of documents.
  - Samples of documents.
  - Volumes per time period.
- Document output, including:
  - Type of reports.
  - Samples of reports (e.g., manual reports, automated reports, online queries).
- Determine areas for improvement, such as:
  - Data receipt and preparation.
  - Data input and validation.
  - Automated processing.
  - Management and administrative activities.
- Perform a return on investment analysis, including:

- Cost analysis to perform remedial action.
- Benefit analysis.
- Return on investment calculations.
- Rank improvements according to priority and implement the changes in the following order:
  - Mandatory changes (i.e., changes that improve the integrity or security of the systems).
  - Return on investment calculations.

In addition to the financial benefits derived from the remedial actions, operational analysis results in qualitative benefits. One benefit concerns knowledge of the systems functions. As time elapses and staff members leave, much of the knowledge concerning a system's functions is lost despite documentation. With operational analysis, however, knowledge of the system's functions is disseminated to a larger audience, which increases the staff's awareness level of the system's functions.

Another qualitative benefit derived from operational analysis is improved communications among various departments. Through participation in operational analysis, the systems development staff becomes committed to improving the productivity of the overall system. Finally, by working together, the attitude of the personnel involved improves, and they find it easier to work together in the future.

One example of the benefits derived from an operational analysis concerns a food service company that performed an operational analysis on 13 of its major systems. The analysis showed both qualitative and quantitative benefits. The qualitative benefits were twofold. First, while evaluating the systems, the end-user departments became aware of existing but unused facilities. Use of these facilities increased the effectiveness of the system and the productivity of various departments. Second, some minor security and integrity problems were identified and resolved, but more important, the company felt confident that its internal financial controls were sound.

The quantitative results were much more substantial. For an investment of $90,000, the company was able to realize an annual savings of $250,000 on one system. Conversely, replacement would have cost well in excess of $3 million.

Managing the Large Project

Most major development projects are so complex that they require rigid process control. The traditional approach of establishing requirements and then translating them into designs, code, and operational procedures in phases is a frustratingly slow, labor-intensive, often manual process. Therefore, most organizations should select and use a structured systems development methodology, such as METHOD/1 or Applied Information Development (AID), or automated approaches to systems development, such as CASE. Both of these areas are beyond the scope of this chapter, however.

Minor development projects, however, must be structured but do not need to be encumbered with all the structure required of major development projects. Minor development includes all the key elements of a structured methodology but is scaled down in proportion to the size of the particular project. These key elements include a purpose statement, the project work plan, the test and acceptance plan, the training plan, the conversion and implementation plan, and any miscellaneous documents.

The purpose statement briefly defines the purpose and scope of the project. The project work plan includes a brief description of each task to be performed in the sequence in which these tasks are to be executed. Each task is uniquely numbered and typically can be accomplished by one person in not less than one day but not more than five days. A minor development project typically includes 10 to 20 tasks but can include as few as two and as many as 60. The work plan should include the following information:

- A unique identification number.
- A one-line task description.
- The name of the individual performing the task.
- Estimated hours for the task.

The test and acceptance plan is a brief outline explaining how unit testing and integrated testing will be accomplished. It identifies who performs the test and who validates the test. This plan defines the acceptance criteria for the project and the user staff responsible for acceptance. The training plan explains what training is required and how user training will be accomplished. The conversion and implementation plan explains any conversion that may be necessary and how the system change should be implemented.

Miscellaneous documents are any other information that may be pertinent to the project. These can include work requests, changes to the database, new database formats, and any new screen or report layouts.

In most cases, because of their size, minor development projects are enhancements to existing systems rather than development of new systems. If an overview of the existing system is not available, it should be developed and should accompany all project reviews.

REPORTING STATUS TO USERS AND SENIOR MANAGEMENT

The last step in the simplified approach to project management is status reporting. Systems development managers do not need elaborate written documentation for a project to be successful. In many cases, elaborate written documentation is viewed negatively and is considered too bureaucratic by both management and users. In addition, it is almost always distasteful to IS professionals.

The key to success in reporting the project status to others is having the right documentation at the right points during the project. Documentation may vary from having little or nothing for emergency, mandatory, and enhancement projects to having deliverables for each phase of the methodology and minutes from project walkthroughs for major development projects. Finally, the documentation includes a status report that consolidates the activities for all types of projects: development, enhancement, mandatory, and emergency.

Deliverables. A project manual is maintained for each major development project. This manual includes the deliverables specified by the methodology for each phase of the project. The manual is a working document and includes copies of any associated documentation (e.g., system overview, correspondence). A similar, though much abbreviated, project manual is maintained for minor development projects. This manual is usually a single deliverable rather than a series of deliverables, as is the case for major development projects.

Regardless of the medium (i.e., document or repository), the deliverables are evolutionary — they increase in number as the elements of the development project become available. Deliverables for emergency, mandatory, and enhancement projects need not be any more than completion of the service request document and an update of standard system documentation when the project is complete.

Minutes. Almost every structured development methodology includes a structured walkthrough of the deliverables at the end of each development phase. Systems development managers should discuss the priority and status of emergency, mandatory, and enhancement requests at monthly user committee meetings. If the systems development department does not hold such meetings, it is in jeopardy of losing the opportunity these projects present. Systems development managers should discuss the priority and status of minor and major development projects at monthly or quarterly executive steering committee meetings.

Minutes are issued for committee meetings as well as for structured walkthroughs. The minutes should identify attendees and agreements based on an agenda issued before the meeting or walkthrough. Such minutes are often carefully read by participants and interested parties. Errors and oversights are quickly called to the attention of the systems development manager or committee member.

It is often difficult for committee members to make positive recommendations about the structure and priority of a software development project, but it is usually far less difficult for them to identify obvious errors and oversights. Systems development managers should distribute the minutes to as wide an audience as possible. If nothing else, minutes provide a running commentary on the progress of the project. They are a communications medium, and it is far better to err in favor of overcommunicating than undercommunicating.

Status Reports

The status report can be issued monthly or quarterly. The status report is a consolidated document that includes the status of all projects — both application software development and such support projects as computer center, database, and technical service projects. This document should be concise; highlighting important accomplishments, summarizing all projects, and concluding with a concise description of the status of each project. Each project's status description should include something similar to the following: a description of the major development project, the targets for major milestones, and a list of the accomplishments achieved during the period.

The status report should identify problems that could potentially interfere with meeting the target dates and should suggest some solutions. Finally, the status report should include the project plans for the next period.

Other projects (e.g., enhancement, mandatory, emergency, and minor development) should be presented in summary form. Only major accomplishments or problem areas are highlighted. It is usually beneficial to supply the following statistics on these projects: the number received since the last status report, the number completed, the number in process, the backlog number, and the amount of labor hours expended.

Talking Status Report

Structuring projects as emergency, mandatory, enhancement and development is an opportunity for parallel development. Multiple project teams can work on different aspects of the same system. However, in this scenario, one group can undo what another has accomplished.

This effect is mitigated, in part, by the talking status report. A structured walkthrough of the status report in the presence of all project managers allows each manager to discuss the status of their projects and what they intend to address in the coming reporting period. In an open forum, the project managers have an opportunity to query the implications of other teams' changes, thereby avoiding some of the pitfalls of different teams simultaneously working on different aspects of the same system. The talking status report ensures that everyone in the IS department understands the current status of projects, and it verifies the integrity of the information.

Systems development and computer center managers should hold a weekly coordination meeting. The agenda for this meeting is to discuss any pending changes or potential conflicts among IS groups. These managers should also hold a short meeting each morning to discuss any emergency projects that were initiated during the last 24 hours. This ensures that recurring problems are being addressed and that permanent solutions are being identified and implemented for any emergency projects.

Communication

The purpose of these techniques is to promote communication. Project deliverables communicate the requirements, design, and implementation plans for the information systems. The meeting minutes communicate the collective agreements among the participants in the systems development process. The status report communicates the collective status of all systems development projects, and the talking status report improves coordination. The greater the communication, the less likely that some aspect of a project will be overlooked or that some participant will do something to jeopardize the success of the project.

PROJECT MANAGEMENT SOFTWARE

Project management software assists systems development managers in managing time, costs, and resources more effectively. Many of the products are designed to plan, track, and analyze activities that can range from simple enhancements to multiyear development projects. Originally, project management software was solely for mainframes, but today some of the most effective project management software is designed for microcomputers.

Most software products provide a set of tools to assist developers plan a project, create and define activities, assign resources, apply resource costs, schedule resources, and perform in-depth analysis of possible project scenarios. The what–if type of analysis available in most project software permits developers to answer such common questions as "What if we add more resources?" "What is the best way to reduce the elapsed time?" or "What do we save if we complete one month sooner?"

Some of the more valuable features of project management software include

- Program Evaluation Review Techniques (PERT) charts or network diagrams to provide a visual representation of the relationship between two tasks.

- Gantt charts to depict the start and end dates of activities.
- Automatic scheduling to derive a project's end date based on the start date and the duration of the intermediate tasks.
- Cost allocation to control such costs as labor, software, hardware, computing resources stated in each task description.
- Automatic resource leveling to determine the optimal task schedule.
- Resource calendars to track holidays, vacations, and other time restrictions.

Some common DOS-based microcomputer products include: Harvard Project Manager from Software Publishing Corp., Microsoft Project from Microsoft Corp., CA-SuperProject from Computer Associates International, Inc., Project Outlook from Strategic Software Planning Corp., and Topdown Project Planner from Ajida Technologies, Inc. For the Macintosh computer, there is Micro Planner from Micro Planning International and MacProject II from Claris Corp. Most of these projects can determine finish date, critical path, and duration, and they provide tools for managing resources, costs, and schedules.

RECOMMENDED COURSE OF ACTION

Project management is a technique that must be revisited many times. In addition, this process can become complex because the requirements for project management change as information technology changes. However, it can be simplified by returning to fundamental project control techniques. The four-step process outlined in this chapter achieves this goal. In addition, the minutes, status reports, and other communication meetings ensure that the project participants have a common understanding of requirements, problems, and progress.

Project management techniques are not to be used independently. To manage projects successfully, the systems development department must have a structured development methodology and at least one committee to develop priorities and other procedures (e.g., a cost/benefit analysis procedure, a feasibility study procedure, an operational analysis procedure). The most essential prerequisite, however, is the desire to put the process in place and a belief that it will yield better information systems.

Bibliography

1. Miller, H.W. "The Chief Information Officer as an Information Architect." *Information Executive* (Spring 1989), pp 3135.
2. Miller, H.W. "Creating an Evolutionary Software System: A Case Study." *Journal of Systems Management* (August 1990), pp 11–18.
3. Miller, H.W. "Developing Information Technology Strategies." *Journal of Systems Management* (September 1988), pp 28–35.

4. Miller, H.W. "Information Technology: Creation or Evolution?" *Journal of Systems Management* (April 1991), pp 23–27.
5. Miller, H.W. "The Leaning Tower of Technology." *Information Strategy: The Executive's Journal* 4 (Spring 1989), pp 17–21.
6. Miller, H.W. "Opportunism: Nine Steps to a Better Information System." *Chief Information Officer Journal* (Summer 1990), pp 24–30.

Chapter 4
Collecting Project Information

Ralph L. Kliem

During the course of any project, whether information systems or engineering, it is easy to get wrapped up in the technology and forget about the importance of documentation in general. It becomes even easier and more tempting to forget about project management (PM) documentation completely. People tend to view PM documentation as "administrivia" during the early and middle phases of a project, finding later that they should have addressed it throughout the life cycle of their projects. The situation becomes quite apparent as senior management and auditors start asking for copies of PM documentation. Frequently, there is a mad rush to develop PM documentation or it is just not done, thereby frustrating everyone from team members to executives.

ADVANTAGES, CHALLENGES, AND OPPORTUNITIES

PM documentation offers several advantages. These include:

- Collecting data to develop meaningful metrics
- Enabling the projection of future performance
- Ensuring that appropriate controls exist
- Getting new employees up to speed
- Protecting the company from legal action
- Providing a record of performance
- Providing an effective means of communication
- Serving as a tool to evaluate performance

Despite the advantages, PM documentation is not done because preparers often believe that:

- Documentation is too time consuming
- Documentation commits them to the written word
- Documentation is not as interesting as the technological issues
- They lack the requisite skills or knowledge
- The right tools are not available

0-8493-9998-X/00/$0.00+$.50

- Documentation will provide a permanent, negative record of performance
- Documentation is administrivia, not a significant activity

Whatever the reasons, PM documentation often does not get done. It is treated as an outcast, either handled poorly or ignored totally — not, however, without cost.

Failure to develop and maintain PM documentation results in missed opportunities, including the opportunity to:

- Communicate effectively
- Comply with contractual or legal obligations
- Determine the level of success or failure for specific tasks and for the entire project
- Focus on the important activities of the project
- Identify best practices
- Provide lessons learned for future projects
- Reduce the learning curve of new team members

CATEGORIES OF DOCUMENTATION

The number and types of PM documentation are infinite. For classification purposes, however, the documentation can fall into one or more of these categories: schedule, cost, quality, and resources.

Schedule documentation deals with the sequence of activities and their start and end dates. Common examples are bar charts, network diagrams, and tabular reports.

Cost documentation deals with planned and actual expenditures. Common examples are a tabular report on expenditures up to a given point in time for a task or an entire project and an S curve chart reflecting the difference between what should be and was spent up to a given time.

Quality documentation deals with level of workmanship. Often, these documents consist of charts, diagrams, matrices, etc., that reflect past performance and future trends. Common examples are Pareto diagrams, line charts, and scattergrams that display defect or error rates.

Resource documentation deals with assigning and using people, tools, supplies, facilities, etc. Common examples are organization charts and resource reports on past and potential usage.

Not all documentation can be neatly categorized as being schedule, cost, quality, or resource. In reality, each document can fall into two or more categories. Exhibit 1 reflects the relationship of these categories to one another.

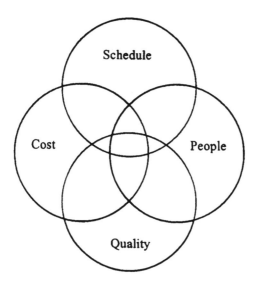

Exhibit 4.1. Relationship of the Categories

LIFE CYCLE RELATIONSHIP

Knowing into what categories a PM document falls helps determine its purpose. What further defines its purpose, however, is its level of importance throughout the life cycle of a project. There are five phases to a project: feasibility, formulation, implementation, installation, and sustaining. The feasibility phase determines whether or not a project is a practical alternative to the status quo. The formulation phase defines in detail what the customer needs and wants and develops alternatives to meet those requirements. The implementation phase involves actually building a product, and the installation phase occurs when the product becomes operational in the customer's environment. The sustaining phase begins when the client assumes direct control over the product.

A specific phase of a project will largely determine the level of importance for a specific document. Some documents are important throughout all phases of a project, while others are significant for only one or two. Exhibit 2 shows common PM documents and their relative importance in a phase.

PM documentation should not be developed unless it meets certain criteria. Too often, projects either produce too much or too little, without forethought about the reasons for its existence.

Exhibit 4.2. Common PM Documents

	Feasibility	Formulation	Implementation	Installation	Sustaining
Activity description form	NA	P	P	P	NA
Activity estimating form	P	P	P	S	NA
Activity status record	NA	P	P	P	NA
Change control log	NA	P	P	P	P
Change request form	NA	P	P	P	P
Contingency plans	S	P	P	P	P
Employee assignment form	NA	P	P	P	NA
Estimated labor usage form	P	P	S	S	NA
Estimated labor usage per activity form	NA	P	P	P	NA
Estimated nonlabor usage form	P	S	S	S	NA
Estimated resource (nonlabor costs) form	NA	P	P	P	NA
Gantt chart	P	P	P	P	NA
Lessons learned	NA	NA	NA	NA	P
Memorandums	P	P	P	P	P
Minutes	P	P	P	P	P
Network diagram	NA	P	P	P	NA
Newsletters	NA	P	P	P	S
Organization chart	NA	P	P	P	P
Post-implementation review report	NA	NA	NA	NA	P
Predecessor–successor schedule report	S	P	P	P	NA
Problem occurrence form	NA	P	P	P	P
Problem report	NA	P	P	P	P
Project announcement	NA	P	S	S	NA
Project cost report	P	P	P	P	NA
Project procedures	NA	P	P	P	NA
Project status report	S	P	P	P	NA
Purchase order form	NA	P	P	P	P
Record of actual daily labor usage form	S	P	P	P	NA
Record of actual resource (nonlabor) usage costs	NA	P	P	P	NA
Resource cost estimating form	P	S	S	S	NA

Exhibit 4.2. Common PM Documents *(Continued)*

	Feasibility	Formulation	Implementation	Installation	Sustaining
Resource cost report	P	P	P	P	NA
Resource histogram	P	P	P	P	NA
Resource utilization to-date report	S	P	P	P	NA
Risk control log	NA	P	P	P	P
Statement of work	NA	P	P	P	P
Work breakdown structure	NA	P	P	P	NA
Work flows	NA	P	P	P	NA

P = Primary importance; S = Secondary importance; NA = Not applicable

THREE KEY QUESTIONS

In today's highly computerized environment, too much PM documentation can lead to information overload, giving people the ability to produce more with decreasing value. The distinction between what is and is not important becomes blurred. The result is frustration on everyone's part. Conversely, too little PM documentation can lead to information "underload," causing people to guess what is and is not important. Again, the distinction between what is and is not important becomes blurred. Again, too, the result is frustration on everyone's part.

The key, then, is to answer three simple questions to determine what documentation, and how much is necessary.

1. *Does the documentation further the achievement of the goals of the project?* That is, does the effort and the consequent results contribute toward successful completion of a project?
2. *Does the documentation have a customer for it?* A customer must need the documentation. If not, then, it raises the issue whether the document is even necessary. If yes, then it raises the concern over whether or not the document satisfies the needs of the customer.
3. *Will it serve as the basis for some documentation deemed important?* A document may be unimportant itself, but may become a significant contributor of information in another more important document.

If project managers can answer "yes" to any of these three questions, then the value of producing a PM document may substantiate the need to invest the effort, time, and money into its development and maintenance. If no, then its value is questionable.

ORGANIZING IT ALL

Compiling PM documentation can prove challenging and unwieldy, especially as its frequency and amount increase. Fortunately, "tools" exist to handle such circumstances: project manuals, history files, and library.

The project manual is a handbook that contains general information about a project. Its contents often include organization charts, schedules, responsibilities, phone/contact lists, and tables. Each team member has a copy and the contents are kept current electronically or manually. The manual helps to improve communications and coordination. Typical contents of a project manual include:

- Diagrams
- Estimating rules
- Forms
- Minutes
- Phone listings
- Procedures/work flows
- Reporting requirements
- Responsibility matrices
- Service support
- Statement of work
- Work breakdown structure

The project history files are repositories of documentation that is produced on a project. Its contents include memorandums, agreements, schedules, reports, and forms. The files are usually located at the project office or, for smaller projects, at the project manager's desk. The files are useful for conducting research, fulfilling audit requests, and reducing learning curves. Typical contents of project history files include:

- Correspondence
- Document drafts (including marked-up copies)
- Forms (completed)
- Matrices (e.g., responsibility)
- Minutes
- Procedures/workflows (current and canceled)
- Reports
- Schedules (with different updates)
- Work breakdown structure (different versions)

The project library is a central location that contains reference documentation. Its contents often include user manuals, standards, books, and other literature. To be useful to a project team, the library should be centrally located and have a system in place to check out material. Typical contents of a project library include:

- Policies, procedures, and work flows (in addition to the ones in the project manual)
- Project manual
- Publications/literature (including project newsletters)
- Technical documentation (e.g., user manuals)

DELIVERY

There are three different delivery vehicles for project documentation: hard copy, client/server, and the Web.

Hard copy has its advantages. It is:

- Easy for most people to use
- A familiar medium of communication
- Easy to reproduce
- Easy to update or make changes

There are disadvantages, too:

- Keeping track of copies is difficult.
- Copies are easily lost.
- Outdated or wrong copies may be circulated.
- Specific information is difficult to find in a large pile of papers.
- Maintenance overhead is required.

Despite the disadvantages, manual copies have remained for a long time, thanks largely to the immaturity and limited availability of information technology. However, with client/server technology becoming more prevalent, a "paperless" environment is less than a figment of imagination and a large possibility.

Client/server technology, which shares IT power with the user, not only offers the capability of developing documentation, but distributing it to the right person in the right amount at the right time at the right place — at least in theory. To develop and maintain documentation in a client/server environment, however, means satisfying specific requirements. The standards must be established for PM documentation, software, and hardware. For people to use the software and hardware, a technical support infrastructure must exist to realize the advantages of developing PM documentation via client/server technology. The advantages of developing PM documentation via client/server technology include:

- Providing an easier and faster method to distribute documentation electronically
- Providing access to more recent versions of documents
- Providing opportunity for people to communicate necessary changes to the documentation

There are disadvantages, too, including:

- Establishing overhead to provide technical support to users
- Investing substantial sums of money in hardware and software
- Investing time, effort, and money in training people
- Putting in place administrative activities to address security, backup and recovery, etc.

The delivery tool that is dramatically affecting the development and distribution of PM documentation is Web technology, whether over the Internet or an intranet. To use Web technology, each project team member requires software (e.g., browser), hardware (i.e., with sufficient RAM), and expertise (e.g., developing Web sites). Web technology offers several advantages:

- Documentation is easy to access
- A high level of expertise is not required
- Information and software can be quickly circulated
- Graphics and text can be mixed

Web technology also has its disadvantages, including:

- Delivering documentation slowly, especially at peak usage periods
- Requiring a technical support infrastructure to maintain the technology
- Requiring heavy investment in software and hardware, especially as the project grows in size
- Producing "junk" documentation, from e-mail to non-value-added reports

The advantages of Web technology far outweigh the disadvantages, which explains its tremendous growth, in general, and in project management, in particular. To maximize its advantages requires keeping the following considerations in mind:

1. Web technology requires looking at documents as information delivery "vehicles," not just containers of data. The former looks at delivering information that the user specifically requests, whereas the latter provides an "untailored" delivery of data. Untailored data still require the user to siphon information from excess data. The latter delivery is often described as "paper under the glass," meaning that an electronic copy is simply a hard copy in different form on a screen.
2. Web technology requires setting standards on the contents and usage of the Web site. Someone functioning as a "gatekeeper" to ensure that no irrelevant or outdated documentation is on the Web site can help establish and enforce standards.
3. It requires informing team members that Web pages do not lessen the need to apply the principles of communicating information clear-

ly. Web pages should hold information that has the characteristics of conciseness, clarity, completeness, and grammatical correctness. A tendency exists to feel that Web technology "throws out" all the rules of effective communication. Web pages frequently become cluttered with distracting icons and wordiness. Like writing on paper, the perennial questions to ask when developing material for a Web site include: Who is my audience? What will the audience use it for?

CONCLUSION

PM documentation can play an instrumental role in the success or failure of a project. Project managers and team members often need to appreciate that fact. Yet, not many of them really do until it is too late. Then everyone suffers — team members, project managers, customers, and auditors.

Chapter 5
Risk Management: The Safety Net for Project Schedules and Budgets

Polly Perryman Kuver

It has happened in every systems development manager's lifetime: the project was canceled before the system ever made it out of coding and test. Even more common, the project cost twice as much as originally budgeted. In the U.S. alone, these percentages translate into billions of corporate dollars. Taking these statistics into account, along with the need for more complex systems and an ever-growing demand for the automation and processing of higher volumes and sensitive information, it becomes imperative do a better job of estimating project costs and schedules. Accomplishing this requires strong management and team involvement from initial project planning through the development life cycle.

Applying principles of risk management supports the quality improvement and improves cost estimation by identifying and mitigating potential risks before a project begins. Risk management puts processes in place to ensure management receives organized risk information early enough to apply corrective actions that will allow realistic schedule and cost estimates and assure successful completion of the project. The same risk management principles increase team involvement by providing a vehicle for reporting potential problems and increasing the team's stake in the overall success of the project. A significant risk that is not identified and mitigated will become a real problem at some point during the project.

COMPONENTS OF RISK MANAGEMENT

The composition of risk management includes:

- *Identification:* increasing awareness of what the project is about so that potential problems in meeting the project goals are readily identified.
- *Report:* putting a mechanism in place the makes it easy for staff at all levels of the project to report things viewed as potential problems.
- *Analysis:* assessing, categorizing, and authenticating reported potential problems as risks; determining the impact the risk represents and then ranking risks for mitigation processing.
- *Mitigation:* exploring alternatives for feasibility, listing alternatives as options, and prioritizing the options.
- *Adjustment:* selecting the option that best minimizes or eliminates the risk and obtaining agreement from everyone affected by the risk and the selected mitigating action.
- *Compensation:* making the changes to the project plan and implementing the approved mitigated action.

Role of Processes and Phases

Processes that move work forward from requirements definition to design to development to test are part of the very nature of software development projects. Taking action to ensure that the processes being used on a specific project or to be used by all approved projects within an organization are defined as fundamental in establishing a risk management program. Whether the processes are defined formally in a set of procedures, or informally within a series of intraproject e-mail messages, does not matter so long as everyone on the team is performing the same steps and producing the same output within each of the project phases and new personnel joining the project have a point of reference on how things are being done.

The defined processes must include a predictable level of output at the end of each project phase. The output should in all cases provide focused information about what was accomplished or decided upon during the current phase and what is planned in the next phase. As the next phase is planned, the project team should identify any incident that could impede the delivery of the process output. Each incident needs to be assessed as a risk and alternative; corrective action must be planned if the risk is significant. During the phase review, the output should be evaluated to determine if the planned corrective action was effective and if any new risks have surfaced.

For example, the output of the requirements definition and analysis process in an organization may call for a list of requirements to be documented and approved by the customer, who may be internal or external. If the negotiation of specific functions or performance capabilities pertinent to the requirements are delayed because the throughput benchmark specifications from a vendor will not be available until past the planned conclusion of the requirements phase, this will affect the output product — which represents a potential risk to both the schedule and system design. The system designer, feeling fully responsible for solving the requirement problem, may not pass information along in a timely manner if the project does not provide a mechanism for informing management. The potential risk then compounds itself by reducing the options for mitigation.

This type of situation is not unlike the project management for the construction of a skyscraper in New York City or the tunnels in Boston. Managers of these projects demand and get a constant flow of information from lawyers, building inspectors, crew chiefs, and tradesman. The gathered information is used to identify risks such as rising cost of concrete or other goods or a change in the city ordinance that may be about to be passed. Once identified, the risks can be mitigated — goods can be purchased earlier than scheduled to avoid the budget impact and paperwork to grandfather the building design can be proposed as a rider to the new ordinance. The bottom line is that the potential risk is identified as early as possible in a manner that provides maximum reaction time for managers to mitigate risk. Buildings go up. Roads are built. Lessons can be learned.

The primary lesson is to keep the flow of information moving from system designers, coders, configuration management specialists, and technical writers to project managers. Factors such as new technology, challenging schedules, constrained budgets, indecisive or unrealistic customers, and insufficient staff are just a few of the reasons to get the team involved in potential risk identification.

As the team begins to view risk management as part of overall quality, the direction of the project toward successful completion becomes smoother. The defined processes provide a road map for both management and the team to use in assessing status effectively. Everyone needs to participate.

RISK IDENTIFICATION

Problems are inherent in every software development project. The size, scope, and nature of the problems vary from project to project, but no project escapes problems altogether. All too often, problems reach "fire drill" level before they are even identified. This situation in itself presents a risk to a project. To mitigate the "fire drill" risk, two things must be done. The first is to increase team awareness about the goals of the project. This includes customer, corporate, and project quality standards, schedule and budget constraints, and the implications the system under development will have in the production environment. The awareness does not necessarily mean management needs to reveal exact dollars and cents against company policy or better business judgment. It does mean providing a sufficient level of information, such as the percentage of dollars the project represents to the 5-year plan or the margin of budget error tolerable before the project would have to be canceled. This information helps team members at every level to personalize their stake in the success of the project.

The second part of problem identification is promoting the idea that problems are expected and being able to identify them early ensures better quality of the product and fewer crisis situations for the team. To ensure cooperation, the project team needs to be comfortable in speaking out and identifying potential risks before they become real problems. In other words, there is no room for a "shoot the messenger mentality," and there is no room for unprofessional taunting about "stupid" submissions.

REPORTING RISKS

All potential risks, once identified, need to be reported up the chain of command. It should be understood that whenever a person uncovers an event or situation that may have a negative impact on the project, it should be brought to the attention of a person responsible for risk management and entered into a central database. Sometimes, a person does not know if the potential risk is theirs to report. In such a case, the person should feel comfortable bringing the matter to their supervisor or, better yet, not being afraid of stepping on toes, anyone's toes, in reporting it. The caution of "toe-stomping" is eliminated in risk management when it is understood that the reporting helps managers by supplying better information to use in making decisions. When the mechanisms for reporting fosters greater involvement by everyone on the team, the success rate of risk management is increased. Since potential risks may be identified by anyone from secretaries working on the project who may know that someone is planning to change jobs, to system application programmers who may find glitches in the design as development takes off, it is important that the reporting mechanism is simple and convenient to use.

Whether this mechanism is as simple as sending e-mail to a central person who carries the responsibility for collecting risk information or an on-line reporting system to which everyone on the program has access, each person involved in the project needs to be made aware of the what the mechanism is and know how to use it. Additionally, controls need to be put in place to ensure that each person acts in accordance with the reporting process.

Once the potential risks are reported, there needs to be a person or team responsible for their disposition. This can be a trained risk analyst, senior engineer, or team of engineers who assess the potential risks to determine if they represent a real risk. A technique for handling reported potential risks that do not constitute a real risk must also be put into place so that the team understands that it will not impact the project.

RISK ANALYSIS

In order to determine if a potential risk reported is a real risk — as opposed to being an existing problem, an issue, or a gripe — it is essential to have a single risk definition. For the purposes of this chapter, a risk is being defined as an incident that could have one or more negative consequences on the project, that the incident has some degree of occurrence probability, and that there are options for preventing or minimizing the incident. Within this definition, there are three conditions that must be met in order to confirm a potential risk as a real risk.

Confirming Risks

The first condition states there will be one or more negative impacts on the project. For example, the design for an imaging system relies on vendor X to complete development of the upgrade of data capture software so that it will meet higher scan rates, and vendor X just notified the lead engineer on the imaging system project that they are two months behind schedule. At a minimum, this could cause a late delivery of this piece of software, which will negatively impact the imaging project's schedule. However, if the software upgrade does not meet the higher scan rates, it could require the purchase of additional scanners and possibly a larger operations center. Another example might be a change in the customer's requirement, resulting in additional time and resources being needed and causing potential budget and schedule issues to surface.

The second condition states there is a probability the incident will occur. Because the vendor called to say that testing of their product is behind schedule, the probability of late delivery is very real. The incident of this delay needs to be analyzed for the imaging project at this point to determine points of impact.

The third condition states that there are options for overcoming the impacts of the event. For example, if the selected hardware is not delivered on time, one option might be to select a different vendor who will guarantee delivery on time. Another option might be to allow both conversion and unit testing to proceed for functionality, with testing of performance pushed out.

In a situation where there is a probability of the customer adding requirements, thus impacting the delivery schedule through increased work effort, one option might be to plan for a limited number of schedule changes with the customer in advance or to establish a release management process for adding new features to the delivered system. In either case, the customer must be able to agree to the mitigating action in advance.

Suppose that the hardware delivery is delayed as the result of a fire, flood, or some other act of nature. In this instance, the incident could not have been foreseen. It is a real problem that now has to be dealt with in real-time. As such, it does not constitute a risk since there are no options except to deal with it. The situation cannot be mitigated to reduce the impact since the event has occurred and the impact exists.

In the case of added requirements, use the Year 2000 effort as an example to emphasize the fact of the importance of meeting schedule demands. The customer adds requirements because new regulations are imposed upon them for doing business, so they have no choice. Work is increased. At first, it might seem as though there are still options available, such as hiring additional professionals, so this may still be considered a risk. However, bringing more people to the effort may not be possible due to learning curves, availability of qualified people, or budget constraints, which eliminates its risk status. Resolving the two conflicting requirements becomes an issue that management will have to contend with in order to find some satisfactory way to bring closure to the issue. Issues cannot be treated as risks.

Identifying Consequences

After a risk has been confirmed, the consequences associated with the risk must be identified and documented. The work performed to qualify a potential risk includes establishing a probability of occurrence factor. This is accomplished by evaluating the probability of occurrence and rating the probability from 1 to 5. Use 1 as the least likely that the incident will occur, and 5 as the highest likelihood that it will occur. In an organization where defined metrics are available, such as Goddard Space Flight Center, a model developed by the Software Assurance Technology Center (SATC) is used. This model relies on metrics collected on quality standards (established by the project manager). The SATC Model is used to predict the risks that will affect predefined milestones in the project. These predictions are based on traditional risk classifications of low, medium or moderate, and high.

To evaluate risk effectively within these classifications, the classifications must be quantified using clearly stated criteria. For instance, does a classification of *low* mean that:

- The probability of occurrence suggests no alternative measures are needed?
- The magnitude of loss is minimal, so do nothing?
- There is ongoing corrective action that will overcome the risk's effects?
- All of the above are valid?
- None of the above are valid?

The quantification of the classification criteria for each independent project or all projects within an organization should reflect the needs of the project manager in terms of successful delivery of quality product.

Neutralizing Risks

Do not be surprised if during this analysis effort, some risks are neutralized. This happens when the project plan has already made allowance for the incident based on previous data, or if other conditions of a true risk are missing. Other times, seemingly benign risks on the surface may expand as a result of the consequences in other areas of the project.

An example of a neutralized risk might be that someone reports on a very real upcoming situation where currently installed scanning equipment does not meet the vendor throughput projections. The system design took this possibility into consideration as potential risk and made provisions for additional scanners to be installed prior to the point at which the volume of items would be ready for scanning. The risk management principles worked as soon as the person reported the inadequacy of the currently installed scanners in relationship to projected volume. It worked because everyone on the team was thinking and contributing to the success of the effort.

Once a probability factor is established, the risks need to be categorized into types of risk; that is, which areas are impacted by the risk? Knowing which areas will be affected by the occurrence of the potential event, ensures that the right people will be involved in the next phase of risk analysis. This part is mitigation.

MITIGATING RISKS

Mitigation is the process of evaluating the risk and finding alternatives to the conditions that precipitate its existence. In other words, what is wrong, and what can be done to eliminate or reduce the impact of what is wrong? Factors that should be considered in setting evaluation criteria are: probability of occurrence, frequency of occurrence, technical outcome, cost impacts, and schedule impacts. It is here that the options for resolving risk are listed. Should it be discovered during this part of the analysis that an incident must be corrected and does not have options, it leaves the risk list and is noted on another list named "issues" or "unresolved items." Issues are dealt with differently than risks. It is important to look for issues that will require management help.

The next step is to identify the action or actions that will eliminate or substantially reduce the classified risks. Naturally, this activity focuses on risks classified first as high and works backwards to those classified as low. The alternative or corrective actions will vary depending on the phase of the development life cycle in which the risk occurs and which future phases the risk impacts.

Each valid alternative should be assigned a numeric value that suggests the feasibility for implementation, cost implications, schedule ramifications, and the level of risk reduction it represents. This information should then be presented to the project manager, who has the ultimate responsibility for making the mitigation decision. The mitigation portion of the work is complete when the option values have been assigned and a selection from the options can be made to minimize or eliminate the risk.

Documentation of the mitigation options is important because it provides an audit trail that can be used throughout the project to update the project plan, bring new people over the learning curves, manage customer expectations, and apply lessons learned to future projects. The documentation may be maintained using a spreadsheet with columns for: Risk, Subordinate Risks, Priority, Options, Option Value, Selected Resolution, Resulting Value. The resolution selected from each of the options must meet with management and customer approval. Maintaining good documentation during the analysis will help achieve their understanding of the problems and their approval for corrective action.

RISK ADJUSTMENT

Adjustment is the process of selecting the option that best mitigates the risk. This can be as simple as the project manager highlighting the option of choice on a list, or it may involve the creation of detailed mitigation plans to be "sold" to management and customers when there are significant cost and schedule impacts.

RISK COMPENSATION

Compensation is the actual implementation of the approved changes to the project, based on the project manager and the customer's agreed-upon resolution. Make certain that the project team understands that the method to be used to mitigate the risk will reduce frustration and complaints from the onset. There should be a defined process for implementing correct actions since that will reduce the chance of compounding risks by the tension and frustration caused by crisis management and chaotic change.

RECOMMENDED COURSE OF ACTION

Considering all the benefits a solid risk management process brings to a project, it appears that no project should function without it. History shows that risk management has been done on the fly with whatever people may be available to fight the risk fire. The structure imposed by a risk management process goes a long way in eliminating chaos, which is a risk in itself, from a project.

The implementation of the risk management process does not need to be a big, formal deal. In fact, on small projects, it may be determined that the best process calls for an agenda item called risk to be added to daily team meetings. Under the time allocated for risk discussions at the meeting, someone takes notes to make certain that the potential risks identified during the meeting are recorded. The same person would note options that come out of the discussion and prepare a report on the status of risk resolution. The responsible person can be the lead engineer, a member of the quality assurance group, or a senior staffer attached to the project management office. The entire team should be kept abreast of what is going on. Everyone has an opportunity to participate in the problem-solving of the project and, as a result, therefore has a greater stake in the success of the project.

On larger projects, a single person may be given responsibility for the risk management process during the staffing of the project. The person may even be given the title of Risk Analyst and have the authority to form action teams from the pool of engineers working on the project to assist with the analysis and resolution phase of the process. Depending on the organization requirements of the project, the risk analyst may be part of the quality management group or be a senior staffer acting independently and reporting directly to the project manager.

The important thing is to put some structure into managing risk. When this is done, completion of the project can be reached. The project does not have to become another statistic of failure. While the biggest benefit of risk management occurs during the initial project planning phase, it is important to continue to process throughout the entire project life cycle.

Recommended Reading

Charette, Robert N., *Software Engineering Risk Anaysis and Management;* Intertext Publications, McGraw-Hill Company, 1989.

DeMarco, Tom and Lister, Timothy, *Peopleware;* Dorset House Publishing Co., 1984

Hyatt, L., and Rosenberg, Dr. L., *A Software Quality Model and Metrics for Identifying Project Risks and Assessing Software Quality,* Paper presented at the 8th Annual Software Technology Conference, Utah, April 1996.

Chapter 6
Guidelines for Making and Using Project Estimates

Larry D. Runge

Although software quality — or the lack of it — is often cited as the most troubling problem software developers currently face, in many cases, the lack of quality in software is directly related to how hard the developers were pushed to get something out the door fast. This is a problem that has its roots in software estimating.

For example, a billion-dollar subsidiary of a Fortune 100 company decided to rewrite a major system critical to the success of the business. The vice president of systems made an initial estimate by comparing the system with other systems he had developed. He estimated that the rewrite would cost approximately $1 million and that the project could be completed in one year. He passed this cost estimate on to the president of the business, saying that it could vary as much as 30 percent higher or perhaps 20 percent lower. He hedged his bet by stating that the project would take two years to complete.

Because the project manager who was put in charge of the rewrite had never been responsible for a project of the magnitude now facing him, he turned to his key analysts; between them, they developed an estimate that exceeded $3 million and allowed approximately two years for completion.

The vice president, dismayed at the doubling of his initial estimate, worked personally with the project manager to refine the projection, and they lowered it to $1.8 million. The vice president then obtained the president's approval for the new budget and schedule, and work started on the project.

The project appeared to be proceeding well until a year later, when the vice president was informed of some problems. The project manager had been regularly providing the vice president with glowing reports of his

0-8493-9998-X/00/$0.00+$.50
© 2000 by CRC Press LLC

progress. The vice president received monthly accounting reports on the cost of the project but, in the spirit of delegation and empowerment, declined to audit them, depending instead on the project manager's reports. Subsequently, the accounting department informed the vice president that the project was $1 million over budget.

The project manager was replaced. The more experienced project manager brought in to replace him informed the vice president after several weeks of careful estimating, that the project would exceed the budget further and it was unlikely that the original schedule could be maintained. The vice president was able to cover the cost overrun by canceling another project; however, attempting to extend the original schedule would have caused major problems for the business (as well as being disastrous for the career of the vice president). The vice president, therefore, insisted that the project be completed according to the original schedule.

When time for delivery came around, the new system was nearly completed. However, it contained hundreds of known bugs and was unstable and difficult to use; it was missing critical modules, and others were jury-rigged. The vice president pushed it into implementation anyway, insisting it was complete and that he had delivered on his original commitments.

The hasty implementation proved to be a catastrophe for the business, not only requiring a doubling of personnel required to do the same level of work as before but actually causing the business to lose customers. What was touted as a wonderful new system was quickly recognized as the albatross it was, and the company became the laughingstock of its industry. Most missed schedules may not turn out to be the nightmare that this one was, but inaccurate estimates and missed schedules are typically the rule, rather than the exception, in the systems world.

In fact, software estimating is as much art as science. As much as systems developers would like to regard their profession as an engineering discipline, they simply do not have the tools and techniques necessary to accurately predict software costs and schedules. Then again, perhaps too high a standard for goals has been set.

THE PROBLEM WITH ESTIMATES

Business managers often complain that systems developers cannot make accurate estimates for their projects. After all, they say, civil and building contractors can predict the amount of time it takes them to put up a bridge or a building. Before the same is expected of software developers, it is important to examine the building industry more closely. An average story in a building is 10 feet high, and an average ceiling in that average story is a little less than 8 feet high.

The missing two feet are above the ceiling with a few wires and pipes running through the space. All this wasted space is there for two reasons. First, contractors cannot be sure exactly how much room they may need for the wiring and pipes. Second, they need to have room in case they forget to plan for something or some new requirement comes up. So they increase the human space by 25 percent to be able to accommodate future needs without having to tear the building down and start over.

In the electrical engineering field, electronic components often have an associated accuracy tolerance. A resistor may come with a 5 percent tolerance, a 10 percent tolerance, or a 20 percent tolerance. The tolerance is marked on the resistor by means of a color band. The point being made is not that the component performs only within 20 percent of the value specified, it is that the user understands that the value may vary as much as 20 percent.

The two key points are that the estimates do not have to be exact as long as the user understands that they are not and that they can always be refined later. In fact, not only do the estimates not have to be exact, it is impossible to make them exact. Regardless of how proficient systems development managers are with their estimating tools, every project has its own set of requirements and challenges and bears little relationship to what they have done before. Again, an estimate is supposed to be a tentative evaluation or a rough calculation.

Yet software developers are typically seen as providing advanced actuals. Estimates are not seen as preliminary calculations, which may vary 20 percent to 30 percent, but as a promise to deliver the system on June 12th, at 5:46 pm, for a cost of $132,553.27.

Thus, the real problem with estimates is not just that they are inaccurate, it is that the people receiving them do not understand how imprecise they can be. The most important step in presenting estimates is to ensure that the person requesting them understands that they are imprecise and not the precise advanced actuals that many business executives believe or are led to expect them to be. However, software development managers must still make every effort possible to ensure that the estimates they provide are as accurate as humanly possible under the circumstances. The following section examines the most popular methods of estimating software.

METHODS OF ESTIMATING SOFTWARE

With the exception of an outright guess, software estimating falls into three basic categories (see Exhibit 6.1): top-down estimates, bottom-up estimates, and like-comparisons. The first two are associated with work units, and the last is a comparison of a proposed project with other, completed, projects that are similar in nature. Although each technique has its

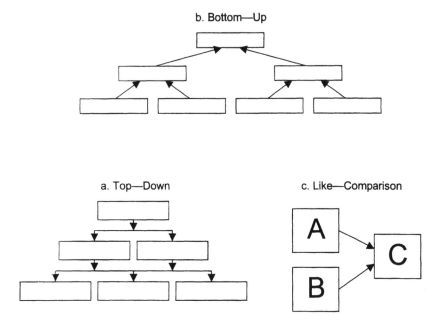

Exhibit 6.1. Basic Categories of Software Estimating

strengths and weaknesses, in a properly estimated project, all three should be used. Within these three categories, there are several separate estimating methods.

The Work Breakdown Structure. The work breakdown structure is a disciplined approach for identifying all the components of a structure (e.g., a bridge, an airplane, or a computer program). Starting at the highest level, each item is broken into its constituent parts and these are numbered (see Exhibit 6.2). Once a structure is decomposed to its lowest level, the costs, schedule, and dependencies can be projected for each individual work unit. This allows a rigorous approach to estimating and tracking, and most formal estimating methodologies depend on this process. However, it takes a significant expenditure of time and money to decompose a project into its work breakdown structure.

This approach was popular from the 1970s through the late 1980s. The methodologies based on it were rigid, inflexible, and expensive and required reams of supporting documentation. This approach was appropriate for the systems and the tools of the time, but to achieve a reasonable level of accuracy, as much as 50 percent of a total project's final cost might be required just for making the estimate. This was not money lost — by this time, all the requirements would be, in effect, completed. However, execu-

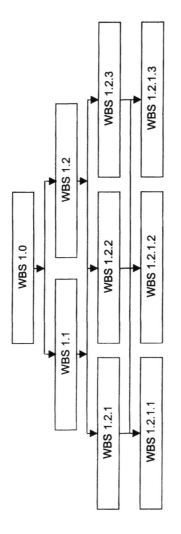

Exhibit 6.2. Sample Work Breakdown Structure

tives were not well disposed to spend hundreds of thousands of dollars just to determine a reasonably accurate estimated cost of a project, so other"techniques" were typically brought in.

Other "Techniques." Often, the scientific wild-eyed guess method of estimating was used to provide a preliminary estimate until the more rigid methodologies could provide a better assessment. SWAG stands for, more or less, scientific wild-eyed guess. The true strength of SWAG estimates is that they are usually based on a comparison of a proposed system with experience gained by completing a similar project — or one as close as possible to that being proposed. In the case of the SWAG estimate, the developer has a rough, intuitive idea of how long the project might take and uses this for the basis of the estimate.

A similar method, often used by senior IS executives (e.g., vice president or CIO) is the ozone ranger method of software estimating. In this approach, the executive — before talking to the staff — plucks an estimate out of the ozone and provides this to the president. Business executives and managers love these estimates, because they sound too good to be true. Of course, because they are made with no basis in reality, they are too good to be true.

A software estimating method in favor with non-systems executives who wield the power necessary to enforce it is called the stake in the sand. In this approach, a senior executive — generally either the CEO or CFO — simply selects a date and decrees that the project will be completed by then. Of course, the danger with this approach is that it often forces the delivery of software that is incomplete, just to meet the arbitrary schedule.

All experienced project managers prefer Dutch dike estimating over any other technique. If a dike is built so high that the water can never slosh over its top, all is safe — just set the estimates so high that they can never be exceeded. The downside to this otherwise excellent approach is that it encourages inefficiency and perpetuates bad habits on the part of the software organization. In addition, because the estimates are always so imposing, companies often either cancel planned projects or outsource them.

A more rigorous estimating technique is called the two-by-four estimating method. It is actually two methods, performed at the start of each of the four major phases of any given software project: analysis, design, construction, and testing and installation. This approach is the most applicable to today's tools and systems and is examined in more detail in the following sections.

THE TWO-BY-FOUR ESTIMATING METHOD

The first step in this method is to perform an initial estimate by comparing the overall scope of the planned project with another project that matches it as closely as possible. This like-comparison provides a rough metric for comparing subsequent estimates. For example, a company planning to convert from one hardware platform and database to a second may have learned that another company in a similar line of business spent $8 million performing a similar conversion. This can be used as a ballpark estimate. Although the various factors at play are likely to cause the first company's own conversion to run from as little as $4 million to as much as $16 million, if the business can afford only $150,000, it is at least obvious that management should rethink the proposed conversion.

Once the conversion has been decided on, all the potential units of work should be identified. This is done from the bottom up. All the screens, programs, and reports the system will be expected to provide are inventoried and then grouped upward into logical applications, until the highest level is reached (see Exhibit 6.3).

For a quick estimate, the total number of work units can be multiplied by whatever figure is used at the individual company for labor estimates to arrive at the total projected person-years effort required to complete the project (three weeks per work unit is recommended to provide a very rough cut). This figure should be multiplied by $100,000 to obtain the rough project cost. (The $100,000 is approximately what it would cost to hire a contract programmer for one year. Thus, this rough estimate is based on doing the project entirely with contract personnel. This figure is recommended even if less-expensive internal programmers are to be used for the job. Internal employees may have to be supplemented or replaced with contract labor, which would automatically create a cost overrun. If no contract personnel are hired, using this amount as a basis for an estimate provides an additional cushion for other unexpected expenses. If one of the Big Six consulting groups is to be used, this figure should be doubled or tripled; $100,000 was obtained by multiplying $50 an hour times 40 hours per week times 50 weeks per year.)

This quick cost estimate should approximate the cost obtained by performing the initial comparative estimate, for example, within a tolerance of 50 percent lower or 100 percent higher. These tolerances are meant to be inexact.

Exhibit 6.3. Bottom-Up Inventory

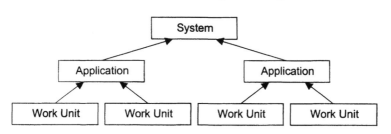

Exhibit 6.4. Table for Estimating Software Work Units

	Analysis	Design	Build	Test and Install
Trivial	4	8	16	12
Easy	8	16	16	28
Average	16	24	40	40
Complex	36	40	80	88
Extremely Complicated	48	60	120	140

The next step is to have experienced programmers examine the work units and give each a complexity rating. They should determine how easy or difficult it will be to program each unit. The categories listed in Exhibit 6.4 may appear to take shape only as individual work units are studied and compared. Once each work unit has been weighted in this way, the units can be compared using a programming estimating table, as shown in Exhibit 6.4, to determine the amount of time required to complete each of the four phases for each of the individual work units. In all but the most trivial project, this is a tedious task.

This procedure actually provides five initial estimates: one is the total estimated cost and effort, and the other four are the cost and effort required to complete each of the four software development phases. Once development starts, progress is monitored against these initial estimates. This information can then be saved and factored into the next project's estimates.

At this point, the like-comparison and bottom-up estimates should have produced a general idea of what the cost and effort for the project is going to be; although more accurate than other less-structured estimates, they can still be misleading. A top-down estimate can provide a further degree of accuracy. The top-down estimate is most easily done with a PC and project management tool. Although these tools may not be applicable in today's Rapid Application Development environment — it can be difficult to keep the data in these current with what is happening on the actual project — they are definitely useful for performing top-down estimates.

The concept of a top-down estimate is simple, even if its execution is a bit more cumbersome. In general, all the work units are plugged into a project management tool, people requirements are added, dependency connections are established, and any remaining items likely to add cost and time to the project (e.g., software, Central Processing Unit processing costs, or management and supervision required) are added. A typical project has 20 to 30 categories of these.

Once all of this information is in the tool, it can be used to generate preliminary schedules and cost estimates. Because these are treated as from tasks or applications and the tool breaks these into their constituent parts, the estimate is made from the top down. This new estimate will be higher than the bottom-up estimate, but there should not be a 100 percent increase between the two. If there is, the alarm bells should go off, and it is necessary to wade back through all the calculations to see why they varied so greatly.

Depending on the development methodology, it may not be possible to perform top-down estimates for each of the four basic stages. If it is possible, it should be done; if not, a single estimate for the total project should suffice.

At this point, it is practical to add an estimating factor of 10 percent to 20 percent to the estimates. Like the space left above the ceiling in a skyscraper, this estimating factor allows a cushion against the things that might have been missed and against the unpredictable things that will occur and hamper the project's completion. This should be compared with the initial comparative estimate, and if there's a large difference, it is important to understand why. It may simply be due to the cavalier characteristics of comparative estimates, but it is worthwhile to check anyway, lest something significant has been missed. In the hectic, ill-defined, intellectually complex world of software development, this happens more often than most would care to admit.

Finally, another 15 percent should be added to the estimate as a contingency but tracked as a separate column. As the project proceeds, progress must be tracked against the overall estimate — not at the work-unit level. Despite all the scientific precision that has been applied to this estimate, it remains an inexact process. Some work units will be estimated too low, others too high. Ignoring the work unit and tracking at the highest level allows these differences to be canceled out. Otherwise, the project is likely to become bogged down with excessive administrative nonsense that will hardly be appreciated by the project team.

The alternative to two-by-four estimating is to take the Generally Accepted Accounting Principles approach. Theoretically, the first GAAP estimate would be more accurate than the first two-by-four estimate, because all the requirements analysis and most of the design will have already been performed. In the real world, it is extremely unlikely that anyone would ever have the luxury of spending the huge amounts of money that GAAP estimating requires just to determine an estimate.

As each major stage of the project is completed, the entire two-by-four estimating process is repeated. The exception to this is that the 15 percent contingency is not reestimated. It is estimated once, at the start of the project, the business leader is informed of its purpose, and withdrawals are then tracked against it. Both top-down and bottom-up estimating techniques are used at the start of each of the four major stages of a software development project.

A FIVE-STEP PLAN

The basic process of estimating software projects can be described in a simple, five-step plan.

Step One. First, it is important to recognize the limitations of the estimates. Atomic scientist Niels Bohr said, "Prediction is very difficult, especially concerning the future." Although software developers may be experts with their tools, each new job is unique in its own way. Developers should do everything to ensure that their estimates are as accurate as possible under the constraints put upon them by the business, but the estimates are estimates, not advance actuals.

Step Two. Estimating is most effective if all the applicable estimating methods available are used. The reality of the business world is such that these methods' use has to be tailored to the needs of the businesses. If possible, the following three estimating techniques should be used:

- Top-down
- Bottom-up
- Like-comparison

During different phases of a project, each of the three may serve as the primary estimating mechanism. However, all three should be used whenever possible to provide a means of checks and balances. This combination of the three is called the two-by-four estimating technique.

Step Three. As professionals, software development managers must acknowledge the inherent inaccuracy of estimating methods to those who are making decisions based on them. Regardless of the amount of effort put into making them, they will always lack absolute precision. It is crucial that this message is conveyed to those outside the field — especially when providing estimates to senior executives. Senior IS executives who have made commitments based on wishful thinking rather than on technical reality must realign their thinking.

Step Four. It is essential to recast estimates at each of the major four stages of software development: requirements, design, construction, and testing and implementation. Each new suite of estimates will be more precise than the one preceding it and will underscore the true state of progress. These revised estimates must be taken back to the sponsors of the project, even if it seems likely that they may cancel the project should they find that the original estimates may have been too optimistic.

Step Five. The project's adherence to schedule should be managed according to the overall estimates and not at the work-unit level. Regardless of how disciplined the estimating approach and how detailed the execution, software estimation is not a science. Managing at the top level allows inaccuracies at the bottom level to cancel themselves out. In addition, micromanagement adds a substantial — and costly — administrative burden to the project, and only increases the likelihood that the estimates will be missed. Finally, the project will have been approved at the top level and this is the level at which it will be tracked by the sponsoring executive. (An executive is interested in total cost, date of completion, and the benefits that are to be returned — not in what day the programming of a given subroutine was started and whether it took the programmer four hours or six hours to complete and unit test it.)

RECOMMENDED COURSE OF ACTION

Inaccurate estimates are not the real problem in the software world. The problem is that people are inadvertently misled into believing that estimates are far more precise than they could ever be for the amount of time and money allocated to make them. Just as is done in other engineering disciplines, software engineers must educate their customers. Ensuring that the estimates are as accurate as possible, however, should remain the goal. To do this, multiple estimating techniques should be used to perform each estimate and the project should be reestimated at the completion of each major stage of a development project.

Chapter 7

A Model for Estimating Small-Scale Software Development

Abbas Heiat

Estimating the effort required to develop an information system is an important project management concern. As a result, a number of models have appeared in computing literature over the past 25 years. Cot, Bourque, Oligny, and Rivard have identified more than 20 estimating models, which were developed to provide a better understanding of software development and its estimation process. Of these, the two most common are Lines of Code (LOC) and Function Points (FP). These models have advantages and disadvantages, discussed in following sections of this chapter. These models, however, are not as well adapted to today's small business environment.

In recent years, a large number of small businesses have used computer technology to automate their operations. Unfortunately, only a few studies have investigated small-scale information systems in the context of small or large organizations. With the rise of end-user computing, the trend toward the information center concept has become widely accepted. By having end users do their own software development work, the larger organizations, too, are supporting a plethora of small information system applications.

Delone, Montazami, and Raymond have identified several critical success factors for information systems in small business environments. Requirements analysis and estimation of the effort required to develop the software are the most important parts of information system planning and control. This chapter reports the results of an empirical study designed to estimate efforts required for developing small-scale information systems, as compared to the LOC and FP methods.

LINES OF CODE (LOC)

LOC has two steps in the effort estimation process. First, the number of lines of code required for the information system is estimated. Second, the total effort is calculated using the formula developed based on historical data of previous projects. The formula is of the following form:

$$EFH = c(LOC)^k$$

where EFH = the estimated effort in man-months or man-hours
  c and k = constants
  LOC = the estimated number of lines of code in the application software

For example, an application requires 1,000 lines of code. According to the estimated formula,

$$EFH = 17.45 \ (1,000) \ 0.39 = 256.1$$

The main limitation of the LOC model is that it depends on the accuracy of an early estimate of lines of code. This estimate is usually based on the systems analyst's past experience. Certainly, organizations find it difficult, if not impossible, to locate experienced analysts who come up with an accurate estimate of the system size using a LOC model.

Another problem with the LOC model is that it does not provide accurate estimates even after the detailed design requirements are specified. An interesting observation comes from a report by Conte, Dunsmore, and Shen.[1] Given the detail design specifications, several experienced project managers were asked to estimate the size of 16 completed projects. Even with the detail design specifications at hand, expert software project managers consistently underestimated the actual system size.

A third problem with LOC model is that it does not take into account the resources available to the systems development team. These include, for example, the types of language used in coding, software tools, and the skills and experiences of the team itself.

FUNCTION POINTS (FP)

An alternative method for estimating systems development effort was developed by A. J. Albrecht.[2] Albrecht introduced the concept of function points (FP) to measure the functional requirements of a proposed system. In FP modeling, system size is determined by first identifying the type of each required function in terms of inputs, outputs, inquiries, internal files, and external interface files. To calculate the value of function points for each category, the number of functions in each category is multiplied by the appropriate complexity weight. The total systems effort is then calculated by multiplying the sum of function points for all categories by the technical complexity factor (TCF). The TCF is determined by assigning values to 14 influencing project factors and totaling them.

The information-processing size is determined by first identifying the system components as seen by end users and classifying them as five types, namely the external (i.e., logical) inputs, outputs, inquiries, the external interfaces to other systems, and the logical internal files. The components are each further classified as simple, average, or complex, depending on the number of data elements in each type and on other factors. Each component is then given a number of points depending on its type and complexity, and the sum for all components is expressed in unadjusted function points (UFPs).

The technical complexity factor (TCF) is determined by estimating the Degree of Influence of some 14 component general application characteristics. The degree-of-influence scale ranges from 0 (i.e., not present or no influence) to 5 (i.e., strong influence throughout). The sum of the scores of the 14 characteristics [i.e., the total degrees of influence (DI)] is converted to the TCF using the formula:

$$TCF = 0.65 + 0.01 * DI$$

Thus, each degree of influence is worth 1 percent of a TCF, which can range from 0.65 to 1.34.

The intrinsic relative system size in function points is computed by the formula:

$$FPs = UFPs * TCF$$

The first step is to build a table that can be used to total the unadjusted function points. The second step is to determine and quantify the effect of factors that influence the complexity of the entire system. For example, the more complicated the communication requirements are, the greater the project effort. If no communication were needed between the users or workstations, a rating of 0 would be used for the data communications. Exhibit 7.1 illustrates these steps.

The third step is to insert the computed values for the total degree of influence and total UFPs into the following equations and solve them:

$$TCF = 0.65 + 0.01 *(41) = 1.06$$

$$FPs = 278 * 1.06 = 294.68$$

The final step is to insert the computed FPs into an estimated equation and solve it:

Exhibit 7.1. Determining Unadjusted Function Points and the Total Degree of Influence

Description	Level of Information Processing Function			
	Simple	Average	Complex	Total
External Input	$2 \times 3 = 6$	$5 \times 4 = 20$	$3 \times 6 = 18$	44
External Output	$3 \times 4 = 12$	$2 \times 5 = 10$	$4 \times 7 = 28$	50
Logical Internal File	$0 \times 7 = 0$	$4 \times 10 = 40$	$2 \times 15 = 30$	70
External Interface File	$2 \times 5 = 10$	$2 \times 7 = 14$	$1 \times 10 = 10$	34
External Inquiry	$10 \times 3 = 30$	$5 \times 4 = 20$	$5 \times 6 = 30$	80
Total Unadjusted Function Points				**278**

ID	Characteristic	DI
C1	Data Communications	2
C3	Performance	4
C4	Heavily Used Configuration	1
C5	Transaction Rate	5
C6	Online Data Entry	5
C7	End-User Efficiency	3
C8	Online Update	4
C9	Complex Processing	2
C10	Reusability	1
C11	Installation Ease	2
C12	Operational Ease	3
C13	Multiple Sites	2
C14	Facilitate Change	1
Total Degree of Influence		**41**

Notes: 0 = Not Present or No Influence, 1 = Insignificant Influence, 2 = Moderate Influence, 3 = Average Influence, 4 = Significant Influence, 5 = Strong Influence Throughout.

Effort Hours = 585.6 + 15.12 (FP)

Effort Hours = 585.6 + 15.12 (294.68) = 5041.16

The best approach to using the FP model is to first build a record of projects at the organization and then to develop and estimate a model specific to the experiences of the organization.

Albrecht argued that the FP model makes intuitive sense to users, and it would be easier for project managers to estimate the required systems effort based on either the user requirements specification or logical design specification. Another advantage of the FP model is that it does not depend on a particular language. Therefore, project managers using the FP model would avoid the difficulties involved in adjusting the LOC counts for information systems developed in different languages.

Critiques of the FP model appear in reviews by Kemerer, Wrigley and Dexter, Symons, Low and Jeffery, Vicimanza, Mukhopadhyay, and Prietula. (Several of these are listed in the Recommended Reading section at the end of this chapter.) Three concerns emerge from these reviews. First, the FP model fails to produce reliable estimates of the system development effort. Second, the FP model does not use information about the system being developed that is captured early in the analysis phase with structured analysis tools. Third, procedures originally developed for FP counting are labor intensive, require experience, and do not lend themselves easily to data collection and processing in a small-scale software development environment.

MODELS FOR DATA-STRONG SYSTEMS

The main objective of an estimation model is to determine the amount of effort that is required to produce the specified information system. Tom DeMarco has developed a specification (i.e., Bang) metric to estimate system development effort.[3] His main hypothesis is that the information content of outputs of an information system is a function of the information content of inputs of that system. It follows that system development effort, too, is a function of the information content of the specified requirements.

DeMarco's metric is developed for data flow diagrams (DFDs). The purpose of a Data Flow Diagram is to represent the flow of data in an information system. This graphic tool is used to show the basic components and flows of a system. DFD are drawn in increasing levels of detail, starting with a high-level summary of the system and proceeding to more detailed lower-levels of detail. In Exhibit 7.2, the context diagram illustrates the highest level of Data Flow Diagram. This chart depicts the relationship of a registration system to the students and the academic affairs office. Four types of symbols are used in Exhibit 7.2: rectangles, rounded squares, arrows, and open-ended rectangles. Rectangles represent external entities, i.e., organizations, departments, or people that are external to the system being developed. They either provide input to or receive output from the system. A rounded square represents a process. Processes often transform data from one form to another. Arrows represent data flows, pipelines that carry packets of data of known composition. Sometimes data flows are forms or documents. An open-ended rectangle represents a data store, an entity in which data is stored.

The overview diagram in Exhibit 7.2 shows the data flow at the next level of detail. The process of establishing multiple levels of diagrams, each expanding on the amount of detail provided in the one above is called *leveling* or *exploding*. Exhibit 7.3 contains two figures, diagram 2 and diagram 4, which expand the approve schedule and the record schedule, which are part of the overview diagram in Exhibit 7.2. In the overview diagram (Exhibit 7.2), the approve schedule is labeled as process 2. In diagram 2 (Ex-

Context Diagram

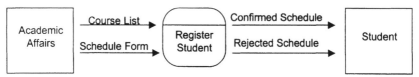

Overview Diagram

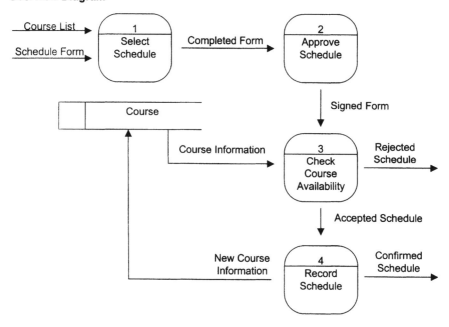

Exhibit 7.2. Context and Overview Diagrams

hibit 7.3) the processes within the approve schedule are labeled 2.1, 2.2, and 2.3. This numbering system is carried down to the lowest-level diagram. In diagram 4 (Exhibit 7.3), which expands the record schedule, the processes are labeled 4.1, 4.2, and 4.3.

DeMarco's model includes 12 different primitive counts (p-counts) of a system's components. A component is considered to be primitive if it is not partitioned into subordinate parts. For example, processes 1, 2.1, 2.2, 2.3,3, 4.1, 4.2, and 4.3 in Exhibits 2 and 3 are functional primitives. DeMarco contends that for process-oriented (i.e., function-strong) systems, the functional primitives count should be the best indicator of the efforts required to develop those systems.

Diagram 2

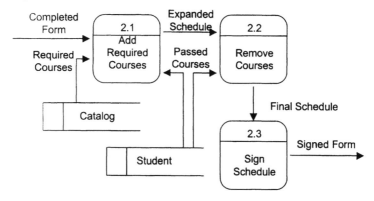

Diagram 4

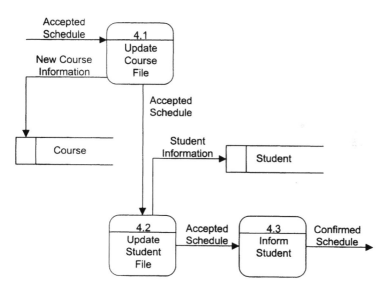

Exhibit 7.3. Diagrams 2 and 4

Many business systems, however, are data-strong systems. A data-strong system is concerned with inputting, accessing, and outputting a large amount of data rather than with processing operations. For a data-strong system with significant database applications, DeMarco recommends the count of objects in the database. To account for complexity of objects, some correction is required. The number of relationships that an object has with other objects may be used as weights. The effort required then is a function of the sum of the corrected objects over all objects.

THE REIO MODEL

This chapter presents a model that builds on DeMarco's proposed model for data-strong systems. The steps to the REIO model are:

- Given a set of leveled Data Flow Diagram, data stores are located on each level.
- The data flows arriving and departing at each data store are counted. For example, in Exhibits 2 and 3, one data flow is flowing in and one is flowing out of the course data store. Therefore, the count is 2.
- Corrections are made for the complexity of the relatedness of a data store or the entity it represents. The first column in Exhibit 7.4 lists the number of relationships (REs) computed in step 2. The corresponding corrected numbers are listed in the second column. In the example presented in step 2, the corrected number would be 2.3.
- The total count is the sum of the corrected REs divided all data stores.
- The total number of data flows that connect the system to external entities are counted. In the context diagram (Exhibit 7.2), there are four data flows that connect the system to the external entities. Therefore, the count would be 4. This number is added to the sum calculated in step 4 to arrive at the total count for the system as a whole.
- For the student registration system as shown in Exhibits 2 and 3, the total count for the system as a whole is computed as follows:

Data Store	REs (Data Flows)	Corrected Res
Course	2	2.3
Catalog	1	1
Student	2	2.3
Total Corrected Res		5.6
Number of data flows that connect the system to external entities		4
Total Count (REIO)		9.6

- The final step is to insert the value for the total count (REIO) into an estimated equation.

The following general equation was modeled for empirical estimation of the amount of effort required for developing a small-scale information system:

$$EFH = f\,(REIO)$$

where EFH = number of man-hours (or man-months) of effort required
REIO = corrected total number of data flows arriving at and departing from data stores (relationship-entity) + total number of

Exhibit 7.4. Relation Weighing of Data Source

RE (Number of Relationships)	Corrected Numbers
1	1.0
2	2.3
3	4.0
4	5.8
5	7.8
6	9.8

data flows that connected the system to external entities (inputs/outputs)

The data used in this study came from projects completed for private and public organizations in Billings, MT. Projects selected had the following attributes:

- They were small in size. The projects' sizes range from 325 to 2,940 lines of code.
- They were all written in a 4GL database programming language.
- They were developed by a small team of one to three systems analysts and programmers.
- Structured specification tools including DFD, E-R diagrams, and data dictionary were used in the development of the applications.
- They maintained auditable time-keeping records.

Based on the above criteria, 35 projects were selected. Regression analysis was used for evaluating and testing the accuracy of REIO, LOC, and FP models. Equations were estimated by ordinary least square estimators. Forecasts of the dependent variable, EFH, were computed for each equation using historical data covering the sample period. To compare and evaluate the accuracy of the estimators, the absolute value of the percentage error of the forecasted values with respect to the actual amount of the development effort-houses (EFH) for each project was calculated.

Overall, the regression results are satisfactory, producing high values of coefficient of determination (R2), and large regression coefficients relative to their standard errors. The Durbin–Watson statistics indicate that all regressions are free from first order serial correlation in disturbances. The results for the proposed REIO model is as follows:

$$EFH = 72.59 + 6.45 \, REIO$$

$$\text{t-values} = (5.4) \ (12.36)$$

$$R^2 = 0.83$$

$$D.W. = 2.13$$

$$MRE = 9.04\%$$

It was mentioned earlier that in the final step the computed value for the total count (REIO) is inserted into the estimated equation to calculate the effort hours required for developing the desired application. In this case:

$$EFH = 72.59 + 6.45(9.6) = 134.51 \text{ hours}$$

ADVANTAGES OF THE REIO MODEL

LOC models, as mentioned earlier, depend on the accuracy of an early estimate of lines of code required for developing the application. This requires using highly experienced analysts and programmers for estimating software development effort. Certainly, most organizations find it difficult and costly to employ experienced estimators for their small-scale projects and end-user computing. As such, it is recommended that the REIO model be used instead of the LOC and FP models for the small-scale software development effort.

A major reason for using REIO as an estimator is that the data stores (entities) relationships and the number of external input–output data flows can be computed easily at an early stage of the systems analysis — even before the data dictionary and the user requirement specifications document is completed. An early estimate of the software development effort is of great value to all organizations. It is a critical success factor for information systems in small business and information centers in larger organizations. Often lacking large pools of financial resources, small businesses need tight project management and controls at low costs. The function point approach is a labor-intensive, costly procedure. Experience in the application of function points is an onerous requirement. In contrast, the REIO method is a simple, pragmatic, and labor-saving approach that works well in small business environments.

Whereas results presented in this chapter appear promising, there are the following limitations. First, the regression analyses have been carried out with only small applications. Therefore, the results cannot be generalized to large applications. Models developed in small environments do not work very well uncalibrated in larger environments, as might be expected. Second, the REIO model developed in this study is designed for use in data-strong applications. Finally, the system development process is a complex and multidimensional process. It is affected by a number of project attributes, including the size of project, software development tools, analyst and programmer experience, and software development methodology. In this study all of these factors have been held constant. Systems analyzed varied only in size and complexity.

CONCLUSION

The REIO model has been developed to estimate the size of small-scale information systems requirements in a 4GL software development environment. The proposed model may be applied relatively early in the systems development life cycle. The model estimates the information systems size by counting data stores, external entries, and the relationships among these objects. Compared to the LOC and FP models, the REIO model appears to be less costly and easier to apply in small-scale software development environments.

Notes

1. S.D. Conte, H.E. Dunsmore, H.E., and V.Y. Shen, *Software Engineering Metrics and Models* (Menlo Park CA: The Benjamin/Cummings Publishing Company, Inc., 1986), p. 214.
2. A.J. Albrecht. "Measuring Application Development Productivity," *Proceedigns of the IBM Applications Development Symposium,* Guide/Share (October 1979), pp. 83–92.
3. Tom DeMarco. *Controlling Software Projects* (New York: Yourdon Press, 1982).

Recommended Reading

Chidamber, S.H. and Kemerer, Chris F. "A Metrics for Object Oriented Design." *IEEE Transactions on Software Engineering* 20, no. 6 (1994).

Costello, Rita J. and Liu, Dar-Biau. "Metrics Requirements Engineering." *Journal of Systems Software* 29:39–63 (1995).

Fenton, Norman. "Software Measurement: A Necessary Scientific Basis." *IEEE Transactions On Software Engineering* 20, no. 3 (1994).

Henry, Lauri and Cassidy, Judith. "The Information Resource Center: Control Mechanism for the End-User Environment." *Journal Of Computer Information Systems* XXXIV, no. 2 (Winter 1993–94).

Kemerer, C.F. "Software Cost Estimation Models." *Software Engineers Reference Handbook* (Butterworth, Surrey, U.K.: 1991).

Kizior, Ronald J. "Function Point Analysis: A Primer." *Interface* 15, issue 1 (1993).

Low, G.C. and D.R. Jeffery. "Function Points in the Estimation and Evaluation of the Software Process." *IEEE Transactions of Software Engineering* January 1993, pp. 64–71.

Matson, Jack, E., Barrett, Bruce E., and Mellichamp, Joseph, M. "Software Development Cost Estimation Using Function Points. *IEEE Transactions On Software Engineering* 20, no. 4 (1994).

Rainer, Kelly, R. "Toward Development of the End User Computing Construct in a University Setting." *Decision Sciences* 24, no. 6 (1993).

Teh, Jack. "The Applicability of Nolan's State Theory in Small Business Environment." *Journal of Computer Information Systems,* Summer 1993, pp. 65–71.

Vicimanza, S.S., Mukhopadhyay, T., and Prietula, J.J. "Software-Effort Estimation: An Exploratory Study of Expert Performance." *Information Systems Research,* December 1991, pp. 243–262.

Chapter 8
Strategic Planning for Acquiring and Managing Computer Resources

Robert DeMichiell

In the early years of automation, acquisition of information technology was placed completely in the hands of the IS staff. Information systems professionals identified the basic applications and solicited assistance and bids from selected vendors. IS designed the database, acquired the computers, developed or bought software, and implemented systems. The process was complex only for those issues directly related to technical feasibility and database design. Applications priority, the development schedule, user training, processing control, and other project management concerns became more important over the years.

To remain competitive, organizations must acquire and use information technology resources effectively. Numerous options in information systems development have evolved owing mostly to the proliferation of microcomputers and the movement toward distributed processing and client/server networks. With the introduction of new decision support and systems development tools, including prototyping methods, and users' growing computer literacy and independence, serious attention must be given not only to receiving financial return on investment but also to acquiring quality products from multiple vendors who are reliable. This chapter emphasizes computer resource planning with an integrated procurement process from assessment through allocation a process that is outlined in Exhibit 8.1.

0-8493-9998-X/00/$0.00+$.50

Establish Framework for Planning	Develop Strategies, Procedures, and Roles for Information Technology
Computer Resource Management Model (CRMM) Stage I: Assessment Stage II: Acquisition Stage III: Allocation	Collaborative Strategies for IS Professionals and Line Managers

Prepare a Formal or Informal Request for Proposal (RFP)

Analysis and Design for Requirements Definition
Authority and Control
Action Planning Teams
Information Technology Assessment
End-User Computing Issues
Applications Portfolio Priority System
Organizational Impact

Assess Organization for Managing Contract Negotiations

Hardware, Software, and Services
Additional Software Issues
Contracting Terms and Conditions

Acquire, Allocate, and Renegotiate Computer Resources

Exhibit 8.1. Integrating Master Plans with Action

THE MASTER PLANNING IMPERATIVE

Some framework is needed to place an organization's business objectives in proper perspective and, ultimately, to translate plans for meeting the objectives into action-oriented solutions. Many end users perceive that immediate hardware and software solutions are commercially available. On-the-shelf solutions usually prompt users to ask two questions:

- Why should there be such a long wait for quality results in the organization's applications development cycle and procurement process?

- Can formal applications be purchased, perhaps by end-user departments, rather than developed?

Users may rush to bypass what they perceive to be lengthy procurement and development processes. Small pockets of funds in departmental budgets are available for such independent solutions and vendors are quick to respond with delivery of hardware and software. Total investment by these independent groups over a long time period is, however, costly and financially unsound. As line managers assume more operating responsibilities in today s information-based organization, IS management will continue to know less about all applications.

Problems with User-Controlled Operations

When IS management is relegated to only monitoring routine data processing activities, information processing capability becomes stagnant. IS management can respond by supporting or ignoring user-developed systems. For IS, the search for a more comprehensive solution is encumbered by the ongoing demands for immediate response, quality enhancement, cost containment, increased productivity, cash liquidity, just-in-time manufacturing and inventory, outplacement alternatives, and organizational downsizing moves.

In user-controlled and independent operations, daily operating procedures often conflict. Departmental data sets are separate entities, and because the data elements may not have unique definitions, data integrity is at risk. In addition, some fiscal status reports for senior corporate management require information from several operating functions. Unless the distributed databases are integrated to a master system with true connectivity to the mainframe, the process requires manipulation of user data files.

When IS and users fail to cooperate, many problems can arise. For example:

- Funding for in-house or outside consultants to help operations run smoothly is often unavailable.
- Neither IS nor the users have the time or expertise to assess requests properly.
- Problem assessments often involve personnel with competing motivations and objectives.
- End users do not provide accurate information concerning application requirements.
- Over-eager vendors provide solutions to organizational problems without an implementation plan.
- Insufficient attention is given to vendor contract terms, conditions, and systems deliverables.
- User documentation is either too technical or too simple, and user literacy is not considered.

- Contingency measures for delayed installation or maintenance of new applications are not identified.
- The roles of IS and end users after implementation of new systems are unclear.
- Access to the computer system by other departments or organizations is undefined.
- Expectations among end users, IS, consultants, and vendors are not delineated.

COMPUTER RESOURCE MANAGEMENT MODEL

To minimize or eliminate some of these conflicts, a long-range master plan with complementary short-term solutions should be established to produce a responsive, manageable operating environment. Traditional organizational models, although applicable for many segments of computer-related management issues, do not address all of these issues.

Case data supports a Computer Resource Management Model (detailed in Exhibit 8.2) that encompasses three managerial stages of assessment, acquisition, and allocation of information technology. Case study data collected from educational, government, and business environments uncovered a model for helping organizations implement computer resources, addressing the concerns of users. Thirty-eight case studies were examined over a decade for attributes relating to managerial issues of information systems planning and implementation. Conclusions were converted into operational action items, including collaborative strategies for IS and line managers, developing a Request For Proposal, and managing contract negotiations. Later sections of this chapter discuss these conclusions in that order.

Addressing User Expectations

The data revealed that user expectations generally are not addressed. If the organization chooses to examine literacy levels, the review usually occurs after acquisition of computer resources. User activity is a function of computer literacy and computer fluency. Computer fluency levels affect management procedures, responsibilities and accountabilities, resource constraints, priority of applications development, and overall risk-return analyses.

Applying computer resources to the right tasks, computer literacy levels of all personnel, and end-user computing philosophy are all integral parts of the planning and control imperative. For many organizations in which there is frequent change of computer capabilities in hardware, software enhancements, and distribution of computing, a formal declaration of authorities for computer systems procurement does not exist. There is a difference between organizational policy for centralized control and the reality of the situation when users acquire and implement standalone, low-

Exhibit 8.2. Computer Resource Management Model (CRMM)

STAGE I: ASSESSMENT

Management of the Organization
  Structure and Modification Mechanisms for Change
  Philosophy, Goals, Decision-Making and Managerial Styles
  Operating Procedures and Work Flow (Formal and Informal)
    Organization Charts: Hierarchy, Project, or Matrix
  Levels of Authority: Responsiveness and Control
Perception of Automation
  Strategic and Operational Feasibility: Definition of Feasibility
  Business Function Operations
  End-User Information Systems Literacy, Fluency; Power Users
  IS Professionals: Education, Expertise, Interests
  Current and Future Requirements; Untapped Opportunities
  Planning
  Organizing for Automation or Automation Changes
    Control Issues: IS and End-User Applications Development
    *Task Forces: TQM System and Authority
    Impact on Organization (Local, National, International)
  Request for Proposal Guidelines
    Development, Production, and Implementation
    Technical, Economic, Legal, Contractual, Administrative Issues
    Level of Specificity, Scope, Constraints

STAGE II: ACQUISITION

Contents of Selection Plan
  Authority, Review, and Control of Process
  Organization, Scope, Timing, Constraints
  Communication and Ethical Issues (Internal and External Reporting)
  Validation and Confidentiality
  Continuity and Continuance of Selection Committee
Implementation of Selection Plan
  Master Plan Conformance: Business Plan and IS Plan
    Application Priorities and Schedule, Organizational Impact
    Computer System Redesign, Resource Changes, and Constraints
Make-or-Buy-Decisions
  Hardware, Peripherals, Data Communications, Software
  Support Services (Consultant On-site, Off-site), Modification, Maintenance
Contract Negotiation
  Solicitation of Bids
  Terms and Conditions of Contract: Mandatory and Desirable Requirements
  Data Collection, Evaluation System, and Analysis
  Clarification of Bids, contract Award, Installation, and Acceptance

STAGE III: ALLOCATION

Master Plan Conformance and Continuous Evaluation System Renegotiation

Exhibit 8.2. Computer Resource Management Model (CRMM) *(Continued)*

Organizational Assessment, Annual RFP Modification
The Three Stages Revisited: Assessment, Acquisition, and Allocation

* The underlying concept for the total quantity management (TOM) approach is to have cross-functional task forces with authority.

---

cost PCs. Strategies are needed to develop a master plan. The preferred approach is one in which strategic initiatives and action statements drive the process to integrate information technology into business practice.

COLLABORATION BETWEEN IS PROFESSIONALS AND LINE MANAGERS

Several design and acquisition issues demonstrate the large scope of the process. The planning effort is a tremendous undertaking, and the frequent change of key personnel can discourage systematic approaches. However, if the organization is willing to commit time to the project at the outset and focus on creating an adaptable long-term solution, then this approach is beneficial to the organization. The financial portion of the contract focuses on cash flow and tax breaks. A phased-in approach with documented milestones and prioritized applications can be implemented. In this way, some results can be realized while the process unfolds.

Vendor relationships should be developed for the long-term with negotiations based on predetermined issues. Procedures establish not only the impact of business programmatic changes, but also the opportunities afforded by technology updates on computing resources. As hardware and software products proliferate and their costs decrease, other extensive systems studies and procurement groups do not have to be reestablished. Historical records are helpful in preventing duplication of effort.

The proposed Computer Resource Management Model uses committees and task forces to focus on design of the best system for the whole organization. A committee should assess technology in all facets of the organization before any procurement action is taken.

All facets of end-user computing become planned activity. Software development by users becomes part of the total effort and should not produce any independent databases or file incompatibilities. Overall benefits of this approach are to reduce costs, minimize risks, use available resources properly, and improve management. The key concept is to quickly develop the master plan, appoint the right people to a loosely coupled network structure of task forces, and produce results on a timely schedule.

Forums

Senior-level managers, including corporate information officers, must provide forums where ideas can be introduced and emerging strategies can be converted into action. Because information technology must be mobilized to support these strategies, the specific responsibilities of the task forces must be identified at the outset.

Line managers and IS professionals must reach a detailed formal agreement addressing the use of information technology for making gains in personal productivity, adding business value to the organization, enhancing the image of the firm, and improving the quality of products or services. Forums should not be complaint centers for current operating problems; these comments could be handled by a separate action team concentrating on those issues.

Forum activity should be visionary. Forums should assess corporate strengths and use them to grasp opportunities in the near term and in the long range picture. Other collaborative strategies are outlined in Exhibit 8.3.

DEVELOPING THE REQUEST FOR PROPOSAL

The Request for Proposal document provides specific deliverables. The effort spent developing a solicitation document should equal the expected return from the information-processing capability.

Strategies incorporated in this document should emerge from task force discussions, findings, conclusions, and recommendations. The selection team for information technology concentrates on procurement, but it will have the benefit of the wisdom, experience, and cross-functional perspective of task force activity to justify its request for proposal (RFP).

Actions to Consider in RFP Development

The Race for Installation. Analysis and design activities are costly and usually do not show any immediate return for the expenditure. Frequently, these phases are accelerated for purchase of hardware and software. Guidelines include:

- Conducting an assessment to make a deliberate decision of the level of detail to be undertaken for analysis and design. Somewhere between the very general specifications and the very specific terms and conditions lies a balanced portrayal of information for the request for proposal (RFP).
- Ensuring that the effort is commensurate with return-investment and risk-return ratios. Identify intangible benefits, hidden costs, and expected productivity gains for new opportunities.

Exhibit 8.3. Collaborative Strategies for IS Professionals and Line Managers

1. Securing top-level support for managing information technology in these key areas:
   - Authorities to control ongoing process by collaborative task forces.
   - Task force makeup: cross-functional teams of IS and line management.
   - Dissemination of information formally to all organizational elements.
   - Implementation plan with flexibility for new users and applications.
   - Strategies with vision and integration of information technology into business plan.
   - Decision-making criteria and impact on information technology procurement.
   - Requirement for planned implementation for migration to new technologies.
   - Creation of new reward systems commensurate with project oriented work.
   - Support of an educational program for new organizational structures.
   - Encouragement to design and implement self-directed teams (task forces).
   - Discouragement of independent information technology activity.
   - Integration of information technology in financial planning process.
   - Requirement that IS, line managers, and vendors meet business objectives.
   - Requirement that IS, line managers, and vendors communicate for effectiveness.
   - Emphasizing strategies with action plans are more effective than crisis reaction.
2. Developing a specific set of objectives for management, including:
   - Scope, constraints, milestones, membership roles, and responsibilities of task forces.
   - Critical success factors and actions needed to exploit them.
   - Identification of corporate strengths and application opportunities.
   - Identification of corporate weaknesses and conversion to strengths.
   - View of future (5 to 10 years) technological advances in hardware, software, services.
3. Creating a forum for ideas, including:
   - Discussion of process and criteria for justification of resources.
   - End-user involvement, including in applications development.
   - Impact of process on organizational philosophy and business practices.
   - Establishment of a communications system using groupware and other mechanisms.
   - Several task forces loosely structured to address issues, problems, and opportunities.
   - Allowance for immediate and long-term timely solutions.
   - Authority clearly established for planning, control, and implementation.
4. Resolving the issues through:
   - Emergence of the most effective and practicable solution for the business.
   - Consideration of technical, economic, operational, political, and human factors.
   - Focus on productivity and total quality management issues.
   - Schedule of activity consistent with task force recommendations.
   - Resolution of application portfolio problems, priorities, and conflicts.
   - Resolution of charging scheme; budget planning and expenditures.
5. Assessing solutions in terms of:
   - Programmatic or staffing changes for alternative solutions.
   - Internal and external impact on organizational structure and workforce.
   - Technology and management advances and their impact on alternative solutions.
   - Focus on business value and less on information technology development.
6. Planning the information technology selection process, including:
   - Schedule for procurement process and evaluation.
   - Immediate, short-term, and long-range acquisitions.

**Exhibit 8.3. Collaborative Strategies for IS Professionals
and Line Managers** *(Continued)*

- Procedures for all phases and all participant roles and responsibilities.
- Full consideration of, and accountability to, task force recommendations.
7. Establishing RFP process and working RFP, including:
   - Comprehensive framework used as continuous reference document.
   - Flexibility on scope and constraints for standard and fast-track processing.
   - Historical record for justified changes to RFP as new information emerges.
   - Continuous dialogue back to task forces for additional information.
   - Focus on the need for long-term relationships with vendors.
8. Addressing design issues, such as:
   - Total systems solution with integrated segments, or phases of migration to new information technology.
   - Inclusion of all computer-related operations in systems design plan.
   - Exploration of standalones, networks, and connectivity concerns.
   - Outsourcing possibilities as integral part of solution.
   - Specific criteria for vendor evaluation and establish evaluation system.
   - Provision for a secure, easily accessible, and comprehensive database.
   - Requirements-driven architecture, not just current computer system adaptation.
   - System for creating and implementing system standards for hardware and software.
   - Provision for physical standards (e.g., optic fibers, equipment service).
   - Pathways for expansion of internal computing to external electronic highways.
   - Database entry, access, and change authorities: who, why, what conditions, how.
   - All levels of management participation: cross-functional task forces.
9. Executing the selection plan by establishing:
   - Time frame for developing evaluated costs for vendor comparisons.
   - Formal procedures for solicitation, contract negotiation, and bids.
   - Definitions of terms used in contract to resolve semantic differences.
   - Clarification of mandatory and desirable requirements.
   - User-driven, business oriented standards and specifications.
   - Product modules, phased-in approaches, application priorities, and schedule.
   - Non-technical evaluation: training, openness for future change, flexibility.
   - Vendor procedures, constraints, responsiveness consistent with client objectives.
   - Confirmation of vendor, line managers, and IS working relationships afterward.
10. Negotiating and renegotiating the contract annually, according to these criteria:
    - Acceptance of systems or services by all key participants.
    - Evaluation standards, procedures, and timing.
    - Insurance that vendors communicate only with authorized team.
    - Product criteria: product quality, performance, reliability.
    - Vendor criteria: trustworthiness, long-term relationship, financial stability.
    - Feedback to appropriate task forces on status of process and any new developments.
    - Development modification procedures, conditions, limitations, and costs.
    - Continuance of this concept of shared participation and ownership of automation.
    - Communications of the process to senior-level management: costs, benefits, trade-offs.
    - Consistency with corporate philosophy for integration of information technology.
    - Commitment to service line management: immediate and long-term plans.

- Ensuring consistency between the desired level of detail required of vendors and the request for proposal (RFP).

Authority and Control of Selection Procedures. Procedures may be documented but not implemented. IS management may not be situated high enough in the organization to provide objective leadership to control computer resources. IS should act to:

- Place IS management at a level high enough to form an action team with authority and responsiveness.
- Establish formal authorities for computer resource allocation with input from end users.

Task Forces or Advisory Planning Groups. The process of managing information technology does not end with advisory group recommendations; it must be a continuous process if it is to have an effect on the organization. Activities center around:

- Creating advisory groups to design, implement, and oversee all aspects of the process.
- Developing operational mechanisms that won t impede progress and that allow for new users, new applications, and new priorities consistent with changing business requirements.

Information Technology Evaluation Team. Because the evaluation process is multidisciplinary (involving end users, technical experts, contracting and purchasing personnel, legal, and finance), the makeup and size of the group depend on the current and intended scope of computing in the organization. Guidelines in this area include:

- Selecting a team with expertise for proper evaluation of the product or services sought.
- Assigning as chairperson an experienced business operating manager with leadership abilities.

End-User Computing. End users must be an integral part of the procurement process to achieve success in using that information technology effectively. Issues of applications development and other related user activity must be addressed at the outset by:

- Formalizing end-user and IS relationships for each aspect of procurement.
- Documenting specific objectives that exploit strengths and reduce weaknesses.
- Capitalizing on new business opportunities made possible by technology and people.

- Ensuring that the management of information technology is consistent with business planning.
- Providing for mainframe connectivity and hardware and software compatibility.

Administrative versus Other Types of Computing. This issue is philosophical, power-based, and political. Computing resources are, after all, an expensive budget item. Policy guidance should be established. Examples are: administrative versus instructional use of computers in higher education; administrative versus research and development for business. This activity involves:

- Tapping members of the computer selection group to examine and suggest solutions for conflicts (total fund allocations and schedule for implementation).
- Creating a system for measuring computer literacy level of all administrators, staff, and computer professionals.
- Establishing organizational standards and incorporating these capabilities in request for proposal (RFP) requirements.

New Technology's Impact on the Organization. Although it is not always possible to anticipate the full impact that computer systems upgrades will have on an organization, some assessment of how new technology will affect the organization should be a goal at the outset of the process. The request for proposal (RFP) represents not only technical and financial specifications for computing, but also indicates future areas to be supported by technology.

NEGOTIATING THE CONTRACT

It is important to promote an atmosphere in which philosophy, discussion, and action merge to produce the best solution for each unique party. Contract negotiation suggests a lengthy process. Because arbitration and debate are encouraged by these guidelines, terms and conditions are examined extensively. Conclusions resulting from a discussion of issues form the basis of a written document that is then enforceable. If areas of dispute arise, there is a reference document on which to base the arguments. A self-assessment guide for managing contract negotiations is presented in Exhibit 8.4.

The purpose of a written agreement is to ensure that all parties understand the terms of the requested service. To deflect timely and costly litigation, not only should the client prepare a document for computing capability acquisition, but the document should also be reviewed by legal staff.

Exhibit 8.4. Self-Assessment Guide for Managing Contract Negotiations

Hardware, Software, and Services
Strategic and operational cost/performance data, support services, and training.
Requirement for vendors to respond to predetermined format.
Individual component costs, depreciation factor, and discounts.
Data communications issues: definitions of system responsibilities.
Phase-in methods: annual modifications and business disruptiveness.
Purchase, lease, or other payment plans, with proper comparison of bids.
Maintenance specifications: end-user standards and requirements.
Operational capability demonstration and references.
User-friendly systems and applications software.
Concurrent usage of system: response peak loading and priorities.
Processing throughput measurement.
System expandability: memory, communications channel, and user stations.
Connectivity and compatibility issues for internal and external systems.

Additional Software Issues
Ownership, site licensing, maintenance: intellectual property issues.
Ethical and leadership issues with all aspects of use of software.
Conversion terms and conditions: data entry, programming, and testing.
Memory requirements and compatibility with system upgrades.
Levels of priority: utilization, recovery, debugging, and file management.
File protect options for updating and enhancements.
Customizing features: buyer allowances and prohibitions.
Control of processing schedule: end-user options.
Acceptance criteria and time frame for trial period.
Termination clauses.

Other Contracting Terms and Conditions
Backup system: procedures, costs, and responsibilities.
Training requirements: computer literacy assessment and location of users.
Documentation of all phases of management of information technology.
Implementation planning: computer literacy assessment and location of users.
Documentation of all phases of management of information technology.
Implementation planning: schedules and actions.
Technical assistance from vendor: constraints, costs, and accessibility.
Multivendor systems: authorities and responsibility tree.
Cost guarantees and time period for which applicable.
Replacement of hardware, software, peripherals: cost for upgrades.
Confidentiality issues of contract negotiation and implementation.
Formal negotiation procedures: time frame and conditions.
Account management: personal contacts afterward and for implementation.
Cancellation provisions and payment schedule for changed arrangements.
Protection against natural disasters.
Provisions for major organizational changes (including mergers and acquisitions.)
End-user involvement through all phases of contracting.
Noncompliance penalties: timeliness, completeness, and opportunities lost.
Site preparation: physical conditions, remote sites, and cable installations.

CONCLUSION

Organizations need a concrete strategy when procuring computer resources. The Computer Resource Management Model discussed in this chapter can be used by the average nontechnical administrator and the IS professional. This model, derived from case data collected over a decade from a variety of organizations, is based on universal concepts that apply to information technology assessment, acquisition, and allocation.

An organization does not have to apply the entire process(selection plan, Request For Proposal, negotiation) in order to realize the benefit of automation. The computer resource management model approach applies to any type of organization at any staff level (division, department, or individual end users).

Some people may wonder if a formal request for proposal (RFP) is really necessary and practical in terms of the effort needed to draft it. The answer is "yes." In order to be competitive today, response is important. In addition, accurate, complete, and reliable information is critical to success. Organizations that have operational objectives, make creative use of the right information getting to the right people at the right time, and employ structured, documented approaches to computer resource management are competitive.

Some form of request for proposal (RFP), even if it addresses only a few carefully selected and important issues, is necessary. The questions it asks of users and IS professionals in justifying a purchase and relating it to business operations is invaluable and practical.

It is especially important that organizations adopt some form of master plan for computer resources now that solutions proliferate and more informed users engage directly in information technology. The new tools must be used for the right applications. Prototyping methods can be highly successful if the organization fully supports the technique. End-user computing and user-developed applications require formal agreements with IS staff. The Request for Proposal, or some similar solicitation document, together with the selection plan and contract, can help avoid costly mistakes and serve as the basis for the solution.

Chapter 9
Large-Scale IS Project Management
Erwin Martinez

During the past 20 years, many businesses and government agencies have undertaken large IS projects. As anyone who has been involved in such an effort knows, a large-scale project is big in readily quantifiable terms. Duration is measured in years, teams number in the hundreds, and work effort is tracked in tens of thousands of workdays. Furthermore, large projects significantly alter critical business functions. Accordingly, such projects involve a broad cross-section of the business organization, uncover complex cross-functional issues, and fundamentally affect core business operations.

Some industry professionals claim that the best way to avoid large-scale project failure is to stop doing large-scale projects. This suggestion sounds simple, but it ignores the state of corporate and government information systems today. Many big businesses and government agencies have delayed investing in technology, whether because of fear of change or the pursuit of short-term profits. In doing so, some have allowed their information processing infrastructure to approach a state of collapse. As a result, large-scale projects are necessary to help these organizations make up for years of inadequate response to competitive pressures, customer demands, changing business conditions, and growing business volumes. Like it or not, large-scale projects are a necessary evil.

Because large-scale projects are so challenging to manage, they frequently fail to deliver the anticipated results. But this failure is not due to the use of so-called bleeding-edge technologies or nontraditional, unproven methodologies. Most large-scale project failure can be attributed to breakdowns in project management fundamentals.

Attention to the basic principles of project management is especially important in ambitious efforts in which fundamental mistakes quickly grow in magnitude. For instance, a one-month delay on a five-person project may be recoverable through increased staffing or overtime. On a 300-person project, however, a similar slowdown has disastrous consequences. Likewise, alienation and distrust among six users are much easier to overcome than such feelings among 300 or 3,000 users.

To improve the chances for project success, IS professionals must ensure that the essential project management functions are identified and earnestly performed. This chapter proposes a project management model and offers recommendations on how companies can prepare themselves for a large project and implement this model both before and after a project has begun.

A MODEL FOR LARGE PROJECT MANAGEMENT

Responsibility for the success of any project resides in the people of the organization who must do the right things at the right times. Each large-scale project embraces a set of essential functions that must be actively performed at the executive, project, team, and analyst/doer levels. These essential functions are interdependent yet distinct, and define a complete framework that addresses the activities critical to a project's success. Ignoring, understaffing, deemphasizing, or circumventing any of these functions invites failure.

Unfortunately, many of these functions are often merely appended to someone's job title, added to the duties of an already-overloaded team or team member, or ignored outright by the people to whom they are assigned. Therefore it bears repeating that these functions must be actively performed.

Reality Check

To recognize the four levels of responsibility in Exhibit 9.1 is not to endorse a hierarchical structure of organizations; it merely acknowledges current reality. Despite the appeal of flat organizations, large projects demand accountability, coordination, and effective division of labor. Because the prevailing structure of an organization will not change to accommodate a project — even a strategically critical one — successful project managers and team members must comprehend and work within existing structures.

Project management holds a project together up and down the organization and across it to business and IS constituencies. Those performing the essential functions at each level coordinate and manage the creative shape of the end products, connect each team with its constituencies, and administer and control project processes.

Executive-Level Functions. When change is under way, members of large organizations usually look to the top to see where the enterprise is headed. Many senior executives fear large-project failure and thus approve such projects while distancing themselves from the nuts and bolts of managerial responsibility. This wait-and-see attitude can provide a false sense of com-

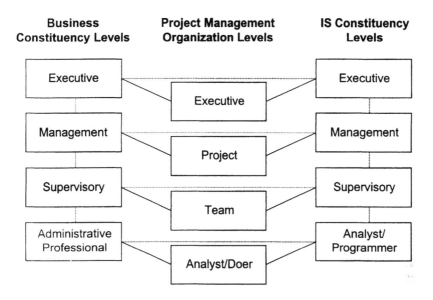

Business Constituency Levels	Project Management Organization Levels	IS Constituency Levels

Exhibit 9.1. Project Management Communications Structure

fort, but it is a formula for project failure. Active executive support and sponsorship motivates employees to get involved in the project by providing a measure of security to everyone in the organization.

In addition to contributing to a successful project launch, executive involvement helps to ensure that the business vision is articulated and that the project is managed toward attaining this vision. Without sufficient executive involvement, the risk is that the strategic business mission will be supplanted by tactical project objectives. A common loss of focus occurs when meeting an interim milestone date for finalizing the design becomes more important than designing a system that enables the organization to attain the business vision. In this scenario, the project team often takes shortcuts by performing incomplete analysis or leaving complex business issues unresolved. Unfortunately, while these actions may result in a short-term success (i.e., meeting the design deadline), the system ultimately implemented will likely fail to meet the true business objectives.

Several executive-level functions (see Exhibit 9.2) address the need to communicate frequently and comprehensively with business and IS constituencies not included in the project team, and to build and maintain positive relationships among all interested parties. This goes beyond ensuring technical adherence to a business mission or an information technology strategy. Without active participation by leaders within the organization who will inherit the system when the project is finished, building a work-

Exhibit 9.2. Executive-Level Functions

Functions	Purpose	Results if Ignored
Strategic Business Decision Making and Policy Setting	Speak for the business; sponsor the project; make final decision	Lack of business ownership
Strategic Business Vision Guardian	Maintain project's focus on enabling the business vision and strategy	Becoming irrelevant to the business; loss of funding
Relationship Management	Maintain cooperation of business community, communicate project issues and status with business; communicate business input to project	Alienate business communicate; implement solutions unacceptable to the business
Business Operations Expertise	Ensure realistic focus and workable solutions; interrogate project team for completeness	Incomplete business solution; unplanned rework
"Devil's Advocate"/Creative Challenging	Challenge ideas, solutions and people to achieve excellence	Incomplete business solution, increased errors and unplanned rework
Strategic IS Vision Guardian	Ensure solution supports IS strategy	Tendency toward uncoordinated, unproven, and mismatched technical solutions; alienation of IS community
Detailed Project Oversight	Focus responsibility and accountability; serve as chief project executive	Unaccountable project; out-of-control project
Quality Assurance	Build quality into solution; detect quality problems; ensure follow-through to remedy quality problems	Lack of quality; unplanned rework
Contract Administration	Maintain adherence to agreed-on scope and terms; make changes to scope and terms explicit	Incomplete scope; Incomplete solution; legal disputes
Legal Advisory	Ensure that solutions keep with in established law and regulation; resolve legal issues	Solutions that violate established law and regulation; unplanned rework; legal disputes
Financial Control	Ensure prudent project financial planning	Unplanned cost overruns; incomplete projects
Administrative Support Infrastructure	Maintain level of Organization	Disorganization resulting project inefficiency and poor communications

able solution is extremely difficult. Furthermore, regardless of how good the system is, it often will be rejected if key constituencies were ignored or alienated along the way.

In short, executives must assume direct oversight of the project, managing the effort in much the same way that they oversee business operations and maintain profit-and-loss responsibility and accountability. They must ensure that a discipline of administration and control is actively in place to plan, manage, and report on project activities. Executives also must help identify and resolve the most severe resource shortages, business problems, and technical issues. Ultimately, the responsibility for whether the project succeeds or fails rests with executive management.

Project-Level Functions. Project-level functions constitute the traditional project manager's role. But while these functions are generally handled by one person in small to midsize projects, the complexities of large-scale efforts require significantly more attention than can be provided by a single project manager. Therefore, it would not be improbable, in very large projects, for the 11 functions in Exhibit 9.3 to be managed by more than 11 people. The advantage of this scenario is that it promotes the deployment of people with specialized skills to areas most in need of those skills, thus avoiding the common pitfall of using essentially meaningless rules-of-thumb (e.g., "The company always take a solid IS manager and a full-time business manager and lets them handle all projectwide activities").

For example, the skills needed by a project manager are much different from those required by the systems architect. A project manager must be adept at planning, controlling, orchestrating, and monitoring activities and resources, as well as at collecting information and building consensus. Technical skill, such as in-depth knowledge of the latest software packages and hardware platforms, matters less than the ability to direct team activities, track results, and anticipate potential roadblocks. Conversely, a systems architect must be able to build creative business and technical solutions. Instead of focusing on the logistics and orchestration of the project, the architect is charged with identifying, designing, and assembling the correct combination of technical components that solve the business problems at hand.

In large projects, these tasks are too consuming to combine. Assigning these responsibilities to a single person invites failure — not to mention burnout on the part of the unfortunate individual.

An important distinction must be made, however, between recognizing the number and variety of projectwide functions and roles, and diffusing responsibility away from a single or small group of project managers. There should always be a focal point for project responsibility and ac-

Exhibit 9.3. Project-Level Functions

Functions	Purpose	Results if Ignored
Project Management	Manage daily details; anticipating, planning, oversight and control, data collection and reporting, results tracking and response analysis	Project failure; disorganization; unscheduled rework; poor quality, missed schedule; incomplete, unworkable solution
Systems Integration Architecture	Ensure cohesive, integrated, quality solution; coordinate activities of application, data and technology teams; under- stand the whole picture of the evolving solution	Unworkable solution; unplanned rework; poor quality
Business Change Management	Ensure business acceptance of solution; prepare business for entire scope of change	Business rejection of solution; solution unworkable in operation
Quality Assurance	Build quality into solution; detect quality problems; ensure follow-through to remedy quality problems	Lack of quality and unplanned rework
Issue Management	Track and resolve business and technology issues	Delay; unworkable solution
Scope/Change Control	Control scope according to business value	Incomplete or unworkable solution; delays
User Coordination and Relationship Management	Involve user experts as appropriate; maintain user cooperation and goodwill	Lack of business acceptance; unidentified issues or requirements
IS Coordination and Relationship Management	Involve technical experts as appropriate; ensure adherence to standards; maintain IS cooperation and goodwill	Lack of IS acceptance; unidentified technical issues or requirements; unplanned rework; lack of adherence to standards
Technical Configuration Administration	Coordinate details of development environment; coordinate building of production environment	Delays; lost work, unreliable solution
Morale Officer	Maintain project team focus on goals in context of broader perspective; provide communications channel to project management and project executives on morale issues	Poor morale; quality problems or delays
Administrative Support Infrastructure	Maintain level of organization; support greater project efficiency; improve communications; administer project reports; control system, library, support staff, logistics, gofers	Disorganization resulting from project inefficiency and poor communications

countability — whether in a few leaders or a single person — so that there is no confusion about who is in charge.

Team-Level Functions. Large-scale projects require a set of focused and coordinated teams. Two types of essential functions are prominent at the team level (Exhibit 9.4).

Exhibit 9.4. Team-Level Functions

Functions	Purpose	Results if Ignored
Business Process Redesign Architecture	Design Improvements/efficiencies into business tax workflow using new technology	Failure upon implementation unworkable, incomplete solution
Applications Architecture	Design application solution; resolve interfacing issues	Project failure; unworkable, incomplete solution
Data Architecture	Design data solution	Project failure; unworkable, incomplete solution
Technical Infrastructure	Design production, development and communications architecture	Project failure; unworkable, incomplete solution
Facilities Architecture	Design physical workspace and conditions in new business environment	Business inefficiencies; business rejection of solution
Knowledge Transfer Coordination	Ensure orderly transition of specialized knowledge/skills from project team to maintenance personnel; manage team training	Failure after implementation; unworkable, incomplete solution
Change Management Coordination	Develop program to introduce business and system change; cultivate two-way communications with business and project teams	Business rejection of solution; unworkable solution
Business Operations Expertise	Ensure team's analysis and solutions address core business needs	Unworkable solution
Quality Assurance	Build quality into solution; detect quality problems; ensure follow-through to remedy quality problems	Lack of quality; unplanned rework
Team Leadership	Provide leadership for specific areas, such as programming and integration testing	Incomplete solution; quality and consistency problems

One type, which is guided by those responsible for the systems integration architecture, creatively plans and designs the developing business and systems solution, such as applications or Business Process Redesign architecture. The other type manages and coordinates an aspect of solution delivery, such as change management or knowledge transfer coordination.

Project managers must be aware of numerous potential pitfalls in the direction of team-level essential functions. These include the following:

- Considering the project purely as a technology effort and ignoring or deemphasizing business areas such as change management, process redesign, and facilities architecture.
- Diffusing responsibility for essential functions among several subordinate teams. For example, charging 5 to 10 detail design and programming teams with resolving applications and data architecture concerns will invite future problems.
- Abdicating management of team functions because they are out-of-scope. Large-scale projects implement broad-based change. People's ignoring essential functions ("it is not their job") merely ensures the uncoordinated development of incomplete or unworkable solutions.
- Ignoring essential functions because it was never done that way before. Large-scale projects are different. In smaller projects it may not be necessary to identify and empower an applications architect role, but ignoring this role in a large-scale project can lead to the development of a disjointed solution.

Analyst/Doer-Level Functions. Organizations often overlook the critical importance of managing the analyst/doer-level functions (see Exhibit 9.5). For a large-scale project to succeed, managers cannot take for granted the people who do the work. These front-line individuals are usually the first to encounter unexpected problems and have the most insightful solutions, yet project managers frequently underestimate their importance.

To keep the effort on track, project managers must provide realistic assignments to, maintain the continuity of, and coordinate the personnel in this group throughout the project. Ongoing training in tools, techniques, and methods should be made available to support the needs of project doers as they progress through their assignments. Managers also must maintain morale and enthusiasm for the effort and facilitate quality two-way communication with this, the largest group within the project. Ignoring these issues significantly undermines the productivity of the project.

Some potential pitfalls in managing analyst/doers are as follows:

- *Ignoring the need for specialized skills in favor of using the people on hand.* An easy way out of difficult personnel decisions is to assign in-

Exhibit 9.5. Analyst/Doer-Level Functions

Function	Purpose	Results if Ignored
Analysts and Doers	Provide expertise and availability to perform project tasks	Project failure; disorganization; unplanned rework; poor quality; missed schedule; incomplete, unworkable solution
Facilitation	Help conduct effective meetings; provide expertise in the identification and resolution of issues	Project failure; disorganization; unplanned rework; poor quality; missed schedule; incomplete unworkable solution
Business Operations Expertise	Ensure team's analysis and solutions are complete and workable and address business needs	Unworkable solution
Quality Assurance	Build quality into solution; detect quality problems; follow-through to remedy quality problems	Lack of quality; unplanned rework

dividuals who are available and hope that they can grow into new positions.

- *Underestimating project demands.* Managers may make the mistake of double-counting people ("J. Doe is doing full-time technical support for the integration test, but can't J. Doe run the performance lab, too?") or ignoring team members' off-project responsibilities. The result has a detrimental effect on work quality and timeliness, as well as on team member morale.
- *Ignoring planning estimates.* Some managers have a philosophy of understaffing to get the most out of their people. While this may keep the personnel costs to a minimum, it usually communicates to team members that management does not care enough about project quality to provide enough people to do the job. It also demonstrates a disregard for staff members' personal well-being and private time.
- *Deemphasizing soft skills.* Projects are not merely technical endeavors. It is perilous to ignore the importance of client-relationship building, consensus building, facilitation, business writing, and listening. These skills are just as vital as programming and data analysis skills. When soft skills are missing, projects tend to alienate business clients and develop solutions that are uncoordinated or do not meet real business needs.

Because all of these large-scale project management functions are critical, serious consequences can result when any function is not performed. At the same time, a project manager must recognize that if each function is paid the respect it is due, large-scale projects can provide dramatic business benefits.

PREPARING TO IMPLEMENT THE MODEL

The large-scale project management model is necessarily comprehensive, as many business divisions and IS support units must cooperate and coordinate to successfully complete a large-scale project. Therefore adopting such a comprehensive model requires — first and foremost — the commitment, direction, and follow-through of executive management. Only top executives have the requisite perspective and influence over the whole organization. They may be the only ones able to counter the entrenched cultures that may resist the types of behavior change required to proactively implement the essential project management functions.

Developing an Executive Steering Committee

Executive management should develop an executive steering committee to govern and monitor all project activities. This committee should have active participation by the most senior managers from all involved constituencies, including the executive leaders of the business units, the chief project executive, and the most senior IS executive. Executives in charge of support functions such as legal counsel, financial control, and contract administration (if a significant contractor involvement is planned) also should be on the executive steering committee. The chairperson of the committee assumes responsibility for the executive-level function of detailed project oversight.

Although typical executive steering committees meet monthly, large-scale projects progress and consume resources at such a rapid pace that biweekly meetings may become necessary. The agenda of these meetings should be driven by project milestones — both recently passed and upcoming — as well as by other issues of major importance. At appropriate milestones, the committee members should demand to see demonstrations of working software not only to ensure that requirements are being met, but also to stimulate the project teams. This does not mean that such meetings have to become marathon sessions; it is a fact that meetings of longer than four hours are too fatiguing to be productive.

Defining and Empowering the Project Manager Role

Two of the most important duties of the executive steering committee are first, crafting the project manager role so that it requires project managers to address all of the essential project management functions noted in Exhibit 9.3, and second, giving project managers the authority to ensure that these functions are performed.

For example, in defining the project manager's role, the executive steering committee should call for project managers to work each function into their overall management duties:

- *Anticipating.* What long-term orchestrations are necessary to ensure that essential functions will be in place and active when needed?
- *Planning.* What resources (e.g., people, organizational structures, time, equipment, tools, methods, and techniques) will be required to perform the essential functions?
- *Oversight and control.* How will the essential functions be monitored on an ongoing basis to ensure that they are being actively addressed?
- *Data collection and reporting.* What reporting and communications mechanisms are necessary to obtain useful data on the progress of the essential functions?
- *Results tracking and response analysis.* How will the collected data be analyzed to create useful information, and what mechanisms are available to respond to warning signs in the information analyzed?

Merely defining the project manager's role, however, will be fruitless if the project manager has no authority to act. A common failing of large-scale projects is not that the project managers do not attempt to track the essential functions; rather, it is that they are not empowered to do their jobs. Worse, they even may be blocked from collecting information to enhance their understanding of whether project-related work is getting done. Some areas — such as the legal department or database administration — may be designated as off-limits to their review, counsel, or intervention. This creates a situation in which the project manager is accountable and responsible for the overall success of the project, but is limited in the ability to manage, coordinate, or influence critical project functions.

The point here is not that the project management role should have direct-line authority over all organizational areas that affect the project. The issue is one of giving project managers the authority to review, monitor, and coordinate all of the relevant resources. Although project managers should not control or directly manage the quality assurance function, they should have the ability to ensure that this function is performed, for example. If it is not being performed, the project manager should be able to communicate these concerns to the appropriate management levels and expect remedial actions.

RECOMMENDED COURSE OF ACTION

The flexibility of this model enables organizations to apply it either at the beginning of a project or once a project is under way. Clearly, the model is most effective when implemented before a project commences. In this situation, the first step is to scope and plan the project using any of a dozen or so full life-cycle methodologies. Scope should be defined up front as comprehensively as possible to ensure that all constituencies understand and agree to what is being proposed. Scoping should include a discussion of the business functions involved, tangible and intangible benefits sought, organizations affected, major problems to be addressed, major open issues to be resolved during the project, systems to be replaced, and — if applicable — technology goals and an outline of the target solution.

Conduct Quality Assurance Reviews. Throughout the scoping and planning process, it is important to confirm that the essential functions are addressed both in the project organization and work plan tasks. One way to do this is to conduct midpoint and final quality assurance reviews of the project plan. During these reviews, the planners should walk through their plan and demonstrate that it is workable, that risks are identified, that risk mitigation techniques are employed, and that the essential functions will be performed.

These sessions should be conducted with forthrightness because, if particular individuals are going to be assigned key roles, they must demonstrate that they have the requisite skills, experience, integrity, dedication, clout, and time availability. Everyone must recognize that skirting these issues during the planning stages only delays dealing with them until later when the project is under way. An expert facilitator can help bring these issues to bear in a constructive manner with the knowledge that all participants have the best interests of the project in mind.

Use Organization Charts. Another issue that should be addressed early is the use of organization charts. Project teams often are tempted to avoid using organization charts because they view them as too bureaucratic or formal. Yet discarding organization charts is a formula for overlooking the assignment of essential management functions. How a project is run depends on the styles of the project executives and managers, not on the existence of an organization chart.

Apply the Model to Current Projects. This model also may be used in a project that is already under way — typically, as a checklist for those assuming responsibility for the executive-level detailed project oversight and quality assurance functions. No one would argue that merely using this model as a checklist fulfills the executive oversight or quality assurance roles. These roles have a great deal more substance to them, but the list does guide these individuals to help ensure that nothing falls through the cracks.

Successful large-scale project management is not black magic. Organizational leaders can, however, get better at executing what they already know, at applying their expertise and skills, and at reworking their organizational cultures to more readily accommodate change. In short, they must never forget that mastering and applying the fundamentals is the key to successful large-scale IS project management.

Section II
Managing Business Relationships

Chapter 10
Corporate Lessons for the IS Manager

Robert E. Umbaugh

The drive to integrate new and existing technologies, a need to become even more competitive, and the growth of a more complex organizational environment is making the job of IS managers even tougher than it has been traditionally. There are many forces at work in the IS field, and it is IS management's job to respond to these changes in a positive way that brings value to the organization.

Although the trade press is filled with articles that articulate the problems that the IS manager faces, there are few articles that offer practical advice on what to do about them. In order to survive and prosper, IS managers should broaden their outlook to include the organizational and personnel changes thrust on all levels of IS management: operations, systems development, end-user computing support, programming, data management, communications management, and general management. To achieve this broadened outlook, IS managers will have to learn a few lessons about their changing role in the corporate environment.

THE CHANGING IS ROLE

The expanding role of IS management has several facets. First is the role at the corporate level; many IS executives who once ran supportive, overhead functions are now running functions that contribute more directly to the organization's corporate goals. Sometimes this means acting as product line managers: information is offered as a product of the organization. Having product line responsibility is substantially different from managing a staff group, if for no other reason than the increased attention that responsibility receives from senior management. It also differs in the way performance is measured. Product lines are almost always measured on a profit-and-loss basis — a more direct and immediate measure than most IS managers are accustomed to.

Another difference is found in the allocation of resources. The equipment and personnel needed to prepare products (in this case, information)

0-8493-9998-X/00/$0.00+$.50

for sale are usually allocated with a high priority — often with urgency — as opposed to the lower priority of products or systems for in-house use. If an IS group sells services as a profit-and-loss center directly to paying customers and at the same time continues to provide staff support in the form of systems development and operations for in-house use, conflict is almost certain to arise — and the new IS manager will be responsible for eliminating such problems.

The IS function is also expanding, and therefore changing, by assuming additional duties. Responsibility for voice and data communications, office systems, records management, information centers, and even corporate planning in addition to the traditional IS functions is not uncommon. Assuming responsibility for ongoing support groups means managing organizational integration, and assuming additional responsibility for support groups that do not exist means taking charge of start-up exercises. Neither of these tasks is easy to accomplish, and both demand the attention of the senior management team within the IS department.

The IS manager is even more likely to report at a very high level in the organization. Organizations in which the IS department continues to report at the controller or financial levels can be considered old-fashioned by modern standards. In many organizations today, the IS manager has a higher-placed and better-paying job than does the controller or treasurer, quite a change from 10 years ago. More organizations are placing the IS manager at the corporate-officer(e.g., vice-president or higher) level; many are even forming separate subsidiaries for providing IS services, in which the top positions are president and CEO of the subsidiary. Moving toward one of these two structures is clearly the trend.

Risks and Costs of the Changing Role

All of this additional responsibility and increased visibility is not without both its costs and its risks. The risks are often partially offset by higher pay, more prestige, and other incentives. But savvy IS managers should not lose sight of the need to be aware of the changed environment in which they work.

Politics. Although there is a greater degree of politics at the higher levels of many bureaucracies, politics is not always a dirty word. Politics is nothing more than goal-oriented behavior that has human interchange and social reaction as its primary elements. Politics takes on its darker side when it is used to further personal goals to the detriment of the goals of the organization or its individual members. The best advice for the newly elevated manager is to be highly observant and to avoid, at all costs, giving the impression of manipulating others for personal gain.

Responsibility versus Risk. Having responsibility for a greater number of corporate functions brings with it both greater potential for success and greater risk of failure. Risk management is a well-structured process used to identify areas of possible or probable weakness and to help managers take steps to mitigate those weaknesses. Managers are tempted to try to eliminate risk altogether, which is a futile effort. Risk comes with the job, and the emphasis should be on understanding risk and managing it. Most successful IS managers take risks, but they do so on the basis of conscious calculations. These managers usually perform the following actions in their risk management efforts:

- *Assessing risk.* IS managers can estimate the degree of risk with a simple classification scheme of high, medium, or low. A more sophisticated risk classification scheme would include severity, probability, timing, and the most likely consequences.
- *Identifying the consequences of an action.* Can immediate and decisive action mitigate the risk? Reduce the severity or impact of the risk? Defer the risk to another time frame? Replace the risk with one of lesser impact or result in some other less-negative consequence?
- *Identifying the risk-versus-reward ratio.* Making management decisions involves making assumptions. In many cases, assumptions must be made to form a risk-versus-reward ratio. Precision is not the goal; practicality is. The primary question to be answered is: do the potential rewards outweigh the risk involved?
- *Mitigating negative effect.* IS managers should identify ways to reduce the negative effect of complete or partial failure. In finance, this is called hedging, which is a respectable financial ploy used to reduce risk to predictable and manageable terms. In IS, redeploying resources can be a hedge as can realigning political alliances. The action taken to hedge against potential failure depends on the environment and the degree of risk, but planning for the potential for partial or full failure is a legitimate management activity.
- *Raising the odds of success.* After studying the risk and the need to mitigate against failure, IS managers should use resource application to help raise the odds of success. The cost of the resources must be weighed against the cost of potential failure and some careful judgment is needed. An example of applying resources to reduce risk of failure is the use of consultants to offer needed but rare skills to solve a unique problem.
- *Measuring results.* Too often, managers fail to learn from their past experiences. IS managers should think back to the results of a risky situation and critically assess how well they did in taking the preceding six actions. Were one or more steps skipped? Was the risk adequately understood and did the risk-versus-reward ratio prove true?
- *Taking action.* Inactivity is often more destructive than taking action. If a project is headed toward failure, IS managers should have the determination to terminate the project if necessary. Many managers

have wasted valuable resources trying to rescue projects that they knew or suspected were headed for failure. Taking action will prevent this wasted effort.

Integration. The more functions managers are responsible for, the more need they have to integrate those activities skillfully. Unfortunately, this is not easily accomplished. In the attempt to integrate technologies, some areas do not fit together naturally, and they do not function well when the fit is forced. This is also true of organizations with long histories and many layers of management.

Integrating a new organization or function is not a matter of adding it on as an appendage. The same considerations given to the merger of two corporations should also be given to the merger of two internal departments. These considerations include thinking about different cultures, taking steps to eliminate or reduce redundancy, looking for economies of scale, and streamlining operations.

Time Demands. Perhaps the greatest cost of moving up the management hierarchy is the increased demand on the manager's time — everyone wants just a minute, which, when translated, means at least 20 minutes. In addition to the need to spend time with all the functions and projects for which IS managers have direct responsibility, two other specific activities also place increased demands on their time: corporate activities and social responsibility.

Corporate-level committees, *ad hoc* problem-solving task forces, staff meetings, board meetings, and other sometimes ritual activities will consume huge amounts of time if executives allow this to happen. Some activities, of course, cannot be avoided, but IS managers should not make the mistake of confusing membership on every possible corporate committee and task force with prestige or success. Success comes from results, and managers who devote too much time and effort to many lower-priority tasks often do not produce results.

Corporate officers are usually expected to devote time to social activities that reflect well on their organization. These activities include serving on boards for hospitals, universities, and other organizations as well as fund raising and running for local office. All of these activities are worthwhile, and although IS managers may feel they have a responsibility to their community, they must recognize when they are being offered more opportunities to serve than they can accept.

There are many time management classes currently available to IS managers for the purpose of teaching them to make better use of their time. These programs include such techniques as:

- Segmenting time into 15-minute slices and scheduling activities to fit into these small time slices.
- Grouping similar activities together. For example, returning all telephone messages at the same time of day, usually the end of the day.
- Taking the first 15 minutes of the day to make a plan of things to do rather than just letting the day happen.
- Requesting an agenda for every meeting to decide whether attendance is required and to better prepare in case the decision is made to attend.
- Learning to say no when that is an appropriate response to an invitation to attend meetings, seminars, and other gatherings that require inordinate travel time.

These and other time management techniques can make the entire IS staff more effective. IS managers should consider attending these seminars and then passing some of the techniques onto their staff members.

Need to Delegate. Because of additional demands on their time, IS managers must delegate to subordinates many of the activities they previously performed themselves. Delegation is not without risk. Effective delegation carries with it authority to act, and when managers delegate authority, they must be sure that the recipient of the authority is capable and that effective control and feedback mechanisms exist so that nothing goes wrong. A manager who delegates an activity still retains residual responsibility for the actions of those to whom the activity is delegated.

Other Corporate Issues

The forces that are shaping the job of the chief information officer could also have an impact on newly elevated executives in other areas within the organization, though the nature of the IS function is rarely replicated in other areas. The organizational impact of technology implementation is an added responsibility, however. Not the least of these technologies is end-user computing and the organizational implications of its expanding role. Rarely has such a revolution taken place in the corporate world, and the ultimate fruition of end-user computing has not yet been seen. Most informed observers believe that moving full computing power directly into the hands of users at all levels of the organization will change the way business is transacted in the United States.

LESSONS FOR THE IS MANAGER

Several lessons can be drawn from the issues discussed. These lessons include planning, training lower-level managers, broadening horizons, using formal processes, organizational impact, moving from technician to integrator, and assessing and managing risk. These are discussed in the following sections.

Planning. Books, seminars, and the trade press all extol the importance of careful planning, and yet many organizations do little, if any, truly effective planning. One thing is clear, however: all successful IS managers understand planning concepts and use those concepts to manage their organizations.[1] IS consultants point out that they rarely find an IS department in significant trouble if it has a well-conceived plan and capable management.

No substitute exists for carefully thinking through the organization's mission and objectives and setting down specific plans to achieve those objectives. The most important advice that the IS manager or aspiring manager can follow is to learn how to plan and to do it well. Execution is much easier when the manager has a well-constructed plan to follow.

Training Lower-Level Managers. A traditional method for training lower-level IS managers is the apprenticeship. Trainees work under one experienced manager until they are ready to assume more responsibility. More likely, however, an opening occurs because of turnover, and then everyone in the management chain moves up one step, ready or not. The shortcomings of this system are obvious. More formal methods for preparing future IS managers must be developed because the demands on these managers will be even greater than those on current managers.

One area not covered in most training programs for IS managers is basic business functions, including a better grounding in planning, budgeting, decision making, change management, finance, economics, organizational theory, behavioral science, work planning, ethics, and the effects of governmental regulations. All of these subjects can be studied in either a formal or informal program designed to develop the skills of technical managers so that they can manage technology. Just as managers must learn to do a better job of planning, they must train their staff to do a better job as well. As managers delegate more responsibility to others, it becomes even more important to ensure that the members of their staff are well trained and ready to move into positions of responsibility.

Broadening Horizons. Many of today's IS managers have come up through the data processing ranks, and this experience has served them well. As they take on greater responsibilities, however, they must broaden their vision of the organization for which they work. This is particularly true if they want the technology they manage to make a direct contribution to the strategic direction of that organization.

In marketing, the term *work the territory* means to understand the marketplace, its needs, its opportunities, and its quirks. IS managers must do the same thing — learn more about the business and strengthen the bonds to those who manage other parts of it. Understanding the management network helps ensure a smoother transition into it.

Using Formal Processes Within IS Functions. The IS department has been quite successful in using technology and information systems to make other departments more efficient and more effective. The time has come to apply that same technology to the work of the IS department. Development centers with programmer's or designer's workbenches properly supported with hardware and staff can substantially increase productivity. Systems to help workload scheduling, project management, change control, and configuration control are available and should be used. IS managers must strive to develop processes that help move systems analysis and system design activities toward repeatable success.

Structured techniques, prototypes, fourth-generation languages, and standard systems architecture are all practical and proven devices that yield better-quality products and greater productivity. The integration of computer technology for use by the IS department itself must be a major objective for IS managers.

Another source of help in the search for better control and efficiency is the internal auditor. IS managers at all levels should view the auditor as a management tool to be included in all phases of IS activities.

Organizational Impact. Most action taken by the IS department affects some other part of the organization and, in today's environment, it is common for that action to affect entities outside that organization. IS managers should be aware of the impact their department's actions can have on the rest of the organization and, if possible, should make sure the impact is positive.

Current technology allows organizations to be linked electronically, and most are taking advantage of this technology to become more closely aligned with their customers and suppliers. These linkages are usually the responsibility of the IS department. Such intimate linkages make it imperative that IS managers take a global view of their organizational responsibilities and that they be especially sensitive to the immediacy with which their organization can either enhance or ruin customer and supplier relations.

Moving from Technician to Integrator. Although the manager's need to move away from being a technician might be obvious, the need to move toward being an integrator might not. On a macroscopic level, an efficient IS manager is a master integrator — one who can integrate technology, management information, strategy, organizational change, and people.

Assessing and Managing Risk. Risk is inherent in all human activity. IS managers should not avoid it, because only by taking some risk can they move forward. Taking risk recklessly is foolish, but managing risk is a sound practice. The business of IS managers is rife with risk, and the better they learn to manage it, the more successful they will be.

UNDERSTANDING THE CHALLENGES

IS managers and their staff live in a world of change. Understanding the forces causing that change will make the transition to the inevitable restructuring of the organization a little easier. Some of the trends affecting IS management are changing organizational structure, cost effectiveness, creative use of technology, and implementation of strategic business systems. Understanding and studying these trends as well as the lessons described previously should position IS managers for their future challenges.

Changing Organizational Structure. As end-user computing becomes more instrumental in the use of computing technology in the organization, and as technology moves into more and more parts of the organization, there will be continual shifts in the balance of power. Although centralized IS will control less of the computing resources, it will continue to be responsible for the backbone systems that, to a large extent, drive the organization. The IS function will also continue to be responsible for the communications net that ties the organization together. The result will be a change in role for IS, but not especially a diminution of responsibility. The challenge is to predetermine who is responsible for what in a formal document that spells out roles, responsibilities, and authority. These changes should not be left to chance.

Cost Effectiveness. There is considerable pressure on all parts of the organization to keep costs down and to become more productive. In many cases, there have been across-the-board budget cuts. In the IS department, this is difficult to manage because there is usually a high ratio of fixed costs to variable costs. The risk management techniques discussed previously can be helpful in addressing this issue.

Creative Use of Technology. Although end-user computing has opened many new doors for the application of technology, it remains true that most new technology enters an organization through IS. This is especially true of heavy-duty technology — that which requires a higher level of technical sophistication to assess and implement. The responsibility for adopting new technology will continue to be a centralized one in most organizations and in some, in which that responsibility has evolved to users and mistakes have been made, it is being returned to the centralized IS staff.

Implementing Strategic Business Systems. The push to use information processing technology for strategic advantage (and that term has many different meanings depending on application, business line, and economic environment) is catching some IS departments unprepared. Rapid response with little room for error is called for and some IS managers are not comfortable operating in that mode. The need to support the primary business product is critical. IS managers are learning that they will have to be tied more closely to the primary business product if they are to continue to be key players on the senior management team.

CONCLUSION

The role of a high-level manager or corporate officer with primary responsibility for information and information processing technology is undergoing change. Members of the IS staff, at any level, who wish to improve their management skills should be alert to the changing environment in which they work.

The intensity of the challenges facing IS managers and their staff will not diminish; in fact, they will in all likelihood become even more intense as information becomes an increasingly vital part of the corporate arsenal. IS managers should review the key points in this chapter, especially the section on risk management, and formulate objectives that focus on improvement in these areas.

Note

1. G.W. Laware, "Strategic Business Planning," *Information Systems Management* 8 (Fall 1991), pp. 44–49.

Chapter 11
Partnership: The Key to Successful Systems Development in a TQM Company

Christine B. Tayntor

Total quality management (TQM) changes the way many companies work. Simply put, a Total Quality Management company delivers what the customer wants without defects in the shortest possible time.

Some IS professionals mistakenly believe that TQM does not affect the IS department because it has little or no contact with outside customers. TQM companies recognize two types of customers: internal and external. For the IS department, this means that the people who used to be called users are now internal customers.

This name change involves more than semantics. The shift to TQM requires a fundamental change in the way IS departments operate. Unlike other initiatives that are frequently one-time efforts, TQM is based on continuous improvement. TQM companies are committed to improving quality, decreasing costs, and reducing cycle time each year.

This challenge represents a double-edged sword for the IS department. To increase their responsiveness to customers, other departments request new or improved systems from the IS department. The IS department therefore faces heightened expectations from its own customers, an increased workload, and the need to improve its services while also decreasing costs.

0-8493-9998-X/00/$0.00+$.50
© 2000 by CRC Press LLC

Although achieving such goals is undoubtedly difficult, IS departments can increase their chances of success by developing a partnership with customers and suppliers. This chapter outlines ways in which IS professionals can develop such partnerships and the caveats they should consider when establishing them.

UNDERSTANDING THE NEW PARTNERSHIP

Webster's definition of partnership includes such phrases as "close cooperation" and "specified rights and responsibilities." Although accurate, these phrases do not fully capture the relationships essential to successful systems development projects in a Total Quality Management company.

In the context of systems development, partnerships involve working relationships that are based on equality. The focus on equality is key because traditional systems development projects involved relationships based on subordinate and superior roles. IS professionals typically played the dominant role, and customers and suppliers had minimal or supporting roles. Total quality recognizes that each of the three parties has different skills and will, at different stages of the project, assume different roles.

There are two other critical elements to partnership: mutual dependency and shared success. Each of the partners requires the others. Systems being developed today are mission critical. Unless IS provides a high-quality system, its customers' profitability may be threatened. Similarly, without the support of its customers and their continued demand for new or enhanced systems, the existence of the IS function is threatened. The relationship between IS and its customers is therefore symbiotic. The relationship between IS and its suppliers should be analogous to that between IS and its customers.

If a successful partnership is based on mutual dependency, it is also founded on the premise that successes are shared. The much-touted win–win situation is one hallmark of a healthy partnership. This concept is often new to the relationship between IS and its suppliers.

In the past, suppliers were viewed as companies that provided a product or service for which they were paid. TQM partnerships recognize that suppliers are key to the delivery of a system and that their stake in the project should be more than purely financial. Although the bottom line is invariably profits, a good supplier partnership involves long-term advantages to both parties as well as short-term payments to the supplier. It may also involve working together in new ways.

CUSTOMER PARTNERSHIPS AND EMPOWERED WORK TEAMS

The key partnership in any project is formed by IS and its customers, without whom a project cannot exist. In contrast, relationships with vendors may or may not exist and, if so, do not span the entire project life cycle. Developing a partnership between IS and what were formerly called users is essential to the success of the project.

Within a Total Quality Management environment, projects are typically initiated by empowered work teams. These cross-functional groups of employees define the problem and then develop and implement a solution. The team, with its emphasis on working together for a common solution, provides the origin for building a partnership between IS and its customers.

Unfortunately, in some organizations, an IS professional is not a member of the original team and is contacted only when solutions have been identified. This is too late. The first challenge IS faces is developing a good working relationship with its customers so that it is invited to participate in all teams that might recommend new or modified systems as a solution to a customer's problem.

The following guidelines will help IS professionals become effective team members and partners.

Understanding the Role of IS on Teams

Although many members of the IS organization have different responsibilities during a project, the IS project manager serves as a member of the cross-functional team and as such is the liaison between the team and the rest of IS. This individual's relationship with team members and the roles that he or she plays determine the success or failure of the partnership.

Although any number of team members from various departments participate in different ways, specific roles are typically assigned at meetings. (See Exhibit 11.1.) Some of these, such as time keeper and process monitor, may be filled by different team members at each meeting; others remain constant for longer periods and continue even outside the formal meetings.

Although the champion should not change during the project, many of the other roles — including team leader — benefit from change as the project phases change. For the IS project manager who traditionally assumed leadership responsibility throughout the project life cycle, the adjustment to taking a leadership role only during the development phase can be difficult.

Exhibit 11.2 depicts the roles the IS project manager, the key customer contact, and the supplier should play during the various stages of the project. During the project life cycle, the IS project manager assumes two major roles: consultant and team leader. This introduces the second guideline.

IS as an Effective Consultant

Empowered work teams typically begin their projects by defining a problem statement. This seemingly simple but frequently complicated step is

Exhibit 11.1. Team Roles in a TQM Company

Role	Responsibilities	Comments
Champion	Initiates project, provides support, formally recognizes accomplishments	Should always be a member of the customer department. Normally is a high level manager
Leader	Chairs meetings, guides team	
Scribe	Takes notes (usually on flip charts) during team meetings to document discussion items and decisions	
Recorder	Formally documents meetings and project status, typically through memos	Role is not restricted to meetings
Process monitor	Ensures that code of conduct and TQM principles are followed	
Time keeper	Ensures that agenda is followed	
Facilitator	Guides team in effective use of TQM techniques	May be an outside consultant engaged for one or more key meetings

essential to ensuring that all team members share a common understanding of the task they are undertaking. Once the problem has been clearly identified, the team begins to analyze it, determining the causes for the problem. Only after the causes have been outlined and ranked according to importance does the team seek solutions.

Exhibit 11.2. Primary Roles and Responsibilities of the IS Professional, Customer, and Supplier by Project Phase

Phase	IS Professional	Customer	Supplier
Initiation			
Outline problem to be solved and form team	Team member	Leader	None
Analysis			
Define requirements and propose solution	Consultant and Recorder	Leader supplier	Prospective
Development			
Build solution	Leader and consultant	Team member	Team member
Implementation			
Roll-out solution	Co-leader	Co-leader	Team member

During these first two phases, initiation and analysis, the IS project manager's primary role should be as a consultant to the project — a team member who provides specialized expertise to help identify solutions to the problem. The project manager's responsibility is not to define the problem but rather to work with the other team members as they outline the problem and search for the underlying causes. There are several facets to the role of consultant: student, educator, adviser.

The IS Professional as Student. As a student, the IS team member seeks to understand the customer's business needs and then applies its own knowledge of technology to help the team resolve the problem. The caveat during this stage is to have no predetermined solutions and to erect no barriers. The project manager must not steer the group toward specific solutions. In this stage of the project, creative thinking is particularly important and no idea should be discounted.

The IS Professional as Educator. At the same time that the project manager works with the team to understand an underlying business problem, he or she serves as an educator, helping other team members understand technical capabilities.

If the problem is slow response to market changes, for example, the team may determine a cause to be sales representatives' lack of awareness of a competitor's recent price changes. As part of the first stage of this problem's resolution, the project manager may introduce the team to on-line bulletin boards as well as to faster communications links. Similarly, if the problem is that current company policies are not being followed and the team determines that a leading cause is the sheer volume of updates and the unavailability of clerical support to file those updates, the manager might introduce the concepts of document scanning and online text search capabilities.

The key element in both preceding examples is the project manager's introduction of the types of technology that might prove helpful. At this point, it is not the project manager's responsibility to propose a solution but merely to facilitate the problem-resolution process.

Speaking the Customer's Language

It bears repeating that all explanations should be understandable by all members of the team. The objective is to help customers resolve their problems, not to turn them into technical experts. Greater bandwidth, intelligent routers, and fiber-optic links are all important to IS. The customer, however, cares about the result: faster processing.

To minimize the number of acronyms and technical jargon its IS organization uses, one company instituted the acronym bucket. Each time someone uses an acronym or technical term without translating it into easily understood language, he or she must put a dollar in the acronym bucket. The money is typically donated to charity at the end of the year. This company's favorite charity is grateful for the tendency of IS professionals to use technospeak.

The IS Professional as Adviser. Once the team has identified potential solutions, the role of IS changes to adviser. This is where the IS professional combines analytical and technical expertise with the business knowledge gained during the earlier steps to help the team develop a recommended technology solution that enables process improvements.

The first key to success is to ensure that all recommendations are clearly explained in terms the customer understands and that potential benefits are expressed in business language. If, for example, the IS professional recommends installation of a local area network (LAN), the justification should include quantifiable benefits.

The Customer Comes First

Customer satisfaction should never be compromised. During the recommendation stage, it is essential that the IS representative help team members make decisions that reflect customers' needs, regardless of their impact on the IS organization. Most IS organizations support infrastructure standards, including data bases and programming languages. Some have policies stating that all software must be developed internally. In a Total Quality Management environment, such standards are questioned and, when it is to the customers' advantage, overridden.

Company A, for example, had a standard that the only databases it supported for client/server computing were brand * and brand Y. A major project team identified a software package that best met its needs, but it was written in a previously unsupported language and used a database other than * or Y. It was also the least expensive of the software packages that had been evaluated. The choice was a clear one. IS could insist on following its standards, which would have made gaining buy-in from its own organization easier, or it could prove that it was truly customer-focused and support the product that best met its customers' needs. Company A made the right choice, and although not everyone within the IS organization was pleased with the decision, the customer was delighted. IS demonstrated its willingness to be a full partner.

Beyond Managing: Being an Effective Leader

During the development phase of the project, the IS project manager becomes the team leader, assuming primary responsibility for the technical implementation of the software and hardware. IS has traditionally assumed this role; however, in a TQM environment, it is essential that IS perform as a leader rather than as a manager.

As was the case with the name change from "users" to "customers," this difference involves far more than semantics. Old-style managers were one step removed from the actual work. They established the overall schedule, then controlled and monitored the process. In contrast, leaders are active participants, people who are willing and able to perform many of the tasks. They may write specifications, test software, or install hardware — tasks that previously would have been delegated.

The leader's role is to guide the team rather than control it. This shift in responsibility is most evident in the schedule-setting process. IS team leaders form part of the group that develops the schedule, but they do not arbitrarily establish that schedule. Although in the past, IS set the pace of the project, customers' needs now dictate the schedule, a situation that frequently results in highly compressed time frames. In this environment, IS must adopt the whatever-it-takes approach, including the options of outsourcing or using packaged software, to facilitate the development of software and ensure that customers' requirements are satisfied.

Making the Customer a Co-Leader

IS professionals should insist that customers help lead the implementation. Just as IS professionals must often change their behavior to be successful in a Total Quality Management environment, customers must also make some adjustments, especially during implementation.

Some customer team members probably believe that their responsibility ends once a solution has been defined. This was, after all, the way systems development traditionally occurred. IS needs to counter this perception with the very real fact that the project's success is predicated on customer participation. The odds of success are enhanced if a customer — typically the same person who was the team leader during the initiation and analysis phases — serves as a co-leader with IS during implementation.

This shared responsibility is one of the hallmarks of partnership and successful projects, for implementation is far more than installing software. It includes training system users, then coaching and encouraging them until the system becomes embedded in their daily work. These tasks are far more effective when performed by members of the customer department than when IS professionals assume full responsibility.

The shared leadership role at this stage provides a clear statement that the project is owned by the customer department. When the IS department and its customers work together to resolve problems and both departments understand their respective roles, the project has an excellent chance of success.

FORGING SUPPLIER PARTNERSHIPS

Speed is one of the mantras of a Total Quality Management company. Translated into IS terms, speed frequently may mean that companies that previously developed all software in-house may discover that the only way they can meet their customers' time frames is to buy packaged software. Others that relied exclusively on inhouse staff may find that they have to hire contract programmers to supplement their staffs rather than provide specialized skills training. Still others may outsource entire projects, retaining only project management responsibilities. Each of these scenarios involves a new player: an outside supplier.

In the past, the relationship between IS and its suppliers was simple. The supplier provided a product or a service; IS paid for it. Working relationships were frequently strained because of aggressively negotiated contracts that left both parties feeling that they had lost. The environment was not conducive to amicable relationships, nor did it foster success.

Total quality management requires that suppliers become part of the project team with IS and its customers. There is, of course, a contractual aspect to the relationship — as there should be in any partnership. Although the contract is the key element in the relationship with a supplier, even the best contract cannot guarantee success. The following guidelines can help IS professionals turn previously neutral or even adversarial relationships into partnerships.

Ensuring a Commitment to Success

The supplier should have the same commitment as the other partners to the project's success. If the project is a critical one for IS and requires highly trained staff working extensive overtime, the supplier must be willing to guarantee that it will meet these commitments.

One way to determine the supplier's commitment, in addition to contractual provisions, is to evaluate the skills of staff the supplier is willing to commit. Will the project be staffed with new recruits and only one or two senior staff members, or has the supplier agreed to provide experienced staff with the specialized skills that the project requires? What provision is there for overtime? Will the supplier commit to a fixed price contract with bonuses for superior quality work or faster implementation?

Equal Stakes Make for Equal Partners

The supplier's stake in the project should match that of the IS department. If the project is mission critical for IS customers but one of the supplier's smallest undertakings, chances are that the relationship will not be a true partnership but rather a traditional supplier/customer arrangement. In this case, IS is likely to believe that it is not receiving enough of the supplier's resources and attention. Conversely, if the project is a relatively small one for IS but is the supplier's largest contract, IS must wonder whether the supplier can meet its commitments. Good partnerships are based on equality.

Making the Supplier a Team Member

Once a supplier has been selected, a representative should become an active part of the team, attending meetings and participating as any other team member would. Because most companies prefer to maintain control, suppliers are not usually team leaders. However, as is the case with the IS representative during the project's earlier phases, the supplier can serve as an adviser, providing specialized knowledge and skills to the rest of the team.

Because suppliers in a TQM project are expected to perform at nontraditional levels, they should have nontraditional incentives. Company B, which treats suppliers as full partners, trains its suppliers' staff along with its own. Including suppliers in total quality training provides them with a deeper understanding of the company's culture and needs. Other companies establish preferred supplier status, which allows designated suppliers to take advantage of quantity discounts on goods and services ranging from communications and PCs to car rentals. Company C works with its preferred software suppliers during their sales cycle, helping them win new accounts.

Partnerships with suppliers are frequently more difficult for IS to establish than are partnerships with IS customers simply because there is little precedent for working together as equals. The relationship is, however, essential to the project and, if properly developed, can be a key element in the project's success.

ELEMENTS OF A SUCCESSFUL TQM PROJECT

Some companies may be uncomfortable with these new working relationships. They are, however, strategies for developing true partnerships.

The most important element to a successful project is having the right staff — from customers to IS professionals to suppliers. It is that simple — or that difficult.

There is no doubt that systems development in a Total Quality Management environment requires a different set of skills than those needed for traditional project management. The differences are felt at all levels of the organization. Most companies find that a three-step approach is needed to ensure that IS staff members are adequately prepared for systems development in a TQM environment.

The Right IS Staff

Evaluate Existing Staff. A checklist similar to the one shown in Exhibit 11.3 helps identify gaps between expected and current skill levels of the project manager. Although the checklist is typically completed by the project manager's immediate supervisor, it may also be a helpful self-assessment tool for the project manager.

Before any evaluation, IS managers should meet with their staffs to discuss the changed roles and responsibilities and the concomitant new skills required of IS staff. Although change is a fact of life in TQM companies and employees know that performance standards are continually being raised, IS managers should outline the specific changes that affect their department.

Train when Appropriate. The preceding skills analysis identifies employees whose skills can be upgraded through training. Such training should occur as quickly as possible because staff will not be fully functional without it.

Replace Staff Who Have Wide Skills Gaps. It is an unpleasant fact that not all employees will make the transition from traditional company structures to TQM. Some people are comfortable only in a strict hierarchical organization in which IS professionals control all aspects of systems development. Others have superb technical skills but lack the interpersonal skills necessary to function as a member of a team. No amount of training will erase these behavioral gaps.

If IS as an organization is to be successful, it must accept the fact that some employees must be replaced. Here, too, the change should occur as quickly as possible. Speed not only benefits the organization as a whole, but it is even preferable to the employees who will be replaced because it erases the uncertainty that accompanies periods of change and allows them to continue their careers, albeit with other companies. Although company policies vary widely, many companies provide outsourcing assistance as well as severance payments to employees who no longer meet the company's profile of a successful IS professional.

Although the transition can be painful, particularly when long-term employees are unable to meet new standards, developing a fully qualified, trained staff is necessary to successful systems development in a TQM company. Failure to recognize the need for staffing changes or delaying their implementation creates additional problems and slows the development of a fully qualified, trained staff.

The Right Suppliers

Selecting the right suppliers presents a different challenge than upgrading internal staff, but it is no less important to the overall success of the organization. The following guidelines aim to make the process easier.

Exhibit 11.3. A Checklist to Evaluate Skills Gaps Among Project Managers

Employee Name: _____

Date Prepared: _____

Prepared By: _____

Skill	Definition	Level Needed[1]	Current Level	Gap[2]	Will Training Eliminate Gap within Six Months?[3]
Project Management	Ability to estimate, schedule, track and control projects.				
Oral and Written Presentations	Ability to express concepts clearly and concisely; exhibits poise when making presentations to groups				
Persuasion/ Influence	Ability to convince others of appropriate strategies and tactics				
Negotiation	Ability to achieve win–win agreements				
Supplier Management	Ability to manage outside suppliers, ensuring that time and quality targets are met.				
Vision	Ability to see beyond the current problem; to anticipate and articulate future needs and include them in the immediate solution				
Technology	Knowledge of current and emerging technologies and the ways in which they can be used to meet customers' needs				
TOTAL GAP[4]	n/a	n/a	n/a		

1. Level needed and current level are rated on a scale of 1 to 5, where 5 is the most critical.
2. Gap is the arithmetic difference between level needed and current level.
3. This column is the rater's evaluation of the employee's ability to upgrade his or her skills through training. If more than six months is required to upgrade skills, the estimated time should be indicated.
4. Total gap is the sum of all previously identified gaps.

Evaluating the Supplier's Corporate Culture and Goals. Because suppliers function as part of the project team and as an extension of the IS department, it is critical that their culture and values be compatible with those of the rest of the team. An aggressive organization will not partner well with one that is collegial. Similarly, one that values short-term profits over long-term customer relationships will be an unlikely partner for a TQM company.

A company can evaluate a potential supplier's culture through the following steps:

- *Asking the supplier for a formal values statement.* Many companies have formal values statements that should be requested and carefully read for similarity with the organization's own goals. Words like "quality" and "customer satisfaction" should appear before "profits."
- *Talking with the supplier's current customers.* Just as a company checks references on potential candidates for internal positions, so should it interview a proposed supplier's current customers. Questions should center on the supplier's ethics, values, commitment to targets, and flexibility when deadlines change.
- *Observing the supplier's behavior.* The questions suppliers ask often provide clues to their values. If the predominant queries relate to the project budget, the supplier is probably driven by revenues. A supplier who asks how quality is measured and what future customer needs have been evaluated is likely to be a better partner for a TQM company.

Negotiating a Fair Contract. A good contract does not necessarily mean the lowest price. Rather, it includes a fair price — one that provides the supplier with a reasonable profit — along with commitments of quality and on-time delivery. If either side emerges from contract negotiations feeling that it will receive less than half the benefits, a true partnership is unlikely. Both sides should benefit equally.

The contract should include measurable performance targets: deliverables, dates, and quality metrics. These should be developed in as much detail as possible during the negotiations because they are key to a common understanding of responsibilities. If the contract specifies the scope of software to be developed, it should also include a provision for modifying expectations if the scope is changed.

Similarly, the contract should outline the consequences of performance — both good and bad. Although it should focus on rewards (e.g., payment and incentives for early completion), it should include explicit penalties for nonperformance. Just as good fences make good neighbors, good contracts make good partners. Both delineate boundaries.

Stipulating the Need for a Single Contact within the Supplier Organization. Although the need for a single contact is typically specified in the contract, its importance should not be underestimated. The compressed schedules that are one hallmark of TQM projects do not allow IS professionals time to deal with multiple individuals and to worry about whether all information is being communicated within the supplier's organization.

Requiring Frequent Communication. In the ideal project, the supplier's representative works as part of the IS department and shares the same offices. In reality, however, suppliers may be located in a different city, state, or even country. In such cases, frequent communication is essential.

The daily phone calls and faxes certain to occur during certain phases of the development process should be supplemented by regularly scheduled, formal communication. The communication should be mutual and verbal rather than in the form of generic status reports from the supplier to IS. When face-to-face meetings are impractical, teleconferences should be used. Such meetings or phone calls aim to identify problems and concerns and to develop solutions that are formulated jointly by the supplier and the IS representative. All decisions should be documented in writing.

Frequent, candid communication is also the key to a successful partnership between IS and its customers. Although the two groups are unlikely to have a formal contract, it is important that each understand the other's responsibilities and that both groups keep the other informed of successes as well as of potential problems. Regular meetings should be scheduled to review the project status and, when discussions are not purely technical, customers should be included in meetings with suppliers.

Throughout the project all three groups — IS, its customers, and its suppliers — must work together in what Webster calls "close cooperation." Though each has different skills and responsibilities, they are all part of the same team, working to achieve the same goals.

CONCLUSION

Systems development in a Total Quality Management company requires a fundamental change in the way IS operates. Instead of assuming the traditional role of managing and controlling projects, IS professionals must become team players, taking on different roles in different project phases and developing partnerships with IS customers and suppliers. These new roles require new skills, most notably persuasion and negotiation. Not everyone will make the transition successfully, but those who do will reap significant rewards.

Chapter 12
Linking Project Outcomes to Customer Needs

Richard H. Deane
Thomas B. Clark
A.P. (Dennis) Young

In many IS organizations, the primary measure of project success lies in meeting some combination of project specifications, a project deadline, and a project budget. The tendency for the completion of one project to coincide with the start of another leaves little time for strategic and long-term measures of project success.

Because the ability of organizations to learn and improve faster than their competitors may be the only sustainable competitive advantage in the business world of the 21st century, successful learning organizations must do more than measure the end result of a project effort. In these organizations, project success involves a strategic question of whether project outcomes meet customer needs. The extent to which they do not is most often the result of one or more performance gaps in project planning and execution.

To ensure success, IS and project managers should link project planning to control actions that relate customer goals to end results. In other words, IS and project managers must envision and apply a model that translates customer requirements into a specific sequence of management actions. This translation and execution process should be measured, evaluated, and continuously improved so that ineffective practices are corrected or abandoned and effective practices are amplified.

This chapter presents a model that helps IS and project managers assess and ultimately narrow the gaps between customer needs and project

0-8493-9998-X/00/$0.00+$.50

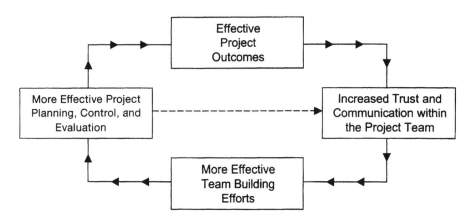

Exhibit 12.1. The Learning Cycle of Effective IT Project Management

outcomes. By identifying and reducing these intermediate project performance gaps, IS managers will systematically improve the project management process in a continuous learning cycle (see Exhibit 12.1). Responsibility for this improvement should not be delegated to a single individual but institutionalized throughout the organization.

THE PROJECT PERFORMANCE GAP

The project performance gap can be expressed as the difference between expected and actual project outcomes:

Project Performance Gap = Project Outcome Expected by Customer –
Actual Project Outcome

IS and project managers who focus on strategic goals recognize that this equation must be modified to reflect the customer's perception of the delivered project outcome. Stated in terms of a performance gap, the new equation reads:

Project Performance Gap = Project Outcome Expected by Customer –
Actual Project Outcome As Perceived by Customer

This second equation still does not ensure project success because it fails to take into account the true needs of the customer. A more representative equation of the project performance gap thus follows:

Project Performance Gap = Actual Project Outcome Needed by Customer –
Actual Project Outcome As Perceived by Customer

A comprehensive model of project success driven by the third equation is presented in Exhibit 12.2.

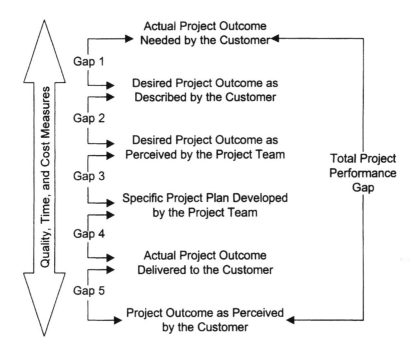

Exhibit 12.2. IT Project Performance Gap Model

PROJECT PERFORMANCE GAP MODEL

Exhibit 12.2 illustrates that an ineffective project result (i.e., total project performance gap) arises from five individual gaps in project performance. The following sections discuss these gaps and provide tips on how to manage them.

Gap 1: Ineffective Statement of Long-Term Customer Needs

The first performance gap occurs when the customer team is unsure, unclear, or unaware of the exact nature of the needed project outcome. Consider the example of a customer team that defines a project requirement for major revisions to a customer order-entry and tracking system. What the customer really needs, however, is a new automated order-entry system design and development effort (i.e., systems reengineering), not a revision to the existing system.

Managing Performance Gap 1. This gap involves a situation in which the project outcome fulfills stated or documented requirements but does not satisfy long-term customer needs nor provide the customer with a business advantage. In the example provided, a project that delivers a revised order-entry system, according to specifications, will not provide an effective solution to the customer's order management needs.

Gap 1 represents a frustrating problem for project teams that do not deal with the customer team as a partner. A project team may suspect that the project requirements are improperly stated but be limited by organizational or contractual constraints on its information access or authority to seek clarification of the true project need. Such situations are more likely to arise in teams dealing with external customers (e.g., teams responding to an invitation to bid or a request for proposal), but they can also arise with internal customers.

The keys to managing Gap 1 are as follows:

- Ensuring that customers initiate interactions with the project team to describe how current business needs are being met (or not met). Likewise, the team should ask the customer to describe how the planned project outcome meets present or anticipated needs. The project team must therefore start the customer interaction process by discussing business needs, not specific project requirements. Customers should be asked to envision and specifically describe their operating environment in terms of what they are trying to accomplish and how they are evaluated.
- Asking key customers to describe the business needs of their own customers and how the project helps meet their needs.
- Using a project team charter to reduce any role ambiguity and conflicts among the project team, customers, and other project stakeholders. The team charter identifies team member roles and operating rules and clarifies how the team will function as it executes the project, particularly in interactions with customer and user groups. A team charter developed consensually and used consistently to guide team interactions actually serves to reduce all performance gaps.

Gap 2: Incorrect Perception of Customer Needs

Gap 2 occurs when the project team incorrectly perceives customer needs. In this instance, the customer correctly understands that a completely new design and implementation of an order management system is needed. However, the customer ineffectively describes the specific project scope, objectives, and constraints, or the project team is unable to understand these key project parameters as expressed by the customer. Often, the project team does understand the general project scope, objectives, and constraints but fails to understand which of these parameters are critical to the customer's interpretation of project quality. Gap 2 often occurs when the project team has a preconceived notion or preference for a given project definition that matches prior projects or its own capabilities.

For example, a project team meets with a customer to discuss a new automated order management system. The customer's primary need is a system that lets sales and marketing personnel verify the status of orders and provides local order-entry clerks real-time access to the order management database. Furthermore, the project must be completed and the system fully operational by August 15, before the start of the Fall selling season.

The project team, however, interprets the customer's primary need as a system that generates daily reports with minimum computer processing time and provides the production division with two automated reports of new orders each day. The project team understands that remote access to the system and real-time access to the database are desirable but incorrectly assumes that these are secondary objectives. Also, the team interprets the August 15 deadline as a target for system installation but fails to incorporate system testing and user training within the scope of the project that must be completed by that date.

Managing Performance Gap 2. Gap 2 problems typically involve an incomplete analysis or incomplete documentation of project requirements, resulting in an inaccurate or perhaps incomplete statement of project needs. IS managers can narrow this gap by:

- *Making diligent use of the project charter.* This three- to four-page document provides a word picture of the project scope, objectives, constraints, assumptions, concerns, risks, and users. Because it is written from a management not a technical perspective, the project chartering process should be used to lead the customer into commitment to the project definition. Diligent use of the charter is also a key tool in preventing scope creep once the project is under way. The project charter sections documenting project scope and objectives are especially important tools in managing Gap 2.
- *Using a classification of primary objectives versus secondary objectives in the project charter.* Primary objectives must be met in full for the project to be considered successful. Secondary objectives are desirable but are not direct determinants of project success.
- *Ensuring that there is significant contact between the project team and the primary customers.* Gap 2 problems are likely to arise when a project team is charged with implementing a project that has been negotiated and designed entirely by the customer and senior management.
- *Ensuring that there is adequate communication between the project team and senior management.* The project charter is an important step in this communication process.
- *Periodically revisiting the project charter during project execution to ensure that the customer and project team do not lose sight of project objec-*

tives. A team may understand these objectives at project commencement but become distracted and lose sight of them over time.

Gap 3: Ineffective Translation of Customer Needs

Performance Gap 3 results from ineffective translation of the customer's needs into the formal project plan. In other words, the project team understands the customer's needs and expectations but develops time, cost, and quality objectives and a project plan that do not fully reflect these needs.

Gap 3 is a common, and often wide, project performance gap simply because of the difficulty of developing a project plan that is directed toward multiple and sometimes competing objectives. The project team may also lack the skills or, equally important, the discipline to plan. Finally, Gap 3 problems may arise because senior managers send signals that planning is unimportant; for example, they fail to proactively review project plans and recognize and reward project planning efforts.

The following examples illustrate this gap. The project team understands the importance of remote sales and marketing access to the data base as a desired feature in the order management system. It does not, however, establish specific software/hardware interface objectives and priorities that allow remote users reasonable access to the system during regular business hours. As a second example, project objectives for the new order management system might be clear but a functional rather than a cross-functional work breakdown structure is developed and a project network is not utilized. The resulting project plan omits important activities (i.e., documentation development and user training) or fails to recognize interdependencies among activities. The bottom line is an incomplete, unrealistic, and unworkable schedule. As a third example, the project plan may not include time for key activities necessary to ensure product quality, such as system testing, approvals, and rework as required.

Managing Performance Gap 3. The third performance gap arises when the project plan is inadequate to meet project objectives. Narrowing Gap 3 starts with careful comparison of the project plan with the project objectives for consistency. It is imperative that shortcomings in the plan be recognized before the plan is actually executed. The keys to managing Gap 3 thus lie in:

- Using the work breakdown structure as a means of verifying the approach to meeting each customer need and objective. If each project objective in the charter cannot be associated with identifiable sections of the work breakdown structure, IS managers and project leaders must clarify how the objective is being met through the project.

Conversely, they need to question the value added by each portion of the work breakdown structure that does not appear to be related to an identifiable project objective in the charter.

- Verifying consistency between the project charter, the work breakdown structure, the project network, the schedule, and the budget. Every project objective in the project charter should be related to identifiable activities in the project network. The project schedule and budget should be compatible with cost and duration constraints as stated in the charter.
- Verifying every task interaction among subprojects and submodules. Large, complex projects do not fail because there are too many details but rather because the project team and the customer fail to understand the interdependencies among activities and subprojects. The project network provides an excellent opportunity to foster discussions regarding the interaction of individual activities and subprojects.
- Using a team-based structured validation process for reviewing the baseline schedule and budget. The project team and customers should ask validation questions such as:
  - Is the critical path intuitive and logical in terms of its location, and is the project duration reasonable for this type of project? Are there surprise activities on the critical path? If so, why?
  - Has a resource plan been developed, and is it compatible with the schedule?
  - Is the budget reasonable based on projects of this type? Has a cash flow plan been developed and approved by management?

Proactively discussing and evaluating decisions concerning time/cost trade-offs. Even if the original baseline schedule is chosen, a discussion of time/cost trade-offs raises vital issues, such as the financial and strategic value of reducing the project duration.

Gap 4: Ineffective Execution of the Project Plan

Gap 4 arises when the project work plan is adequate to achieve customer needs but the project team is unable to execute the plan. The numerous reasons why a project plan is not properly executed include:

- A flawed project control process.
- Inadequate technical expertise.
- Uncontrollable external interventions.
- Failure to prevent project scope creep.

In the case of the order management system, the project team is unable to execute what is an adequate plan because it lacks expertise in database design or the requisite hardware cannot be supplied in a timely manner by the customer or a vendor. Compounding slippage eventually causes project failure.

Managing Performance Gap 4. Implementation of an effective control process is, of course, essential to managing the problem of ineffective execution. Accurate measurement of progress is a necessary element of the control process for executing the project. The keys to narrowing Gap 4 thus include:

- Ensuring that an agreed-upon set of metrics for measuring time, cost, and quality performance is consistently followed throughout the project.
- Regularly conducting project team meetings to evaluate progress, identify/diagnose problems, and develop corrective interventions.
- Remaining alert to environmental threats to the project effort and proactively responding to them. Because some external circumstances can make even the best planned projects go awry, a control system must implemented that allows quick adjustment to the project effort after external threats to success are identified.
- Empowering project team members to report both good and bad results in control meetings. Because some managers seem to want to hear only good news in project meetings, poor intermediate performance results are swept under the rug or discussed offline.
- Developing a response to every deviation from the project plan, no matter how small.
- Updating the plan as required so that the team always has a current credible plan for the remainder of the project.
- Demonstrating commitment to the discipline of the project control process and ensuring commitment from upper management as well. Managers who routinely cancel project control meetings or ignore intermediate project status reports send the project team a signal that the control process is either unimportant or simply not worth the time and effort it requires.

Gap 5: Ineffective Communication of Results

Gap 5 represents the project team's failure to effectively communicate results to the customer. In other words, the team does a poor job of documenting or otherwise communicating that project outcomes do indeed meet customer needs. Gap 5 problems may arise from lack of communication or from miscommunication (e.g., overzealous promises). In most cases, the seeds of the Gap 5 problem are planted during project planning or project execution, even though the gap is not recognized until project completion.

Continuing with the example provided, the project for the order-entry management system has successfully met the established and agreed-upon objectives and will serve the customer's real business need. However, the customer has received inadequate communication during project execution. Upper management in the customer's organization became actively involved with the project four times to resolve problems. The final project report is poorly written by the project manager based on the assumption that the new system is running and everyone seems satisfied. The result is a customer who does not understand what was actually accomplished.

Managing Performance Gap 5. IS and project managers should address the problem of ineffective communication throughout the project rather than at project end. The keys to narrowing performance Gap 5 are:

- Developing a specific customer communication plan. A regular channel of communication to the customer is coordinated with a plan to keep senior management informed. The communication plan identifies the format, timing, and distribution of project communications. Regular project status reports to customers must be concise and consistent.
- Establishing a horizontal communication plan among project team members. Simply stated, all project team members must be "playing from the same song book." IS and project managers can test the effectiveness of the communication plan by regularly surveying team members to determine if they feel informed regarding the project status.
- Ensuring that the final project report addresses each and every project objective as identified in the project charter, which should be used a guide in writing the report.
- Celebrating project success.

The total IT performance gap thus implies a gap between the actual outcome needed by a customer and the customer's perception of the result. It can result from any one of the five single gaps or from a combination of them. Because the five gaps are always cumulative (i.e., they never offset each other), it is inadequate to measure only the total IT performance gap. Rather, the total gap must be analyzed and addressed through one or more of the other gaps.

Exhibit 12.3 provides a summary of how specific elements of the project management process should be used to prevent performance gaps.

RECOMMENDED COURSE OF ACTION

The framework provided in this chapter is designed to help IS managers create a learning project environment. By addressing intermediate gaps in the project planning and control process, IS managers will improve the entire project management process.

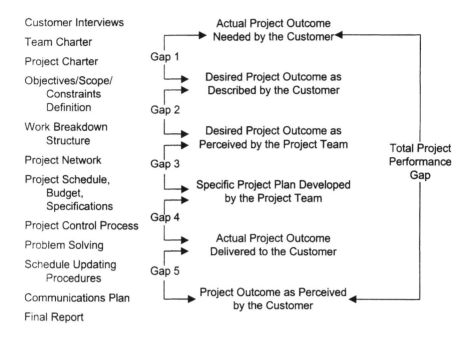

Exhibit 12.3. Project Performance Gap Model

Although an overall gap in project performance is always the result of one or more of the five intermediate gaps, project team members are likely to disagree as to where gaps existed in a particular project. Addressing and resolving such a disagreement is the first step to improving the project management process, because it helps focus team thinking.

Bibliography

1. Zeithmal, V.A. et al. *Delivering Quality Service: Balancing Customers Perceptions and Expectations.* New York: Free Press, 1990, p. 46.

Chapter 13
Managing End-User Development in a Client/Server Environment

John Windsor
Leon A. Kappelman
Carl Stephen Guynes

Client/server computing is growing in popularity, driven by two major factors. Top management believes client/server technology saves them money, and users believe that in an environment in which the information systems department is not responsive enough, client/server computing can solve all of their needs. Unfortunately, neither case is necessarily true. In fact, client/server-based end-user computing is a two-edged sword — with both edges cutting the IS department.

The major problem with client/server technology is that neither top management nor end users fully understand all that is involved in providing an organizationwide computing infrastructure. Top management can easily understand that the hardware for a client/server system costs less than a mainframe, but they have a very difficult time understanding multiplatform software costs, the costs of controls to protect data integrity, or why support costs rise. For their part, end users have little or no understanding of why they cannot upload their local data to the organizational database. Often, end users want significant access to the organizational database, and such concepts as controls and data integrity have little meaning for them — until problems actually occur.

0-8493-9998-X/00/$0.00+$.50

SYSTEMS DEVELOPMENT MANAGER'S ROLE

As cheaper workstation technologies increase the drive for direct exploitation of available information, systems development managers (SDMs) need to change their approach to end-user development. That is, rather than opposing or resisting the migration, SDMs need to keep in sharp focus the lasting business benefits that end-user development can bring; no longer can they position themselves between the end user and the technology.

The goal of end-user development is to allocate responsibility and facilitate the information system (IS) construction process. Although traditionally SDMs have been responsible for IS construction in a client/server environment, today the end users often take on this responsibility, and development is possible only when end users understand the technology and process. Therefore, a partnership of end users and SDMs is an effective means for establishing the appropriate control and support measures needed for systems implementation.

The leadership for implementing an end-user-developed system can be placed with a user, but that position must be guided and supported by the IS department. All the knowledge SDMs gained from years of handling problems in standardization, documentation, testing, maintenance, and performance should be shared with the rest of the organization.

In matters of security, too, SDMs are in an excellent positions to play strong roles in protecting the systems and data that are the lifeblood of the organization because, historically, they have been charged with helping to maintain the integrity of the organizational database and have established extensive controls to protect that data. Going forward, they should be concerned with where organizational data is being downloaded and with the stability and security of the networking systems that are installed throughout the organization.

MANAGING END-USER COMPUTING

SDMs can reduce the risks of end-user development by developing an effective strategy for controls, which must both foster organizational efficiency in using limited information resources and provide support to maintain high-quality systems. Key areas of control include vendor selection, software and hardware selection, and data security; two primary dimensions to a control strategy are levels of control and mechanisms of control. Examples of levels of control are high control (i.e., IS controls all development), moderate control (i.e., IS approves development activities), and low control (i.e., IS maintains a hands-off policy). Examples of mechanisms of control are standards, policies, and procedures.

Each area requiring control should be evaluated and the appropriate level and mechanisms of control applied. Balance is important, because too much control restrains the benefits of End-User Computing, and too little control allows all the risks associated with end-user computing to flourish. A fine line, of course, exists between support and controls, and some of the best support mechanisms also provide control benefits.

Depending on how much they know and how well they can communicate, end users require varying levels of assistance, including help with product evaluation, purchasing, training, application development, testing services, application consulting, software and training libraries, user groups, and backup facilities. Simultaneously, IS needs to demonstrate to end users why controls are needed.

User-Developed Systems: Disadvantages

The sense of ownership that can be such a positive factor for user involvement in application development may also create major problems. Systems may be viewed as "belonging to" the user departments, creating situations in which hardware and software purchases introduce products that are incompatible with the existing system. Users may even develop the attitude that the system must be modified to meet their design decisions, rather than the users adhering to company standards.

Data. The ownership problem can extend to user-developed data and databases, which in fact must be viewed as organizationwide resources that must be used effectively. As data becomes associated with a particular user department, the development of private data bases can be a major problem. In addition, the rest of an organization depends on timely data. However, as a department develops private databases, the importance of updates to the organizational database diminishes, in their eyes, and they may not see to the task with as much diligence as is necessary. Consequently, the data used for decision making by the rest of the organization becomes out of date.

Software. The ownership of software creates a similar problem. As a department develops software that provides enhanced decision-making capabilities, department users' willingness to share the software may well decline. In addition, the private software bank creates situations in which other users are forced to develop the same tools on their own, wasting precious organizational resources.

User ability to identify correct and complete requirements for an application is limited. Users know their own needs, but that does not make them good analysts. Often the user needs the assistance of an IS professional. On their own, users may:

- Apply incorrect formulas or models.
- Use incomplete or outdated information, or both.

- Develop applications that already exist.
- Select untested or inappropriate software.
- Lack adequate knowledge of the importance of quality-assurance pro- cedures.
- Overpay for hardware, software, and support.

Other activities normally performed by SDMs can be neglected by end users. They may fail to:

- Follow organizational standards or guidelines.
- Test assumptions or models.
- Train other users adequately.
- Document an application adequately.
- Maintain an accurate inventory of software, hardware, and data.
- Maintain security.
- Provide for backup and recovery.
- Follow software licensing agreements properly.

User-Developed Systems: Advantages

Potential benefits for user-developed client/server systems do exist. Cli- ent/server systems can speed up the application development process, be- cause projects do not have to compete for scarce mainframe or programmer resources. Fewer bottlenecks lead to faster response time and may have an impact on reducing the systems development backlogs found in most organizations. In addition, powerful desktop workstations can run applications that are impractical to run on the mainframe. Central Process- ing Unit-intensive applications, such as graphics and data analysis, often require client/server computing's distributed processing and shared data to be efficient. This is because the server, regardless of the hardware plat- form, can be freed up to process other applications when such intensive applications are run on desktop workstations.

User development can also relieve a shortage of system development personnel. Better systems can sometimes be developed by knowledgeable users who know the needs of their jobs and the organization. Although us- ers sometimes need some assistance from SDMs, the user-developed sys- tem minimizes the necessity for a middleman.

Ultimately, end-user-developed systems provide more control to the us- ers. Users usually get systems quickly by developing the systems them- selves, and they turn out to be more satisfied and committed to them.

TECHNICAL PROBLEMS IN CLIENT/SERVER ENVIRONMENTS

By nature, client/server-based end-user computing creates a diverse envi- ronment. Multiple platforms, vendors, and technologies require a variety of support that is not otherwise necessary, and SDMs can play a pivotal role in juggling them all.

The Effects of Diversity

For example, client/server-based end-user computing requires more diverse technical support than mainframe-based systems, as it allows an organization to use hardware and software from many different vendors. Support contracts may be required with each of these vendors, so to minimize the difficulties of having multiple vendors, a company must establish internal hardware and software standards.

Client/server systems require more technical experts because of the diversity of technologies that must be brought together to create an effective system. For example, most developers understand either the mainframe system or the microcomputer, but not both. Because an organization may have a shortage of skilled and experienced developers, creating client/server applications involves more trial and error than does developing older, well-understood mainframe applications. Developers may need to go through extensive training to learn the new technology. Therefore, in addition to retraining current employees, a company may have to consider hiring specialists in local area network (LAN) administration, DBA, application development, project management, and technical support for users.

A Lack of Standards

As with most developing technology, client/server computing does not have agreed-upon industry standards. Currently, no standard exists for retrieving, manipulating, and maintaining complex data, such as graphics, text, and images, and standards must be established before combining products from different vendors becomes a reality in client/server technology.

In the communications arena, structured query language (SQL) is a standardized data-access language that enables communications among various PCs and an organization's data bases; however, each database management system (DBMS) vendor has its own SQL dialect. This adds to the complexity of building transparent links between front-end tools and back-end database servers.

Additional problems arise when an organization is to take advantage of its investment in existing computing resources — typically a mainframe — while moving into a client/server environment. The ability to communicate with the mainframe as if it were a server is available through several protocols, most typically TCP/IP. However, client software is mostly based on other protocols. The network hardware needed to include the mainframe in the client/server system is an additional expenditure, generally not included in the prices quoted by software vendors. Finally, most client/server software that is compatible with the mainframe links only to specific software on the mainframe. The company must either have current versions of that software or maintain both platforms at compatible levels.

A Scarcity of Tools

Serious security and access control issues also must be considered. Right now, the lack of automatic backup and recovery tools is a big deterrent for organizations considering moving to a client/server environment. Backup and recovery procedures have been improving, but logging procedures are still inadequate. Until these tools are developed, organizations cannot place mission-critical applications on client/server platforms.

Because the server is usually the central location for critical data, adequate physical security and operational security measures need to be taken to ensure data safety. A large number of tools perform security and control functions on mainframe systems, which have been dealing with data security for many years. All of these mainframe tools can help with the client/server effort, but they are not designed specifically for client/server environments.

Today, there is still a lack of client/server-oriented communications, diagnostic, and applications tools. These troubleshooting tools are more powerful than they were three years ago, but they are less robust than those readily available for mainframes.

There is also a lack of good tools for converting existing applications to client/server routines. This forces client/server users to either write new client/server applications from scratch or use the existing applications on the mainframe. Most organizations have invested in millions of lines of mainframe code that cannot be easily converted to client/server use, so mainframes will be required for many more years.

TECHNICAL BENEFITS IN CLIENT/SERVER ENVIRONMENTS

In a client/server-based end-user computing environment, users begin to feel direct involvement with the software, data, hardware, and the system's performance. They define their critical needs and allocate the resources they are willing to spend on those needs. Such involvement is the foundation for building a sense of ownership, which has long been a corporate objective, because ownership results in numerous benefits. In fact, research has shown that a key to the success of any new development project is user involvement in the process of developing and implementing their own information systems.

If installed properly, client/server systems should reduce IS department operating costs, because the hardware typically uses replicated configurations, thereby allowing a greater coverage of the sophisticated support environment. In addition, client/server systems provide a better return on technology investments, because they allow niche or specialized technology to be configured as "common resources," which are widely available within the computing environment. If the proper controls are in place, client/server computing should allow greater access to organizational data and information while providing for appropriate data security.

Traffic Reduction

In the client/server environment, the workstation controls the user interface. Most commonly, the user interface commands are processed on the client (i.e., the workstation). This frees the server to do other types of computing. Because the server is free of user interface and other types of computations performed by the client, it is able to devote more resources to specific computing tasks, such as intensive number crunching or large database searches. Also, controlling the user interface at the client keeps each keystroke off the network.

Full data files do not need to be sent to another workstation for processing, as in networked microcomputer-based environments; only answers to requests from the clients are sent. Because the client receives only the data requested, network traffic is reduced and performance is improved. Access is also easier because resources are transparent to users. The reduction in both file and keystroke traffic dramatically cut down on network use and cost.

Improved Performance

Client/server systems allow organizations to put applications on less expensive workstations, using them instead of expensive mainframe and midrange systems as clients or servers. Existing mainframes can be used as enterprise data management and storage systems, while most daily activity is moved to lower-cost networked platforms. Server performance is also cheaper than equivalent mainframe performance. Microcomputer millions of instructions per second (i.e., MIPS, a performance measurement) can provide a cost advantage of several hundred to one, compared with mainframe MIPS. Another cost advantage is that client/server database management systems are less expensive than mainframe DBMSs. Moreover, the client/server model provides faster performance for central processing unit-intensive applications, because much of the processing is done locally, and the applications do not have to compete for mainframe central processing unit time.

Database servers centralize the data and enable remote access. Client/server computing allows multiuser access to shared databases. With client/server computing, users can tap into both the data that was stored in their departments in the past and any other organizational data that they need to access. In addition to access to more data, users have broader access to expensive resources, use data and applications on systems purchased from different vendors, and tap the power of larger systems. With client/server computing, users have access to large databases, printers, and high-speed processors, all of which improve user productivity and quality.

Client/server computing allows organizations to extend the lifespan of existing computer equipment. The existing mainframes can be retained to perform as servers and to process some of the existing applications that cannot be converted to client/server applications. Client/server computing is flexible in that either the client or the server platform can be independently upgraded at any time. As processing needs change, servers can be upgraded or downgraded without having to develop new front-end applications. As the number of users increases, client machines can be added without affecting the other clients or the servers.

CONCLUSION

The successful implementation of client/server-based end-user-developed systems requires involvement by top management, representatives from user groups, and systems development management, because only with all three can a balanced approach take place. For example, it is possible for IS to become so involved with the decision and selection process that it ignores the organization's strategic concerns. For their part, the end users may not see the value of careful and reasoned selection and end up with a solution that, at the beginning, may seem to meet their requirements but in the long run may not solve their real business needs.

The major issues to be considered would include ways that the system could improve efficiency, minimize costs, provide a competitive advantage, and reduce cycle time. Developers should build a model of the organization's workflow and data flow, which helps in designing networks and in determining how data should be distributed. The tools that are selected are determined by the data and systems requirements and require a great deal of investigation before a decision is made on which application is appropriate for the system's particular needs.

The users must be made aware of the client/server technology and the benefits that it can provide. A knowledge of the proposed client/server solution should be disseminated to all concerned groups. This knowledge is key to the proper use of the technology, as the users are in a better position to evaluate the technology. If the users can use the system and it solves the business problem, the chance for systems success is high.

Chapter 14
Managing User-Driven Systems Development

Kwasi Amoako-Gyampah
Kathy B. White

Integrated systems development projects involve people from different departments who use different languages, have different objectives and different types of training, and yet must work together closely on a unique task. The organizational structure that defines departments can create a barrier to communication between the people involved in these development projects. Time pressures in systems development exacerbate communication problems.

Information managers are continually trying to better manage and control integrated systems development projects. Numerous models have been developed providing technical support for the project manager (e.g., critical-path modeling, budgetary spreadsheets, and activity flowcharts), but there exists a great need for a formal approach to managing the organizational and human requirements for successful systems implementation. This lack of a formal approach to the softer side of systems integration can contribute directly and indirectly to systems development failures.

BENEFITS OF USER INVOLVEMENT IN SYSTEMS DEVELOPMENT

Effective integration of systems projects requires the involvement of the eventual users of the system during all phases of the project. The benefits of user involvement are that it:

- Provides a more accurate and complete assessment of user information requirements.
- Furnishes expertise about the organization and the processes that the intended system is going to support, expertise not usually held by the systems developers.

0-8493-9998-X/00/$0.00+$.50
© 2000 by CRC Press LLC

- Helps avoid the development of unacceptable features and reduces the risk of system failure in complex projects.
- Decreases user resistance and the potential for sabotage.
- Leads to greater user acceptance, and satisfaction with the system.
- Gives users a sense of ownership of the system.

Merely involving users through their membership on committees or having them to sign-off at different phases of system development is not enough. There is the need to induce positive interest in the user group with regard to the group's involvement in the systems development effort.

Traditional Project Management Approaches

With the projected benefits of user involvement in mind, some approaches have been suggested for integrating system projects. These approaches can be classified generally as project management tools. They consist of mechanisms for linking the project team's work to the users at both the managerial and lower levels. Examples of these tools include:

- The selection of a user as project manager.
- The creation of a user steering committee.
- A user-managed change control process.
- Frequent and detailed distribution of project team minutes to key users.
- The selection of users as team members.
- A formal user-specification approval process.

Another tool could be the use of a liaison. This role is typically assigned to the project manager who is charged with expediting communication links.

These elements all attempt to put a structure in place that allows for co-ordination and communication. The assumption is that if the structure is in place and the appropriate committee meetings are held, the process of integration and coordination will occur. These activities are, however, very loosely defined (unlike the technical side of project management), and very often there are no mechanisms in place in most organizations for the checks and balances required for integration to achieve the desired results. There needs to be a distinction between structural integration and the effective management of the involvement process.

COMMUNICATION BETWEEN IS STAFF AND USERS

User steering committees and formal and rigid communication structures by themselves can act as barriers to systems implementation and, therefore, affect system success. Once structural integration has occurred and the various committees, teams, and other structural units have been set up, user involvement in systems development must be deliberately managed for it to be effective. It is important to ensure that interactive communication occurs. Two-way communication is needed between project teams, between project teams and users, and between users and managers on any changes in systems components and project schedules that might affect them. There must also be the provision of adequate feedback. In addition, this form of integration requires communication that conveys to users that their input is valued and will be sought constantly.

It is crucial to find mechanisms for bridging the barriers between users and designers. Merely saying effective communication is important is not enough. It is essential to demonstrate how effective communication can be achieved and to recognize the distinctive competencies of the users and the designers.

A Case Study

A large manufacturing company (with 1990 sales of more than $500 million) implemented a $14 million computer system for order tracking and customer service. To facilitate the discussion, the company will be referred to as LMC and the system as Milltek. The system affected 12 different departments at five plant sites of the company, as well as 280 users in different locations across the country. Four months after the system was installed, there were more than 1,000 program request changes waiting to be addressed. Because of the many changes required, the users preferred to do things manually rather than use the newly implemented system.

Before the implementation of Milltek, LMC essentially had a piece-meal approach to information systems. Each functional unit within the organization had its own IS unit with little integration between units. The IS group within each unit tried to develop systems specifically tailored to its needs, and whereas some of these units had fairly advanced systems, they were not tapped into by other functional units.

The objective for the development and implementation of Milltek was to implement an information system that integrated all the information processing needs of the various units of the organization, with the aim of maximizing overall goals as opposed to individual functional goals. It was the perception of senior management that the system had to be developed and implemented as quickly as possible, and a project duration of one year was established. The project was initiated in March 1990, and the system went online in January 1991.

The specific user-involvement techniques used at LMC as part of the development and implementation effort were as follows:

- A project team consisting of 15 personnel from a consulting company and 10 people from LMC.

- Two project managers from LMC were appointed, one for system implementation and the other for applications development.
- A business unit sponsor's team that consisted of senior vice-presidents from the plant sites was formed. This team met once a month with the project team, and members of the business unit sponsors were to solicit input from their units.
- There was an IS steering committee comprised of senior management personnel, including the president of the company and the vice-president of IS . This committee was responsible for establishing direction and priorities for Milltek, ensuring adequate LMC participation in the project, approving major project output, monitoring and reviewing status, and monitoring and controlling the overall LMC-consulting team relationship.
- Several subteams were put in charge of training, development of procedures, software development, and hardware selection.
- Weekly project meetings were held and chaired by the vice-president of IS.
- User sign-offs were expected at different phases of the project (e.g., software selection), after changes to previously agreed-upon units, and during development of screens and other critical units.

Several other aspects of user involvement were also evident during the development of the system. Different levels of users were involved at different phases to get the users to "buy in" to the system. In addition to training sessions, pilot sessions were held with some users and their input was sought through phone conversations and one-on-one meetings. These efforts were in line with the key success factors for the project, which had been identified as solid reporting and responsibility relationships, frequent and timely meetings, active participation of all members of various project teams, and user project sponsors and owners.

To summarize, all the necessary elements of traditional user involvement were in place. The required integration between users and project teams did not occur, however. The users indicated their level of involvement was minimal, and the system was perceived as unsuccessful. For the organization as a whole, lack of success was evident from the fact that 40 percent of its customers were not receiving invoices for three months following the implementation. For the users, the system lacked the credibility, accuracy, and user-friendliness that they had expected. To improve user acceptance and satisfaction, attempts were made to quick-fix one thing after another, but this further undermined user confidence in the system. Although senior management indicated its dissatisfaction by getting rid of one of the project managers and other senior IS personnel, the users preferred to do things manually rather than use the new system.

Shortcomings of Traditional User-Involvement Tools

During the development and implementation of Milltek, a cycle clearly developed where one series of actions on the part of the systems designers (including consultants) and the users led to another set of actions. This could have been avoided through proper management of the user-designer interaction.

Miscommunication. To begin with, the system was intended to centralize islands of information systems within the organization. This created a perceived loss of power with regard to the control of information for some users. To the extent that the systems development group was perceived as being responsible for the reallocation of this power, effective dialogue was needed to alleviate user concerns. Although some of these issues were acknowledged, there was no follow through.

For example, a memo from the head of the consulting team to the president of the company during the early stages of the project noted that ownership and commitment were necessary for long-term success. Another memo revealed that before converting any future application, the company needed to spend substantial time in verifying the business units' understanding of the new system and new business practices. Walkthroughs and simulated conversions (in which the key users will use the system to support their operations in simulation mode before conversion) were recommended.

Following the implementation of Milltek, however, a memo by the internal auditor revealed that LMC did not take the time to mold the system to its business. Business practice changes were not discussed in detail with all those affected. This clearly indicates the lack of effective communication. There was a stated intention to get the users involved, but beyond that, no mechanism existed for monitoring the process.

Lack of Leadership. The business-sponsors unit and the steering committees were very ineffective. Members lacked the initiative to participate and did not solicit input from their units as expected. In fact, before systems implementation and right after, some key members of the business-sponsors unit left the company. In addition, some of the subcommittees gradually ceased to function after software selection , although their input was still needed.

A contributing factor to some of the issues discussed was the lack of clear authority on the part of the various committees in dealing with the external consulting team. A memo from the project manager to the president of LMC revealed that the consultant's style created animosity between LMC personnel and personnel from the consulting team. User involvement was discouraged by the consultants — especially at the lower levels — and the consultants preferred working with higher levels. On most occasions when user sign-offs were required, senior-level users were used instead of the actual end users.

The consulting team also discouraged the involvement of the procedures and training group within the organization in the design process. As a result, the benefit of their knowledge on the existing systems was lost and the group was completely handicapped when it came time to prepare procedures and participate in systems testing and user training.

Semantic Gaps. Project team members as well as the consultants felt that the users did not follow procedures or take the time to listen; as a result, they discouraged further user involvement by referring to the user group as being unsophisticated. Semantic gaps existed between the user groups and the system designers. The consultants (as members of the systems group) did not understand the business practices sufficiently, and the user groups were perceived as lacking understanding. These gaps could have been addressed if sufficient mechanisms had been provided for monitoring the interaction process through effective communication and feedback.

Uncoordinated Activities. There did not appear to be a person clearly in charge of coordinating activities. The consultant group had indicated, during the planning phase, the need for an individual (from within LMC) with project management responsibility to the user community, yet the preference by the consultant team to deal directly with senior management rendered the position virtually powerless. In fact, the LMC project manager designated for this activity resigned.

The people in charge of training were required to develop training modules and screens without seeing the actual program screens to be used. The net effect was that the training received by users was poorly designed and did not take into account the specific business practices at LMC.

Very often, changes were made to the system without informing all the affected participants. For example, a few days before the system went online, major changes were made to the system and none of the trainers was informed. As a result, the system went online without any written documentation to support the system.

Again the internal auditor's memo revealed that countless unanswered questions from the grass roots level came up in training classes and adequate time for hands-on training was not provided. At one of the company sites, no one except the plant manager knew that a new system was being implemented until about a month before the system went online, although there were about 40 users at this site.

METHODS FOR BETTER MANAGING USER-DESIGNER INTERACTION

The analysis of the LMC systems development and implementation example suggests that user involvement goes beyond those elements expressed by traditional project integration. User involvement is a process with many issues and activities that have to be adequately managed.

The basis for some of these activities is the recognition of the importance of negotiations when developing integrated information systems: negotiations between the designer team and user group, between user groups, and between different project teams. These activities recognize the political environment in which systems development occurs and the many conflicting issues surrounding their development. The suggested elements are aimed at building consensus, enhancing the perception of user involvement, and monitoring the effectiveness of the involvement process.

Project Managers Should Be Known to All Project Participants. Traditional project integration requires that a user be selected as the project manager. It is equally important that this manager be known to all project participants. In many organizations, very often, a large proportion of the user population may not know the individual who is the project manager for a particular system.

Identifying the Right Type of Users. Some users might lack the desire to be involved; this group of users can be identified early to avoid conflicts later on. Those who want to participate should be motivated to do so, but it is important to clarify roles and expectations. For example, if external consultants are involved and they choose to deal directly with top management rather than users, it may undermine the influence that the users think they have with regard to their ability to suggest changes to the system.

Allowing Users to Make Suggestions and Informing Them as to the Outcome. Users should be asked to make suggestions or improvements to the system development effort, but they should also be informed as to whether or not their input is assimilated into the project plan. If no feedback is provided, but users see changes occurring to the system or the system proceeding as usual, the feeling is going to be that the designers do not really want any input from users. This affects the desire of the users to be involved in subsequent development activities.

Providing Effective Feedback Mechanisms. There are going to be misunderstandings because of semantic barriers, perceptions about roles and expectations, and the complexity of the project. It is important for users to know whom to contact in the event there are questions or misunderstandings during any phase of the development process. A mechanism is needed so that user problems or questions can be fed back to the development team for corrective action. A mechanism should also be in place to let the designers know if the users are gaining the right type of understanding. If the users are not receiving adequate clarifications or timely answers to their questions, and if the designers have no way of knowing this, then the expected level of integration will not occur.

Communicating Schedule Revisions and Reasons for Changes to Users and Other Project Participants. This is necessary to align expectations regarding the project timeline with reality and to lessen any pressures that might be imposed on systems developers and users alike with respect to project completion. User involvement sometimes suffers when designers face tremendous pressures to complete the project on schedule. It is not desirable for users to perceive that the value of their input is going to suffer because of the time pressures. It is important that users are kept abreast of any such schedule changes.

All project teams should consistently communicate to other teams any changes in their plans or the status of project activities that affect the work of others. At LMC, the training and procedures unit was severely handicapped in its efforts by not being aware of all the changes that were being made to the system during the development process. The results of planning meetings should be published and distributed to applicable personnel. Furthermore, the different roles of internal systems developers, outside consultants, and project managers should be clarified so that everyone knows who to inform when changes happen.

Establishing a Climate of Trust. Project teams should exchange ideas in an open, frank, and trusting manner. A positive climate of trust fosters user involvement and satisfaction. The importance of trust to the negotiation process cannot be overemphasized. A positive climate also lessens any perceptions of manipulation that the user groups might have and reduces any dysfunctional behaviors.

The preceding items are aimed at finding ways in which the user-designer interaction process can be managed effectively. They should be viewed as an important step in developing a formal approach to managing the people interfaces during systems development. They should not be perceived as all-inclusive. Essentially, they should be viewed as guidelines for developing mechanisms that allow the user-interaction process to be monitored and controlled.

CONCLUSION

In IS projects that involve complexity and state-of-the-art technology, it is sometimes difficult to state clear, concise, and complete requirements. In such environments, sophistication and flexibility are required of both users and designers. The more the user is able to deal with change and ambiguity, and the more there is ongoing interaction between the user teams and the systems development team, the more successful the systems development will be. The perceived success of the implementation effort often depends on the interaction between the systems development group and the user group.

In the development of information systems, it is important to ensure that the input from the users is understood and, if appropriate, that the input is incorporated into the development of the system. In addition, to the extent that there are benefits to having users involved in systems development, user input should be sought and encouraged.

The reality is, however, that most of this process is very much left to chance. If the right person with strong communication skills happens to be in charge of the project, it may occur. Otherwise, real communication problems are present. Managers need to put in place mechanisms to ensure that the proper level of interaction between systems developers and users is occurring.

Some of the measures outlined in this article can serve as a basis for managing the user-involvement process. Although traditional project management methods (e.g., having users on project teams, establishing steering committees and project subgroups) give structure to integrated systems development projects, these methods by themselves cannot ensure adequate user involvement and satisfaction. Interactive communication is necessary to clarify roles and expectations, remove any negative perceptions and barriers, and monitor the effectiveness of the interactions between users and developers.

Chapter 15
Tips for Effectively Managing User Expectations During Systems Development

Dana T. Edberg
Fritz H. Grupe

End-user computing (EUC) managers are in the paradoxical position of having to foster the rapid diffusion of digital technologies through their organizations while at the same time having a restrain users from moving beyond realistic limits during its implementation. At times, EUC managers may tire from the amount of effort expended encouraging, convincing, cajoling, and educating users to accept the idea that new times call for new solutions. At other times, managers must strive to keep up with users who are impressed by what the local PC vendor has told them they can accomplish with the latest software, or by the latest magazine article on object-oriented methodologies and client/server technologies, or by what is happening at other companies. Users' and EUC managers' perceptions may also come into conflict when projects are completed. Users may find that the project failed to deliver the features they expected or delivered the wrong functions. EUC staff assertions that the users were given what they asked for seldom placate a disappointed user.

In the context of major application development projects, users may develop unrealistic expectations about the following:

- The goals and objectives of the project.
- The scope of their involvement in the development effort.

0-8493-9998-X/00/$0.00+$.50
© 2000 by CRC Press LLC

- The time to completion and the costs of development.
- The actual functional ability of the system.
- The impact the system has on their operating procedures.
- The ease with which future modifications can be incorporated into the system.
- The amount of training it will take to learn to use a new system.

Managers must recognize the potential disruptive effects of erroneous user expectations. When users are disgruntled with the results of past projects, resources and support for future projects is withheld. Impatience and poorly defined time projections lead users to develop their own applications. Users begin to mistrust the statements of EUC personnel and view them as purposely deceptive. Users start to perceive EUC personnel as a blockade to the development of new applications rather than as cooperative facilitators for these tasks. As a result, jobs are lost and a cycle of increasing failure presses EUC further backwards. In some instances, companies have elected to outsource their EUC function rather than attempt to correct the problems experienced during systems development.

Most EUC managers have at least a few stories to tell about how users were disappointed during a systems development project. Those same managers, however, may not be able to tell what steps they took to alleviate those mistakes and prevent their future occurrence. The vast majority of EUC managers have realized that users have a crucial role to play in systems development efforts. But what they forget is that users often do not understand the technologies that are in use well enough to play their role effectively unless they are assisted by EUC staff. It is the responsibility of EUC managers to effectively manage user expectations during systems development so that everyone involved in a project understands what can, and cannot, be delivered at the end. If EUC managers elect not to shoulder this burden, it is possible that new systems development may slowly move into the hands of inexperienced and untrained end users who are experimenting with the latest heavily advertised software package.

EUC has experienced many successes with systems development and it is important to search those successes for patterns to discuss those aspects of the process that can be modified to improve the overall rate of success. This chapter summarizes some of the tips of the trade; discussing how EUC managers can improve their success rate with users' perceptions of project development by better managing users' expectations.

UNDERSTANDING THE BUSINESS, ITS GOALS, AND ITS ENVIRONMENT

Although not responsible for actually creating programs, programming failures were often attributed to user inattention and lack of understanding of their own business processes. No longer — projects must now meet true user needs and solve real business problems. New EUC personnel should be trained in both business applications and information systems. College students should take heavy doses of accounting, finance, marketing, and operations management along with their information systems courses. Leading-edge organizations are sending their analysts, designers, and programmers into user departments to enhance communications, to improve products, and to ensure adherence to user needs. Those that keep their staff in-house use such techniques as joint application development (JAD) to force their staff to deal with user needs more directly.

RESPONDING TO USER REQUESTS FOR ASSISTANCE

EUC managers should work with a small, well-structured information systems' steering committee to create a comprehensive business systems plan containing the overall objectives of information systems tailored to the requirements of the organization. The steering committee should also have the responsibility for establishing project priorities on a periodic basis. This plan, and the resulting project priorities, are invaluable assets when evaluating proposals for new systems development and for explaining why proposed projects must be eliminated, delayed, or modified.

Vision can haunt CIOs as well as presidents. One computer center director found that in the absence of such a plan, negative decisions became personalized. He, rather than the company, would not support installation of a departmental network; he denied the acquisition of a new database; and he would not support the purchase of a new LAN. The availability of a commonly agreed-upon, long-term perspective for computing within the broader business perspective is instrumental as an educational device, as a neutral decision making tool, and as a guide for users interested in projects that are likely to find support. An effective business systems plan can prevent EUC from becoming enmeshed in the wrong projects. A new project may be hatched by a verbally powerful manager who heard a few complaints and decided to use an exciting but unproven technology with the temporary availability of some funding. Some users may be pleased with the results, but the majority may question why this project was started and whether EUC really knows what it is doing.

CREATING AN ORGANIZATIONAL STRUCTURE DESIGNED AROUND USER FUNCTIONS

Many EUC managers are struggling to reorganize the structure of their department to make it more effective in meeting user demands. In the past, it was possible to organize along technical lines; separating operations and communications from programming, and systems development from data base administration, the information center, and other user support functions. To manage user expectations, the EUC department must be structured to better facilitate EUC staff knowing and even anticipating user requests. For example, a utility company has changed its structure from the traditional lines by looking at the business functions they support and creating small workgroups headed by business managers with systems knowledge who have the responsibility for supporting specific application functions. This company pools their more technical communications and database personnel — providing their services to the work groups on a per-job basis. A similar structure is being used by both a county government and a manufacturing company. Both of these organizations have flattened their structures by eliminating middle management and upgrading all development project personnel to programmers and analysts.

EUC is not exempt from reengineering. Honest communications must be matched with a willingness to redesign and adapt procedures to suit changing times. Users want help in addressing their problems. They do not want to sit through lectures about standards, security, control procedures, and the like that simply introduce new constraints on their options. Successful implementations of new systems usually require EUC to modify its procedures, to retrain its staff, and to reorganize its operating mechanisms. When old relationships with users do not work, they must be changed fast.

ASSUMING THAT USERS CAN HELP THROUGHOUT THE SYSTEM DEVELOPMENT LIFE CYCLE

Systems development is not a spectator sport. Most users are already transitioning to a new technological world. They expect to change for good purpose. They expect to adapt to reengineered work flows when the changes result in more efficient operations. They expect to learn new skills and they do not want to be in technological backwaters.

Managers of successful projects uniformly report that a key reason for the success of new applications is the participation of knowledgeable users. Each major project should have a development committee that remains intensively committed to working with systems developers throughout the effort. One judicial systems development group found that their interpretation of only one address in a person's address history on a screen display being sufficient for court administrators was wrong. As a result of weekly review and evaluation meetings with users, this error was discovered early in the process before screen designs were finalized and before data structures were frozen. The success of a military inventory control project was attributed to the daily interaction key users had with the development team. Even the development of mundane business systems can profit from user input. A manufacturing company used a JAD approach for the development of a new accounts receivable system and found that they were able to create the system much more quickly than their original estimates. They attributed the speed of development of the

JAD meetings; because their analysts did not have to meet separately with users and then frequently have to return to ask the users more questions, they were able to complete system design in an intense, concentrated week rather than a longer, more spread out period of time.

Some EUC units develop formal contracts with their users to establish the level of their involvement early in the process. Formal contracts do not only specify how, when, and which users will be involved, they also improve user expectations by clearly identifying the objectives of the project and which features the user can reasonably expect to receive.

AVOIDING OVERPROMISING AND UNDERPROMISING

Some EUC managers, in their zeal to acquire access to new technologies, deliberately low-ball cost estimates as a hook to acquire new facilities, equipment, and staff. This phenomenon is also one used by computer vendors to acquire new customers. The short-term commitment invariably leads to user disillusionment, however, as project scopes are reduced and actual costs are raised. A director at a machinery manufacturing plant used low cost estimates as a means of gaining management support for a new materials requirements planning system. By the time the project was cancelled, it had tripled in cost, the director had been replaced, and her successor had a difficult time overcoming user skepticism for starting on a desperately needed personnel system.

Quoting time and costs for ill-defined projects is, of course, especially dangerous. One manager was asked to estimate the costs for a facilities management system that was to be discussed at a senior-level management meeting several hours later. His off-hand estimate, carefully qualified as to the high degree of uncertainty with the minimal information he was given, came to be the official figure for the life of the project. Naturally, the costs were considerably higher so his credibility was damaged.

SELECTING ACHIEVABLE, APPROPRIATELY SIZED PROJECTS

Although some technologically sophisticated, asset-rich organizations are capable of mounting a total, top-down redesign of their information architecture, most are not. Specific high-priority projects must be mounted one at a time. The creation of a business systems plan with a prioritized projects listing should help EUC managers define, and communicate to their users, the most important projects needed to be completed. It is the EUC manager's job, however, to be sure that the projects include in that listing are ones that can be solved by the application of automated information systems. Managers should avoid including a project on that list simply because it is a problem and needs to be solved. Solutions to some problems may not be easily structured in a computable fashion.

KNOWING AND ACCOMMODATING ALL USERS

A tendency exists to fill project development committees with higher-level officers who have a broad view, can commit resources, and make decisions that stick. As important as these characteristics are, other users should be involved. Lower-level users (e.g., the clerk who accepts and records payments and the picker who retrieves items from inventory) must be involved because they are often more familiar with current procedures, legal requirements, and implementation problems than are their superiors. One consultant found, to his dismay, that a final system was not acceptable to a county social services department simply because the clerks did not think that the new system looked like a system they had been using. The manager of the office provided the key requirements for the system, but was unwilling to force her staff to use the newly developed but more efficient system. Upper-level managers should be saved for the IS steering committee, and the people who will be responsible for the use of the system should be fairly represented on the development committees.

USING PROJECT MANAGEMENT TECHNIQUES

A person capable of controlling and managing a project should be assigned as the leader of a systems development project. Important projects deserve expert leadership and sometimes the most effective project manager may not be in EUC. Many EUC units place a respected user in charge of the project development committee to encourage greater ownership of the project and to foster greater learning about technological opportunities and limitations. If project leadership is to be kept within the EUC organization, the personnel must understand the key concepts of project management including planning, estimating, communication, establishing milestones, tracking, and controlling. It should be part of the departmental culture to use a standardized approach to project management for every major project. Standardized does not have to mean time-consuming; it should mean a uniform process that is generally accepted as reliable in an organization.

Personnel should be encouraged to keep projects moving; to start and end each phase of the project on time. Users can tell that a project has stagnated when communication drops off, when staff start hedging their estimates of delivery times and costs, and when a project suffers from higher than usual staff turnover. Adequate attention should be given to techniques for installing the software smoothly, for training staff at the right time, and for issuing suitable documentation. All persons involved should have access to evaluative information so that they can understand where the time and money is being deployed on a project. If this information is disseminated among project team members, specific milestones should be well-known before questions about progress arise.

COMMUNICATING REGULARLY AND HONESTLY

EUC staff should accept users as their peers, not as their subordinates. Users are informed professionals who deserve details and frank appraisals about a project's status. They are vitally concerned with the system's success and deserve accurate briefings on any problems encountered. They can recommend alternatives that often eliminate problems, but can only provide that service when they are asked questions. Frequent communication enables managers to provide users with details, concepts, and insights that are essential for building an effective partnership. Managers should engage in technology transfer with their users. Above all, they should find solutions, recommend directions, remove obstacles, and display a positive can-do attitude that supports users rather than fights them or tries to shift responsibility to them.

EUC managers should answer questions and deal with problems honestly and completely. It could just be that they do not understand the problem or the solution users see. Managers should accept and act on users' feedback. They should respond to objections and fears as they arise.

It is essential for EUC managers to establish a communications channel that will work best in their company. A large governmental organization found it difficult to schedule acceptable meeting times for face-to-face meetings with project participants. After initial JAD sessions were over, it was hard for the members of this organization to find a way to continue to meet when necessary. Their consultant said that they should simply schedule regular meetings and require participants to attend until the project was complete. This organization found that regular meetings were time-consuming and unproductive, however, so it was a better fit for them if they used electronic mail to communicate the additional details necessary to complete their project. Another company set up a large, physical bulletin board that was used to post ideas, messages, and notes during the development process.

APPROACHING SYSTEMS DEVELOPMENT FROM THE USER'S POINT OF VIEW

Systems developers can be enamored with cutting-edge technologies. They want to be in the forefront of their trade employing image processing, expert system, Computer-aided software engineering tools and object-oriented programming. Users not only care little about the specific workings of these technologies, they are often confused by them. The users are worried about the piles of paper that get higher and higher, about the lag in their service time, and in the efficiency with which bills are paid. They want to improve their operations. Users want to know what their managers can do for them and how a new system will assist them, not what they can do for their manager or how the technology will benefit the organization in general. They are not interested in the company buying new technological toys. An emphasis on hardware and software, on acronyms and buzz words, retards rather than facilitates communication.

EUC managers must recognize that their users have probably previously had some negative experiences with computer systems development. They know the new technologies are rarely as cheap to build, as easy to implement, as modern as they expected, or as productive as they seemed when the decision was made to create the system. Managers must deal with their insecurities and not simply plow ahead. Users need feedback on the emerging system and they need to provide feedback on how the systems does or does not meet their needs.

EVALUATING USER SATISFACTION BOTH DURING AND AFTER DEVELOPMENT

An EUC manager should know how end users feel about the EUC department. The manager should know whether users are satisfied in general with the service they are receiving, as well as whether or not a specific project has met their goals and expectations. This information can be obtained informally by talking with project participants and other managers in a company, however, the process is subject to wide variations in validity depending on who is speaking with whom. The best way to evaluate user satisfaction is to formalize the process by creating a brief questionnaire routinely given to users. Users should identify for themselves their perceptions of EUC, and a specific project, by answering concrete, objective questions about how they are using EUC services and the system in question. EUC managers can help a user understand their own perceptions by asking them to crystalize those feelings on paper. Those questionnaire answers can then be used to validate problems with the system and act as input for future enhancements. If the user is perceiving a problem where one perhaps does not appear to exist, it is vital that managers neutralize that concern before it becomes part of the folklore of the company for future development efforts.

Evaluation should also be done informally. After a project has been in operation, managers should revisit users to find out if they are using the system correctly and effectively. They can check whether the documentation is helpful to the users by watching to see if it is being used correctly, or at all. In systems that have many user options, it has been found that most of the previously trained users are under-using system capabilities and new employees may not be using the system at all. With a small investment in retraining, EUC can boost its users' satisfaction ratings.

TOOTING THEIR OWN HORN

Perceptions are equivalent to reality. If users are in fact in error when they think EUC is unproductive, unsupportive, behind the times, or irrelevant, it is the fault of EUC. Every system is perceived to be mission-critical to the user, but EUC is not. Managers must find ways to let users know about their contributions to the enterprise's success. Success stories let people know that EUC is productive, that new technologies have a role to play in their company, and that their investment in EUC is paying off. Managers might consider publishing a regular, but infrequent, newsletter that not only details a given success story but also explains some new feature that your users want or need to know about. If managers include training material, as well as marketing information in their newsletter, they will have a better chance of it being read by users.

CONCLUSION

EUC managers have the opportunity to manage how users perceive EUC and the systems development process at their organization. If they do not take this opportunity, they can be assured that users will be sharing their perceptions with each other and defining their own opinions of EUC effectiveness without any input from the EUC department. In these times of business reengineering and reevaluation of the way an organization performs its daily operational tasks, EUC managers have an excellent environment to create new processes to manage user expectations. They should take the time to figure out how they can direct user perceptions to have a more positive view of EUC, and systems development in particular, preferably before they are asked to do an analysis of the advantages and disadvantages of outsourcing that next large development project.

Chapter 16
Project Teamwork: How To Make It Happen

James R. Coleman

There is a great deal of emphasis on the need for teamwork. It should be on the need for *good* teamwork. If a project requires a variety of skills, has multiple tasks, and shared resources, it usually involves several individuals working together to accomplish it. If the job eventually gets done, then teamwork of some variety has happened. The question is "How well did they work together?"

To determine if teamwork is effective, the following questions should be asked:

- Was the work accomplished in the minimum amount of time, with the resources available?
- Did the individuals performing each task have all information, tools, or material available to them when they needed it?
- Was there any uncertainty on the part of the team members about who was responsible for what?
- Did the individual elements fit together nicely the first time, or was a lot of rework required?
- Were formal team meetings confined to quick status reports, news essential to the entire team, and issues appropriate for group discussion, such as development of high-level specifications?
- Did the project require very little management intervention?
- Did the work meet the goals of the project?

If the answer to any of these questions is no, then the teamwork needs to be improved. Think about last two or three projects done by the team. How do they stack up?

0-8493-9998-X/00/$0.00+$.50
© 2000 by CRC Press LLC

THE THREE ESSENTIAL ELEMENTS

Three activities where astonishing levels of teamwork are common have been studied. They are aircrew coordination on an antisubmarine warfare aircraft, professional motor racing teams, and team sports at the college and professional level.

Crew interaction on an antisubmarine warfare aircraft is one of the most dramatic examples of teamwork ever observed. The aircraft is required to operate at dangerously low altitudes, performing a series of aggressive maneuvers, for long periods of time. Data from multiple sensors must be received, logged, and processed. Decisions have to be made and actions taken. Delays of a few seconds make the difference between a successful mission and lost contact.

What is remarkable is not that this is routinely done well, but that it is was done well by hundreds of crews, with whatever individuals are assigned. Equally remarkable is the fact that individual members can be replaced without seriously degrading the performance of the crew. Somehow, the skills of the group can be maintained in an environment of constantly changing personnel.

In the case of the racing teams and organized sports, one member of the team usually gets all the headlines (drivers, quarterbacks). However, it is inevitably the group that executes the best as a team that enjoys the most success. How many people remember the name of the quarterback for the University of Nebraska during the past NCAA football season, yet Nebraska thoroughly trounced Tennessee and superstar Peyton Manning to win the national championship. It was able to do this because it was better as a team at executing the plays.

These activities represent the achievement of very high levels of teamwork, but they largely depend on repetitive drill for developing it. The luxury of constant drill is not available in the business world. However, there are three elements common to all these teams that define why they work so well; which can use project managers to improve the teamwork in their own projects.

The three essential elements of good teamwork are:

- Each member of the team must thoroughly understand the process and the relationships of the individual parts of the process to each other.
- All members of the team must be adequately skilled in their function or part of the process.
- Each member of the team must be committed to the success of the team as a whole rather than to success as individuals.

When these elements exist, uncertainty largely disappears.

UNDERSTANDING THE PROCESS

Understanding the process is not easy. It requires careful analysis. Fortunately, in the case of repetitive processes, if the work is done well, it only has to be done once. Remember, everything else depends on how well the manager and all the team members understand the process.

This is the point where most businesses fail in their effort to improve teamwork. Excuses given for not properly analyzing and specifying development processes are usually some variation of "We don't have time for that." A better statement of why process design is poorly done would be "We don't know how." That situation is at least correctable. A full course on process design is beyond the scope of this chapter, but, since it is fundamental to achieving teamwork, at least a look at the basics is worthwhile.

Every process consists of three parts, inputs, a transform, and outputs. Each input has to come from somewhere and contain certain items. The transform operates on those items and turns them into something else (outputs). The outputs have to go somewhere and are required to contain certain data, information, or material.

Most processes can be further broken down into subprocesses. The trick is to break them down *properly*. The breakdown should be according to function, not organizational department. Most process designs require at least three levels of breakdown. Very seldom will even the most complex processes require as many as five levels. It is easy to get carried away with breaking down the process. If it is getting out of hand, it would probably be a good idea to rethink the way the process has been partitioned. As a general rule, process breakdown should continue until each subprocess is easily accomplished by one individual or small task group.

The function of each process or subprocess should be clearly stated, but it would be a mistake to be specific about *how* the transformation is done. This allows the individual or group responsible to create and change procedures as necessary to fit their situation. Each individual subprocess should appear as a black box to the rest of the system. This means that, as long as the input or output structures are not affected, the specific procedures for the transform can be changed and revised without affecting any other part of the system.

The form and content of the inputs and outputs should be specified *explicitly*. Identify the direct and ultimate sources and destinations of the material. While it is easy to get carried away with breaking down the process, it is almost impossible to overdo the documentation of inputs and outputs.

Processes can be diagrammed in a number of ways. *Remember,* the objective is to enable those who are is given the responsibility for one part of the process to understand exactly what they are supposed to accomplish, where the needed input is coming from, what form the input will have, where the output is supposed to go, and what form that output needs to have.

The best way to develop a good process design is to involve those who will eventually be assigned to projects. These are the professionals who understand what is necessary for the development project to be successful. It is highly unlikely that one individual could create a good process design without utilizing the knowledge and experience of all the professional resources available.

TRAINING TEAM MEMBERS

Once a good process design document exists, it is relatively easy to train the personnel. They need to be trained to do three things:

1. Understand the process as a whole, and how their work fits into it.
2. Trust their teammates.
3. Do their job first, and then make themselves available to help anywhere else they are needed.

Process Training

Plan your training to ensure *understanding* of the process. This understanding is, after all, the key to making it work. Remember that this is training in the process, not specific disciplines. The manager is trying to give the team members a project organizational structure that will allow them to do their best work.

Training to Trust

Training people to trust their teammates takes a little more thought. Most people are reluctant to believe that the process will truly function as designed. This lack of confidence usually is the result of experience with poorly organized teams. This is not due to any character flaws in the personnel, but is usually a self-defense behavior. In teams where process is poorly defined and teamwork is poorly understood, the natural tendency is either to try to control as much of the activity as possible or to try to shift any blame to another area. Show the team members that the objective of the process design is to define individual responsibility clearly.

The key is to emphasize that *everyone* have a clear understanding of what is required. Point out that as long as everyone performs his or her individual function, the process as a whole will work well. If it does not, it is probably the fault of the process design, not the individual. Most people will be happy to concentrate their efforts on their function once uncertainty is eliminated.

Training in *How* to Assist Others

When people realize they are being evaluated as a team, it is not difficult to get them to help each other. There are two problems that usually happen here. First, there is a tendency to meddle instead of assist, and, second, there is often a reluctance to do menial work. Preventing these can be more difficult than might be imagined.

Point out that the objective is to assist where needed, not to take control of other functions. In most cases, the need for assistance falls in the category of simple administrative help or legwork. These things are not perceived as heroic efforts, but they are just as essential as anything else. Emphasize how they can free up time for a teammate to apply specialized skills to the core problem. Teach them that assistance in specialized skills areas should be given *only* when it is requested and *only* when they are fully qualified to give it.

In the case where a more experienced or knowledgeable person is assisting one who is not at the same level, it is certainly appropriate to share experience and knowledge. However, this must be done in an attitude of teaching or coaching instead of simply taking over the work. The most experienced people should be given a little special training in how to do this. Ensure that they understand the difference between valuable assistance and destructive meddling.

GETTING THE REQUIRED COMMITMENT

The key to obtaining commitment is making the team members understand that they will be evaluated only as a team, not as individuals. In fact, individual performance simply does not matter if the team as a whole does not perform well.

Once this has been said, it is important to be consistent in applying it. It is also essential that management understand this philosophy and is willing to back it up. *Only when people understand that they are being measured as a team will they start performing like one.* This sounds like common sense, but it is the second most common cause of teamwork failures. Under no circumstances, should a manager single out an individual for praise or criticism. All team members must be treated as equally important. If the process is well designed, all functions are part of an essential chain. Even if the most mundane function fails, the effort of the entire team is compromised.

Expect a fair amount of uneasiness about this method of evaluation. No matter how often it is said that this is the way it will be done (and it should be said often), managers will have to prove that they really mean it.

WHAT ABOUT THE "NON-TEAM-PLAYERS"?

Undoubtedly, there will be one or two individuals who simply do not function well in a team environment. Unfortunately, these people tend to be either very experienced, or very skilled in what they do. If this happens, find some other way to use their talents. If you leave these individuals in the team during the formative stages of teamwork attitudes, they will guarantee failure. If their skill set is essential, try to use them as an internal technical consultant, but do not make them responsible for any functions. These people are usually very valuable to an organization. Do not waste them! Just do not let them get in the way of developing effective teamwork.

PUTTING IT ALL TOGETHER

This chapter is about developing teamwork, not about project management. However, teamwork has no value unless it is applied. With this in mind, how to manage a project will be touched on briefly.

The trick is to *make the project plan match the process design*. This sound obvious, but, more often than not, project plans are organized by department and tend to be very linear. A great deal of effort went into to analyzing and specifing the process; use the work!

Gantt and PERT charts are wonderful tools, but they have serious limits. It will be found that the process design creates a large number of dependencies, and some things will probably have to be blocked. It may be necessary to have a few tasks that include more than one function. Most of the common project management software is going to be difficult to use — not impossible, but difficult. Just make sure that the plan does not conflict with the process design.

Concentrate on ensuring that the requirements of the process inputs and outputs are met. Do not worry too much about discontinuities in the project plan. If the process design is good and the team members are properly trained, the project will be completed in just about the minimum time anyway.

WHERE TO GET HELP

With all of this information, why would help be needed? The answer is because this chapter touched only lightly on some very important technical areas.

First, if readers are new to some of these ideas and cannot find help within their organization, they should *get some outside help!* A good consultant can save immense amounts of money and time. More importantly, they will prevent mistakes that will cause the initial effort to fail. There probably will not be a second chance. Here are a few things to look for in selecting a consultant:

- Find one with some background in both structured design and leadership development.
- Beware of consultants who are too attached to any particular buzzwords. This usually indicates a lack of flexibility.
- Look for a consultant who approaches this type of situation as a teacher. The manager is going to have to continue this work long after the consultant has collected his or her check and gone.
- Beware of anyone who claims to be able to solve all the problems. Such individuals tend to rely on "canned" solutions that may or may not be appropriate to the organization.
- If a consultant is hired, work together. Managers should make sure that they and their management are committed to the effort.

For internal help in process design, look in the IT or systems engineering departments. There is likely to be someone with knowledge of structured systems design. The techniques of that discipline will provide an excellent framework for doing the process analysis. Some modification of the specifics is necessary, but the principles are the same.

DOES THIS REALLY WORK?

In terms of the original set of questions for evaluating teamwork, how will these techniques help?

- Was the work accomplished in the minimum amount of time, given the resources available?
  If the process design is good, it will eliminate uncertainty and enhance communication. It also defines precisely what work has to be done. If the project plan matches the process, all the work will be done and in just about the minimum amount of time.
- Did the individuals performing each task have all the information, tools, or data available to them when they needed it?
  This is a function of the design and adherence to it.
- Was there any uncertainty on the part of the team members about who was responsible for what?
  The process design explicitly defines what functions are required. All that is necessary to do is assign responsibility by function.
- Did the individual elements fit together nicely the first time, or was a great deal of rework necessary for the project to make sense?
  The process design defines the required interfaces.
- Were formal team meetings confined to quick status reports, news essential to the entire team, or issues appropriate for group discussion, such as development of high-level specifications or functional baselines?
  Once the higher-level issues of the project are decided, the ususal purpose of formal meetings is to maintain communication. With a good

process design, communication is a provided for by the input and output specifications. Uncertainty is eliminated, interfaces are defined, and points of coordination are right there for all to see. Formal meetings may then be used simply for short status updates, or to pass along information useful to the team as a whole.

- Did the project require very little management intervention?
  Beginning to get the idea?
- Did the work meet the goals of the project?
  Adherence to the process design will ensure the project goals are met.

Chapter 17
Team Building for IS Success

Raghu Nath
Albert L. Lederer

As today's IS executives implement the large-scale redesign of business processes to maximize the payoff from information technology, user relations become increasingly important. Wide-scale business process redesign can seriously threaten users and engender more resistance than any of the more-limited projects of bygone years. Fragile user relations can thwart even the best redesign plans.

At the same time, users have more options than ever before. For smaller projects, they can easily choose external systems integrators over the internal IS department. In many firms, they can create their own departmental IS groups and build information technology applications themselves.

All of this leaves today's IS managers more pressed than ever to successfully manage user relations. It leaves them with the challenge of building user cooperation and trust and generating the user enthusiasm required to carry major projects through to their successful conclusion.

One way to meet this challenge is through a process called team building.

TEAM BUILDING FOR IS SUCCESS

Team building is human process intervention — that is, it is a well-defined method of changing people's attitudes and behavior. Its primary goal is to create a climate of trust and cooperation among a group of people. Team building draws users and IS professionals together to identify common goals and work together to achieve them.

The expected outcomes of team-building sessions for IS professionals and users are:

- IS participants develop an understanding as well as an appreciation of the plans and objectives of the users.

- User participants develop a similar understanding and appreciation of how IS can contribute to their plans and objectives.
- IS and user participants develop a climate of mutual trust and openness.
- IS professionals and users identify a few pilot projects for collaborative work to set a precedent for future work.
- IS professionals and users develop a mutual understanding of each other's roles and responsibilities.

Building such trust and understanding is not an easy task. It requires specialized skills. Thus the expertise of the team-building leader is key to the success of the effort. Several major universities offer programs for training team leaders. They include the University of Pittsburgh, the University of California at Los Angeles, Harvard University, Case Western Reserve University, Pepperdine University, and Bowling Green State University. Their training programs involve participants in team-building sessions, leadership of team-building sessions under the supervision of an experienced leader, and study of the theory of team building and organizational development. The programs are typically offered as part of doctoral programs in business administration or social sciences. None specializes in team building for IS professionals and users.

This chapter details the process of team building for IS professionals and users and provides a brief case history of successful team building in a manufacturing firm.

PARTICIPANTS IN TEAM BUILDING

Team building requires no formal training of participants, but it does make demands on them. Most important, participants must keep an open mind, be willing to share their ideas, and be willing to listen to the ideas of others. Users should be able to reveal their plans and objectives, and IS professionals should be able to listen and express how they think they can help users realize those plans and objectives. Users need to be able to hear IS professionals' ideas and evaluate them critically. Above all, each side must have confidence and trust in the other.

User Participants

Team building treats both internal users (those inside the company) and external users (those outside it) as customers. However, the dynamics of team building vary for each type of user.

Internal Users. Organizational structure and politics greatly affect internal users, so the team leader must assess an organization's structure, culture, and politics before conducting team-building sessions. Cultural and political problems can make it virtually impossible to create a climate of trust and cooperation among IS managers and internal users.

Conducting a user satisfaction survey in advance is essential to detecting underlying problems. Severe dysfunctional issues are later discussed by the leader in in-depth focus groups of internal users before team-building sessions are held. Use of the survey as a diagnostic took is discussed in detail in a later section.

External Users. External users are not a part of the same organizational system, and their power relationship with IS managers differs from that of internal users. External users generally have more options for obtaining services from other suppliers and as a result can be more demanding. They may also be more objective about the IS department's services. It is, therefore, necessary to survey them too.

Selecting IS and User Participants

Like their user counterparts, IS professionals are surveyed to allow for objective selection of participants who represent all levels of the IS group as well as the spectrum of attitudes toward users.

Similarly, a stratified sample of both internal and external users is selected to participate in the team-building sessions. Here, again, stratification allows for representation of different levels of users as well as of the spectrum of attitudes in the user community. Although the sampling is done scientifically, many subjective factors must also be considered. Thus, the selection of users for team building is both an art and a science.

The Team Leader

The team leader should not only have training in team building but also experience in working with people from diverse organizational levels and with an assortment of attitudes. A skillful and experienced team-building leader is therefore essential and should be carefully selected by the IS department.

After IS and user participants have been selected, they are interviewed by the team leader. The interviews have two goals:

1. To enable the team-building leader to establish rapport with participants before designing and conducting the sessions.
2. The leader uses the interviews to design a team-building session that meets the specific needs of the organization. The session lasts approximately three to five days depending on the complexity of the issues. Ideally, it is held off site so that participants are not distracted by their daily responsibilities.

The team-building process can also include sessions for project teams.

TEAM-BUILDING SESSIONS

There are two types of team-building sessions: goal-oriented and interpersonal.

The Goal-Oriented Session. The goal-oriented session emphasizes the development of acceptable goals through the process of joint planning. Team building helps build the cooperative climate necessary for successful joint planning.

Goals are developed based on the needs of the users as well as the ability of the IS professionals to meet those needs. Thus, they tend to be realistic and achievable. Once goals are mutually set, participants clarify and assign specific roles and responsibilities so that each participant knows who is to do what and when.

The Interpersonal Session. The second type of team-building session emphasizes interpersonal relationships. It helps develop a climate of trust between IS professionals and users that, in turn, leads to a spirit of mutual understanding and cooperation.

In most organizations, both types of team-building sessions are necessary, although more work may be needed in one area than in another. Sessions include talks by the leader followed by problem-solving sessions for carefully formed groups of IS and user participants, and then reports by these groups to the full group.

SURVEY FEEDBACK: A DIAGNOSTIC AND BENCHMARKING TOOL

Survey feedback is an essential partner to team building. As explained previously, the initial survey is designed to identify specific user needs. With the help of a survey team of IS professionals and users, the team-building expert designs a questionnaire that addresses the specific needs of the organization. The customized survey is administered by the survey team and the data analysis is conducted by the team-building leader to ensure confidentiality. The results of the survey are compiled for each different type of user. They are fed back to the survey team as well as to IS management and a user group for validation of results.

One questionnaire uses scaled items with numerical responses from prior team-building sessions of IS professionals and users. It measures user satisfaction along three dimensions:

1. The IS product
2. IS support
3. Relationships with IS professionals

When such an instrument is used, focus groups of both IS professionals and users should modify the items to fit the language of the organization. The groups should also generate additional items for the questionnaire.

The questionnaire is administered to a sample of users. Results are then statistically analyzed to identify related groups of items called factors. The factor analysis may generate other dimensions in addition to the three mentioned. Another statistical analysis is conducted to check the reliability of the questionnaire, and the numerical responses of all subjects are then added up for each factor.

The initial survey and the interviews conducted following selection of participants make up the diagnostic effort for the team-building session. The survey data provide input for the design of the session, but they also serve as the benchmark for measuring future progress.

The factor totals from the first survey provide the initial reading on the organization. After the team-building sessions, a second survey is taken and its factor scores are computed. Changes from the first and second survey are then calculated. These changes should meet the goals and expectations of the first team-building session. If these goals are either under- or overachieved, reasons are identified through interviews with users and IS professionals. Thus, the survey shows the organization's improvement in user relations and identifies areas for future improvement.

Survey feedback and team building are interrelated activities. Together, they provide a powerful way of developing a climate of trust and cooperation between the IS department and users leading to the joint development of goals, activity schedules, and the assignment of roles and responsibilities. Done effectively, they can dramatically improve the chances of the successful development and implementation of major information systems.

TROUBLESHOOTING THE TEAM-BUILDING PROCESS

Exhibit 17.1 summarizes the steps to using team building for IS success. Following them carefully minimizes the likelihood that these problems will occur:

- Surveys, interviews, and focus groups often uncover sensitive, political issues that require handling by user or IS executives. If such issues are not resolved before the team-building session, the sessions may be unproductive.
- Despite precautions, conflicts may erupt during the team-building session. These may concern business or interpersonal issues. Ideally, many are handled outside the sessions, but severe interpersonal conflict must be dealt with during the team-building session. Careful selection of an experienced leader is therefore crucial.
- Budget and time constraints may necessitate compromises with the ideal program. For example, holding the team-building sessions in a remote setting may be infeasible. The ability to alter the design of the team-building session is also necessary.

Exhibit 17.1. Steps for Team Building for IS Success

Initial Survey

The survey is developed in collaboration with users and IS professionals. After it is administered and results are analyzed, interviews are conducted with both groups to clarify issues identified by the survey. Focus groups are conducted to gain further insights into the survey results.

Selection

Based on the results of the survey and in consultation with IS and user executives, participants for the three-day team-building sessions are selected.

Interviews

Interviews are conducted with the selected participants to reveal their expectations for the upcoming session and hidden or sensitive issues that may impede the goals of the session. If, during the interview process, significant resistance surfaces, the three-day session may be postponed so that the resistance can be addressed. In any case, the data from the interviews help fine tune the design for the three-day team-building session.

Three-Day Team-Building Session

The session aims to develop a climate of trust, openness, and collaboration between users and IS professionals.

One-Day Team-Building Sessions for Project Teams

A one-day team-building session is conducted with each project team to identify roles and responsibilities of users and IS professionals and thus to help develop a healthy psychological contract between them.

Two-Day Follow-Up Session

When project teams have completed their work, a two-day off-site session is held to receive their reports and develop an implementation plan.

Implementation

As projects are implemented, consultation is provided to project teams as requested.

Evaluation

The survey is again repeated. Results of this second survey are compared with the initial survey and discussed in a one-day session with users as well as with IS executives. Problems encountered during the implementation stage are identified so that they can be corrected in future cycles.

AN EXAMPLE OF SUCCESSFUL TEAM BUILDING

A high-tech manufacturing firm with $1 billion in annual sales recently implemented a successful team-building program for IS success. The following section gives a brief history of its experience.

Background

For many years, the organization had been known for the high quality of its sophisticated software. At times, the 900-member IS department had more than 200 project teams at work. Occasionally, top management received some minor complaints from business executives that IS services had not met their standards. Before the team-building program, the IS department hired consultants to train its IS professionals in such project management skills as forming project teams and managing team meetings.

Then, in 1990, a major customer voiced serious complaints about the deterioration in performance of one of the organization's software products. After meeting for a one-day session, an IS management team began investigating the complaints.

Preliminary Planning

A preliminary planning meeting was held with the IS management team to explain team building. The IS management team then decided to include survey feedback in its team-building effort.

The organization already had a technical team charged with developing a significant new information system. Two more teams, a survey team and a consultants group, were also established. In addition, a divisionwide coordinating council was established with two representatives from each team. A full-time internal coordinator led the program and headed the coordinating council. The IS management team provided overall guidance.

Customer Satisfaction Survey

The organization's external customers were categorized into three groups: two groups of major customers and one of several different customer organizations.

Then, two distinct levels were identified within each of the organization's seven internal business units. The first was authorizing executives — individuals with the authority to commit funds for IS projects. The second comprised the end users who actually use IS services.

A customer satisfaction survey was designed in collaboration with the survey team. The team tested the survey with selected customers and prepared a final version. It administered this instrument to a large sample of customers, who returned the surveys anonymously.

Survey data were analyzed separately for the three customer categories and seven business units. Based on the analysis, some authorizing executives were interviewed and focus groups were conducted with some end users. These provided further insights into what was needed to meet customers' needs and expectations. A three-day team-building session for the IS management team was designed based on the findings.

The Team-Building Session

The IS management team discussed three major issues at the team-building session. The first centered around the results of the customer satisfaction survey, the interviews with authorizing executives, and the focus groups with end users. As a result, the IS management team compared its practices with those of organizations that have high customer satisfaction.

The second issue was the strengths and weaknesses of the IS department. The IS management team compared its strengths and weaknesses against those of its competitors.

The third issue emerged from the first two. It focused on developing a vision based on customer satisfaction and on creating strategies to implement the vision. During the discussion of these issues, the focus was on human as well as team processes such as values, attitudes, interpersonal relations, communication, decision making, and planning.

The major result of the three-day team-building session was a commitment by the IS management team to build a consensus on team building throughout the organization. This was to be done through a process of cascading team-building sessions within the IS department. To facilitate these sessions, 20 people within the organization were designated for training as team process consultants.

Training the Team Process Consultants

The designated team process consultants were selected from different levels of management using two criteria. First, they already had to have demonstrated some skill at facilitating change. Second, they had to be viewed positively throughout the organization.

A five-day off-site training session was designed to provide team skills to the selected individuals. At the end of the session, the participants formed an ongoing team that was to meet regularly. Also, these process consultants were assigned in pairs to the cascading team-building sessions.

All-employee meetings were also held. Half of the IS staff attended a morning meeting and half an afternoon meeting. Employees were assigned to small groups led by the team process facilitators. The groups met monthly to ensure interactive communication between top management and staff.

As the team building cascaded downward in the organization, the vision as well as the strategies were converted into specific action plans. A key component of these action plans was to establish a collaborative relationship with the users through joint team-building sessions.

Projects

One key IS project was selected from each of the seven business units and the three categories of customers. A team-building session was conducted at the beginning of each of these projects. This session involved key people from the IS department and the user organizations. It focused on developing a collaborative climate to achieve consensus on project objectives and on the activities needed to attain these objectives. Also, roles and responsibilities were clarified and assigned. Finally, monitoring and tracking mechanisms were mutually established to ensure two-way communication throughout the life cycle of the project.

Evaluation

A systemic evaluation of the program was conducted. It comprised three elements: a customer satisfaction survey, interviews with customer executives, and focus groups with end users. The data were compared to the benchmark data collected at the beginning of the program.

The evaluation indicated significant improvement in user satisfaction. During the interviews and focus group sessions, the typical response was positive and indicated strong commitment to continuing the program.

The major improvement was in user relations. Users felt that a collaborative relationship had been established with the IS department that would help in further team-building sessions. Although there were improvements in the product and support areas, the evaluation identified several issues that needed additional work.

Lessons Learned

The organization incorporated what it had learned from the evaluation into the next cycle of program development and implementation. Lessons learned included:

- *Separating internal and external users into different sessions.* When both internal and external users were combined in the same session, many internal issues surfaced that took considerable time to resolve. During this period, external users were uncomfortable and felt that they did not need to be present. In fact, in a few cases, involvement in some severe internal differences embarrassed them. This necessitated a modification of the team-building design. Although internal and external users did learn from each other in the combined sessions, it is more effective to keep them separate.
- *Limiting the number of participants.* The first team-building session had 22 participants. Because the IS and user issues were so complex, the sessions ran well into the late evening. Limiting the number of participants to 12 would have been more efficient during the three-day session.
- *Keeping programs planned during team building reasonable.* The euphoric atmosphere of the off-site meeting encouraged participants to develop an ambitious program that required considerable time and money to implement. Thus, during implementation, both users and IS

professionals were overworked. In fact, many of them worked late in the evenings and on weekends without additional compensation. Although their efforts evidence the success of the team-building program, the extra hours became problematic. Thus, it is essential that programs be kept within reasonable bounds so that they can be implemented within budgetary and time constraints.

The organization's internal staff is managing the next cycle of program development and implementation with minimal help from the outside consultants. Thus, the process of team building helped launch a continuous process of improvement in the organization.

Chapter 18
Survival Skills for the Information Systems Professional

Clinton O. Longenecker
Jack L. Simonetti
Mark Mulias

The advent of more user-friendly information technology has taken much of the awe out of the information management business. Most business professionals are becoming computer literate out of necessity. This newfound technical awareness frequently causes many users to oversimplify the complexities and demands of managing large-scale information systems and projects, sometimes creating unrealistic expectations among users.

In many organizations, IS professionals are experiencing stress because of changing user attitudes, current trends toward reengineering, the decentralization of the IS function, outsourcing, and contracting. There is a migration away from tightly controlled, highly centralized corporate IS departments to smaller, dispersed, decentralized IS operating groups. Organizations that historically demanded the right solution at any cost are now being asked to provide the right solution at the right price.

IS customers in most environments have a growing host of needs that cannot be satisfied by technical aptitude alone. IS professionals need to develop a better understanding of customer expectations and become more proficient at satisfying customer needs to avoid the consequences of customer dissatisfaction. The purpose of this chapter is to encourage EUC managers and all IS professionals who provide support to end users to develop better customer-oriented systems and skills.

IS FOCUS GROUPS: A CASE STUDY

The suggestions and advice that follow are the consensus of five-person focus groups conducted with 75 experienced IS professionals from three For-

0-8493-9998-X/00/$0.00+$.50
© 2000 by CRC Press LLC

tune 500 organizations. Participants were asked to answer the following questions based on their experience:

- What do users want from IS professionals?
- What specific skills does it take to be an effective IS professional in today's environment?

After participants answered these questions individually, they were assigned to focus groups to discuss their responses and to come to a consensus. Responses across all 15 groups were then compared and tabulated according to top customer expectations and IS skills that a significant majority (at least 65 percent) of participants agreed were necessary to operate successfully in today's IS environment.

What Users Want from IS Professionals

According to the focus group participants, users want technical expertise in terms they can understand. They want assistance in identifying project requirements and direction, leadership, and guidance on technical applications. At the same time, they want practical applications that support strategic direction and business decisions. Users want IS products and services that provide value to the organization and help them better serve external customers.

Users also appreciate it when IS professionals share ownership of the users' projects, communicate with them regularly and remain accessible for consultation during and after the project's completion. Users want an IS department that is flexible in responding to change and realistic about the commitments they make to users. Quality assurance , commitment to a satisfactory finished product, and prompt response in fixing customer problems should all be provided in a cost-effective and timely fashion.

Experienced IS professionals take these requests seriously in light of the fact that sophisticated users have more systems options than ever before and are more willing to experiment in seeking ways to reduce cycle time and improve quality.

Survival Skills for the IS Professional

According to the focus groups, to survive professionally, IS staff members must have:

- Up-to-date technical skills.
- Strong interpersonal and communication skills.
- A business-solutions orientation.
- The ability to operate effectively in teams.
- Strong project management skills.
- Effective planning and organizing skills.

- Analytical and creative skills.
- Flexibility and adaptability in changing circumstances.
- A responsive attitude toward customer needs.
- The ability to be a teacher and coach.

A recurring theme emerged in the focus group findings. The key survival theme IS professionals emphasized could best be described by the word *balanced*. IS professionals must be technically proficient and up-to-date in their areas of expertise. They should, however, balance technical competency with a growing list of skills that have frequently been deemed less than critical for the IS professional in the past — skills relating to business and customer orientation.

Focus group participants considered strong interpersonal and communication skills to be among the most critical skills for survival in the IS field. In addition, IS professionals must be able to operate effectively in the team environment that pervades most organizations. Project management and effective planning and organizing skills must be developed by IS professionals to increase their ability to provide a quality product. Participants made it clear that the IS professionals most effective on the job possess and develop skills that better enable them to provide a value-added service and product to their organizations.

The systems professional has the challenge of developing the ability to think analytically while at the same time being able to be creative and innovative. One chief skill IS professionals should cultivate is coaching. The IS professional should be able and willing to coach others in operating the system. Coaching requires a close working relationship between the customer and coach (i.e., the IS professional) because the coach provides advice and assistance and gives timely and constructive feedback when work needs improvement or greater efficiency is required. The coach must relay this feedback in an understandable language and in an effective, motivating way. This activity includes working with both fellow IS team members and users.

IMPLICATIONS FOR THE EUC MANAGER

Managers in the IS field are being asked to do a better job of serving customers, reducing cycle time, reducing costs, and providing more usable business solutions. Technology can provide significant assistance in this regard. IS professionals are responsible for keeping the organization technically up-to-date, advising which technologies the organization should invest in, maintaining and developing the organization's technical infrastructure, and keeping the organization technically positioned in the marketplace. The attitude, orientation, and approach IS professionals take toward their users becomes important, especially when outside service providers are able to offer equivalent technical expertise.

IS departments and group managers should address each of the following critical questions that focus on the customer-oriented issues raised by the focus groups:

- Who are the customers?
- What are their needs?
- Is IS in tune with the overall strategy of the business and current operating objectives?
- Are users requesting projects and services that are in line with the current goals of the organization?
- Is IS fully aware of its strengths and weaknesses as an IS provider from the point of view of the users?
- Has the IS department developed a mission statement that clearly makes customer service and satisfaction a priority?
- Does IS have a clear understanding of users' needs? Has IS developed service standards that result in actions to meet those needs?
- Has IS educated users on how the system operates and how they can help expedite projects?
- Does IS have systems in place to solicit ongoing customer input and provide performance feedback to ensure user satisfaction?
- Is IS attempting to nurture relationships and develop partnerships with users to better work together and understand each other?
- Is IS responsive in attempting to remove organizational barriers that limit its ability to serve users?

Without strong technical infrastructure, responsive customer service is virtually impossible, but by addressing these issues and EUC manager can better develop a customer service orientation that supports and makes effective use of that infrastructure.

To support these efforts, specific management practices must be developed to encourage individuals to focus on and develop the IS survival skills identified in this study. IS managers interested in improving customer service as a performance dimension should consider developing the practices discussed in the following sections. These activities can assist managers in creating a customer-oriented IS environment operated by professionals with balanced technical, business, and people skills. Managers play a key role in creating this customer-oriented climate.

Developing a Department of Professionals with Balanced Abilities

Although hiring technically competent people is a necessity, technical skill alone does not guarantee value will be added to the organization. The full breadth of abilities needed should be defined and a selection process designed to assess the candidates' complete package of both technical and soft skills. IS professionals with balanced skills give the department *more* flexibility and can help with the critical issues of solving business problems and providing customer service.

Making Customer Service a Component of the Job Description

Departmental customer service standards must be defined and established within the context of the individual IS professional's job. A typical job description identifies specific duties. Specific customer service standards should likewise be identified for the purpose of creating accountability for how to best serve department users.

Providing IS Support Staff with Feedback on Customer Service

Ongoing performance feedback is an effective mechanism for reinforcing appropriate behavior and encouraging the change of inappropriate behavior. Managers are typically in a position to provide feedback on certain aspects of an employee's job. Customers are also an invaluable, although typically untapped, source of critical performance information that can provide meaningful feedback for IS professionals. Most IS professionals hear only negative feedback from users because usually no system exists to channel comments other than complaints. Ongoing customer satisfaction devices should be developed, with customer input, to provide balanced feedback for IS professionals on both technical and interpersonal areas of improvement.

Training for Well-Rounded IS Professionals

IS professionals are accustomed to receiving ongoing technical training in their discipline. However, IS professionals also need training activities in other critical, so-called soft areas such as communication, team-building, customer service, project management, and coaching skills. In addition, professionals need activities aimed at developing a business orientation within the context of the larger organization. Cross-training outside the IS function and assignments on task forces or cross-functional teams offer excellent opportunities for development of other, less technical skills that are necessary for balanced professional development. Training resources should be targeted to help develop the right set of skills for the right person to avoid misusing resources and talents.

Evaluating and Rewarding Performance

One of the key issues in encouraging IS professionals to become more balanced is the issue of accountability. IS professionals must be held accountable for improved customer relations activities and their ability to solve business problems. Therefore they must be evaluated and reviewed on their complete performance, not simply the technical dimensions of their jobs. Appraising performance should not be a once-a-year affair but an on-

Exhibit 18.1. Self-Assessment Development Questionnaire

Instructions: Readers should evaluate themselves in each of the areas listed below. Results of the questionnaire can be used in planning professional development.

	This Area Needs Improvement	This Area is Satisfactory	This Area is a Strength
1. Written communication skills	☐	☐	☐
2. Verbal communication skills	☐	☐	☐
3. Listening skills	☐	☐	☐
4. Ability to operate effectively as a team player	☐	☐	☐
5. Project management skills	☐	☐	☐
6. Planning skills	☐	☐	☐
7. Organizing skills	☐	☐	☐
8. Time management skills	☐	☐	☐
9. Business experience in operations	☐	☐	☐
10. Business experience with external customers	☐	☐	☐
11. Innovative and creative abilities	☐	☐	☐
12. Ability to cope with change	☐	☐	☐
13. Attitude in coping with change	☐	☐	☐
14. Customer service orientation	☐	☐	☐
15. Ability to teach/coach others	☐	☐	☐

going activity that is formalized a minimum of twice a year. Rewarding the right types of performance with appropriate compensation, job opportunities, and assignments can have a strong motivating affect on the IS professional accustomed to being evaluated on purely technical merits.

PERSONAL IMPLICATIONS FOR THE IS PROFESSIONAL

Honest responses to each of the questions in the self-assessment development questionnaire in Exhibit 18.1 can identify areas for improvement. The exhibit lists those key areas that will propel IS professionals to success and long-term career survival. Any skills found to be needing improvement should become part of a personal development plan that identifies specific steps necessary to bolster performance. Development activities individuals can pursue include self-help readings, seminars and workshops, requests for cross-training assignments, expanded involvement in professional organizations, seeking out a mentor or coach, and volunteer activities to acquire experience. The important issue is that IS professionals take responsibility for their own long-term development in addition to any organization-sponsored activity.

Customer service, quality, and continuous improvement are the keys to survival for any organization; the same is true for the individual. IS professionals must think of success as being defined by how well they meet customer needs, and doing this requires a person with balanced technical and soft skills that are not always easily acquired.

Chapter 19
Assessing Customer Perceptions

Naomi Karten

Major discrepancies often exist between how an organization perceives its performance and how its customers do. Sometimes, customers perceive responsiveness and effectiveness to be better than the staff itself does; more often, the reverse is the case. These discrepancies can account for problems the staff faces in achieving a high level of customer satisfaction.

Few organizations take action regularly (or even periodically) to assess customer perceptions of their performance. For some organizations, the reason they focus so little attention on customer perceptions is that they believe they already know how their customers perceive them and do not feel the need to attempt to learn more. For other organizations, assessing perceptions is seen to be just one more task in an overflowing work load, and one that does not generate sufficient benefits to justify the effort.

Fortunately, total quality and continuous improvement programs have led many EUC groups to conduct customer satisfaction surveys, and the results are giving them better insight into changes they need to make to improve their effectiveness in serving customers. This chapter looks at how one banking institution, Mega-Bank, decided to use a more direct and more personal approach that involved its customers as key players in the assessment process.

REASONS FOR CONDUCTING AN ASSESSMENT

At Mega-Bank, organizational changes produced by numerous mergers and reorganizations had put significant stress on relationships between EUC and customer departments. The bank has a corporate headquarters and four affiliate banks in several states. Incompatibilities in hardware, software, and standards existed among the multiple locations, resulting in project delays and confusion. Redundancies in systems responsibilities added to the confusion as management undertook to centralize certain EUC functions and to consolidate, distribute, or eliminate others. Which group

0-8493-9998-X/00/$0.00+$.50
© 2000 by CRC Press LLC

in which location a customer should contact for a particular type of support was unclear to many customers; at times, the staff itself was unsure.

This organizational turbulence created frustration among customers and led many customer departments to attempt to do more of their own computing. Although some of these customer departments were technically astute, others lacked sufficient expertise for the applications they were now developing, and the quality of the resulting applications was far from certain.

EUC management decided to undertake an assessment of customer perceptions. The objective was to obtain detailed customer feedback to support a reexamination of EUC services and to identify changes that would be needed to help them improve both EUC performance and the way this performance was perceived. Although a survey approach was initially considered, it was dismissed as a method that would yield considerable data but only superficial insight into their customers' perspectives. In this case, management decided to use interviews and group discussions. Although this approach would result in feedback from far fewer customers overall than a corporatewide survey, that limitation would be more than offset by the quality of the feedback EUC would gain from direct interviews and discussions.

GATHERING CUSTOMER FEEDBACK

Making Customers Team Members

To plan the assessment process, an EUC team was assembled, headed by a vice president and made up of representatives from corporate headquarters and each of the affiliate banks. Team members concluded that their success in gathering useful feedback would be enhanced if they invited customer representatives to fully participate in the assessment process — not just in providing input, but in actually helping to plan the assessment process and then carrying it out. This idea was uncomfortable for some of the team members; it proved, however, to be one of the keys to the success of the effort.

The EUC team identified customer representatives from each of several major divisions of the bank and invited them to take an active role in the effort. All invited customers were either managers or high-level staff members who had the authority to represent and speak on behalf of their division. Each customer selected was one with whom at least one member of the EUC team had had extensive contact and a reasonable comfort level.

Although various bank initiatives up to this point involved representation from multiple customer and EUC departments, few such cross-functional efforts had ever taken place that were not project-specific. As a result, the EUC team had no way of knowing whether the designated customers would be willing to participate. Although a few customers dropped out because of conflicting priorities, eight customers, representing a cross-section of bank functions, became members of the perception assessment team.

INTERVIEW PLANNING

It was in the interview planning process that the customer representatives became fully involved, by agreeing to take responsibility for identifying appropriate interview candidates in their own divisions and for arranging the interviews. Each customer scheduled three to five interviews, with from one to four customers each, and each interview was to be jointly led by one customer and one EUC representative.

In choosing this approach, one concern is that customers might be unwilling to express negative views about EUC in the presence of an EUC representative. In this case, however, the team decided that the opportunity to hear the customer perspective directly, rather than filtered through a subsequent summary report, would be helpful in understanding the customer perspective and therefore was worth the risk. In addition, by participating in the interviews, EUC members were able to ask interviewees to expand on or clarify points that they might otherwise misinterpret.

Being Open-Ended

Customer team members felt strongly that interview candidates could provide the best quality feedback if they knew in advance what they would be asked. The intent, after all, was not to surprise customers with trick questions but to learn as much as possible about the customer perspective on EUC service. Customers also felt that they could broaden the scope of the feedback by encouraging interview candidates themselves to gather additional feedback from their peers or others with whom they worked on various projects or committees. Accordingly, a sheet of interview questions was prepared and distributed to each interview candidate in advance, with the request that each person discuss the listed topics with as many others as possible before the scheduled interview.

Team members agreed that questions should be left as open-ended as possible to stimulate discussion that would offer insight into the customer perspective. As a result, they decided to focus the interviews on customer perceptions of whichever of various EUC services each customer had had experience with.

Among the specific services and processes listed in the interview sheet were:

- Sources of technical support.
- Access to data.
- Hardware/software acquisition and installation.
- Product evaluation.

- Systems development support.
- Project management.
- Standards setting.
- Service request process.
- Communications about new services or products.

The interview form asked interviewees to indicate, for each of these services and processes, the nature of their experience with those services they were familiar with. Specifically, customers were asked:

- What they viewed as the strengths and weaknesses of the EUC service-process.
- How they viewed EUC performance with regard to the service or process.
- What types of changes they would recommend.

In addition, they were asked to comment on their general perception of EUC and their concerns about the increasing role of technology in their areas, and to suggest other EUC services not currently available that they would like to receive. In this process, the interview forms were used by interviewees as a tool for jotting down notes in preparation for the interview.

THE INTERVIEW PROCESS

All interviews were conducted during a two-week period; in total, there were 24 interviews with a total of 44 customers. Each interview lasted approximately one hour and in most cases was led by the customer team member; the team member asked clarifying questions and took notes. Because customers were welcomed into the process they felt comfortable about speaking their minds, whether expressing positive or negative comments about EUC performance.

To make interview comments easy to analyze, customer feedback from each interview was edited and documented as a series of individual items, with each item constituting either a comment or a recommendation. The result was 20 to 40 items per interview. Most customers had relatively more contact with two or three services and processes than others, and their comments focused on these areas.

To further support the analysis of customer feedback, comments pertaining to each of the services and processes were collated from all customers and documented. The result was a comprehensive look at customer perceptions, both by customer and by service or process.

SAMPLE FINDINGS FROM INTERVIEWS WITH CUSTOMERS

EUC groups are often surprised by some of the results of their perception assessment efforts. Almost invariably, they find their customers perceived them positively in some ways and negatively in other ways that they had not appreciated before. They also find evidence that customers misunderstood certain services or do not fully appreciate how they can benefit from them. Customers also experience frustrations that the EUC staff is unaware of.

The findings are almost always an eye-opener, and so it was in this case. Some customer comments confirmed the EUC staff's own assessment. For example, the service request process was a mangled maze, according to EUC, and customers agreed. But several issues that EUC did not appreciate as problems turned out to be, and others that it assumed were problems were not. The interviews produced findings in several areas that differed from what EUC expected.

Peer Support Issues. Customers use the Help Desk considerably less than was thought. Although the Help Desk was kept extremely busy, many customers ignored it altogether and relied on other customers to help them with problems.

Customers were also frustrated by a lack of awareness of how their peers at other affiliates were using systems services.

Documentation. Customers were more aware of their inadequacies in documenting their own applications than the EUC staff realized. Customers stated they would do a better job of documentation if they had an easier way to do it.

Procedures. Despite the major effort that had gone into preparing a comprehensive policy and procedures guide, many customers were unfamiliar with its contents, and some did not even know of its exitence.

Domains of Responsibility. Customers frequently did not know who to call when they experienced problems. The division of responsibilities between the central EUC group and affiliate groups aggravated this situation.

Communication. Some customers felt that communication among departments was deficient, resulting in a lack of awareness of the support each of several departments was providing to a given customer area.

Communication about the impact of systems initiatives that affected all affiliates or spanned functional boundaries was often lacking. According to some customers, their EUC contacts sometimes did not know about these systems initiatives until they learned of them from their customers.

Acquisition Process. The PC acquisition process was seen to be extremely cumbersome, frustrating some customers and totally mystifying others.

Applications Development. Some customers were doing as much applications development as possible themselves and wanted to continue doing so. Others, however, felt EUC should take responsibility for more of the computer work now being undertaken in customer departments, so that customers could once again focus on their areas of business expertise.

Training. Training was much more highly regarded than expected. However, advanced training was perceived to be a growing need, and some customers felt they already knew more than the training staff.

GROUP DISCUSSIONS

To supplement the interview, the review team met to discuss these customer perceptions and to share their own. These discussions were, by design, loosely structured. Although an agenda was used to guide the discussions, it was found that an unsolicited topic or two invariably emerged as hot buttons for the customer representatives, and time spent on these issues would provide greater insight into the customer perspective than forcing the discussion to follow through on the remaining agenda items.

One such issue was the future technological direction in which EUC would lead the company. Customers perceived EUC as slow in making decisions about technological directions. To customers, the resulting delays impeded their efforts, because they did not want to risk moving in a direction that might necessitate conversations to different platforms and different products later on.

Customer frustration on this issue was not news to the EUC participants, but they had not, up to this point, attempted to explain what was taking place during what customers perceived as delays. The resulting discussion about the nature of the EUC decision-making process did not reduce customer frustration; customers still perceived the long wait as a delay that impaired their productivity, though they came to appreciate that the problem was not as simple as sluggish decision making.

Group discussions were also held on other issues raised in the interviews, such as a cumbersome service request process, the growing confusion about whom in EUC to contact for what service, and frustration over the EUC staff's lack of awareness about systems efforts in progress elsewhere in the bank that customers felt they should be kept informed about. Such an exchange of ideas among customer and EUC participants made two things clear: that customers had not had the opportunity to sound off about their concerns to an audience of willing listeners, and that much of what the EUC staff was hearing it had either never realized or fully appreciated before.

In this case, EUC participants attempted to correct what they viewed as customer misperceptions about their services, although when several customers reflected similar misperceptions, it became apparent that these were not isolated perceptions and that flaws existed in the way EUC communicated information about itself and its services.

Uncovering Common Problems and Solutions

Whereas interviews solicit the views of a few customers from a single functional area, customer/EUC group discussions help to identify issues of common concern. By including representation from multiple customer areas, these discussions provided the opportunity not just for EUC staff to hear customer feedback, but for customers to hear from each other. Customers became aware of similarities in experiences and viewpoints about EUC services, the impact of technology, and changing information needs.

One of the most valuable outcomes of these discussions was not anticipated: the very process of soliciting feedback about customer perceptions improved those perceptions. Several customers had never before been asked for their opinion in an open forum. The opportunity to do so led customers to have an improved attitude about IS and resulted in new joint efforts never anticipated as a consequence of the perception assessment process.

For example, on the issue of the service request process, IS and customer team members decided to improve the process. Forming customer/IS teams to address this issue was not an objective of these meetings; nevertheless, despite the fact that they were under no obligation to do so, *ad hoc* groupings of IS and customer representatives formed to explore a solution, a testament to the relationship-building value of the effort.

OUTCOMES AND BENEFITS TO IS

The findings of the perception assessment process yielded considerable information that the EUC group was able to take into account and act on in deciding how to improve its service strategies and performance. The EUC staff knew it needed to clarify EUC services, improve communications with customers, and streamline several processes. EUC also needed to do more to understand the impact of technological change and growing technical sophistication among customers on the way work was being done in the customer divisions.

The process generated additional benefits as well. EUC learned not to underestimate the willingness, and even the eagerness, of customers to describe both what worked and what did not work for them. In addition, EUC came to appreciate that customers represent a broad constituency comprising different needs and expectations, and therefore a range of differing perceptions about EUC services and performance. The same support that one customer area found excellent another found flawed, and what was important to one was not necessarily important to another. This finding served to remind EUC neither to view nor to treat customers as one large homogeneous group and underscored the importance of taking the full gamut of customer views into account in their planning efforts.

Planning for Ongoing Feedback

Although the assessment of customer perceptions was initially seen as an effort to be done once, it became clear that both EUC staff and customers could benefit in at least three ways from continuing to gain customer feedback on an ongoing basis:

- Periodic interviews and group discussions would ensure that EUC staff would learn about customer concerns early on, before small problems had a chance to loom large.
- Ongoing efforts would communicate to customers that their opinions mattered and would give them a forum through which they could share their views.
- Perhaps most important, holding periodic discussions, independent of any specific projects, would help to promote strong customer/EUC relationships, which could have only a positive impact on all customer/EUC efforts.

FINAL THOUGHTS

A process for assessing customer perceptions can reveal information about how an organization provides services to its customers and how well customers are making full use of EUC services. To help organizations gather information from customers and make the best use of the feedback to improve service, the following recommendations are offered.

Attain a Common Ground Among EUC Participants. Before holding perception assessment sessions with customers, first ensure that there is a meeting of the minds between EUC participants. EUC representatives themselves have different and often strongly held views about such things as the purpose of a perception assessment process, the changes that will be made as a result of it, the ways customers should be involved, and topics that should be discussed at joint meetings. It is not necessary to reach a consensus on every issue, but these meetings are not the place to dispute differences. It is advisable for EUC staff members to compare their views before involving customers to identify differences in perspective that could affect the success of the venture and to establish a common ground.

Weigh the Advantages and Drawbacks of EUC Participation in Customer Interviews. Some customers do not want to speak negatively about EUC, even if they have negative views, and may require coaxing before they speak openly about their perceptions. The presence of EUC staff at these interviews could serve as a deterrent and thereby undermine the value of the interview.

On the other hand, EUC staff members who participate in such interviews almost always gain insight into customer views that they had previously been unaware of. To reduce customer reluctance to describe problems, questions should be structured so they focus not on EUC *per se,* nor on the interviewer, but rather on the issues, activities, services, or processes under discussion. Interviewees feel less as though they are making accusations or issuing complaints when they can speak about the strengths and weaknesses of various services rather than the strengths and weaknesses of those who deliver the services.

Ask for Concrete Examples. When customers use such terms as cooperative, unresponsive, flexible, or slow, to describe EUC, it is important to clarify precisely what they mean by these terms. Without concrete examples, EUC runs the risk of making false assumptions about what customers have in mind. One of the things that made this particular group successful in assessing customer perceptions was that its face-to-face approach enabled the staff to ask customers to expand on their views and to describe actual situations that led to the resulting descriptions. Surveys or other impersonal forms of feedback can make such clarification difficult and may lead the EUC staff to draw inappropriate conclusions about actions it should take to maintain or improve performance.

Ensure That Customers Are Full Participants in the Effort. One of the keys to success for this company was that customers were invited not simply to offer feedback but to have a say in the entire process and to play a significant role in its execution. The actual expenditure of time did not amount to more than several hours for each participant, yet by being involved, customers felt they had a stake in the effort and wanted it to succeed.

Promise Nothing, but Do Something. EUC staff should ensure that customers understand at the outset that the perception assessment effort is intended to identify problems, not solve them, and that appropriate solutions or changes will be considered afterward on the basis of the group's findings. EUC staff should also ensure that customers are not inadvertently led to expect specific changes as a result of the assessment feedback.

Managing customer expectations about actions to be taken is extremely important; otherwise, the entire effort can decrease, rather than increase, customer satisfaction. At the same time, while promising nothing specific, it is important for EUC to take at least some small action as quickly as possible afterward — and to communicate to customers that it has done so — to ensure customers that the EUC staff really was listening and took their input seriously. Involving customers not just in the perception assessment process itself but also in the subsequent planning of changes to be made as a result of the assessment can only help to further strengthen the customer/EUC relationship.

Section III
Effectively Managing Outsourced Projects

Chapter 20
Outsourced Systems Development
Raoul J. Freeman

The outsourcing of large-scale systems development activities is becoming more prevalent, yet the success of these activities is not. In many cases, the repeated failure of large-scale outsourcing projects is caused by lack of management attention to a common set of factors. Given the magnitude of investment involved in large-scale efforts, IS managers must learn to manage these factors before a system is approved for funding and in a way that ensures on-time and within-budget delivery of effective systems. This chapter draws from the experience of several large-scale systems development efforts in the public sector to present recommendations that help ensure the success of large-scale outsourced development projects.

CHALLENGES IN LARGE-SCALE PROJECTS

Well-known failures in the area of large-scale systems development include the State of California Department of Motor Vehicles (DMV) registration system, the Denver Airport baggage-handling system, and the Bank of America trust system. Failure, however, is not reserved to the well known. A study of 24 large U.S. companies reports that 68 percent of major projects using client/server technology overshot their schedules, 55 percent overspent their budgets, and 88 percent involved significant redesign. Large projects (i.e., those in excess of 5,000 function points) are canceled about a quarter of the time, and projects in the 10,000 to 20,000 function-point range are canceled half the time. About 67 percent of projects that are completed overshoot their original schedules and budgets by nearly 100 percent.[1]

IS managers responsible for projects that are significantly larger than others they have managed face challenges not only regarding day-to-day management and integration but also in terms of their ability to conceptualize whether the scale factor will affect system operation. Missed intermediate milestones in large projects involving new technology require special attention, because the development is occurring in relatively uncharted territory. It is at these milestones that managers need to make decisions to

0-8493-9998-X/00/$0.00+$.50
© 2000 by CRC Press LLC

continue the project, cut back on functionality, or spend additional money. If such decisions are postponed, the sponsors of the system may find themselves at a point of no return.

FACTORS TO MANAGE IN LARGE-SCALE PROJECTS

Analysis of outsourced systems development projects ranging in value from $1 million to $100 million and involving, among others, the State of California, County of Los Angeles, and Los Angeles Unified School District revealed several factors that significantly contributed to failure or delay in multiple instances. In each project, managers failed to give appropriate consideration to one or more of the following areas:

- Acceptance testing standards.
- Contract specifications, especially:
  - Measurable business effects or outcomes.
  - Requirements specifications.
  - Arbitration and cost-reimbursement clauses.
  - Mechanisms for settling management disputes.
- Project management and metrics.
- Resource reserves for system implementation.
- Software examination.
- Length of the development cycle.
- Independent quality assurance.
- Technology transfer.
- System ownership.

Because absence of proper attention to these factors contributes to failed systems development efforts, management of these factors is a vital, although not necessarily sufficient, ingredient for ensuring project success.

DEVELOPING APPROPRIATE ACCEPTANCE TESTING STANDARDS

Standards for acceptance testing should be adopted for all systems development efforts. IS managers should ensure that any deviation from such standards is approved by an independent technical body and that wherever possible a parallel acceptance test is conducted.

Parallel testing need not be conducted in real time, which can reduce costs, but any live or parallel test must be sufficiently long to ensure that conditions occurring at significant calendar times throughout the year are experienced. There must be no cold turkey starts of a system without adequate testing of critical system capabilities, and there must always be a fallback plan in case of failure.

IS managers should ensure that proper documentation of the acceptance test is maintained and that *ad hoc* judgment is not allowed to substitute for contractually obligated performance. When the new and the old systems can accept the same transactions, comparison is facilitated. When they cannot, a set of specialized transactions needs to be devised to fit the new system.

Under such circumstances, it is possible to encounter a reconciliation-of-reports problem between the new and old systems. IS managers should not let the issue rest with a promise from developers that these minor errors will be fixed down the road. Independent sign-off that the acceptance test plan meets standards and that the test actually done corresponds to the planned test helps ensure that the area of acceptance testing does not become the cause of a failed development effort.

ENSURING CLEAR AND COMPREHENSIVE CONTRACT SPECIFICATIONS

IS managers must ensure that technical contract specifications are clear and based on design objectives. Before a request for proposal (RFP) is issued, the IS manager should hire independent technical and legal professionals to review and approve the specifications.

Such a review should focus not only on what is included but also on possible areas of omission (e.g., lack of a binding-arbitration clause). The contract should clearly delineate resources to be supplied by the vendor and the user in terms of number of person hours, qualification of personnel, calendar time when people are to be available, hardware, documentation, and training. The manager must also ensure that all contracts contain specifications to cover various contingencies.

Independent review of contract specifications clearly has costs in terms of money and time. Is the insurance worth buying? Although managers have to make that judgment for themselves, it is a well-known fact that ambiguous contract specifications lead to lawsuits.

In Los Angeles County, independent review by outside legal counsel following review by in-house counsel has produced valuable results. In addition, independent technical review outside of the sponsoring agency is being instituted through a new office of the chief information officer. Previously, independent departments or users issued their own RFPs without central oversight.

Specifying Measurable Business Effects or Outcomes

IS managers should ensure that measurable outcomes or expectations from the implementation of a system are included in contracts at the outset, preferably as stipulations but at a minimum as goals. Examples of such outcomes include a reduction in the amount of manual labor required and increases in the efficiency of service (e.g., the amount of paperwork needing to be redone will be reduced from two percent to one percent). Failure to meet such specifications would be cause for cancellation of the project and for arbitration damages.

IS managers should ensure that the amount of manual intervention and support required by any new system once operational is also detailed. Lack of this specificity can lead to delivery of all kinds of fancy systems that do not achieve business outcomes.

Consider the example of a new order-entry system. High-level business outcomes for the system could include the following:

- Reductions in staff that save * million dollars a year.
- Reduction of one minute in the average length of time a customer spends on the phone while the clerk fills in the screen.

These expected outcomes might be difficult to include in a contract, however, because a vendor might balk at being responsible for total user information performance and the actions of user personnel. Still, an effort to include such outcomes should be made.

Specifying Business and System Requirements in Clear and Cost-Effective Terms

IS managers must ensure that contract specifications clearly reflect the user's business requirements. It should not be assumed that a given system will magically meet specific user requirements even though it may contain laudatory general capabilities. The full requirements of the user must be anticipated for several years, and systems acquired must be flexible enough to accommodate such requirements.

System requirements should be based on the system's handling most, but not necessarily all, transactions. Automated handling of 100 percent of transactions may necessitate the development of excessive code and generate additional development expense.

Ensuring that a stated requirement accurately reflects the needs of the user can be accomplished through independent evaluation of business and systems requirements. Some RFPs have been found to contain 20 to 30 pages of minute requirements, many of which the user did not need, and to omit others that the user did need. If an outside agency is hired to evaluate requirements, it should be made liable for the validity of its findings.

Including Binding-Arbitration and Cost-Reimbursement Clauses

IS managers must make every effort to ensure the inclusion of a contractual requirement for binding arbitration to handle disputes and a penalty structure agreed upon by both sides. Penalties, such as treble damages for revenue losses resulting from lack of system performance, should be immediately payable without further legal recourse. Los Angeles County, for example, lost a substantial amount of money from inaccurate Medicare and Medicaid billing resulting from information produced by an outsourced system that turned out to be faulty.

Contracts should stipulate that a vendor guarantee financial resources to cover the cost of a fallback position that permits the continuation of the client's essential user services. Alternatively, contract provisions should ensure that the user is reimbursed for losses incurred as a result of curtailment of essential services. The size of a performance bond, if any, should be commensurate with the size of the project and the dollar magnitude of the operation it concerns.

Is it realistic to try to include binding-arbitration, cost-reimbursement, or measurable-effects clauses into contracts? Although it has been difficult to include such clauses into public contracts in the past, progress is being made in this area. Smaller vendors, however, are still hesitant or incapable of providing these type of guarantees.

Developing Dispute-Settlement, Change-Control, and Early-Warning Mechanisms

Because any project involving a user and a developer will have disputes and changes, IS managers must ensure that appropriate mechanisms are in place to meet such contingencies as they arise. Basic management practices and alertness warrant that such mechanisms be enforced as well; a sound structure that is not enforced serves no purpose.

Any systems development contract should therefore include a variety of levels for settling disputes, starting with gentle persuasion and ending with CEO summits. The failure of lower-level management to settle a matter or escalate it to a higher level of review should be a cause for disciplinary action. Failure to meet milestones or provide deliverables should be pursued within the managerial chains of both contractor and user.

IS managers should ensure that the outsourcing contract contains an adequate mechanism for change control that is fair to both the user and contractor. Early-warning conditions must be specified, and IS staff must be kept cognizant of development or implementation progress. Potential problems should be brought to the attention of appropriate managers.

DEVELOPING EFFECTIVE PROJECT MANAGEMENT

Project management is a major factor in the success or failure of systems development efforts. It involves tracking progress and then making changes to keep projects in control and heading along the path to completion in an efficient manner. Projects should be managed by an experienced project manager who has been involved in the development of systems of the same dollar magnitude. When an individual with this experience is not available internally, IS managers should consider hiring someone to fill this function.

Effective project management requires establishing a standard — including well-defined project review cycles — that considers deliverables, effectiveness of what is delivered, metrics (e.g., function points), and tightly defined reporting formats. Progress tracking can only be accomplished when there is a well-defined and unambiguous measure to track. Function point analysis meets this criterion and is suitable as well for change control and measurement of scope creep (i.e., percent change in function points between phases of the software development life cycle). The methodology is also readily communicated to users.

IS managers should recognize that use of any metric can involve the fudging of numbers at lower levels. This is particularly commonplace with percentage of completion estimates. A savvy manager, however, should be able to detect or have a feel for how things are going. If they are going badly, the manager should know how easy or difficult the cure or fix is going to be.

Some managers, however, simply do not want to face up to the fact that a project is in trouble. Although these managers know, either overtly or subconsciously, when a project is in trouble, the seemingly dire consequences of shutdown or other drastic remedial action lead them to decide not to acknowledge reality and just hope for the best. Some of the factors that play a role in such cases follow:

- Top management, for its own political agenda, has made successful completion of the system a matter of paramount importance.
- IS managers find continued operation under the present system such a distasteful prospect that even a slim chance at producing a better system is deemed more desirable than an aborted effort or rescoping of functionality.
- Managers have developed an affection for the new system that hinders them from acknowledging the tell-tale signs of failure.
- The reward/punishment system favors going forward.

Disregarding the facts, for whatever reasons, can cause IS managers to continue a development effort that should be curtailed or altered. Once certain levels of commission are passed, it becomes increasingly difficult to stop a project. The manager gets more deeply enmeshed and hangs on to increasingly unrealistic hopes for success.

ALLOCATING SUFFICIENT BUDGET RESOURCES FOR IMPLEMENTATION

The success of outsourced systems development also depends on the sufficient budgeting of resources for system implementation, including user training, dual operation, conversion, physical facility changes, and documentation. To accommodate peak personnel requirements during implementation and changeover, IS managers should consider the use of temporary employees and overtime and allocate funds for these purposes.

Training funds should be budgeted not only for the people doing the training but also for the people taking the training. These individuals require overtime or replacement help to do their jobs while they are being trained. IS managers should advise user managers in advance of the need for such allocations.

Because a thorough evaluation of implementation costs increases the price of a system, some IS managers do not conduct full cost evaluations. In addition, overruns in development or programming costs lead managers to co-mingle implementation funds with operating funds or even with other funds for development of the system.

The practice of robbing Peter to pay Paul or banking on the idea that there always will be a way to find the money for implementation is fraught with danger. It usually results in inadequate or shoddy implementation. The saddest of all development experiences is to see the hard work of systems development go to waste or at a minimum used inadequately because of improper implementation. The following sample scenario illustrates the results of this practice.

A lack of implementation funds for a newly development welfare-payments system causes users to be improperly trained. As a result, a number of transactions are mishandled. Needy members of the public do not receive their allotted benefits. The media picks up on this, and the system is accused of having all sorts of glitches. Government committees hold hearings, and consultants and advisory committees are called in to investigate what was in fact an effectively developed but poorly implemented system.

The preceding scenario could have been avoided had the IS manager set aside adequate funds for implementation and safeguarded the funds from other use. An independent assessment of the adequacy of implementation resources also helps to avoid problems later on.

EXAMINING SOFTWARE

In any turnkey system, provision must be made for examination of the source code. This examination provides an assessment of how easily user-required changes can be accommodated, as well as the ease with which the user can assume control of the system if necessary. Examination of the source code can be done by user personnel or by an agreed-upon third party and should address the documentation and structure of the code, methodology used in development, ease of change, modularity, and programming language.

SHORTENING THE LENGTH OF THE DEVELOPMENT CYCLE

The length of time between the inception of system specification and the end of system implementation must be kept to a minimum. IS managers should endeavor to cut major systems development projects into smaller more manageable projects that have shorter lead times and are more amenable to careful oversight.

The rapid pace of changing requirements and technology mandate that the development cycle never be allowed to exceed two years. Projects with estimated completion time exceeding two years should be redefined; IS managers should consider using ready-made software and integrating if possible. Although this approach might seem inefficient, the nature of today's development environment warrants its use.

REQUIRING INDEPENDENT QUALITY ASSURANCE

Large-scale outsourced systems development efforts benefit from independently monitored quality assurance. Hiring an independent entity represents an additional expense, but it provides an insurance policy for management that is justified by the high stakes of large projects. Los Angeles County is using this approach to ensure that when a user department outsources a large-scale project, an independent contractor monitors vendor quality and adherence to standards.

ENSURING TECHNOLOGY TRANSFER

IS managers need to ensure that appropriate technology transfer to the user agency or department occurs. This transfer involves the careful delineation of the information that must be transferred to the sponsoring agency and of the form in which the information will be transferred. Managers who leave these issues up to contractor personnel are courting disaster, particularly in the area of system maintenance.

MANIFESTING SYSTEM OWNERSHIP

Because having a high-level manager take a personal interest in a system (i.e., manifesting ownership) helps keep everybody involved in the development on their toes and ensure that things get done, personal attention by user and IS managers at all levels is certainly another key ingredient of a successful outsourced development effort.

How can an IS manager tell that system ownership has occurred among colleagues? The amount of time other managers spend on the project and the number of questions they ask regarding the system are some of the indicators of system ownership. But most important is an attitude that demonstrates involvement.

CONCLUSION

The need to specify requirements and objectives has been a prime consideration throughout this approach. Sometimes, however, such specificity is not available, as is the case when a project involves changing conditions or the development objectives become determined as the project progresses. Such conditions are not ideal for outsourcing, except perhaps on a time and materials basis, and reinforce the need for careful consideration of the outsourcing decision.

Once such a decision has been made, IS managers should actively manage the factors known to have a direct effect on the success or failure of development efforts. Before a system is approved for funding, a manager must secure detailed presentations from the contractor describing how these factors have been addressed. Furthermore, periodic checks should be made during the systems development life cycle to ensure that management of these factors has been kept on track.

Does consideration of all the factors ensure a project's success? Not necessarily, but it does improve the project's chances of success. IS managers who follow the recommendations provided in this chapter help ensure that if outsourced systems development efforts fail in the future, it should at least be for reasons other than the ones described here.

Note

1. R. Garner, "Management Meltdown," *Open Computing* (January 1995), pp. 36–42.

Chapter 21
Applications Maintenance Outsourcing

Joseph Judenberg

The issue of the strategic value of information systems has given rise to the concept of selective outsourcing. This approach entails outsourcing selected data processing functions or applications. Activities with little strategic implication are more likely candidates for outsourcing than functions that are more strategic in nature. It is generally agreed that strategic activities should be kept in-house. One form of selective outsourcing that has significant benefits and opportunities in the current IS environment is application systems maintenance outsourcing.

IS managers who want to accelerate the move to new technology — whether it is client/server, object orientation, or multimedia — know that this migration requires qualified, dedicated resources. Because IS must continue to be responsible for the legacy systems that currently support the business, there is significant contention for management attention, knowledgeable resources, and project manager focus. Outsourcing of applications maintenance is a potential solution to this dilemma.

BENEFITS OF OUTSOURCING MAINTENANCE

Applications system maintenance is defined as the performance of those activities required to keep a software system operational and responsive after it has been accepted and placed into production. It includes two major sets of activities:

- Promptly fixing software problems that cause the system to be nonoperative or to perform incorrectly.
- Implementing changes, improvements, and enhancements to the system.

When an outside firm is selected for outsourcing software maintenance for an applications system or group of systems, it assumes responsibility not only for implementing corrections and enhancements, but also for managing the process.

Although each situation is different, companies have achieved benefits from properly structured maintenance outsourcing arrangements. Opportunity areas and benefits of selective outsourcing include:

- Freeing up existing maintenance staff to work on new development activities.
- Improving internal staff morale by removing the perceived drudgery of maintenance and providing opportunity to work with new technologies.
- Offering potential career paths for employees not moving to the new technologies.
- Reducing costs of providing maintenance.
- Supporting fluctuating maintenance demand with external variable costs rather than internal fixed costs.
- Improving service to applications system users with more responsive systems modifications and enhancements.
- Allowing management to focus on high-priority areas.

Several of these benefits directly relate to IS management's need to support new business initiatives through technology.

Staffing Issues

The usual approach is to hire new staff to work on applications development requiring newer technologies. When it is difficult to find staff, consultants are usually engaged, but this approach poses some serious problems.

Existing staff members may feel neglected because they are relegated to maintenance work and not given the opportunity to advance their skill levels, while new employees or consultants are given the more exciting assignments using the latest technologies. Many of the IS department's current employees have knowledge about the business that could be valuable in development of the new applications. In addition, the cost of hiring consultants or new employees with the required skills is often high.

Applications maintenance outsourcing offers an effective solution to these problems. Retaining a firm to assume responsibility for maintenance of one or more legacy systems is a strategy that frees up existing staff members so they can be trained in new skills and can bring to bear their accumulated knowledge of the business. Retaining the in-house staff is usually less costly than hiring new employees and can be more cost-effective than hiring consultants. The cost of outsourcing maintenance should be significantly lower than the cost of hiring a firm to provide new development capabilities.

Use of maintenance outsourcing also provides a solution to another problem faced by organizations moving to new technologies. Studies have shown that a higher than expected percentage of the existing staff will not make the grade on newer technologies. Approximately 20 percent or more do not even want to learn new skills. Of those that do learn, about 20 percent are unsuccessful. The outsourcing arrangement can be structured so that the outsourcing supplier acquires some of the existing maintenance staff. This ensures knowledge and continuity in the systems maintenance work and accommodates those employees unwilling or unable to adapt to the new environment.

Assessing the Maintenance Outsourcing Supplier

The most critical factor in a successful maintenance outsourcing arrangement is finding the right supplier. Although terms and conditions must be defined and a contract executed, flexibility and mutual understanding for the other party's interests are crucial and yield the spirit of cooperation that's needed to sustain an ongoing relationship that benefits both parties.

Key issues and questions to consider in assessing an outsourcer are as follows:

- Prior track record:
  - Does the firm have a history of performing similar tasks? It is advisable to evaluate the number of engagements and their success as described by the references provided by the outsourcing firm.
  - Have current clients achieved the benefits they were seeking? Are these benefits similar to what your organization expects?
- Proven staff and management:
  - Does the firm have a large staff experienced in maintenance and in the applicable methodologies and approaches?
  - Will the individuals to be assigned have relevant business or applications experience?
  - What is the quality and experience level of the management team to be assigned, and how long will they be committed to the contract?
- Level of commitment:
  - Is maintenance outsourcing a key business for the outsourcer firm?
  - Is there a corporate commitment in support of maintenance outsourcing, as evidenced by a corporate support staff, corporate tools and methodologies, adequate local support, and a general sense that this business is important to the firm?
- Personnel issues:
  - Does the outsourcer have an approach for absorbing the organization's employees if necessary? Does the approach protect these employees' interests? Is it consistent with your organization's human resources policies?

- Phased approach to assuming responsibility:
  - Does the firm have a standard, proven approach for assuming total responsibility?
  - During the transition period, are tasks and responsibilities for them clearly delineated?
  - Are the costs for transition defined and attributed?
- Methodology for managing maintenance:
  - Does the supplier have a methodology that defines all the phases in the maintenance life cycle, all the tasks to be performed during these phases, and responsibilities for such tasks?
- Appropriate procedures:
  - Either as part of the methodology or as stand-alone tools, does the supplier have formal, documented procedures for managing service requests, testing, and quality assurance?
- Project management discipline and tools:
  - Is there a management control tool that tracks service requests and the tasks required to accomplish them?
  - Are regularly scheduled status reports defined and required?
  - Is level of service (discussed in more detail in the next section) tracked and reported on?
- Use of automated tools to improve performance and service:
  - Does the supplier bring to the job automated tools that support the maintenance team in analysis, documentation, and testing?

LEVEL OF SERVICE

An outsourcing arrangement, by definition, is different from typical contracting arrangements. The outsourcing supplier should assume greater responsibility for successful performance of the function being outsourced, sharing not only rewards but risks as well. The supplier should therefore be willing to provide services on a fixed-price basis.

First, however, the supplier and the contracting company need to agree on a level of service to be provided. The supplier can then guarantee the agreed-to level of service for a monthly fixed price.

The level of service should define minimal levels for each area; if additional services are needed, these can be contracted for at an additional fee. The service areas and some samples of service criteria include:

- Responsiveness to production rescue:
  - Hours for providing production rescue.
  - Approach to off-hours coverage.
  - Speed of response to emergency maintenance.
  - Number of hours per month provided for production support.
- Amount of work:
  - Number of change requests completed.

- – Number of change requests by category.
- – Amount of work completed versus estimated.
- – Percentage of work completed on schedule.
- – Function points affected or changed.
- Quality of work:
  - – Quality of delivered product (subjective).
  - – Meantime between failures.
  - – Average number of incidents.
  - – Average time to correct.
  - – Failures per XXX lines of code.

STEPS FOR INITIATING AN OUTSOURCING ARRANGEMENT

When initiating a maintenance outsourcing arrangement, a structured approach, with discrete predefined activities and events, is advised to ensure optimal results.

Identifying a Pilot System. In undertaking the first such initiative, it is prudent to begin with a pilot. The size of the pilot project has to be large enough to make it worthwhile for the outsourcing supplier, but from the standpoint of the user organization, starting with a pilot minimizes risk and allows the organization to devote the resources necessary to ensure success. A pilot system also provides enough information that can be used to evaluate whether the effort should be extended to additional systems.

Identifying Potential Suppliers. Although there are always advantages to soliciting several suppliers to bid, there may also be significant benefits in dealing with a single supplier. If there is a firm that meets the criteria (such as outlined previously), is familiar with the systems in question, and with whom there is an existing positive relationship, these benefits may override the advantages of competitive bidding.

Assessing the Systems Environment. A major activity is conducting an assessment of the existing environment. Some of the issues to be addressed during this assessment include:

- Defining the scope and size of the systems.
- Evaluating the quality (e.g., stability, maintainability) of the systems.
- Assessing service requests and backlog history and trends.
- Evaluating presence and quality of procedures.
- Determining current level of user satisfaction.

This assessment provides the baseline for:

- Defining (with the supplier) the level of service desired or required.
- Developing a fixed-price bid.
- Determining required staff levels (during transition and beyond).
- Identifying opportunities for improving the environment.

Determining Feasibility. Based on the results of the assessment, the feasibility of outsourcing can be evaluated. Are there opportunities for improvement? Is there reason to believe that an outside supplier with existing procedures, tools, and methodologies can be more successful? Are there issues that might preclude outsourcing?

Defining Level of Service. Using the findings of the assessment, a minimum level of service should be defined for each of the relevant categories (e.g., production support, enhancements, user support).

Soliciting and Evaluating Proposals. Using the qualitative and quantitative data uncovered during the assessment, the next step is to solicit proposals from the identified suppliers. These proposals should include the desired level of service and a fixed-price bid should be requested, based on this service level. In addition, the user organization must request pricing parameters for effort to be supplied over and above the minimum level of service. Proposals should also include plans for transition and the requirements to be imposed on the contracting firm, both during and after transition.

Reaching an Understanding. On the basis of the proposal of the selected vendor, the relationship with the vendor, and the benefits desired, the contractual agreement must be negotiated. (Pertinent issues relating to the contract are discussed in more detail in the next section.)

Initiating the Pilot Outsourcing Effort. In addition to the steps required to initiate and phase-in the outsourcing arrangement, monitoring and tracking procedures should be defined in advance. These procedures should be designed to allow an evaluation of the success of the effort and to support a decision on whether the desired benefits were achieved. This work will help the organization decide whether to continue the arrangement or even extend outsourcing to additional systems.

THE CONTRACT

Under a partnership approach, he contract should not be viewed as the sole means for holding each party to its obligations. A strong partnership relationship, in which each organization has incentives to strive for a common goal, is far more likely to yield successful results. That said, in the end, the contract is the vehicle for articulating and reviewing what each party expects from the other, and there are several key issues to review.

Thoroughness and Comprehensiveness. As the vehicle for ensuring that everyone understands and agrees to the terms and obligations, the contract should be as comprehensive as possible, defining all pertinent issues. It must discuss the obligations of each party, costs, duration, terms, and conditions. Care should be given to anticipating future needs as well as those known up-front. Where it may be premature to resolve or even discuss an issue, the contract can include language on how and when the issue will be raised and resolved.

Flexibility. Although the contract should be explicit about issues known at the outset, it must provide flexibility for future situations. The contract can be viewed as a set of master terms and conditions, with details about the specific work required, and the compensation for that work, treated as additional components. Each system to be maintained could have a separate component defining its level of service and associated fixed price. Additional work to be defined during the course of the arrangement can be dealt with in additional components, without requiring renegotiation of the underlying contract. Unanticipated events can be treated the same way.

Duration. Although the supplier will require a minimum timeframe to make the effort worthwhile, there also needs to be some escape clause in case the effort does not work out as envisioned. This can be accomplished through objective criteria for termination (where possible), payments to the vendor to compensate for early termination, and lead time for termination.

Incentive. The contract should be structured so that the supplier has an incentive to improve the environment. When the supplier can share in the benefit, there is an incentive to improve the stability or maintainability of the systems through restructuring, reengineering, or improved documentation. Such improvements can provide benefits to the contracting organization through better customer service or reduced cost of processing.

RECOMMENDED COURSE OF ACTION

The use of maintenance outsourcing can help a user organization achieve its strategic objectives. Such an arrangement relieves management of many of the day-to-day burdens of maintenance and thus allows management to dedicate more attention to strategic activities. Redeployment of IS staff currently assigned to maintenance can enhance the size and quality of staff assigned to new development activities. Reduction of maintenance costs can support increased expenditures in strategic development activities.

To achieve these potential benefits, management should adhere to the following steps:

- *Developing a plan to guide the activities.* This involves identifying a set of activities to be pursued, responsibilities for all tasks, and key decision criteria. The benefits desired should be defined in advance so that ongoing monitoring can determine whether the desired benefits are being achieved.
- *Defining the baseline.* An outsourcing assessment is necessary to define the existing environment from both a quantitative and a qualita-

tive perspective. When this is accomplished, key objectives can be defined.

- *Defining a desired level of service using the findings of the assessment.* Level of service is of paramount importance in selecting a supplier, in establishing a fixed price, and in evaluating ongoing performance.
- *Selecting a maintenance outsourcing supplier.* The selection must be made carefully and wisely, ensuring that the supplier has the required credentials, experience, and tools and resources. It may be best to select a firm with whom the organization is already comfortable or with whom it feels confident it can develop a partnership relationship.
- *Exercising due diligence in establishing contract terms and ongoing expectations.* At the same time, it is vital to recognize that a partnership approach or philosophy holds the greatest promise for success. Maintaining the concept of partnership during the contract process provides the opportunity to structure an arrangement that can foster an environment of shared risk as well as shared benefits.
- *Monitoring performance and results on an ongoing basis.*

Chapter 22
Outsourcing Network Management and Information Systems

Nathan J. Muller

With computing and networking environments getting ever more powerful, complex, and expansive, an increasing percentage of the corporate budget is being used for their support. Much of this money is spent on such brick-and-mortar aspects of computer operations as hardware and software and lines and circuits. In addition, many companies can no longer afford the salaries of qualified technical people to run computer systems and networks or skilled programmers to develop the sophisticated applications needed to run the core business.

Instead of hiring, training, and retaining internal staff to perform cabling, hardware maintenance, systems integration, and network management functions, companies can become far more competitive by focusing internal resources on strategic or business-specific applications that can add measureable value to the enterprise in the form of new products and services. Overhead functions that support these efforts can be offloaded to outside organizations for a monthly fee.

With the current competitive environment and the trend toward downsizing, many companies are experiencing hiring freezes and staff reductions, coupled with increased pressure from senior management to get more work done in less time. All of this is occurring at the same time the enterprise is becoming more and more dependent on an information systems network that must be operational 24 hours a day, seven days a week.

Consequently, many companies are turning to service firms that specialize in managing networks, integrating diverse computer systems, or developing business applications. Outsourcing involves the transfer of network assets or staff to a vendor, who then assumes profit and loss responsibility for some or all of the client's network and data processing operations.

0-8493-9998-X/00/$0.00+$.50
© 2000 by CRC Press LLC

APPROACHES TO OUTSOURCING

There are two basic approaches to outsourcing — each of which can benefit organizations facing tough financial times. First, the outsourcing firm can buy a company's existing information systems and network assets and lease them back to the company for a fixed monthly fee. In such an arrangement, the outsourcer can also take over the network management payroll. This relieves the client of a cash outlay, which can be applied in turn to its financial recovery.

The outsourcer maintains the data communications equipment, upgrading to state-of-the-art systems within the budgetary parameters and performance guidelines in the agreement. In some cases, equipment leasing is part of the arrangement. Aside from its tax advantages, leasing can protect against premature equipment obsolescence and rid the company of the hassles of dealing with used equipment once it has been fully depreciated.

With the second type of arrangement, the company sells off its equipment and migrates the applications to the outsourcer's systems. Often, these are managed by the company's key personnel, who have been reassigned to the outsourcer's payroll and receive a comparable benefits package. Because the outsourcing firm may provide a wide array of services to a broad base of clients worldwide, employees can even find new career opportunities with this type of outsourcing arrangement.

OUTSOURCING TRENDS

The trend toward outsourcing is not new in the information systems arena. Service bureau activity, in which in-house data centers are turned into remote job-entry operations to support such applications as payroll, claims processing, credit card invoicing, and mailing lists, has traditionally been associated with data center outsourcing. Under this arrangement, mainframes are owned and operated off site by the computer service company.

As applied to networks, however, the outsourcing trend is quite recent. An organization's LAN may be thought of as a computer system bus, providing an extension of the data center's resources to individual users' desktops. Through facilities, data center resources may be extended further to remote locations. Given the increasing complexity of current data networks, it is not surprising that companies are seeking ways to offload management responsibility to those with more knowledge, experience, and hands-on expertise than they alone can afford.

In this context, outsourcing firms typically analyze the user's business objectives, assess current and future computing and networking needs, and determine performance parameters to support specific data transfer requirements. The resulting system design may incorporate equipment from alternative vendors as well as the exchange facilities of any carrier. Acting as the client's agent, the outsourcing firm coordinates the activities of equipment vendors and carriers to ensure efficient and timely installation and service.

In a typical outsourcing arrangement involving WAN facilities management, an integrated control center — located at the outsourcing firm's premises or that of its client — serves as a single point of service support at which technicians are available 24 hours a day, 365 days a year, to monitor network performance, contact the appropriate carrier, or dispatch field service as needed, perform network reconfigurations, and perform any necessary administrative chores.

WHAT TO OUTSOURCE

Networks are growing rapidly in size, complexity, and cost; technical experts are expensive and difficult to find and keep; new technologies and new vendors appear at an accelerating rate; and users clamor for more and better service while their bosses demand lower costs and increased work performance. Consequently, the question may no longer be whether to outsource but what to outsource.

The prevailing view among users is that outsourcing commodity-like operational functions, sometimes called tactical functions, is a low-risk proposition. It is possible to save both money and headaches by letting someone else pull wires, set up circuits, and move equipment. Outsourcing mission-critical or strategic functions, however, involves more of a risk to the company. If the outsourcing firm performs these functions poorly, for whatever reason, the client company's competitive position could become irreparably damaged.

One way for a company to take a partial step toward outsourcing is to outsource network management for the second and third shifts and weekends, while keeping control over the more critical prime time. As confidence in the vendor grows, more can be outsourced.

TYPICAL OUTSOURCING SERVICES

The specific activities performed by the outsourcing firm may include:

- Routine equipment moves, adds, and changes.
- Integration.
- Project management.
- Trouble ticket administration.
- Management of vendor-carrier relations.
- Maintenance, repair, and replacement.
- Disaster recovery.

- Long-term planning support.
- Training.
- Equipment leasing.

Each of these is discussed in detail in the following sections.

Moves, Adds, and Changes

Moves, adds, and changes constitute a daily process that can consume enormous corporate resources if handled by in-house staff. This process typically includes such activities as:

- Processing move, add, and change orders.
- Assigning due dates.
- Providing information required by technicians.
- Monitoring move, add, and change service requests, scheduling, and completions.
- Updating the directory database.
- Handling such database modifications as feature, port, and password assignments.
- Creating equipment orders upon direction.
- Maintaining order and receiving logs.
- Preparing monthly move, add, and change summary reports.

In assigning these activities to an outside firm, the company can realize cost savings in staff and overhead, without sacrificing efficiency and timely order processing.

Integration

Current information systems and communications networks consist of a number of different intelligent elements: host systems, LANs and servers, cable hubs, and facilities, to name a few. The selection, installation, integration, and maintenance of these elements requires a broad range of expertise that is not usually found within a single organization. Many companies are therefore turning to outsourcing firms for integration services.

The integration function involves unifying disparate computer systems and transport facilities into a coherent, manageable utility, a major part of which is reconciling different physical connections and protocols. The outsourcing firm also ties in additional features and services offered through a public switched network. The objective is to provide compatibility and interoperability among different products and services so that they are transparent to the users.

Project Management

Project management entails the coordination of many discrete activities, starting with the development of a customized project plan based on the client's organizational needs. For each ongoing task, critical requirements are identified, lines of responsibility are drawn, and problem escalation procedures are defined.

Line and equipment ordering is also included in project management. Acting as the client's agent, the outsourcing firm negotiates with multiple suppliers and carriers to economically upgrade or expand the network without sacrificing predefined performance requirements. Before new systems are installed at client locations, the outsourcing firm performs site survey coordination and preparation, ensuring that all power requirements, air conditioning, ventilation, and fire protection systems are properly installed and in working order.

When an entire node must be added to the network or a new host must be brought into the data center, the outsourcing firm performs acceptance testing of all equipment before bringing it online, thus minimizing potential disruption to daily business operations. When new lines are ordered from various carriers, the outsourcing firm conducts the necessary performance testing before cutting them over to user traffic.

Trouble Ticket Administration

In assuming responsibility for daily network operations, a key service performed by the outsourcing firm is trouble ticket processing, which is typically automated. The sequence of events is as follows:

1. An alarm indication is received at the network control center operated by the outsourcing firm.
2. The outsourcing firm uses various diagnostic tools to isolate and identify the cause of the problem.
3. Restoral mechanisms are initiated (manually or automatically) to bypass the affected equipment, network node , or transmission line until the faulty component can be brought back into service.
4. A trouble ticket is opened:
   - If the problem is with hardware, a technician is dispatched to swap out the appropriate board.
   - If the problem is with software, analysis may be performed remotely.
   - If the problem is with a particular line, the appropriate carrier is notified.
5. The client's Help Desk is kept informed of the problems's status so that the Help Desk operator can assist local users.
6. Before the trouble ticket is closed out, the repair is verified with an end-to-end test by the outsourcing firm.
7. Upon successful end-to-end testing, the primary customer premises equipment or facility is turned back over to user traffic and the trouble ticket is closed.

Management of Vendor-Carrier Relations

Another benefit of the outsourcing arrangement comes in the form of improved vendor-carrier relations. Instead of having to manage multiple relationships, the client needs to manage only one: the outsourcing firm. Dealing with only one firm has several advantages in that it:

- Improves the response time to trouble calls and alarms.
- Eliminates delays caused by fingerpointing between vendor and carrier.
- Expedites order processing.
- Reduces the amount of time spent in invoice reconciliation.
- Frees staff time for planning.
- Reduces the cost of network ownership.

Maintenance, Repair, and Replacement

Some outsourcing arrangements include maintenance, repair, and replacement services. Relying on the outsourcing firm for maintenance services minimizes a company's dependence on in-house personnel for specific knowledge about system design, troubleshooting procedures, and the proper use of test equipment. Not only does this arrangement eliminate the need for ongoing technical training, the company is also buffered from the effects of technical staff turnover, which is usually a persistent problem. Repair and replacement services can increase the availability of systems and networks while eliminating the cost of maintaining inventory.

Disaster Recovery

Disaster recovery includes numerous services that may be customized to ensure the maximum availability and performance of computer systems and data networks:

- Disaster impact assessment.
- Network recovery objectives.
- Evaluation of equipment redundancy and dial backup.
- Network inventory and design, including circuit allocation.
- Vital records recovery.
- Procedure for initiating the recovery process.
- Location of a hot site, if necessary.
- Installation responsibilities.
- Test run guidelines.
- Escalation procedures.
- Recommendations to prevent network loss.

Long-Term Planning Support

A qualified outsourcing firm can provide numerous services that can assist the client with strategic planning. Specifically, the outsourcing firm can assist the client in determining the impact of:

- Emerging services and products.
- Industry and trends.
- International developments in technology and services.

With experience drawn from a broad customer base, as well as its daily interactions with hardware vendors and carriers, the outsourcing firm has much to contribute to clients in the way of assisting in strategic planning.

Training

Outsourcing firms can fulfill the varied training requirements of users, including:

- Basic communications concepts.
- Product-specific training.
- Resource management.
- Help Desk operator training.

The last type of training is particularly important because 80 percent of reported problems are applications oriented and can be solved without the outsourcing firm's involvement. This can speed up problem resolution and reduce the cost of outsourcing. For this to be effective, however, the Help Desk operator must know how to differentiate among applications problems, system problems, and network problems. Basic knowledge may be gained by training and improved with experience.

Equipment Leasing

Many times, an outsourcing arrangement will include equipment leasing. There are a number of financial reasons for including leasing in the outsourcing agreement, depending on the financial situation. Because costs are spread over a period of years, leasing can improve a company's cash position by freeing up capital for other uses. It also makes it easier to cost-justify technology acquisitions that would have been otherwise too expensive to purchase.

Leasing makes it possible to procure equipment that has not been planned or budgeted for. Leasing, rather than buying equipment, can also reduce balance sheet debt, because the lease or rental obligation is not reported as a liability. At the least, leasing represents an additional source of capital and preserves credit lines.

With new technology becoming available every 12 to 18 months, leasing can prevent the user from becoming saddled with obsolete equipment. This means that the potential for losses associated with replacing equipment that has not been fully depreciated can be minimized. With rapid advances in technology and consequent shortened product life cycles, it is becoming more difficult to sell used equipment. Leasing eliminates such problems.

OUTSOURCING LAN MANAGEMENT

As the size, complexity, and expense of local area network management get to be too big to handle, companies consider outsourcing the job. Certain routine LAN functions (e.g., moves, adds, and changes) are regularly outsourced. Such functions as planning, design, implementation, operation, management, and remedial maintenance are increasingly outsourced, and LAN operation and management are the services most needed by many current companies.

Providers of this type of service can be categorized into two groups, with a third rapidly emerging. First, computer makers such as IBM, Digital Equipment Corp., Unisys Corp., and Hewlett–Packard Co. have introduced comprehensive LAN operation and management services packages. Second, management and systems integration firms (e.g., Electronic Data Systems Corp., Andersen Consulting, and Network Management, Inc.) have become less rigid in terms of the services they provide.

The strengths of the computer firms include a sound service and support infrastructure, knowledge of technology, and a diverse installed base. Their weaknesses include an orientation toward their own products and skills that are limited to certain technologies or platforms.

Systems integration and facilities management firms approach LAN outsourcing from the time sharing, data center, and mainframe environments. Their strengths include experience in data applications, familiarity with multivendor environments, and a professional service delivery infrastructure. Their weakness is that they often lack international networking capabilities, though this is changing.

The emerging category of outsourcing firms includes telecommunications companies, including interexchange carrier, regional Bell operating companies (RBOCs), and value-added network providers. Although AT&T has the service infrastructure to become a major player in LAN outsourcing, it must combine the support infrastructure of its telecommunications and computer divisions to ensure success in this area. Although US Sprint Communications Co. and MCI Communications Corp. have developed LAN connectivity and integration services, they have limited operation and management capabilities relative to AT&T.

Among the strengths of these firms is that they typically have a large service and support infrastructure, significant experience in physical cabling and communications, network integration expertise, and remote management capabilities. In addition, they have considerable investment capital available as well as strategic partnerships and alliances worldwide.

The regional Bell operating companies have strong regional service presence, but limited data communications and applications experience.

They are also limited by law to providing only a narrow range of services, limited domestically to operating within designated serving areas, and are subject to close state and federal regulation.

The strength of the value-added network providers is their ability to manage an internetwork of LANs as part of their packet network and frame relay services. Their chief weakness is that they do not have extensive service infrastructures and staff.

The custom nature of LAN outsourcing makes discussion of price difficult. Vendors change users per event, hour, or year for certain service elements; however, LAN outsourcing service packaging and pricing is still determined by the custom bid.

REASONS FOR OUTSOURCING

The reasons a company may want to outsource are varied. They include:

- Difficulty in using technical personnel efficiently.
- Insulating management from day-to-day system problems and decisions.
- Concern about buying expensive technology that could become obsolete shortly after purchase.
- Greater flexibility to deal with fast-changing worldwide markets.

Beyond these considerations, outsourcing arrangements may encompass several strategic objectives. First, to free capital tied up in buildings and equipment; second, to save money in absolute terms on an annual basis in the form of operating expenses; third, to move to more advanced information systems and network architectures; and fourth, to bring in — through the outsourcing firm — the necessary personnel and technical knowledge to consolidate operations that had not been available in-house.

Despite the many reasons to outsource, there are still many concerns associated with putting such critical resources in the hands of outsiders. Many of these concerns can be overcome with experience and knowledge of typical outsourcing arrangements.

Many corporate executives are concerned about giving up control when considering the move to outsource. However, control can increase when corporate management is better able to concentrate on issues that have potentially greater returns. Instead of consuming valuable resources in the nuts-and-bolts aspects of setting up an automated teller machine (ATM) network, for example, bank executives can focus on developing the services customers will demand from such a network and devise test marketing strategies for potential new financial services.

A common complaint among corporate executives is that outsource firms do not know their companies' business. In any outsourcing arrangement, however, users continue to run their own applications as before; the service provider just keeps the data center or network running smoothly. In addition, outsourcing firms typically hire at least some members of the client staff who would have been let go upon the decision to outsource and who are familiar with the business.

Companies that are considering outsourcing should examine their current information system and network activities in competitive terms. Activities that are performed about the same way by everyone within a particular industry can be more safely farmed out than those that are unique or based on company-specific skills. Most important, the company must take precautions to remain in a position to recommend and champion strategic systems and new technologies, which may involve high initial payout and possible cross-functional applications.

As the company opts for external solutions, standards that were internally developed do not suddenly lose their relevance. Oversight of standards that address hardware, communications, and software should remain an internal responsibility to ensure compatibility of information systems and networks across the entire corporation.

In-House Commitment to Outsourcing

Outsourcing can increase service quality and decrease costs, but management control cannot just be handed over to a third party. The fact that work has been contracted out does not mean that company staff can or should stop thinking about it. Typically, there is still a significant amount of supervisory overhead that consumes resources.

Someone within the company must ensure that contractual obligations are met, that the outsourcing firm is acting in the company's best interests, and that problems are not being covered up. Just as important, considerable effort is usually required to establish and maintain a trusting relationship. To oversee such a relationship requires staff who are highly skillled in interpersonal communications and negotiation and who are knowledgeable about business and finance.

THE DECISION TO OUTSOURCE

Strategic, business-oriented issues play a significant role in the decision to outsource. It is essential that potential users take stock of their operations before making this decision. Arriving at the correct solution requires an examination of the company's unique characteristics, including its human resources and technological infrastructure.

For example, it is advisable to compare the costs of in-house operations with the services that will be performed by the outside firm. This entails performing an audit of internal computing and networking operations to determine all current and planned costs for hardware, software, services, and overhead. These costs should cover a minimum of three years and a maximum of seven years and should include specifics on major expenses that may be incurred within that timeframe. This establishes a baseline figure from which to evaluate more effectively the bids of potential outsourcing firms and monitor performance after the contract is signed.

A detailed description of the operating environment should be prepared, starting with computer and network resources. This description should include:

- Hardware configuration.
- Direct-access storage device requirements.
- Backup media and devices.
- Systems software.
- Applications software.
- Communications facilities and services.
- Locations of spare bandwidth and redundant subsystems.
- Restoral methods.
- Applications at remote locations.
- Critical processing periods.
- Peak traffic loads.

The next step is to identify potential outsourcing firms. These vendors can then be invited to visit corporate locations to view the various internal operations, thereby obtaining an opportunity to understand the company's requirements so that these can properly be addressed in a formal proposal.

A company that turns to outsourcing to alleviate problems in managing information systems or networks should realize that transferring management to a third party may not turn out to be the hoped-for panacea. Although outsourcing represents an opportunity for companies to lower costs and enhance core business activities, before such an arrangement is considered, it should be determined how well internal staff, vendors, consultants, and contract programmers are managed. If there are difficulties in this area already, chances are that the situation will not improve under an outsourcing arrangement. In this case, perhaps some changes in staff responsibilities or organizational structure are warranted.

Vendor Evaluation Criteria

Most vendors are flexible and will negotiate contract issues. Each outsourcing arrangement is different and requires essentially a custom contract. It is important to identify all the issues that should be written into the contract. This can be a long list, depending on the particular situation. The following criteria, however, should be included in any rating scheme applied to outsourcing firms:

- Financial strength and stability over a long period of time.
- Demonstrated ability to manage domestic and multinational computer systems and data networks.
- Number of employees, their skills, and their years of experience.
- Ability to tailor computer and network management tools.
- History of implementing the most advanced technology.
- An outstanding business reputation.
- Fair employee transfer policies and benefits packages.

The weights of these criteria should be set by the company in keeping with its unique short- and long-term requirements.

Software suppliers may impose inhibitive transfer fees on licensed software if an outsourcing vendor takes over internal operations. This is often a hidden and potentially costly surprise. The common assumption among software users is that they can just move software around as they please. For the most part, software firms do not allow third parties to provide use to customers without a new license or significant transfer fees. They see this as necessary to safeguard their intellectual property rights. Outsourcing firms hit by these fees must pass them on to their clients if they expect to continue in the outsourcing business. If these fees are sizable, it could sway the decision on whether to outsource.

Requirements of the Outsourcing Firm

The outsourcing firm should be required to submit a detailed plan — with timeframes — describing the transition of management responsibilities. Although time frames can and often do change, setting them gives the company a better idea of how well the outsourcing firm understands the company's unique requirements.

Performance guarantees that mirror current internal performance commitments should be agreed upon — along with appropriate financial penalties for substandard performance. The requirements should not exceed what is currently provided, unless that performance is insufficient, in which case the company should review its motives for outsourcing in the first place.

Satisfactory contractual performance guarantees for network operations can be developed if sufficient information on current performance exists. It is more difficult to develop such guarantees in the applications development arena, and this is why some companies avoid outsourcing this function.

A detailed plan for migrating management responsibilities back to the company at a future date should also be required. Despite the widely held belief that outsourcing is a one-way street, proper planning and management of the outsourcing firm can keep open the option of bringing the management function back into the corporate mainstream. Despite this option, the company may decide that, after the 5 or 10 years of the contract are up, the outsourcing arrangement should be made permanent.

Structuring the Relationship

Companies that outsource face a number of critical decisions about how to structure the relationship. Entering into a long-term partnership with the outsourcing firm can be risky without proper safeguards. As previously noted, poor performance on the part of the service provider could jeopardize the client company's competitive position.

It must be determined at the outset which party will respond to computer system and network failures, and the degree to which each party is responsible for restoral. This includes spelling out what measures the outside firm must take to ensure the security and integrity of the data, financial penalties for inadequate performance, and what amount of insurance must be maintained to provide adequate protection against losses.

The outsourcing relationship must make explicit provisions for maintaining the integrity of critical business operations and the confidentiality of proprietary information. The firm must ensure that the outside firm will not compromise any aspect of the relationship.

The typical outsourcing contract covers a lengthy period of time — perhaps 5 to 10 years. Outsourcing firms justify this by citing their need to spread the initial costs of consolidating the client's data processing or network operations over a long period of time. This also allows them to offer clients reasonable rates.

The relationship must provide for the possibility that the client's needs will grow substantially. The outsourcing firm's ability to meet changing needs (e.g., from the addition of a new division or the acquisition of a small company) should be evaluated and covered under the existing contract.

Companies entering outsourcing relationships must also establish what rights they have to bring some or all of the management responsibilities back in-house without terminating the contract or paying an exorbitant penalty. However, this should not be done lightly, because it can take a long time to hire appropriate staff and bring them up to an acceptable level of performance.

To avoid getting locked into the outsourcing arrangement, organizations should stay away from sharing data centers, networks, and applications software and from relying on customized software, applications, and networks. It can be difficult for a company to extricate itself from outsourcing arrangements when its operations are tightly woven into those of other companies operating under similar arrangements. The contract should be structured so that it can be put up for bidding by other parties.

Contracts should provide an escape clause that allows the user to migrate operations to an alternative service provider should the original firm fail to meet performance objectives or other contract stipulations. Because it is difficult to rebuild in-house systems or network staff from scratch, it is imperative that users do not outsource anything that cannot be immediately taken over by another firm. In fact, having another firm on standby should be an essential element of the company's disaster recovery plan.

CONCLUSION

The pressures for third-party outsourcing are considerable and on the increase. Requirements to service large amounts of debt have made every corporate department the target of close budgetary scrutiny, the corporate network and data center included. In addition, competition from around the world is forcing businesses to scale back the ranks of middle management and streamline operations. Outsourcing allows businesses to meet these objectives.

Although outsourcing promises bottom-line benefits, deciding whether such an arrangement makes sense is a difficult process that requires considerable analysis of a range of factors. In addition to calculating the baseline cost of managing the in-house information system and data network and determining their strategic value, the decision to outsource often hinges on the company's business direction, the state of its current data center and network architecture, the internal political situation, and the company's readiness to deal with the culture shock that inevitably occurs when two firms must work closely together on a daily basis.

Chapter 23
Certification of Externally Developed Software
Craig A. Schiller

For years, the software engineering community has used certification as a means of ensuring that large critical systems (usually government-related) are accurate, correct, and ready for operational use. Certification was used primarily to validate code that was developed locally. It was assumed that commercial off-the-shelf software was not a threat to the system. As applications grew in size and complexity, pressure increased to reduce their time to market, and as the number of individuals involved in commercial software development increased, the number of errors and incidents of malicious code also increased.

The problem is aggravated by an attitude called the shrinkwrapped syndrome that has been inherited from the non-programming world. It is usually assumed that a shrinkwrapped or sealed package is better than an open package. The food and drug industry is highly regulated to build confidence and to protect the public. Unfortunately, the message is so strong that it carries over into such unregulated industries as software development. The result is that usually cautious software engineers place unwarranted trust in shrinkwrapped software. When problems occur, the developer usually has little recourse because commercial off-the-shelf (COTS) rarely includes source code or warranties. If enough other users have experienced a similar problem, then the COTS developer may make an out-of-cycle fix available. Otherwise, if it is fixed, the developer must wait for the next official version release. The local software developer is ultimately responsible for the performance of the system being developed, regardless of whether the source of the problem is traced to developed code or a COTS product. COTS products represent a category of software that may be assumed trustworthy, but the issue exists for all externally developed software (i.e., software that was developed outside of the security professional's control). The difference between internally developed soft-

0-8493-9998-X/00/$0.00+$.50

ware and externally developed software is control of the development process, knowledge gathered during development, and the ability to perform detailed tests based on that knowledge. The controlled gathering of knowledge of an internally developed system is fundamental to the concept of certification. This chapter presents a body of collectable knowledge that may be used to guide the determination of the content and extent of tests to reduce the threat from externally developed software.

CERTIFICATION CONCEPTS USED ON DEVELOPED SOFTWARE

Certification of software developed for government use is a well-documented process. The most recognized description of certification is in the Federal Information Processing Standard (FIPS) 102 publication. The objective of the certification process is to ensure that a system is accurate and correct, that a system meets all applicable federal laws and directives, and that the system security safeguards work as intended. The certification process relies on a significant (but unspecified) development infrastructure.

Software developers may respond in several different ways to meet these requirements. Most attempts to address certification include a formal software development life cycle that provides for the following:

- Clear, testable requirements.
- Traceability of requirements through specification, design, coding, testing, and integration phases.
- Internal controls to ensure that the system that is tested is the same system that was specified, designed, and coded.
- Test results demonstrating that the system met its requirements accurately and correctly, and tests of the security safeguards demonstrating that they work as intended.

Although these processes directly address the requirements for certification, other less direct processes and controls are usually necessary. For example, configuration management processes are necessary to ensure that changes are not introduced without management and technical review. Subcontract management is necessary to ensure that subcontracted work meets requirements; this provides an avenue for recovery should the subcontractor performance fail to meet requirements.

The assurances that software development processes provide to the technical management team making a certification recommendation to executive management should be considered. Executive management should solicit certification recommendations from the discipline experts or technical managers (e.g., certification for the physical environment from industrial security or the facility manager or system certification from the software project manager).

Organizational Process Assurances

Organizational process assurances monitor the product assurance processes for corruption. Common implementations of organizational processes include program management, audit, risk management, internal control systems, corrective actions systems, contract review, internal quality audits, and the use of statistical tools for metrics collection and use. For computer systems products, the acquiring organization may have little visibility into the organizational processes. If the systems developing organization and its processes are well-known (e.g., when the developer is another part of the organization), the product-using organization may be able to accept some of the risk for a reduced testing regime based on the knowledge of the developer's assurance and an examination of the testing results.

Several indications may be drawn by the presence or absence of International Standards Organization 9000 certification (an international quality certification program)and whether the organization has been through a software capability evaluation (e.g., as a part of a government contract proposal). If the organization claims ISO 9000 (i.e., 9001, 9002, or 9003) certification, a copy of the scope statement should be obtained. The scope statement identifies the extent of the certification; the certification may include software development activities. ISO 9000 certification states that the organization performs the stated objectives for the processes covered in the scope statement. The certification process also provides for regular recertification to ensure that the quality implied by ISO 9000 is actively maintained. This certification does not mean that the company puts out a quality product, nor does it mean that the processes are necessarily productive. It does mean that the organization has processes and that it follows its documented processes. This implies that if a copy of the organizational assurance processes can be obtained from an ISO 9000 certified product developer whose scope statement includes software development, the developer may be following those processes. This adds a significant measure of evidence to support the decision made regarding the use and testing of the software product.

For an independent evaluation of the effectiveness or maturity of processes, the security professional may be able to use the results of evaluations or assessments in relation to the Software Engineering Institute's (SEI) Capability Maturity Model (CMM). An SEI software capability evaluation is performed to support the selection of a contractor for some government contracts. An assessment is usually performed by the contractor to determine whether it meets the CMM standard. In general, most assessments have been found to be at least one level higher than the subsequently evaluated level. If a contractor claims to have been evaluated at SEI level 3, then the product user knows (if the evaluation can be substantiated) that the product developer at the time of the evaluation had a mature development organization that has organizational level standards and procedures for configuration management, QA, training, project management, subcontract management, and software development. Similarly, if the developer claims to have been assessed at SEI level 3, he or she is more likely to have project-oriented maturity with defined processes. Substantiating the results of an assessment can only be achieved by having the developer prove these findings. The developer may be unwilling to do that because it may pinpoint company weaknesses.

This issue highlights a significant difference between ISO 9000 certification and SEI evaluations and assessments. ISO 9000 results are intended to be shared with potential customers, and SEI evaluations and assessments are intended to be used only in relation to a specific contract proposal offering. Therefore, SEI evaluations represent only the state of the contractor in relation to the proposal that requires the evaluation. Although the criteria of the SEI evaluation and assessments are more useful to the user of a product in determining the details of key assurance processes, the static nature of the evaluations and assessments and the strong binding to specific contract proposals weakens the criteria s usefulness as a general assurance meter. However, if the system developer has ISO 9000 certification and a previous SEI evaluation, the product user can confidently use the SEI evaluation to support decisions to use the product and reduce the extent of product testing with no perceived severe losses.

In the case of products with potentially severe losses, another form of organizational assurance can be acquired through an external audit. This form of assurance requires the cooperation of the product developer; assurance is only possible if the nature of the product makes this a reasonable request. If little is known about the organizational assurances, the rigor and thoroughness of testing should be increased.

Product Assurance

Product assurance is the core of the quality task, with processes defined for each life cycle phase. Product assurance ensures that the product does what it is supposed to do, that the product does it as well as was expected, and that the product shipped is what it is supposed to be (e.g., all product components are present, it is not an older version, it is not a test version, and it does not contain a virus). Product assurance examples include life cycle reviews (e.g., design review, inspections, and peer reviews) and such processes as requirements management and configuration management. The results of these assurances are produced by the developers. The previous comments regarding ISO 9000 and SEI evaluations also apply to product assurance. Similarly, if the developer s product assurance measures are appropriate to the potential for loss, then the product user may be able to reduce the rigor and extent of product assurances, as long as the user can validate that the product received is the product tested by the developer.

Traditional methods include the concept of bonded software (QA locking the certified product in a penetration-resistant case using a serial-numbered metal band) or storage in a protected library. Newer technologies include the use of digital signatures or cryptographic checksums.

Measures that are less expensive and less effective may be appropriate for Electronic Data Systems Corp. products with less severe potential losses. These measures include site visits, sitting in on development meetings, discussions with the technical staff, and interviews. These assurances are more qualitative than quantitative, but they may add confidence or weight to other assurances.

Personnel Assurances

Personnel assurances include a comprehensive training program that provides instruction at the awareness level up to and including the cognitive level. To provide assurance, the training should be provided to meet clearly stated, testable objectives. To develop a comprehensive training program, the task and skills necessary to meet the organization s needs should be identified. The tasks and skills should also be expressed in terms of roles and responsibilities. Critical roles and responsibilities (including those that are critical during disaster recovery or emergency conditions) should be identified. Roles requiring special attention (e.g., separation of duty, position certification, or profession certification) should be identified.

Clearances and personnel performance reviews also provide assurance. For security-related products with less severe potential losses, more credibility can be given to development teams lead by a Certified Information Systems Security Professional (CISSP) or composed of personnel with other appropriate certifications. For systems products with severe potential losses, it is recommended that an official description of the development organization's roles, responsibilities, clearances required, internal controls guaranteeing separation of duty, and key position qualifications and credentials be identified.

Financial Assurances

Program management reviews address financial assurances. A company's inability to manage its finances can cause a development program to fail. Subcontract management is another facet of the financial assurances. The cost and schedule program data is used to project expenses to allow management to react to financial conditions and trends before they become program-threatening incidents. The source selection process may apply weight to such items as financial stability when making the selection. The loss of financial stability of either the prime contractor or its subcontractors could threaten the customer's ability to maintain the system after delivery, and it has the potential to reduce the quality of the product in response to financial pressures.

If the intended use for the product does not require periodic updates or deficiency resolution from the developer, then financial assurances may not be necessary. If the product is easily replaced by another similar product, then financial assurance is unnecessary. However, if the product serves a critical function (e.g., availability), sensitive function (e.g., integrity), or if the developer provides a key management service to support confidentiality that could result in severe loss, then some financial assurances should be pursued, preferably before acquisition.

Some management aspects of financial assurance can be derived from the availability of SEI CMM evaluation results regarding project management and subcontract management. Other financial assurances can be gained by reviewing the developer's annual report, financial statements, stock ratings, and other indicators from Standard and Poor's, Dunn and Bradstreet, and court filings for bankruptcy. A knowledgeable CPA should be consulted for other available indicators of financial stability.

Operations Assurances

To preserve the quality delivered with the system, the operations community should have processes for receiving, handling, storing, installing, testing, and accrediting the system for operation. The operations community should conduct tests and inspections from an operations perspective to ensure that normal operations perform as expected. In addition, the operations community should develop, publish, and test plans for disaster recovery, continuity of operations, and end-user contingency planning.

Physical Environment Assurances

The physical environment of the operations and development sites can affect the safeguard selection process. A sensitive application, such as NASA mission control, is usually located in a controlled access area (i.e., an area that is not accessible to the public). Additional safeguards required should be considered. A system's certification and accreditation to operate are only valid for a specific physical environment. For systems that are developed for general use or for many different user communities, the developers should clearly describe the physical environment assumptions and expectations used when developing the product.

Logical Environment Assurances

With logical environment assurances, the developer documents the environments in which the product is expected to be successfully executed.

The logical environment includes restrictions (e.g., minimum memory required, maximum records supported, export restrictions), limitations (e.g., supports text files only, specific device requirements), devices tested on, devices not tested but expected to execute on, compatibility issues, and preferred, required, or alternative system parameter settings.

Risk and Vulnerability Assurances

It is not possible to protect a system against all potential threats and exploitable vulnerabilities. Managers use risk management to select the set of potential threats and vulnerabilities that should be addressed. Security professionals determine the value of assets by examining the nature of the asset and its actual or proposed use. This is to assess the value to the organization as well as the potential value to those who might exploit the organization, the existence of vulnerabilities, the frequency of each threat, the potential impact of each threat, and the exploited vulnerability. They may also determine and use a measure of the certainty of the data used and collected. From this information, security professionals may recommend to management a set of potential threats and vulnerabilities to address and a set of proposed safeguards. The contents of these two sets of data depends on the reliability of the data used to make the decisions. In the case of threat and vulnerability data, no certified sources of information are evident. Therefore, certifying the supporting data consists of documenting its source and selecting information to judge its credibility, currency, and accuracy.

External Interface Assurance

Interfaces with other systems and organizations are a potential source of problems for system developers. To minimize the problems from external interfaces, developers create and maintain interface specification and interface control documents for rigorous interface control. Memorandums of agreement or understanding for less rigorous interface control are also created. Systems products may also have documentation or supporting code for developers that include interface definitions. This may be in the form of application programming interfaces or documents that describe file and field formats. Documented external interfaces may allow product users to conduct black box testing. External interface assurances may provide all forms of integrity, availability, and confidentiality assurance.

Other forms of assurance may exist within an organization's development processes (e.g., maintainability, timeliness, responsiveness, documentation, usability, communications, and legality). Following the pattern used for the above assurances, an organization would develop equivalent measure that can be taken for systems products for each form of assurance that is unique to the organization (or otherwise missing from the preceding list).

APPLYING CERTIFICATION CONCEPTS

ISO 9000 describes a series of concerns that a manufacturer should address regarding the certification of materials acquired for use in the manufacturing process. In software, the corollary to acquired materials is externally developed software and data. As the International Standards Organization 9000 standard recognizes, an organization cannot reasonably claim a product is certified unless all internally and externally developed components have been certified for a specified purpose. However, with planning it is possible to certify a product in stages. In the case of software, the product can be certified for general use within an organization (i.e., data has been gathered and some tests have been run and documented that do not have to be repeated when a department performs specific certification of the product). In some cases, general certification may cover all or most of a department's concerns.

There may be no need for certification based on the general use of the product (e.g., a database management system [DBMS]). However, if that DBMS is used to dispense drugs to patients, for example, the concerns for integrity, privacy, and availability fuel a need to certify the DBMS for this intended use. The security professional then determines the degree and type of certification to recommend by examining the general use of the product and the intended use of the product for the type and severity of potential loss. The following is a summary of the tasks essential to certifying systems-related products:

- Determining the type and degree of certification required for general use of the product.
  - Determining the types of potential losses that could result from general use.
  - Estimating the range of severity.
  - Developing likely loss scenarios
- Determining the type and degree of certification required for the intended use of the product.
  - Determining the types of potential losses that could result from the intended use.
  - Estimating the range of severity.
  - Developing likely loss scenarios.
- Gathering identification and assurance information about the Electronic Data Systems Corp. product and developer.
- Prescribing tests on the basis of the type of loss, the severity, likely loss scenarios, and the available assurance information.
- Conducting tests.
- Prescribing corrective action activities on the basis of test results, assurance data, potential types of losses, and potential severity.
- Managing the proposed corrective actions for approval.

- Executing the corrective action activities approved by technical management.
- Preparing and delivering the certification briefing to management.
- Changing the version designator for each product to indicate certification.

RECOMMENDED COURSE OF ACTION

Software that has been developed outside of the organization's control can present certain concerns to the security practitioner. The certification concepts and different types of assurances contained in this chapter form a basis from which to evaluate this type of software. By reviewing the information provided, the security practitioner can ensure that certification for externally developed software follows the correct process.

Chapter 24
Audit and Control of Information Systems Outsourcing
S. Yvonne Scott

Outsourcing is contracting with an outside vendor for the performance of a function that was previously performed by an employee of the company. It is a practice that organizations have been engaged in for some time. For example, most large companies collect payments through a bank lock box rather than having employees receive them at home offices. Similarly, many companies have chosen to have an outside firm process and distribute payroll. These practices are both examples of general accounting outsourcing.

Outsourcing is a reality and is an industry force that warrants the audit community's attention. Any significant change in the established control environment indicates security issues that should be closely examined. In addition, information (and the systems used to generate it) can differentiate a company from its competitors; therefore, information is a valuable asset worthy of protection.

PREVIOUS MISCONCEPTIONS

Outsourcing IS is not a new trend. The use of service bureaus, contract programmers, disaster recovery sites, data storage vendors, and value-added networks are all examples of outsourcing. In addition, such functions as time-sharing, network management, software maintenance, applications processing, limited facilities management, full facility management, and EDI services are now considered potentially outsourced functions. For example, Eastman Kodak entered into a ten-year agreement to outsource its entire IT function in 1989, a deal worth an estimated $100 million. As a result of increased reliance on outsourcing by organizations, a new area of audit responsibility has been created.

0-8493-9998-X/00/$0.00+$.50

Outsourcing is not a transfer of responsibility. Tasks and duties can be delegated, but responsibility remains with the organization's management. Therefore, outsourcing does not relieve the organization or management of the responsibility to provide IS services for internal operations and, in some cases, customers.

Outsourcing is not an excuse for substandard customer service, regardless of whether the customers are internal or external to the organization. Customers do not care how or by whom services are provided. Their concern is that they receive the quality services they need, when they are needed.

The most successful outsourcing deals are tailored relationships that are built around specific business needs and strategies. There has been a definite shift from an all-or-nothing approach to a more selective application of outsourcing. In many cases, deals have been structured to more closely resemble partnerships or alliances rather than service agreements. For example, some of these deals include agreements to share in the profits and products that result from the alliance.

In the internal audit profession, outsourcing is not an elimination of the need to audit the outsourced services. It is the auditor's responsibility to safeguard all of the assets of an organization. Therefore, because information is clearly an asset, the auditor must ensure that its confidentiality, integrity, and availability are preserved.

TYPES OF OUTSOURCING SERVICES

As previously discussed, any agreement to obtain services from an outside vendor rather than providing them internally meets the definition of outsourcing. The following list includes the types of IS outsourcing service contracts that the audit community is being required to address:

- Time-sharing and applications processing.
- Contract programming.
- Software and hardware maintenance.
- Contingency planning and disaster recovery planning and services.
- Electronic data interchange services.
- Systems development and project management.
- Network management.
- Reengineering services.
- Transitional services.
- Limited facilities management.
- Full facility management.
- Remote LAN management.

It should be noted that the first six services in this list have been outsourced for at least a decade. The remainder of the list represents expansions of the other services. For example, facilities management is the use of time-sharing on a broader basis, and remote LAN management is hardware maintenance on a distributed basis.

IMPLEMENTATION REASONS

Outsourcing should be specifically tailored to the business needs of an organization. It appears to be most viable for those organizations with the following characteristics:

- *Organizations in which IS is not a competitive tool.* If there is little opportunity for an organization to distinguish itself from its competition through systems applications or operations, there is less concern over entrusting the execution of these services to a third party.
- *Organizations in which short-term IS interruptions do not diminish the organization's ability to compete or remain in business.* An outsourcing vendor should be able to recover operations in one to two days. It is probably not reasonable to rely on a third party to recover complex systems within one to two hours. Contracts can be structured to specify that the outsourcer must recover within a one- to two-hour timeframe or incur severe penalties. However, if the outsourcer fails to comply with the contract, it is unlikely that the penalty adequately compensates the organization for the long-term effects of losing customers. Therefore, the shorter the tolerable window of exposure, the less viable outsourcing becomes.
- *Organizations in which outsourcing does not eliminate critical internal knowledge.* If outsourcing eliminates those internal resources that are key to the future innovations or products of the organization, the risk may be too great to assume.
- *Organizations in which existing IS capabilities are limited or ineffective.* If this is the case and the organization is considering outsourcing, management has probably determined that additional investments must be made in the area of IS. In this situation, it may make more sense to buy the required expertise than to build it.
- *Organizations in which there is a low reward for IS excellence.* In this case, even if the organization developed and operated the most effective and efficient information systems the payback would be minimal. Because every organization must capitalize on its assets to survive, the effort that would be expended could probably be spent more wisely in other areas.

MOTIVATING FACTORS

Companies have various reasons for outsourcing. Just as the outsourcing agreement itself should be tailored to the individual circumstances, the factors that cause an organization to achieve its objectives through outsourcing are unique.

Because more and more auditors are becoming involved in the evaluation of IS solutions before they are implemented, it is important to understand these motivating factors when evaluating whether a particular solution meets an organization's objectives. In addition, as in all cases in which the auditor has an opportunity to participate in the solution of a business problem (e.g., systems development audits), it is important to understand the overall objectives. In order to add value to the process, these objectives and their potential shortcomings should be considered when evaluating whether the outsourcing agreement maximizes asset use and maintains the control environment. For this reason, the motivating factors often cited by management, as well as some of the reasons why these objectives may not be readily met, are discussed in the following sections.

Cost Savings. As the global economy grows, management faces increased competition on reduced budgets. The savings are generally believed to be achievable through outsourcing by increasing efficiency (e.g., staff reductions, shared resources). However, several factors may preclude cost savings. Comparable reductions in service levels and product quality may occur, and comparable staff reductions may be achievable in-house. In addition, vendors may not necessarily achieve the economies of scale previously gained through shared hardware because many software vendors have changed their licensing agreements to vary with the size of the hardware.

Fixed Cost versus Variable Cost. In some cases, management has been driven to a fixed-cost contract for its predictability. However, service levels may decrease as the cost of providing those services increases. In addition, should business needs dictate a reduction in information systems, the company may be committed to contracted fees.

Flexible IS Costs. Management may have indicated that outsourcing is preferred because it allows management to adjust its IS costs as business circumstances change. However, necessary revisions in service levels and offerings may not be readily available through the vendor at prices comparable to those agreed on for existing services.

Dissatisfaction with Internal Performance. Dissatisfaction is often cited by senior management because it has not seen the increases in revenue and market share nor the increased productivity and cost reductions used to justify projects. Many outsourcing agreements, however, include provisions to transfer employees to the outsourcer. The net result may be that the personnel resources do not change significantly.

Competitive Climate. Speed, flexibility, and efficiency are often considered the keys to competitive advantage. By outsourcing the IS function, personnel resources can be quickly adjusted to respond to business peaks and valleys. However, the personnel assigned to respond to the business needs that determine the organization's competitive position may not be well acquainted with the company's business and its objectives. In addition, short-term cost savings achieved through reactive systems development may lead to long-term deficiencies in the anticipation of the information systems needs of both internal and external customers.

Focus on Core Business. Such outsourcing support functions as IS allows management to focus on its primary business. If IS is integral to the product offering or the competitive advantage of the organization, however, a shift in focus away from this component of the core business may lead to long-term competitive disadvantage.

Capital Availability and Emerging Technologies. Senior management does not want to increase debt or use available capital to improve or maintain the IS function. If IS is proactive and necessary to support the strategic direction of the organization, however, delaying such investments may result in a competitive disadvantage. In addition, precautions must be taken to ensure that the outsourcing vendor continues to provide state-of-the-art technology. Obsolescence can be tempered without the use of capital by negotiating hardware leases that afford some flexibility.

Staff Management and Training. Outsourcing eliminates the need to recruit, retain, and train IS personnel. This becomes the responsibility of the vendor. But regardless of who these individuals report to, IS personnel need to receive training on the latest technologies in order to remain effective. After control over this process is turned over to a vendor, provisions should be made to ensure that training continues. In addition, the cost of this training is not actually eliminated. Because the vendor is in business to turn a profit, the cost of training is included in the price proposal. In addition, this cost is likely to be inflated by the vendor's desired profit margin.

Transition Management. As mergers and acquisitions take place, senior management views outsourcing as a means to facilitate the integration of several different hardware platforms and application programs. In addition, some managers are utilizing outsourcing as a means to facilitate the organization's move to a new processing environment (e.g., client/server). However, knowledge of strategic information systems should not be allowed to shift to an outside vendor if the long-term intention is to retain this expertise within the organization. In such cases, the maintenance of existing systems should be transferred to the outsourcer during the transition period.

Reduction of Risk. Outsourcing can shift some of the business risks associated with capital investment, technological change, and staffing to the vendor. Because of decreased hands-on control, however, security risks may increase.

Accounting Treatment. Outsourcing allows the organization to remove IS assets from the balance sheet and begin to report these resources as a nondepreciable line item (e.g., rent). The organization should ensure that outsourcing is not being used as a means of obtaining a capital infusion that does not appear as balance sheet debt. This can be achieved if the outsource vendor buys the organization's IS assets at book (rather than market) value. The difference is paid back through the contract and, therefore, represents a creative means of borrowing funds.

All of these driving forces can be valid reasons for senior management to enter into an outsourcing arrangement. It should be noted that the cautions discussed in the previous sections are not intended to imply that outsourcing is undesirable. Rather, they are highlighted here to allow the reader to enter into the most advantageous outsourcing agreement possible. As a result, these cautions should be kept in mind when protective measures are considered.

PROTECTIVE MEASURES

Although it is desirable to build a business partnership with the outsource vendor, it is incumbent on the organization to ensure that the outsourcer is legally bound to take care of the company's needs. Standard contracts are generally written to protect the originator (i.e., the vendor). Therefore, it is important to critically review these agreements and ensure that they are modified to include provisions that adequately address the following issues.

Retention of Adequate Audit Rights. It is not sufficient to generically specify that the client has the right to audit the vendor. If the specific rights are not detailed in the contract, the scope of an audit may be subject to debate. To avoid this confusion and the time delays that it may cause, it is suggested that, at a minimum, the following specific rights be detailed in the contract:

- Who can audit the outsourcer (i.e., client internal auditors, outsourcer internal auditors, independent auditors, user controlled audit authority).
- What is subject to audit (e.g., vendor invoices, physical security, operating system security, communications costs, and disaster recovery tests).
- When the outsourcer can or cannot be audited.
- Where the audit is to be conducted (e.g., at the outsourcer's facility, remotely by communications).
- How the audit is conducted (i.e., what tools and facilities are available).
- Guaranteed access to the vendor's records, including those that substantiate billing.
- Read-only access to all of the client company's data.

- Assurance that audit software can be executed.
- Access to documentation.

Continuity of Operations and Timely Recovery. The timeframes within which specified operations must be recovered, as well as each party's responsibilities to facilitate the recovery, should be specified in the contract. In addition, the contract should specify the recourse that is available to the client, as well as who is responsible for the cost of carrying out any alternative action should the outsourcer fail to comply with the contract requirements. Special consideration should be given to whether these requirements are reasonable and likely to be carried out successfully.

Cost and Billing Verification. Only those costs applicable to the client's processing should be included in invoices. This issue is particularly important for those entering into outsourcing agreements that are not on a fixed-charge basis. Adequate documentation should be made available to allow the billed client to determine the appropriateness and accuracy of invoices. However, documentation is also important to those clients who enter into a fixed invoice arrangement. In such cases, knowing the actual cost incurred by the outsourcer allows the client to effectively negotiate a fair price when prices are open for renegotiation. It should also be noted that, although long-term fixed costs are beneficial in those cases in which costs and use continue to increase, they are equally detrimental in those situations in which costs and use are declining. Therefore, it may be beneficial to include a contract clause that allows rates to be reviewed at specified intervals throughout the life of the contract.

Security Administration. Outsourcing may be used as an agent for change and, therefore, may represent an opportunity to enhance the security environment. In any case, decisions must be made regarding whether the administration (i.e., granting) and the monitoring (i.e., violation reporting and follow-up) should be retained internally or delegated to the outsourcer. In making this decision, it is imperative that the company has confidence that it can maintain control over the determination of who should be granted access and in what capacity (e.g., read, write, delete, execute) to both its data and that of its customers.

Confidentiality, Integrity, and Availability. Care must be taken to ensure that both data and programs are kept confidential, retain their integrity, and are available when needed. These requirements are complicated when the systems are no longer under the physical control of the owning entity. In addition, the concerns that this situation poses are further compounded when applications are stored and executed on systems that are shared with other customers of the outsourcer. Of particular concern is the possibility that proprietary data and programs may be resident on the same physical devices as those of a competitor. Fortunately, technology has provided us with the ability to logically control and separate these environments with Virtual Machine (e.g., the IBM Processor Resource/System Management). It should also be noted that the importance of confidentiality does not necessarily terminate with the vendor relationship. Therefore, it is important to obtain nondisclosure and noncompete agreements from the vendor as a means of protecting the company after the contract expires. Similarly, adequate data retention and destruction requirements must be specified.

Program Change Control and Testing. The policies and standards surrounding these functions should not be relaxed in the outsourced environment. These controls determine whether confidence can be placed on the integrity of the organization's computer applications.

Vendor Controls. The physical security of the data center should meet the requirements set by the American Society for Industrial Security. In addition, there should be close compatibility between the vendor and the customer with regard to control standards.

Network Controls. Because the network is only as secure as its weakest link, care must be taken to ensure that the network is adequately secured. It should be noted that dial-up capabilities and network monitors can be used to circumvent established controls. Therefore, even if the company's operating data is not proprietary, measures should be taken to ensure that unauthorized users cannot gain access to the system. This should minimize the risks associated with unauthorized data, program modifications, and unauthorized use of company resources (e.g., computer time, phone lines).

Personnel. Measures should be taken to ensure that personnel standards are not relaxed after the function is turned over to a vendor. As was noted earlier, in many cases the same individuals who were employed by the company are hired by the vendor to service that contract. Provided that these individuals are competent, this should not pose any concern. If, however, a reason cited for outsourcing is to improve the quality of personnel, this situation may not be acceptable. In addition, care should be taken to ensure that the client company is notified of any significant personnel changes, security awareness training is continued, and the client company is not held responsible should the vendor make promises (e.g., benefits, salary levels, job security) to the transitional employees that it does not subsequently keep.

Vendor Stability. To protect itself from the possibility that the vendor may withdraw from the business or the contract, it is imperative that the company maintain ownership of its programs and data. Otherwise, the client may experience an unexpected interruption in its ability to service its customers or the loss of proprietary information.

Strategic Planning. Because planning is integral to the success of any organization, this function should be performed by company employees. Although it may be necessary to include vendor representatives in these discussions, it is important to ensure that the company retains control over the use of IS in achieving its objectives. Because many of these contracts are long-term and business climates often change, this requires that some flexibility be built into the agreement to allow for the expansion or contraction of IS resources.

In addition to these specific areas, the following areas should also be addressed in the contract language:

- Definition and assignment of responsibilities.
- Performance requirements and the means by which compliance is measured.
- Recourse for nonperformance.
- Contract termination provisions.
- Warranties and limitations of liability.
- Vendor reporting requirements.

PROTECTIVE MEASURES DURING TRANSITION

After it has been determined that the contractual agreement is in order, a third-party security review should be performed to verify vendor representations. After the security environment has been verified, the contract can be signed. After the contract has been signed and as functions are being moved from internal departments to the vendor, an organization can enhance the process by performing the following:

- Meeting frequently with the vendor and employees.
- Involving users in the implementation.
- Developing transition teams and providing them with well-defined responsibilities, objectives, and target dates.
- Increasing security awareness programs for both management and employees.
- Considering a phased implementation that includes employee bonuses for phase completion.
- Providing outplacement services and severance pay to displaced employees.

CONTINUING PROTECTIVE MEASURES

As the outsourcing relationship continues, the client should continue to take proactive measures to protect its interests. These measures may include continued security administration involvement, budget reviews, ongoing reviews and testing of environment changes, periodic audits and security reviews, and letters of agreement and supplements to the contract. Each of these client rights should be specified in the contract. In addition, the continuing audit effort typically includes the following types of audit objectives:

- Establishing the validity of billings (the IBM Systems Management Facility type-30 records can be used).
- Evaluating system effectiveness and performance. (the IBM Resource Management Facility indicates the percentage of time the CPU is busy. As use increases, costs may rise because of higher paging requirements.)
- Reviewing the integrity, confidentiality, and availability of programs and data.
- Verifying that adequate measures have been made to ensure continuity of operations.
- Reviewing the adequacy of the overall security environment.
- Determining the accuracy of program functionality.

AUDIT ALTERNATIVES

It should be noted that resource sharing (i.e., the sharing of common resources with other customers of the vendor) may lead to the vendor's insistence that the audit rights of individual clients be limited. This is reasonable. However, performance of audits by the internal audit group of the client is only one means of approaching the audit requirement. The following alternative measures can be taken to ensure that adequate audit coverage can be maintained.

Internal Audit by the Vendor. In this case, the outsourcing vendor's own internal audit staff would perform the reviews and report their results to the customer base. Auditing costs are included in the price, the auditor is familiar with the operations, and it is less disruptive to the outsourcer's operations. However, auditors are employees of the audited entity; this may limit independence and objectivity, and clients may not be able to dictate audit areas, scope, or timing.

External Auditor or Third-Party Review. These types of audits are normally performed by an independent accounting firm. This firm may or may not be the same firm that performs the annual audit of the vendor's financial statements. In addition, the third-party reviewer may be hired by the client or the vendor. External auditors may be more independent than employees of the vendor. In addition, the client can negotiate for the ability to exercise some control over the selection of the third party auditors and the audit areas, scope, and timing, and the cost can be shared among participating clients. The scope of external reviews however, tends to be more general in nature than those performed by internal auditors. In addition, if the auditor is hired by the vendor, the perceived level of independence of the auditor may be impaired. If the auditor is hired by each individual client the costs may be duplicated by each client and the duplicate effort may disrupt vendor operations.

User-Controlled Audit Authority. The audit authority typically consists of a supervisory board comprised of representatives from each participating client company, the vendor, and the vendor's independent accounting firm and a staff comprised of some permanent and temporary members who are assigned from each of the participating organizations. The staff then performs audits at the direction of the supervisory board. In addition, a charter, detailing the rights and responsibilities of the user controlled audit authority, should be developed and accepted by the participants before commissioning the first review.

This approach to auditing the outsourcing vendor appears to combine the advantages and minimize the disadvantages previously discussed. In addition, this approach can benefit the vendor by providing a marketing advantage, supporting its internal audit needs, and minimizing operational disruptions.

RECOMMENDED COURSE OF ACTION

Outsourcing arrangements are as unique as those companies seeking outsourcing services. Although outsourcing implies that some control must be turned over to the vendor, many measures can be taken to maintain an acceptable control environment and adequate audit coverage. Some basic rules can be followed to ensure a successful arrangement. These measures include:

- Segmenting the organization's IS activities into potential outsource modules (e.g., by technology, types of processing, or businesses served).
- Using analysis techniques to identify those modules that should be outsourced.
- Controlling technology direction-setting.
- Treating outsourcing as a partnership, but remembering that the partner's objective is to maximize its own profits.
- Matching the organization's business needs with the outsource partner's current and prospective capabilities (e.g., long-term viability, corporate culture, management philosophy, business and industry knowledge, flexibility, technology leadership, and global presence).
- Ensuring that all agreements are in writing.
- Providing for continuing review and control.

The guidelines discussed in this chapter should be combined with the client's own objectives to develop an individualized and effective audit approach.

Chapter 25
Improving IT Performance as an Outsourcing Alternative

Richard D. Hays

Outsourcing has grown to become a primary force shaping business, especially in the information technology (IT) arena. Owing to high costs, service that is often viewed as unresponsive and frustrating, and a willingness to see IT as an easily substitutable commodity, many organizations have targeted the IT function as a prime outsourcing candidate. Many IT executives have realized too late that their efforts to optimize internal technology have been eclipsed by the pressing need to deal with external communications and service effectiveness issues.

Many outsourcers have reduced costs and improved service levels. Others have found that their strategic focus has been sharpened by eliminating an IT function that was not central to their core technology. Still others have achieved improved access to information technology and expertise as a result of their outsourcing move.

For some organizations, however, the shift to outsourcing their IT function has been much less positive. Horror stories have resulted from the lack of flexibility and control that accompanies this shift.[1] Old problems and complaints that should have disappeared with the introduction of a new IT supplier remained. New limitations on control and flexibility have hampered strategic actions, and some have awakened to rude shocks as unanticipated parts of their agreement forced sudden and unpleasant lessons about the contracting process. For these companies, the promise of IT outsourcing is severely tarnished.

0-8493-9998-X/00/$0.00+$.50

Symptoms of Poor IT Performance

Many disappointed volunteers in the outsourcing movement share a common original motivation and entry process. They were propelled into outsourcing primarily as a flight from a poorly performing internal IT unit (the more satisfied outsourcing companies are more likely to have had an original motivation rooted in broader strategic concerns). Frustration with cost and service quality in the existing IT unit and with repeated unsuccessful attempts to fix the problem have often precipitated a headlong rush to an outsourcing option. With no existing positive model of a well-functioning IT unit available, these organizations have been much more likely to jump into outsourcing for inappropriate reasons or negotiated much less favorable contracts and conditions. In addition, a quick move directly into outsourcing often means that fundamental factors that helped create the initial unsatisfactory IT performance remain unidentified and unaddressed — a neglect that sows the seeds of future discontent, even in an outsourcing mode. The following six symptoms of serious internal performance problems can help determine the level of concern about existing internal service performance within an IT organization:

1. *Conflict.* A high state of conflict and disagreement between IT and customer units is a continuing and dominant feature of the ongoing relationship.
2. *Complaints.* Customer units complain loudly and insistently about poor IT service or high IT costs.
3. *Duplicating service.* Customer units attempt to build their own internal duplicates of IT-provided services to gain better control.
4. *Executive frustration.* Senior corporate executives are frustrated with seemingly uncontrolled IT costs and the continuing need to referee conflicts between IT and its customer units.
5. *Organizational energy.* Considerable executive and managerial time, energy, and effort are being expended in dealing with interdepartmental conflict issues or in positioning for future conflicts.
6. *Customer impact.* The internal conflicts over IT costs or service quality are beginning to have an impact on the interface with external customers.

IT PERFORMANCE TURNAROUND

The risk and uncertainty surrounding outsourcing can be significantly reduced by achieving a performance turnaround in the existing IT unit before the formal consideration of outsourcing. Effecting such a turnaround requires commitment of substantial resources and effort, but yields three important organizational payoffs:

- Confrontation of key performance-limiting issues
- Creation of a solid comparative basis for outsourcing

- Achievement of greater cost and service benefits than outsiders can offer

Confronting Key Performance-Limiting Issues

If an existing IT unit is performing poorly, it is doing so for specific reasons. These reasons frequently have to do with fundamental structural factors that seriously impede the unit's ability to yield solid, cost-effective service. For example, a major source of difficulty for many internal IT units is unclear or conflicting service expectations. Lack of specific articulation and agreement between supplier and user of IT services breeds violation of unstated (but strongly held) expectations. In addition, senior management may want low cost, while line customer units want premium service. In such cases, the IT function is caught in the middle and can satisfy neither.

If these conflicts have not been addressed and resolved, moving to outsourcing only exacerbates problems. When an IT activity is poorly managed, the managers will probably not be any better at managing an external service provider. The question to ask is why executive management would want to bestow the benefits of improving an inefficient operation to an external market. Two responses have been suggested for this scenario. The first is to hire better IT managers, and the second is to improve the performance of the IT function before making the decision to outsource.[2] When fundamental problems such as poor performance or inefficiency are left unresolved, they are much more difficult to improve within the outsourcing arrangement.

Creating a Solid, Comparative Basis for Outsourcing

When moving directly from a poorly performing internal IT unit to outsourcing, a company has a very ill-formed basis for structuring and negotiating a contract. Significant evidence is emerging that shows that IT performance gains have much more to do with the adoption of effective management practices than with economies of scale.[3] Can the organization afford to give away an unknown (but probably large) premium to an outsider, based simply on the ability to bring in effective management?

Without the existence of a well-functioning internal IT unit that is operating within the unique variables and constraints of a particular company, the company has little basis for structuring the contract. The outsourcing contractor is much more experienced and knowledgeable about the factors that will determine final cost and performance — a rather one-sided basis for negotiations.

Achieving Greater Cost and Service Benefits

A well-known research study carefully examined six firms with IT units that were judged by their own company to be performing unsatisfactorily.[4]

Each firm placed its IT function out to bid in an outsourcing mode but, after considering both external bids and a bid from their own internal IT unit, elected to grant a contract to their internal unit (a practice known as insourcing). The performance of each unit was then monitored as changes were made — changes that were more extensive than were possible in the old mode of a totally captive unit.

The results were impressive. Costs were reduced from 20 to 54 percent and, in many cases, service improved as well. It was concluded that internal IS departments, given the freedom and capability to change, often possess strong cost advantages over any outsider and offer greater insight into the unique organizational service needs as well.

The emerging success stories in insourcing are causing new questioning as to why an external agent, using essentially the same people and equipment as the internal unit, should be able to deliver more cost-effective service and produce a profit as well. In fact, once internal IT units start to see the overall problem from this perspective, the challenge to use their own resources to exceed what an outsider could offer can become a positive and motivational vision. They already have the basic resources that would become available to an outside supplier — why not work on the revised perspective, practices, and processes that will provide the same cost and service benefits?

Each of these benefits can be substantial, but the combination of all three provides a commanding reason to seriously consider the turnaround option. Many companies have avoided the turnaround option because of the difficulty in designing and executing such a complex organizational change. However, the change technology and experience base are available to help structure an IT performance turnaround that will most likely succeed (even in cases with low reform success in the past).

DETERMINING THE APPROPRIATENESS OF A TURNAROUND

Individual organizational characteristics determine whether a turnaround attempt should be made prior to outsourcing. While no simple answer exists, affirmative responses to the following questions should bias the IS manager's thinking toward investing in a turnaround effort:

1. *Is IT central to the core business and strategy?* IT is often viewed as a substitutable and replaceable commodity, particularly if historical performance has been poor. However, a more in-depth analysis may reveal that IT is more central to effectiveness of strategic actions than is apparent on the surface. If the overall strategy of the business depends on IT functioning and performance to any substantial degree, outsourcing could mean loss of control and flexibility in a key area — actions that could seriously blunt the overall strategic impact.

2. *Could IT become a source of competitive advantage?* For many companies, IT is more than just crucial to strategic action — it is a fundamental source of external competitive advantage. American Airlines, Otis Elevator, USAA Insurance, FedEx, and Frito-Lay all gain primary competitive advantage from their IT competence. Envisioning how IT could move to a role of providing a basic competitive advantage may be extremely difficult if present IT issues center on adequacy of basic functioning.
3. *Are IT needs complex, relatively unique, and dynamic?* An outsourcing contract can be most effective with fairly straightforward service needs and a moderately steady-state situation. The loss of flexibility as conditions change (i.e., either organizational needs or technology changes) can become a substantial limitation with a rigid contract.
4. *Is frustration with the present IT function a primary outsourcing motivator?* Successful outsourcing arrangements tend to be grounded in strategic analysis rather than based on a flight from a frustrating existing internal unit. Identification of, and assault on the fundamental issues creating the present performance problems is necessary, even in an outsourcing mode.

SETTING UP THE TURNAROUND

Once it has been determined that a turnaround is an appropriate endeavor, the following actions should be taken to help ensure a successful effort. These include:[5]

- *Situational assessment.* IS managers should assess the initial situation to determine the need for change, the general extent of changes needed, and the capability of the parties involved to manage and embrace the change. Asking pointed questions about the general need, the IT unit, and the customer units can help focus thinking about the need to change and make this need more salient to all.
- *Enrollment of stakeholders.* It is important to ensure the continued understanding and support of senior managers, customer managers, and IT leadership in the organizational change process. Top managers and customer unit leaders must have specific information on the need for change, the benefits of a successful effort, required resources, impact on others, and scheduling. IT leaders needs to grapple with the significant issues involved with a major change process.
- *Final commitment.* All of the setup work should be committed to a specific and written document that serves as a public agreement on such issues as the need for the change, the goals of the turnaround, and the general process to be used. Top management, customer unit leaders, and IT leadership all need to have a shared understanding and agreement about the important organizational change ahead. The team that

273

will actually manage the change process will need to organize itself to ensure effective project management.

BUILDING THE INFORMATION BASE

Any successful organizational change effort must be grounded in firm information and analysis. An IT turnaround effort requires a clear vision of the existing problem situation and its cause, detailed insights into the real service needs to customer units, and a deep understanding of their own internal processes and procedures. An effective change plan must be founded on this solid information base.

The process of constructing the needed information base can serve as the launch pad to a new IT culture centered on internal customers — units with service needs that must be identified and filled if IT is to be successful. Extracting the views of these internal customers and other stakeholders regarding the following questions is essential to the construction of an effective IT change plan:

- How do they view present IT service?
- What is their perception of the present IT function?
- What are the service needs?
- What specific topics are causing the most difficulty within the units?
- What is the desired balance between cost and service responsiveness?
- How strongly do the units feel a need for basic change?

Surveys and interviews can provide important insights into the causal forces that shape today's problem situation. Focused exploration of customer unit service expectations can reveal the nature and form of their service beliefs (and provide an opportunity to identify those that may be unreasonable or excessively costly).

DESIGNING THE TURNAROUND PLAN

Once the information base regarding the existing problem, customer service expectations, and existing processes is understood in depth, a plan to direct the IT turnaround effort can be constructed. The plan must set specific and measurable goals, define the needed changes, and identify the required processes for change.

Defining IT Performance Standards

Many of the goals of the plan will be derived from newly defined IT performance standards. Considerable work needs to be expended on working directly with customer units to define these standards. They will reflect both the specific service expectations of the customer units and the practical and professional pragmatics of the IT unit. The standards need to be as specific and measurable as possible and explicitly agreed upon by all as the definition of excellent service. This definition of excellence will serve as the guide for the efforts of the IT unit, as well as the standard used by the customer units to judge service.

The process of negotiating and defining these standards may be one of the most difficult tasks of the entire turnaround, but it is also one of the most important. One survey of IT departments in a variety of industries searched for factors that contribute to high internal customer satisfaction.[6] The IT units that ranked high on service satisfaction had significantly better and more precise specifications regarding the service to be performed than did their less-well-rated counterparts. For these IT units, the considerable investment in defining expectations and clarifying standards paid off strongly in service satisfaction.

FROM PLANNING TO IMPLEMENTATION SUCCESS

Three supporting elements are key to converting a turnaround plan from an abstract concept to an implementation success. They are discussed in the sections that follow.

Aligning the IT Culture

Customer-centeredness must become the driving force of the IT culture. Most poorly performing IT units have an internal culture centered around the enhancement of their own technology or processes. The conversion of this well-established culture to an entirely new focus that targets the service needs of customer units is a prodigious task, unlikely to respond to gentle prodding. Gaining an explicit understanding of the functioning of the present internal IT culture and producing a specific articulation of the desired culture are necessary but difficult and foreign processes for most IT units. Designing the actual cultural changes and reinforcements may be even more foreign.

Developing Service-Oriented IT People

Building the skills and attitudes needed to produce service-oriented people in the IT unit is also a necessary support step for the change plan. Being skillfully solicitous of, and receptive to, customer feedback (particularly negative feedback) is a trainable skill. This skill escapes even many external service companies, but is no less crucial to an IT unit dealing with internal customers. IT agents must provide respectful and responsive service interactions with internal customer units and be able and willing to gain feedback on service rendered — an invaluable element in improving future service.

Ensuring Capability for Service Recovery

Many IT units deliver service adequately but destroy their relationship with customer units when they face service recovery situations. Because the best of service will sometimes fail, the skill that the IT unit has built to recover positively from these unanticipated shortfalls will heavily shape the customer's view of the service they have received. Recovery situations are particularly difficult because of the higher interpersonal skill level and service commitment needed to handle disgruntled and emotionally charged customers who have just received service that violates their expectations.

RECOMMENDED COURSE OF ACTION

At the completion of a successful IT performance turnaround, the company has a greatly expanded range of alternatives. When a cost-effective and service-sensitive IT unit is in place, the motivation for outsourcing erodes. The loss of flexibility and control associated with outsourcing is just too great a cost without the negative prod of poor and costly existing service. The process of creating a truly effective internal IT unit causes fundamental problems to be addressed and, at a minimum, establishes an excellent basis for negotiating an outsourcing contract.

If outsourcing is still a consideration, the outsourcing options themselves become richer as new performance experience is gained. A more sophisticated view moves from asking a simple "outsource or not" question and looks at the effectiveness of selective outsourcing of specific functions. Assessing IT performance and achieving a performance turnaround is thus a practical alternative to outsourcing.

Notes

1. Lacity, M.C., Willcocks, L.P., and Feeny, D.F., "IT Outsourcing: Maximize Flexibility and Control," *Harvard Business Review,* 73 (May–June 1995), pp. 84–94.
2. Earl, M.J., "The Risks of Outsourcing IT," *Sloan Management Review* (Spring 1996), p. 27.
3. Lacity, M.C. and Hirschheim, R., *Beyond the Information Systems Outsourcing Bandwagon: The Insourcing Response,* (New York: John Wiley, 1995), p. 168.
4. Lacity and Hirschheim, p. 36.
5. Hays, R.D., *Internal Service Excellence: A Manager's Guide to Building World Class Internal Service Unit Performance* (Sarasota FL: Summit Executive Press, 1996).
6. Pfau, B., Detzel, D., and Geller, A., "Satisfy Your Internal Customer," *Journal of Business Strategy,* (November–December 1991), p. 11.

Chapter 26
Contracting with Consultants for Computer Services
David M. Massey

Outside consultants are often used to ease the transition to new hardware and software, alleviate staff shortages, meet short-term staff requirements, and assist in the development of in-house expertise. Often the manager in charge of a project makes the decision to use a consultant, selects and hires the consultant, and executes an agreement between the parties. Although this approach saves time, it can lead to legal, financial, and operational problems later in the consulting relationship and obviate the cost benefits of hiring a consultant.

This chapter outlines some of the considerations critical to the process of contracting with computer consultants. Companies that have the benefit of in-house counsel should continue to rely on their legal experts to ensure that the consulting agreement addresses all important legal issues. If in-house counsel is not available, outside counsel should still be used. The guidelines in this chapter should, however, help IS managers make informed decisions about, and better manage, the performance of their legal representatives.

WHY CONTRACTS ARE VITAL

In some ways, a contract is not unlike a computer program. Both use precise language within a structured framework to obtain specific results. The consulting agreement represents the legal essence of the understanding between two or more parties. The law regarding contracts has been built up over centuries of commerce, and its development has sometimes been confusing even to legal professionals.

IS managers would never ask members of the human resources department to draft and negotiate contracts on their behalf, and they would certainly object if the accounting department designed and implemented its

0-8493-9998-X/00/$0.00+$.50
© 2000 by CRC Press LLC

own system. Yet it is common practice in many IS departments to use a standard purchase order to describe the terms and conditions of the consulting agreement. The results are often disastrous because a standard purchase order cannot adequately address the complexities of a consulting relationship.

In addition, it is not uncommon for an organization to send a purchase order to a consultant and receive a letter of agreement in return. In many cases, neither party signs the other's form. Whose form prevails? Is there a contract at all? Most likely, no contract governs either party's form, and general principles of law will apply. The uncertainty and unpredictability of such a situation make a single contract signed by both parties a necessity.

CHOOSING A CONSULTANT

Among the most important considerations in contracting with consultants is selecting the right consultant. Computer consultants generally come in two varieties. Some are experienced professionals who have decided to strike out on their own. In these cases, the client is dealing directly with the person who will perform the work. Most consultants, however, are employed by relatively small, entrepreneurial companies that are prone to high turnover. When dealing with these companies, particularly if they have been chosen because of the reputation or ability of a particular consultant, the client must maintain the right to approve or reject individual consultants assigned to the project. In the event a consultant must be replaced or reassigned, the contract must also specify who will pay any additional cost of training a new person.

Before accepting a consultant, the client should be sure to check references from satisfied customers for whom the consultant recently performed similar work under similar circumstances. Time permitting, a client can interview a consultant in the same in-depth manner as a prospective employee is interviewed.

Because contracting firms vary in size and area of expertise, the first step in choosing a consultant is to develop a list of candidates from which to choose. Sources might include marketing literature or evaluations on file from past experiences, recommendations of IS managers in other organizations, or even the *Yellow Pages*, under Data Processing Services.

As the following sections explain, the type of consultant needed also depends on the type of work to be done.

Routine Assignments

If the work to be done is relatively routine (e.g., system maintenance, coding, and testing under in-house supervision), any firm or individual contractor can be considered. Small or independent contractors often have lower rates, though large firms may be cost competitive if they wish to place employees immediately.

Project-Oriented Work

The success of a project depends on a cohesive, effective project team. A larger contractor with a reputation for project management can choose from among many employees to assemble a team with the necessary skills for the client organization. A clearly structured project-management methodology helps ensure that the project management aspects of development receive the required attention.

Specialized-Skill Assignments

A specialist is often needed when an assignment requires in-depth knowledge of a particular area. If a contracting firm that specializes in the required skill cannot be found, large firms, especially regional or national consulting organizations with a large employee base, should be used.

As in any field, a specialist costs more than a generalist. The client should thoroughly examine the credentials of anyone suggested for a specialist's assignment.

PREPARING THE REQUEST FOR QUOTATION

IS managers usually preface the issuance of a Request For Quotation with one or more informal meetings with each prospective contractor. This gives both the client a chance to see how the contracting firm responds to the request and the contractors an opportunity to review the background and scope of the project and to withdraw if they choose. These informal meetings occasionally foster ideas that can alter the scope and complexity of the project, and the contractor's perspective can encourage new approaches to the problem. Furthermore, a contractor who offers ideas and attempts to review and understand the problem is probably interested in the project and should be considered for the contract.

After the work has been reviewed with the contractors, the request for quotation (RFQ) becomes the key vehicle of communication. A properly prepared and executed request for quotation (RFQ) lays the foundation for a successful project and a satisfactory working relationship with the contractor. However, if it is incomplete, the request for quotation can lead to serious problems. The following paragraphs discuss the sections an request for quotation (RFQ) should include.

Job Description. The RFQ should define all required deliverables. For example, the request for quotation must specify if the job control language and documentation must be delivered with a completed program.

Background Material. A contracting firm's performance can depend on how well its employees adapt to the client organization and its method of operation. Therefore, the RFQ should include background information about the organization, the purpose of the proposed system, and the relevant system interfaces. This information helps the contractor understand how the system will function within its larger environment.

Responsibilities. Because certain items are often ignored in proposed requests, they are not accounted for at project initiation. The RFQ should specify who has responsibility for preparing test data, miscellaneous typing, and documentation.

Work Environment. The work environment can significantly affect the cost of a project. The RFQ should define turnaround times precisely; for example, turnaround time of code compilations and tests should be defined in terms of maximum time or number per day and not in such vague phrases as "reasonably fast turnaround." Workstation configuration and availability should also be specified.

In addition to using precise language, the client should designate an individual to act as a contact with the consultant for questions, problems, and approvals. The RFQ need not name this client contact person but should define the client contact's role within the client organization or project.

Pricing Structure. The RFQ should precisely define how the consultant should structure pricing on the proposal, including the type of contract and the level of detail required. The most common types of contracts are:

- Fixed-price, in which the client pays the consultant a fee for the entire project.
- Time-and-materials, in which the client pays an hourly rate for the consultant's services and provides the means and resources to perform them.
- Not-to-exceed, which is actually a time — and — materials contract with a fixed-price ceiling. The contractor is paid the hourly rate for the limit of the contract, after which time the consulting firm must absorb the cost of any overrun. Such arrangements are advantageous to the client, and few consultants are willing to enter into them unless they are absolutely certain that the scope of the effort is well within the limits of the contract.

A breakdown of pricing by project phase is usually sufficient; however, it is not unusual for a client to request estimates for each project deliverable. An entire contract need not use a single price structure. Occasionally, fixed-price and time — and — materials arrangements are used in different parts of the same contract.

Response Guidelines. The RFQ should state the date and time by which all proposals must be received and the method in which they must be presented. Most contracting firms prefer to give a formal presentation rather than mail the proposal because presentations are an effective marketing tool. They also provide clients an additional opportunity for clarification. When formal presentations are made, each contractor should be given the same amount of time. Because larger contractors have more financial and marketing resources, IS managers should not be swayed by a flashy marketing package but should evaluate the contractor according to the proposal criteria.

Once the RFQs are sent to the prospective contractors, changes or additions to them must be transmitted to each contractor in writing, regardless of the urgency of time.

EVALUATING CONTRACTOR PROPOSALS

The method for evaluating contractor proposals should be established before the request for quotation is released. The evaluation may simply compare the bottom-line price, or it may use a combination of factors, including price, completion time, relevant experience, and approach. Defining the criteria before issuing the RFQ facilitates the quick, logical, objective evaluation of proposals.

Larger, complex projects usually elicit proposals that are equally large and complex, as well as tedious. However, the only way to evaluate a proposal properly is to read it thoroughly. IS managers should pay attention to both the information contained in the proposal and the manner in which it is presented. The care and professionalism demonstrated may indicate the contracting firm's overall attitude.

General Information

Because a proposal is a marketing tool, the contracting firm will not overlook the opportunity to present positive information about itself. Information on the firm's history, mode of operation, past successes, and unique methodologies is often included and should be considered in the decision-making process.

Project Narrative

The section on project narrative should address all points requested in the RFQ in the manner specified. IS managers should be suspicious of proposals that skirt issues or seem vague. A contracting firm that claims that its staff does precise and accurate work should be able to submit a precise and accurate proposal.

Cost is probably the most important item on the proposal, so a careful review of the pricing breakdown is essential. IS managers should review with the contractor any part of the proposal that is not done properly or does not include all requested information, such as specification of the cost of the work for each project subphase. If a firm's bid is extremely low or high, or the bids vary considerably, the pricing breakdown of the proposals should be reviewed to determine the cause of the differences. Any proposals that do not encompass the scope of the project as defined should be either corrected or eliminated. Any changes to proposals must be made in writing and by mutual consent.

When IS managers find it difficult to choose between similar bids, they should conduct a follow-up interview with each contractor. All contractors should be notified of the client's final decision, and managers should arrange a meeting with the chosen contractor as soon as possible to finalize the legal aspects of the contract.

GENERAL CONTRACT PROVISIONS

Contracts used by consulting firms vary from standard preprinted forms for time-and-materials work to contracts drawn up for special projects or fixed-price work. As with any legal document, it is wise to have a lawyer review the contract to ensure that it is fair and reasonable, covers all contingencies, and meets with the client organization's practices, policies, and expectations. The contract should define the scope of the association between the client and the contractor, the liabilities of both parties, and the effort to be undertaken; it should also clearly state the legal rights of both parties. The following sections discuss the topics covered in most contracts.

The Project

The name and description of the project or effort to be undertaken should be included, along with its start and finish dates and any milestones relevant to contract performance. Penalties associated with missing deadlines should be stated.

Individual Rates

Individuals covered by the contract should be identified by name and functional title (e.g., programmer or project leader.) In addition, the type of contract should be defined and individual rates assigned as applicable.

Additional Costs

Any costs exceeding the hourly rate or fixed contract price should be explicitly stated. These include expenses to be billed to the client, rate increases that occur during the contract period, and overtime rates (together with a procedure for authorizing overtime). Fixed-price contracts should include a pricing method for work that is not within the scope of the contract and for changes or additions to the existing contracts.

Payment and Billing

General Issues. The contract should state the billing method, billing due date, and any late-payment penalties. Under a time-and-materials contract, billing for hours expended is usually done biweekly or monthly. Fixed-price contracts may require that a certain percentage of the contract amount be paid at various points in the development effort. Thus it is important to establish and agree on the criteria for measuring the completion of each phase.

The consulting agreement should clearly state the amount of payment due to the consultant and how payment is to be made. Unless the consultant needs an up-front payment to subsidize the work in progress, full payment should not be made until the work is completed. Once consultants have been paid in full, their interest in and commitment to a project usually diminish. For projects of longer duration, payments can be staged to coincide with project milestones.

The consulting agreement must also specify whether payments are net of taxes, or whether the consultant is liable for withholding. Although it is customary for the consultant to handle taxes on consulting fees, the hiring company may agree to withhold and make payments as a convenience to the consultant.

Issues Specific to Time-and-Materials Contracts. T&M contracts are most frequently used by service brokers, small organizations, independent consultants, and consulting firms with many employees but without a stable workforce. Clients should keep in mind that this method of payment may tempt a consultant to extend work until another assignment becomes available.

Fixed-Price Bonus. In some cases, the client may wish to provide an incentive for the consultant to complete a project before its deadline or under budget. This can be done by awarding a bonus directly related to the cost savings if the project is completed early. Because this arrangement motivates consultants to complete projects quickly, clients should ensure that the job is done thoroughly.

Expenses. Some consulting firms charge for expenses in addition to the hourly rate for services. These expenses are typically small and include mileage, parking, and certain supplies. Expenses for meals, travel, and lodging may occur when a contractor from outside the local area is employed. Organizations should seek such consultants only when the skill needed for a project is so specialized or uncommon that it cannot be found locally.

When a client agrees to handle expenses for an out-of-town consultant, the contract should clearly delineate the expenses for which the client is liable. The client usually retains the right of prior approval for expenses and requires that regular periodic expense reports be filed.

Right to Hire. Although not directly related to compensation, the right to hire is sometimes addressed as part of the compensation arrangement with the consultant. Typically, this provision gives the client the right to hire the consultant after a specified period of time and stipulates that the client pay a penalty for earlier hire. As is the practice with employment agencies, the penalty is usually calculated as a percentage of the hiring salary.

THE FINE POINTS OF CONTRACTING

If the RFQ has been properly prepared and reviewed, the groundwork for the contract will have been laid by the time a consulting agreement is needed. The agreement, however, must expand on some of the issues presented in the RFQ, as well as introduce certain new issues.

Scope and Standard of Work

Consulting agreements are often made on a time-and-materials basis without any specifically stated goals. This approach provides a blank check to the consulting firm, and good-faith misunderstandings about what is expected can lead to costly disagreements.

To avoid or minimize these problems, the contract must provide specific descriptions of the expected results and how the success of any end product is to be measured. It is often difficult to describe with precision the desired result of the consulting work and tie the description to a precise timetable and price. If the result of the work is a specific program or system, completion can be measured by appropriate performance tests. When possible, specification of the work should divide the job into small increments for which the manager sets separate prices and timetables.

In addition to the specific obligations described in the written contract, a consultant has a second type of obligation to the client. It is the same as the duty of any other professional — to exercise a level of care appropriate to the relationship. In most cases, the consultant must exercise the same level of skill in performing the job as the average full-time practitioner would exercise. Failure to exercise this standard can be considered negligence and render the consultant liable to the client for loss and damage caused by the consultant's error.

Proving negligence, however, is not easy. For example, the consultant may argue that any errors or omissions were not the result of negligence but arose from adherence to the instructions given by the client. Therefore, the consulting agreement must specify precisely what is expected of each party and what their respective remedies will be if expectations are not met.

Acceptance Criteria

Before any work is undertaken in a consulting relationship, the parties should agree on the criteria upon which acceptance, and thus completion, of each phase of the project will be determined. Every project milestone, from successful compilation of code to completion of an entire processing cycle, should have acceptance criteria and a procedure for documenting compliance with them.

Acceptance is typically documented through the use of a schedule or attachment to the consulting agreement. To avoid possible misunderstandings, each party signs the schedule on meeting each milestone. In the event the agreement is prematurely terminated, the schedules help determine what, if any, payment is due.

Maintenance and Error Correction

Software is inherently complex, and nobody can guarantee that it will be error-free or operate without interruption. The consulting agreement, however, should explain who is responsible for failures, errors, and interruptions. Software authors typically bear this responsibility for a limited period of time, usually from 90 days to a year, during which time they must correct any errors discovered in the software. After this period, the client may wish to extend protection by entering into a separate maintenance agreement.

The maintenance agreement may be an attachment or schedule to the consulting agreement, in which case it will be governed by the terms and conditions of the consulting agreement. It may also be a separate agreement, in which case it will have to address anew all the issues relevant to the consulting agreement. Practically speaking, it is best to consider the issue of maintenance at the beginning of the consulting arrangement.

Ownership of Results

Clients frequently make the mistake of not executing a written contract assigning themselves — as commissioners of the work — copyright of the consultant's work. This agreement should be obtained before work is begun because in addition to clearly defining ownership , the agreement helps define the scope of the work to be done.

It may seem obvious that the party hiring someone to make something should own what is made. Unfortunately, the question of ownership in contract programming is far more complex. Generally, the author of a work owns the copyright. However, when the author is an employee, and the work is created within the scope of employment, the employer owns the copyright.

Work for Hire. In consulting arrangements, ownership may depend on whether the work product is considered a work for hire. Several criteria are used to determine whether a work is a work for hire and therefore whether it belongs to the author or the commissioning party. These criteria include the method of payment, whether there was an express contract for hire (especially one restricting the author's freedom to engage in other related creative activities), whether the author maintained regular working hours, whether the employer withheld income tax, and whether the work was created at the employer's place of business.

The Copyright Act describes nine types of work that are generally considered to be works for hire. Computer programs are not specified in any of these categories, but some of the categories are broad enough to be interpreted as including computer programs. The best advice for programmers is to negotiate copyright ownership up front. Hiring parties should ensure that a written agreement exists if they want to own programs created by consultants.

Whether the original copyright to a work vests in the author or the commissioning party, the author may assign the copyright expressly to any party. Therefore, it is customary for a contract to describe the work as a work for hire that is the property of the client. In the event the work is not a work for hire, the contract usually provides for the author to expressly assign copyright to the client. The common failure to include this provision results in further delays and negotiations.

Warranties, Liabilities, and Indemnification

Warranties, like ownership, may not seem important immediately, but they are critical to consulting agreements because they are not legally required by statute. In some cases, certain warranties from the Uniform Commercial Code (UCC) may govern the consulting agreement. But because UCC warranties are applicable to the sale of goods, they generally apply to hardware or off-the-shelf software. Custom programming is a service, not a good, so the customer purchasing custom software is not protected by these warranties.

It may not be clear from the consulting agreement whether the end result of work is custom software. To avoid any uncertainty regarding warranties, negotiating parties usually include an explicit disclaimer in the contract. To be effective, the disclaimers must be conspicuous and precise; they are therefore generally capitalized in print.

Other warranties are specifically addressed in the following sections. When a warranty is breached, remedies are available. Some are provided as a matter of law. Parties to a contract, however, are free to specify other warranties, a practice that may benefit both parties in the long run. By agreeing up front to liquidated damages — that is, to a specified form and amount of damages in the event of specific breaches — the parties to a contract can avoid costly and protracted litigation.

Consultant's Insurance. Many consultants have errors-and-omissions insurance that covers their liabilities for failure to do the consulting job correctly or on time or for violating third-party rights. If the consultant has such a policy, the client should request a copy of the certificate of insurance before waiving any warranty in the agreement. Often the client will request to be added as an additional insured party so that the policy cannot be canceled without written notice to the client.

Third-Party Rights. Consultants often have prior obligations to companies for whom they have previously worked. They may be obligated to maintain the confidentiality of information, techniques, or processes to which they have been exposed. They may have assigned the rights to material they have created to the companies that hired them. Finally, they may have agreed to restrictions against working in certain areas, with certain clients, or in certain industries.

The consulting agreement should include a clearly written representation and warranty by the consultant that the work to be performed will not violate any third-party rights and that all materials to be delivered under the agreement will be original to the consultant. The client may require the consultant to indemnify the client in the event that any third parties assert claims against the work performed by the consultant. Indemnification is simply an arrangement for one party to make another party whole against any claims airing under certain circumstances. Because this can be a costly proposition , it should not be entered into lightly.

Confidentiality

In the course of their work, consultants are likely to have access to the confidential or proprietary information of the hiring company. Although less likely, the company may also be exposed to confidential or proprietary information belonging to the consultant. Once disclosed, information that may have been considered a trade secret may no longer be protected, unless the disclosing party has protected the information with appropriate confidentiality provisions.

Confidentiality provisions generally outline a procedure for disclosure that ensures that both parties understand the confidential nature of the information being disclosed. The terms of confidentiality must also include the duration of the restrictions, and the remedies available if they are breached.

Because information that has become widely available loses its strategic importance, one remedy available for breach is injunctive relief. An injunction allows the injured party to prevent the breaching party from further damaging the value of strategic information by continued improper disclosure.

Solicitation

While working on the project covered by the contract, the consultant will come in contact with the client's key suppliers, customers, contacts, and employees. The client has legitimate expectation that the consultant will not use any of these contacts for personal benefit, particularly to the detriment of the client.

The restrictions on exploiting the contacts obtained through the consulting relationship are typically of limited duration. Otherwise, the consultant would eventually exhaust the supply of potential customers simply by virtue of having worked with their associates. The scope and duration of the restrictions depend on the work being done, as well as on the nature and extent of the consultant's access to client information.

Before retaining a consultant, clients should ascertain the nature of any applicable restrictions. Because consultants are in a better position to determine whether prior agreements restrict provision of the services required, it is customary for a consultant to warrant that no such restrictions exist or that any existing restrictions do not prevent work on a client's project.

Competition

Competition is handled through a noncompete clause designed to protect the customer's expectation that custom software or similar technology developed for the organization will not be provided to a competitor. The noncompete clause is standard and valid unless it is unreasonable.

Reasonableness is a widely used legal standard that is judged in the courts on a case-by-case basis. For example, a stricter noncompete clause is generally more acceptable in the case of custom software that is work made for hire. Broad restrictions would not be appropriate for more routine work and therefore may not be enforceable.

Restrictions on solicitation and competition are closely related and are often addressed together. Confidentiality provisions are also related. The contract must specify that violation of any of these provisions constitutes a material breach of the agreement.

Disputes and Remedies

The consulting agreement outlines what each party expects of the relationship. Ideally, the expectations are met, and the parties are satisfied with the outcome of the relationship. In reality, it is helpful to know in advance how disputes will be resolved and what remedies are available when they occur.

Consulting agreements are controlled predominately by state law since there is no national contract law. It is necessary therefore to specify which state and law will control the contract. Because courts in one state may adjudicate disputes governed by the laws of another state, the consulting agreement must also specify where disputes will be resolved.

Although there is no inherent advantage in having the client's state law and court system govern a contract, consultants often balk at such a provision if they are from another state. An equitable solution, and one that usually discourages litigation, is the provision that any dispute be resolved under the law and in the courts of the state of the party defending a legal complaint. Faced with the prospect of out-of-state litigation, a potential plaintiff is likely to resolve any disputes without resorting to formal legal action.

Changing the Contract

It is not unusual for the direction of the consulting project to change midway through the assignment. These changes should be documented in clearly written change orders to avoid misunderstandings. Changes may be necessitated as a result of changing needs of the client or of the consultant. Sometimes both parties agree that a refinement or adjustment to the project is required for successful completion.

The consulting agreement should clearly state how the parties will handle the delays and increased costs caused by changes to the contract. When the client initiates changes in the contract, it is customary to extend the time for completion of milestones as well as the deadlines for any completion bonuses; this is not done, however, when the changes are made at the request of or to accommodate the consultant.

Any changes, no matter how minor, should be documented so that their impact on the project is clearly known. The client should retain the right to accept or reject change requests, based on overall impact to the project. Changes to fixed-price or not-to-exceed contracts may require a budget increase. Finally, a client should never have to pay for changes caused by a consultant's error.

Term and Termination

The term and termination of a contract are integral parts of the contract life cycle. These clauses may include a specific length of time for the duration of the contract as well as certain circumstances or conditions that end the contract before expiration of the term. Instead of specifying a time frame for the expiration of the contract, the consulting agreement may simply terminate on completion of the project.

Every contract should provide the right of termination for a material contract breach by the other party. A material breach may include such events as nonpayment, nondelivery, failure to meet specific deadlines, or even bankruptcy. If a breach occurs, one party may wish to give the other time to cure the breach before terminating the agreement. The time allowed for a cure varies according to the nature of the breach, but, in general, it is between 10 and 30 days.

The contract should also provide for termination by mutual consent. Such occurrences should be documented by both parties so that there is no question that the wish to terminate is mutual. If the client wants the right to terminate the agreement at any time, that right should be set forth clearly in the agreement. The client should expect to pay a penalty if this option is taken.

Other Contractual Considerations

To be optimally effective, a contract must include provisions whose purpose is not always clear to the parties. Contract law is old and complex and has been heavily litigated. Some phrases that have crept into common contract usage should be aggressively avoided.

One example is the best-efforts clause. Although both parties expect that the consultant will devote professional and diligent efforts to the project, a best-efforts standard can have unpredictable, and undesirable, implications.

Another common contract provision is the merger and integration clause, which provides that the written contract is the entire agreement between the parties. This seemingly unimportant clause can avoid complications in the event of a dispute.

MANAGING PROBLEMS OF PERSONALITY AND PERFORMANCE

To help a consultant become as productive as possible, the client should prepare the consultant's working environment in advance. Preparation should include setting up a work space and workstation, making any security arrangements necessary for entrance and exit by the consultant, and preparing the system so the consultant can access project data and software. Contact with the consultant should be managed by the client contact, who will help the consultant with orientation, design standards, and project monitoring, among other issues.

A reputable consulting firm selects its consultants carefully and tries to match their abilities with client needs. Nevertheless, problems occasionally arise with personalities and performance. Although the IS manager's participation in interviewing and selecting the consulting firm and consultants minimizes the likelihood of problems, the manager should be prepared to address these issues as they arise.

Nonperformance

When a consultant is not performing as expected, the problem is usually resolved by replacing the consultant. All problems, however, must be documented and explained to eliminate any doubt regarding nonperformance or misunderstanding of expectations. Comparing the consultant's performance against the project plan helps clarify the problem.

Personnel Conflicts

Conflicts between in-house employees and consultants can seriously disrupt a project. The problem may simply be in-house resentment of a highly paid outsider, or it may be a personality clash.

Personality issues are less a matter of performance than of compatibility, and consultants may find themselves, through no fault of their own, in the unfortunate position of clashing with in-house personnel. Personality types that do not fit well in the organization should be detected through careful and thorough interviewing. If personnel conflicts arise, however, the consulting firm should be notified.

Careless Habits

Habitual late arrivals, long breaks and lunches, and early departures should not be tolerated. They should be brought to the attention of the consultant and, if necessary, of the consulting firm.

Missed Deadlines

If the consultant continually misses deadlines, the client should review the project with the consultant and the consultant's managers. Vague specifications, inadequate turnaround, downtime, and overly optimistic time estimates are just a few of the many causes of missed deadlines. The consulting firm should assume its share of cost overruns when it is responsible for delays.

RECOMMENDED COURSE OF ACTION

Contracting for systems and programming services can be a useful staffing alternative. But drafting and negotiating a consulting agreement should not be undertaken without professional advice. Form contracts, or one-size-fits-all agreements, are not sufficient. The procedures described in this chapter are not all necessary for every project. The complexity of the procedures should correspond to the scope and importance of the proposed work. Each consulting relationship is unique and should be approached as such.

Many, if not all, of the problems between a client and consultants can be anticipated and avoided or minimized through use of a clear, well-written consulting contract. When disputes arise, a well-written contract provides a reference point for the assignment of responsibility and for an amicable resolution without litigation.

The consulting agreement is the blueprint by which a project is implemented. By paying careful attention to the details and using professional assistance, IS managers can ensure that the consulting relationship is productive and satisfying for both parties.

Section IV
Managing Special Projects

Chapter 27
SAP Implementation and Control

Frederick Gallegos
Loida Tison-Dualan

The R/3 enterprisewide integrated system may be the answer to the needs of many organizations. After recognizing the threats, accurately assessing its ramification, and developing ways to mitigate the risks associated with R/3, auditors will be ready to begin implementation. The implementation of R/3 should be performed with its unique characteristics in mind. This section will discuss both general implementation guidelines and specific guidelines unique to the R/3 environment.

Understanding the Corporate Culture. The first factor involves understanding the corporate culture of your company in relation to their readiness and capability for change. There is a difference between seeing the necessity for change and being able to actually make the changes. SAP is an enterprisewide implementation that will affect many, if not all of the departments. Thus, understanding each department and their issues are important. Many decentralized organizations may find that their divisions may not welcome change that affects their territory. Thus, resistance to change is common. The implementation team will need to unfreeze the organization or prepare the organization for the change. By educating the users about the R/3 system and involving the user departments in the decision-making process, project teams can develop stronger acceptance of the system change.

Understood and Complete Process Changes. The second critical success factor requires the completion of all business process changes. These changes must occur prior to implementation. Thus, difficult decision-making can be done early. Each company should perform some level of business process reevaluation or redesign prior to implementing SAP. With SAP, the cost and difficulty of changing the way a packaged system is configured after implementation is far greater than that of making the most informed decisions early. It is important to understand the structural and policy decisions that must be made.

In addition, auditors should reevaluate the controls in the newly designed processes. Emphasis should be placed on the new risks associated with the new objectives. Since the controls available in the new system will differ from the previous environment, auditors can perform proactive design phase review to address exposures inherent in the new system.

Communication — Never Enough! The third factor deals with communication. It is important to communicate continuously with new users at all levels in business, rather than in technical terms. Employees who are affected by the new system need to be informed of its progress so that their expectations will be set accurately. People need to be notified many times about change. Communication is the key to managing expectations. When expectations are set too high, people tend to become frustrated, upset and disappointed with the results. When they are set too low, people may have difficulty adapting or are surprised with the extent of the change. Thus, to allow people time to accept and fully use the new system, a rigorous communication program should be adopted.

Auditors evaluating the system development phase of R/3 can ensure that the team is performing communication activities appropriately by reviewing minutes from meetings and workshops, interviewing users and watching for behavioral problems. Lack of communication will create tension and resistance to the system change. By helping employees see their work as part of the whole, or how it fits into the final product, the team can help to communicate that the success of project depends on the efforts of all employees.

Management Support. Acquiring superior executive support for the project is essential from the beginning. Executive management must spearhead the effort to conform with the R/3 structure. Executives need to provide active leadership and commitment during the implementation of R/3. Their efforts to personally engage in the change process will provide the support needed to gain success in this project. Many companies or divisions within an organization will be reluctant to change their business to fit the R/3 framework. Some may become territorial and want to sabotage the project. According to a survey of executives, the common phrase heard is: "the hardest part of implementation is aligning your policies and processes with SAP." R/3 is a centralized, top-down, structured approach. It works well when companies are able to operate within these limits. Executive management must encourage dedication to the reengineering effort.

R/3 requires full reengineering, not just automation. Attention to employee empowerment from the start will ensure success to the business process improvement efforts.

SAP Project Manager Competence. Another relevant critical success factor deals with project management. The project manager should be capable of negotiating on even terms with the technical, business, and change management requirements. Integrated change blends both the organizational and technical solutions into one large-scale change. Many concerns fall between the cracks. With an enterprisewide integrated information system, there is a need to address issues from all perspectives. Thus, the project manager, as well as the project team, should be sensitive to the impact of the new technology, new business processes, and changes in organizational structures, standards, and procedures on the project as a whole. This will help he or she from becoming overwhelmed by the sometimes conflicting requirements of the implementation project.

The Team. A project team that includes both IS and business personnel will find the balance to be more effective. After defining project roles up front, team members should be reminded that they will be expected to shift to non-traditional roles. With R/3, many IS roles shift to the users. Customizing the R/3 software to fit the requirements of a particular function becomes a user responsibility. Users configure the systems by using the tables and functions to run their business in the new way. Tables are modified by the users and systems are maintained by the users. Thus, with many IS responsibilities shifting to the users, the project teams will be more effective when they are composed of not only IS personnel but also by people from the business departments that are affected by the new system. In addition, many companies are strengthening their R/3 project teams by adding outside consultants. These firms are able to provide project leadership support and R/3 and ABAP/4 expertise that are not always readily available in-house.

Project Methodology — It is Important. Another critical success factor relates to the project methodology. The project methodology chosen should act as a road map to the project team. Objectives should clear and measurable so that progress can be reviewed at intervals. Setting measurement goals is a key aspect of reengineering. They demonstrate the effectiveness of actual improvements. System integration projects are complicated and require attention to detail. All interfaces should be documented so that any implication of change will be given the required attention. Whatever the methodology taken, auditors must keep in mind that no single approach will work best at all times. The auditor must evaluate how a particular implementation approach was chosen and assess it's appropriateness to the R/3 project.

Training. It is also important to train users at all levels and provide support for all job changes. The SAP environment will change the roles of many of the employees. Current skills need to be reassessed and new skills need to be identified. The changing nature of the jobs will mean that management will need to provide support via new job definitions, rewards and recognition, and reevaluation of pay schedules. Education reflects a financial commitment to the effort and promotes problem-solving skills. Problem-solving skills empower employees to make effective changes.

It is also important to provide the project team members with the training that will help them succeed in the project, such as training in the technology, the business, and change management issues. Thus, training is not enough, it is only the beginning with R/3. It is difficult to master all the modules because the system is complex. Experimentation is the only way to arrive at the best choice. It also locks in the learning. Users of the system have hundreds of ways to access the same data. They will need to understand what will and will not happen with certain parameters. SAP encourages the "sandbox" approach so that users can understand in elaborate detail exactly what the system is designed to do. Even the team members need to try multiple options before they choose the configuration that works best for them.

Commit to the Change. Problems will definitely arise. Thus, the project team should expect problems. The project scale and complexity of R/3 ensures that problems will surface throughout the implementation effort. The project leader and team, however, must continue to persevere and remain committed to the information system change. Thus, although the project team will run into resistance and problems, commitment to the change will help overcome the tides of reengineering. With management's persistence and consistency, the team will be able to overcome the pitfalls.

In today's client/server environment, corporate success with SAP requires diligence for all the critical success factors; there is little tolerance for mediocre performance. The auditors and project teams that encourage the consideration of these critical factors will set a winning course for their implementation of the R/3 system.

ESTABLISHING SECURITY AND CONTROLS

SAP R/3 imposes a changed computer environment and a stronger reliance on networked computers on an organization. Thus, there is a need for the reassessment of the information security architecture. The security architecture is the foundation of all diverse computing and networking elements of an organization. It is imperative that information security architectures provide for a consistent administration and monitoring tools and techniques, common identification and authentication processes and an alerting capability that meets realistic needs.

This chapter will examine the security features accessible in SAP R/3 and will propose administrative and procedural controls required to ensure the security of the R/3 system. Lastly, it will discuss the impact of R/3's EDI and Internet capabilities on security.

Security Features of the Basis Component. Auditors are challenged with ensuring that adequate controls are in place in information systems. Controls should reduce business risks and security exposures. Fortunately, the SAP BC module has built-in security features. They provide for security-related concerns of applications, data, and resources. The SAP security and control capabilities support identification, authentication, and authorization of system users to ensure that only authorized users are able to access specific transactions, tables, modules, and the entire R/3 system. In addition, SAP programs and data are internally protected from other applications and utilities. Thus, with the SAP security and control features, the complex R/3 environment can be adequately safeguarded.

The effectiveness of the security system depends on the combination of the security measures implemented. Security measures should uniquely define individual users to the system and prove or confirm their identity. In addition, they should determine whether users are allowed access to certain resources. The unique security components of SAP work together to support the identification, authentication, and authorization of the R/3 users.

Log-on Process. The log-on procedure to access the host operating system is independent of the SAP log-in procedure. Generally, users log on to desktops as clients to the main system. During the log-in procedure, the users' ID and password are reviewed for validity against the user master record to ensure that only valid users access the system. System profile parameters can be used to set password length minimums and password expiration times. They can also control the number of times a user can enter incorrect passwords before the system ends the log-in attempt or locks the user against further log-in attempts. In addition, users are not able to log on to the application or database servers. Thus, they are not able to access or corrupt the SAP application programs and data.

User Master Records. To track user access rights, a user master record is created for each user. It contains data such as user ID and the corresponding user password (that is stored in encrypted format). It also defines the user groups, user type, period of validity, user defaults, and user address information. Each master record references an authorization profile. The profiles refer to authorization value sets that define the user's access capabilities.

SAP. SAP is a default super user with unlimited system authorizations. It is used to initially install the system. Although, a user master record is defined for SAP during installation, it does not require one. Deletion of the user master record for SAP can increase the risk of unauthorized access to the system because it will not be subject to authorization checks and therefore has all authorization capabilities. In addition, it has the password PASS, that cannot be changed without creating a new user master record. Thus, it is imperative that the ability to delete SAP is properly restricted.

TSTC Table. This table holds all the transactions available in the SAP system. The table can be used to identify certain transactions that do not need authorization. Transactions are available to users when the user master record lists the object and the user passes the authorization test. Thus, if a transaction is marked as not requiring an authorization check, all users can run that transaction with the appropriate menu option.

Authorization Objects. This feature restricts the ability of users to perform certain functions and access certain information. System elements such as transactions, tables, fields, or programs are represented by authorization IDs that are contained in these objects. Again, authorization is only granted when the user master record lists the object. Otherwise, the user is rejected access. Standard authorization objects control user access and ensure consistency with management procedures and guidelines.

Authorization Value Sets. For each authorization object, an unlimited amount of system access privileges can be defined. A value set is a list of allowable values for each field in an authorization object. There are value sets for all the transactions that a user can execute and the value sets for the business areas a user is able to access and update.

Authorization Profiles. The system uses authorization profiles to minimize the administrative work in managing security. For each task, a profile is set up that matches the authorization object and the authorization value set. However, actual authorizations are not located in the profiles. The user master records contain references to the profiles to which the user is authorized. The system's ability to allocate the same profiles to many users and to allocate the same authorization's value sets to different profiles reduces security administration time and resources.

Additional Authorization Checks. Additional checks can be created using ABAP/4 or by allocating authorization objects with transactions in the TSTC table. When additional authorization checks are defined, the user's authorization value set is tested for that object during the log-on process.

Changes. It is possible to display all user master records and profiles that contain a specific object to determine which users have sensitive authorization objects. Changes to the user master records, profiles, and authorization value sets are logged by the system. Changes to master records and profiles can be reviewed via transactions "SU93" and "SU91." These system logs can be used to control unauthorized changes to users' access capabilities.

Summary of Access Control

In summary, the R/3 process for user access is very detailed. Before a user can initiate a transaction, SAP performs an access checking process. When the user enters the user ID and password, the system checks the user ID and only allows valid users with the appropriate password to gain access. After gaining access, the user can initiate a transaction. However, if the transaction is not defined or is locked in the TSTC table, it is rejected. Further, if an additional authorization check has been defined, the user's authorization value set for the object is tested. It is rejected if the user is not authorized for the additional check. Lastly, the other detailed authorizations of the user (that are stored in profiles and in authorization value sets) are checked by the system to determine whether the user is authorized for the object.

In R/3, user access capabilities are managed by the user master records, authorization profiles, and authorization value sets. To ensure that all user access is consistent with management policies, procedures and guidelines, control must be exercised over changes to user master records, profiles, and authorization value sets. The R/3 system provides standard authorization objects specifically for this purpose. Thus, they can be used to control the actions of the administrator in relation to different user groups. They can also specify the profiles an administrator is able to maintain and the profiles a user is able to add to a user master record. Further, the authorization value sets that an administrator is able to maintain and enter into a profile can also be restricted.

ADMINISTRATIVE CONTROLS

Administrative controls are implemented via documented policies and procedures and are exercised by people rather than the system. These controls address access to data, system development, customization and modification, and maintenance processes. The automated control procedures offered through the SAP system are more effective when reinforced with control procedures. Business-based policies and procedures should be established that address accountability, access control, confidentiality, integrity and security management issues.

Accountability

As users become developers of the R/3 system, they will be customizing the system through changes to the tables. Segregation of duties between the users and the IT department will become imperative in order to ensure accountability. Thus policies should address and monitor segregation of duties. For example, customization should be separated from the production environment and procedures should allow only properly tested and approved changes to be copied into production. Likewise, access to customization functions should be prevented in the production environment and all changes should be approved and require the sign-off by users and IT management. In addition, a detailed security policy should specify the ownership of the system and data and require the documentation of all system changes. Management should review system logs for unauthorized table changes and follow up and investigate any unauthorized use of the system. Lastly, physical access to the servers and workstations should be restricted to authorized personnel only.

Access Control

Access to SAP data and transactions are restricted by the SAP security system. However, standards and procedures will ensure that access rights have been authorized by management, users' accesses are relevant to their duties, and that access rights are not incompatible. Thus, the following segregation of duty procedures should be established:

1. Users' direct access capabilities should be restricted by the operating system and database;
2. Users' access rights should be approved and documented by management;
3. User master records should be assigned for each user to prevent sharing of IDs and passwords;
4. Passwords should be kept confidential and be difficult to divulge;
5. Passwords should be changed regularly;
6. Management should regularly review and follow up on any access violations;
7. Access to the SAP system during non-working hours should be minimized and adequately controlled.

Confidential, Integrity, and Security Management

The environmental controls within SAP can be compromised if access and changes to SAP programs and data from other applications and utilities are not properly restricted. Thus, the following issues should be reviewed to ensure that the security system is not negated:

1. The ability to change the system and start-up profiles should be appropriately restricted;
2. The SAP user master record should not be deleted and users should not be able to delete this record;
3. DYNPROs changes should be prohibited in the production environment and should be restricted to appropriately authorized users;
4. Additional authorization checks for potentially dangerous transactions and should be defined in the TSTC and should not be changed or deleted;

5. Review of users given access as "Batch Administrators" should be performed periodically because these users can perform any operations on all background jobs in the R/3 system;
6. Batch input session files that have been created by an interface program or an internal SAP program should not be modified prior to the release stage;
7. Changes to ABAP/4 dictionary should be adequately tested and authorized;
8. Standard table entries should be removed when not intended to be used for a particular installation;
9. ABAPs should be assigned to appropriate authorization groups so that users cannot execute ABAPs that are not relevant to their work functions.

EDI and Internet Security

SAP R/3 is not immune to the intrusion and exploitation from outsiders. R/3 supports EDI (electronic data interchange) and has recently released Internet capabilities for their R/3 processes. EDI and the Internet make security issues more critical because external intruders can degrade the integrity of the system and jeopardize company assets. Thus, security policies should accommodate the unique needs of EDI and the Internet.

Dangers threatening EDI messages include the compromise of message integrity, message repudiation, disclosure of confidential data, misrouting of messages, and delaying of messages. To ensure that EDI messages arrive at appropriate destinations and are only accessed by authorized users, security mechanisms and procedures must be employed. EDI security mechanisms available include encryption, digital signatures, key management, and sealing. Unfortunately, these tools are not all available within the R/3 system. At this time, they will need to be installed outside the R/3 environment. Therefore, auditors must insure that the overall security architecture includes security mechanisms that support EDI. In addition, procedures should be established that will ensure that information transferred via EDI is complete and accurate.

With the advent of the Internet, computer hackers are becoming more sophisticated. As companies combine SAP with the advantages of the Internet, security threats will continue to multiply. In an integrated system, like R/3, a hacker may be able to compromise not only a small section of the system but all the systems connected to the basic component. Thus, it is even more crucial to ensure that basic Internet security measures are applied. Examples of Internet security measures include installing internal and external firewalls, using security tools to find well-known security problems and holes, and making safe computing practices a condition for employment. Although, SAP provides Internet capabilities, they do not yet provide for the encryption or encoding of TCP/IP packets over the Internet. However, Kerberos security features have recently been released.

People and passwords can become the weakest link in most information systems. Both must be managed effectively to ensure the protection of the R/3 system. Thus, system security features can only be effective when reinforced with policies and procedures that prevent the compromise of security in the R/3 system.

Chapter 28
Keeping Client/Server Projects on Track with Project Management

Ralph L. Kliem

Information systems (IS) developers and end users are always rushing to adopt new computing solutions to gain competitive edge, lower costs, and increase profitability. Such are the forces driving the growth of client/server (C/S) technology. IS developers and end users see C/S technology providing the following benefits:

- Increase end-user autonomy
- Decrease information technology (IT) development cycle time
- Improve business performance
- Improve IT customer satisfaction

These benefits are so enticing that the percentage for C/S spending in an I/S budget keeps growing.

Despite the growth of C/S technology, disenchantment appears to be growing, too. In fact, some companies have reduced their client/server efforts due to migration difficulties. Several reasons for the decline in enthusiasm for C/S technology include:

- Difficulty in people adopting a new paradigm for computing
- Complexity in integrating different technologies from multiple vendors
- Inadequate network management
- Lack of IS professionals skilled in C/S technology
- Upgrade costs

0-8493-9998-X/00/$0.00+$.50

- Poor response times
- Out-of-control network costs
- Weak security
- Unsatisfactory project results

This last reason has shaken the IS industry like an earthquake. Yet, the record is all too clear about the fate of C/S projects. C/S projects cost more than expected, dramatically slide in schedule, and result in a product that often leaves just about everyone dissatisfied.

HOW PROJECT MANAGEMENT CAN HELP C/S PROJECTS

It can help a great deal. Almost three-quarters of C/S and open systems projects are believed to come in late, exceed budget, and fail to meet expectations. The reason? Many systems developers lack project management skills though they possess excellent technical expertise. Some of the factors causing C/S project disappointments and failures include:

- *Unclear or constantly changing requirements.* The inability to "lock-in" on a minimum set of requirements and specifications using prototyping or building models that describe the system to build.
- *Unrealistic scope.* Developing a project that is too comprehensive and would be better developed in releases.
- *Arbitrary schedule dates.* The customer becomes frustrated with the time taken to deliver the initial release and arbitrarily declares a project end-date.
- *Unrealistic expectations.* The customer believes that the new system will be so user-friendly that little or no training is necessary.
- *Unclear responsibilities.* A confusion exists over the responsibility for managing the configuration of software on the client level.

What is Project Management?

To many people, project management is scheduling. Such a notion could not be more false. Project management is more than schedules. It is the knowledge, tools, and techniques for controlling requirements, setting a realistic scope, creating feasible schedules, defining responsibilities, and managing expectations. To accomplish these and other goals, project management uses the following basic processes:

- *Leading.* This is motivating people to perform satisfactorily. It means getting people to commit themselves and to perform in a manner that meets or exceeds expectations.
- *Planning.* This is determining in advance what the project will achieve and when. It entails conducting a realistic road map that people follow to accomplish project goals and objectives. Schedules are a subset of planning.

- *Organizing.* This is arranging resources in a manner that expedites the achievement of goals and objectives. It means using people, for example, efficiently and effectively. It also means, for example, setting up a responsive communications infrastructure.
- *Controlling.* This is determining how well a project progresses according to plans and, if necessary, taking corrective action. It means, for example, collecting and evaluating information regarding cost, schedule, and quality.

The following sections in this chapter examine how these four processes keep C/S projects on track.

LEADING THE WAY TO PROJECT BUY-IN AND SUPPORT

Leading, the first process of project management, can help C/S projects in three ways:

1. Widespread participation
2. Project announcement
3. Statement of work

Widespread Participation

One characteristic of C/S technology is that it affects many people throughout an entire organization. The technology requires end users to have a knowledge of what the product can and cannot do. End users, therefore, cannot help but feel a sense of ownership. Developers need to capitalize on this sense of ownership by encouraging end-user participation throughout the development of C/S systems and applications.

Who Gets to Participate. A problem exists in that difficulty often arises over just who are the participants. Other participants, other than the developers, might include senior executives, strategic planners, program planners, sales and marketing executives, and product managers.

Regardless, project leadership calls for involvement of all parties in the planning and execution of C/S projects. This participation involves forging a partnership with everyone, including remote users, having a stake in a C/S project. The best way to achieve "partnering" is through widespread participation.

Having widespread participation does not mean having a large "core" team to develop the system or application. It does mean that all interested participants have a "say" in the project. This widespread participation offers several advantages, including:

- Building ownership in the results
- Generating effective communications

- Giving everyone an appreciation of the effort to deliver a C/S product
- Establishing accountability for tasks
- Sharing knowledge, tools, and information
- Stopping "turf" battles

Building prototypes, conducting demonstrations, encouraging close collaboration between users and developers, sharing information among developers and users, and setting up cross-functional teams are just some ways to generate widespread participation.

Project Announcement

This is a memo that informs all the proper people that a project now exists. It states the:

- Completion date (e.g., for each release and the entire project)
- Goals and objectives (e.g., for the project)
- Product description (e.g., for clients and servers)
- Project manager and reporting relationship (e.g., steering committee)
- Project name

The project announcement offers several advantages. The most important is that it creates senior management commitment. The presence or lack of executive management support is a major reason why software projects either succeed or do not fare too well.

The project announcement offers another advantage. It gives visibility to the project. In an environment of shrinking or slowly growing IS budgets, the number of C/S projects increase, and the competition over resources can become intense. The right "champion," or senior executive, can increase the opportunity for acquiring sufficient resources.

Statement of Work

The statement of work (SOW) is a written contract between the IS development team and the people receiving the system. The SOW contains these sections:

- Introduction
- Product description
- Constraints
- Schedule
- Budget
- Roles and responsibilities
- References
- Additional considerations
- Signatures

Introduction. The introduction covers the goals and objectives of the C/S project. Goals are broad statements of intent, such as "To build a client/server inventory management system that provides an integrated data base for ordering new parts." Objectives are specific, measurable features, such as "Providing an average response time of no more than three seconds."

Frequently, however, C/S projects start with vague goals and objectives. The goal might be something vague like "Build a distributed database." Objectives may be difficult to measure, like "Build a user-friendly system." Such ambiguity and subjectivity causes "scope grope" — a host of miscommunications and misunderstandings, unrealistic expectations by the user, and oversell by the IS community.

When developing and negotiating the SOW, the principal participants from the IS and user communities must define goals and objectives clearly and concisely. Upon signature of the SOW, all the principal participants understand what the project will achieve.

Production Description. The product description section addresses the major characteristics of the system to build. The advantage of this section is that it addresses issues often overlooked until the project has proceeded too far. Some product description issues addressed include the:

- Application or applications (e.g., document management)
- Architecture (e.g., two or three tier)
- Client applications
- Client operating systems (e.g., UNIX or NT)
- Major features (e.g., graphical user interface [GUI])
- Major functions
- Middleware (e.g., proprietary application programming interfaces)
- Protocols (e.g., TCP/IP)
- Server applications
- Server operating systems (e.g., NT)

Constraints. The constraints section addresses the parameters under which the system must be developed. By identifying constraints early, everyone can obtain realistic expectations. Some constraints discussed include:

- Accelerated schedule
- Lack of certain skills (e.g., C++ programming)
- Level of complexity (e.g., only GUI development vs. multiprotocol networking)
- Limited budget
- Mandatory application development tools (e.g., upper CASE)
- Opportunity for interoperability (e.g., proprietary vs. open systems)
- Organizational receptivity to change
- Standards to follow (e.g., CORBA)

Schedule. The schedule section describes the major milestones and when to achieve them. It emphasizes agreement as to the major activities that must occur and when. It contains, at a minimum, schedule dates for:

- Key reviews and approvals
- Major phases of the project (e.g., specifications, implementation)
- Start and stop dates for the entire project

Budget. The budget section describes the expected cost for the project. This cost represents a high-level approximation. The figure is a composite for items like labor, computing time, application development tools, training, network usage, and support costs.

Roles and Responsibilities. The roles and responsibilities section is significant because it addresses accountability. Roles and responsibilities often become muddied, especially between IS and the user communities during C/S development. In this section, roles and responsibilities for these categories of topics include feasibility, definition, development, installation, and sustaining.

Feasibility includes determining whether to build or buy the C/S components. It also includes assessing the business (e.g., organizational infrastructure) and operational (e.g., network performance) impacts of the C/S system. Definition includes defining the exact performance requirements (e.g., data volume and response time) of the new system; the roles and functions of the client and server; the look and feel of the GUI; the logical and physical design of data and applications; and middleware services and functions. Development includes the development tools to use, the application programs and databases to build, and integration of all components. Installation includes testing individual components and their integration (e.g., the client with the server). It also includes implementation handling issues (e.g., management and scheduling of "cutover"). Sustaining includes disaster recovery (e.g., backup and recovery), network management (e.g., capacity planning), security, and upgrade control.

References. This section cites what the development team and the eventual product must comply with. Company policies, procedures, and methodologies and industry standards are typically listed. Standards listed might be for clients, servers, application development tools, vendor interaction, protocols, security, data base management systems, network management, and user interfaces.

Additional Considerations. The additional considerations section contains information not included in the aforementioned sections that might be of significance to all key participants. Some possible topics include:

- Design considerations for applications and data
- Development methodology
- Development tools
- Personnel issues
- Physical and logical architectural concerns
- Project organizational structure
- Risks
- Scalability and interoperability issues

Signatures. The signatures section, although small, is perhaps the most important because it reflects the key participants (e.g., project manager and end-user management) agreement to a baseline of what and how the product is delivered. From that point onward, the SOW serves as a basis for future decision-making by all participants.

PLANNING TO KEEP BUDGETS, SCHEDULES, AND RESOURCES ON TRACK

Planning, the second process of project management, can help C/S projects in four ways:

- Work breakdown structure
- Time estimates
- Schedules
- Resource allocation

Work Breakdown Structure

Also known as the WBS, the work breakdown structure provides a top-down explosion of all the products and its elements and the tasks and sub-tasks to build them. The WBS offers two advantages: it provides the basis for estimating, scheduling, and resource allocation, and offers a useful checklist for project participants.

For a typical C/S project, a tendency exists to build the application and ignore other significant issues. While developing a WBS, everyone is forced to consider all issues prior to "cutting code." Some significant topics to address in the WBS include the tasks and overall responsibility for security, documentation, configuration, training, administration, and construction.

Security includes defining, controlling, monitoring, and reporting access (e.g., from a laptop) to the new C/S system. Documentation includes developing and maintaining user and technical documentation (e.g., online manuals and architecture diagrams) during and after development. Configuration includes baseline control and reporting of the components (e.g., hardware and software) that comprise the client and server. Training includes developing, conducting, and updating training for users and technical support people. Administration includes maintaining and updating application software, data, and hardware at the client and server levels. It should also include dealing with network management (e.g., handling reliance and performance issues). Construction includes designing and building applications, software, and databases; testing at the client and server levels for component reliability and systems integration; and implementing the new system.

Time Estimates

The WBS is the basis for estimating the time required to complete each task and, consequently, the entire project. Both, in turn, are the basis for building reliable schedules.

On C/S projects, preference is for a speedier life cycle rather under the traditional "waterfall" life cycle for development. Two common ways to achieve a speedier life cycle is by employing reuse and rapid application development (RAD) techniques. While such techniques do accelerate the life cycle, they also tend to turn IS professionals into extreme optimists. The result is often an unrealistic schedule.

The key to estimating is balance. Estimates, by their very nature, cannot be totally accurate. Yet, some estimates are more reliable than others. Reliable estimates account for extreme and normal estimates; such reliability is attained by accounting for the most optimistic, most likely, and most pessimistic times available to perform tasks. By accounting for all three, developers and other participants can produce estimates that generate realistic expectations of what is possible.

C/S projects, however, are unique in comparison with traditional development projects. Some unique factors to consider when estimating include:

- Availability and necessary approvals of end users
- Integration of protocols, products, operating systems, and data
- Learning curve of developers and end users
- Migration from mainframe to client/server technology
- Skill deficiencies
- Need for accelerated development
- Greater likelihood of dealing with unprecedented technical complexities
- Ability to define requirements and be flexible in a changing business environment

Schedules

Schedules reflect the sequence of tasks identified in the WBS and their respective start and stop dates; time estimates are the other input to schedules. Schedules offer several benefits, including:

- Providing start and stop dates for each task and the entire project
- Giving a "road map" that everyone can relate to and follow
- Identifying a critical path reflecting the most important activities to complete
- Provide structure, coordination, and discipline throughout the C/S life cycle

C/S Schedules are Unique. For C/S projects, perhaps the last benefit is the most important. C/S projects are highly specialized and involve considerable employee autonomy. Unless managed carefully, they can easily go awry. Having everyone follow a schedule, however, lessens the opportunity for such situations to occur.

Schedules sometimes counter the benefits (e.g., flexibility, speed, and user involvement) of pursuing C/S development. That is because schedules often contain too many approvals, lengthy duration for tasks, and lack comprehensiveness. The schedules become anachronistic, even counterproductive to the development effort.

Meaningful schedules on C/S projects, therefore, must:

- Be integrated with other C/S projects providing input to the project
- Contain a minimal number of approvals
- Contain short-term milestones
- Have "buy-in" from the people performing their respective tasks
- Reflect use of the latest development techniques (e.g., RAD)

Resource Allocation

With a "workable" draft of the schedule, allocating resources can begin. Adjustments to the schedule can occur based upon the availability or expertise of the resources. Resources can be anything, such as equipment, people, and supplies.

Resource allocation is very difficult on C/S projects. People with certain expertise (e.g., GUI-building; C++ and SmallTalk programming; and protocol coding) are hard to find and, more often than not, other projects compete for or borrow them. In addition, the latest hardware (e.g., UNIX workstations, notebooks) and software (e.g., Visual Basic) tools may not be available.

Resource allocation is essential to successfully execute C/S projects. Three key guidelines for allocating resources are:

- Give preference to critical activities.
- Allocate resources to the most-behind schedule tasks.
- For noncritical activities, give preference to the most difficult or most uncertain tasks.

ORGANIZING FOR ACCOUNTABILITY AND CLEAR COMMUNICATIONS

Organizing, the third process of project management, can help C/S projects in eight ways:

1. Responsibility matrix
2. Organization chart
3. Project history files
4. Project procedures
5. Project manual
6. Project wall
7. Meetings
8. Tools

Responsibility Matrix

After completing resource allocation, the next action is to develop a responsibility matrix. The matrix tells who is accountable for each task. It should include not only application programmers, network programmers, business analysts, and data base analysts, but also vendors, consultants, and end users.

The matrix enables project managers to ask questions like: Are the right people assigned to their respective tasks? Should any last-minute reassignments be made? Has anyone been left out? Are the people assigned jointly to a task compatible?

Organization Chart

The organization chart shows the reporting structure and team relationships among all participants. It serves as a communications and coordination tool. An organization chart for C/S projects should not only show "hard-line" relationships, such as application programmers reporting to a lead, but "dotted-line" relationships, too, such as with vendors, end users, and remote users. The key is to reflect the true cross-functional relationships that exist among all participants.

Project History Files

These files serve as a repository of all the key project management documentation created. Documentation stored in the files includes versions of the schedule and WBS. The advantages of having these files are the ability to produce an audit trail and to familiarize new participants with the project.

Project Procedures

These documents provide instructions on performing the administrative tasks of the project. Topics include change control, schedule performance reviews, and interaction with vendors. Project procedures should be clear, concise, and contain only necessary details.

Project Manual

This book is often in the form of a three-ring binder. It contains useful reference material, such as phone listings; most current WBS and schedule; standards for producing "deliverables" and tools to use throughout the life cycle of the project; a glossary of terms; and procedures. Each participant should receive a copy.

Project Wall

This wall simply contains many important items for everyone on the project to see. It can include a schedule, a high-level work breakdown structure, responsibility matrices, organization charts, system architecture displays, and metrics on systems performance. The benefits of having the wall are providing visibility for the project and facilitating communications among the participants.

Meetings

Basically, three types of meetings work well on a C/S project: checkpoint review, status review, and staff meetings. Checkpoint review meetings are held at the conclusion of a phase (e.g., completing a time box) or major milestone with the expressed purpose of determining whether to proceed. Status review meetings are held to collect information on project performance in regard to cost, quality, and schedule. Staff meetings are held regularly to exchange information.

A key caveat for C/S projects is to ensure that specialization does not lead to miscommunication among all participants. For that reason, meetings should occur frequently and be a vehicle for consistent input and feedback.

Tools

Basically, two types of tools are used on C/S projects: development and project management. Object-oriented, transaction monitoring, computer-aided software engineering (CASE), and GUI-builders tools are just some examples of development tools used. Project management software on the server or client is a tool for managing the project. Regardless of the type, a tool should:

- Accelerate the life cycle
- Build maintainable products
- Create a variety of architectures
- Have import/export capabilities
- Have interoperability

- Have scalability
- Be supported by a reliable, stable vendor
- Meet agreed-upon standards (e.g., OLE, ODBC, TCP/IP)
- Not "lock" the development team into a specific methodology
- Require a minimal learning curve

CONTROLLING VARIANCE AND CHANGE

Controlling, the fourth process of project management, can help C/S projects in two ways:

- Detecting variances
- Managing change

Detecting Variances

A key determinant of managing projects is to track performance according to a baseline and take corrective action. A baseline is usually set against product, schedule, and cost. On C/S projects, the scope can easily expand until finally it becomes unmanageable. A modification here and a slight addition there and suddenly the C/S system is different from what everyone had expected. Such "scope grope" leads to cost overruns, schedule slides, and a complex, difficult-to-maintain product.

Some key considerations for detecting variances on a C/S project are:

- Establish well-defined milestones in the schedule.
- Obtain frequent feedback, hearing not only what one wants to hear, but also needs what one to hear.
- Set a baseline for cost, schedule, and product.
- Set up a mechanism for collecting, analyzing, and assessing status on cost, schedule, and product.
- Start measuring against baselines as early as possible.

Managing Change

One key benefit of C/S development is flexibility, meaning the ability to adapt to changing business needs and new technological developments. While powerful, the benefit can easily allow a project to go haywire, making change management akin to training a Tasmanian devil to dance gracefully. Lose control and the project spins out of control.

Suffice it to say, therefore, it behooves project managers to establish and follow an infrastructure to manage change. This infrastructure should apply to changes in schedule, cost, and product. Some key considerations for managing changes on a C/S project are:

- Conduct frequent, short meetings (e.g., weekly status review).
- Use the baseline established for schedule, cost, and product.

- Explode the product into manageable components for tracking and monitoring.
- Obtain input from all the participants affected by a change.
- Recognize that a technical change may affect other areas (e.g., organizational, business processes) and vice versa.
- Track prototyping frequently, noticing who is participating, how well it meets requirements, and when it must stop.
- Understand that prototyping does not replace testing.

PROJECT MANAGEMENT SOLUTIONS

Despite its reputation for being nothing more than a schedule, project management is based on four processes that can keep C/S projects on track.

- *Leading.* Leadership techniques can be used to manage user expectations so that the final C/S system does not disappoint. They also manage user expectations by creating agreement between IS and the user community about the goal of the C/S project. Finally, the leading process can help ensure overall project success by garnering upper management support.
- *Planning.* Techniques based on the planning process help manage the three fundamental resources required by a systems development project: budget, time, and resources. Estimating time and developing schedules for C/S projects are unique from other systems development projects, but they both rely on the fundamental activity of planning.
- *Organizing.* The organizing process improves communication among every participant in the project and lets systems development managers better plan and reallocate resources. CASE tools and GUI-builders can help automate the organizing process to further ensure success.
- *Controlling.* The controlling process helps systems development managers to manage changes in the project. Change can be either a variance in schedule or resource allocation or redefinition of the project scope. Techniques based on the controlling process can help ensure that a C/S project does not run over budget or schedule, nor become bogged down by new end-user requirements.

By using these basic project management processes, systems development managers can keep client/server projects on track and reap the benefits of this popular computing solution.

Chapter 29
Project Management Solutions for The Year 2000 Crisis

Ralph L. Kliem

INTRODUCTION

Handling the Year 2000 problem has all the elements of a project. It looks like a project. It smells like a project. It feels like a project. It tastes like a project. So the only conclusion is that the Year 2000 problem must be a project. That makes it a good candidate for applying the six basic processes of project management. Then, why do most IS shops treat it like any other maintenance activity?

Four Elements of a Project

Maintenance activities (also known as house-cleaning operations), of course, eliminate problems with or improve an existing system. Often, these activities do not involve a large effort and their impact is restricted to a few subsystems or modules of a much greater system. Typically, they do not involve the release of a complete configuration; the goal is to keep the existing system in working order and implement any changes within a reasonable period of time. Maintenance to an existing system, if well documented and controlled, should not be costly; its schedule for the revision should not be tight; the level of quality is not rigorous; and the expertise required does not necessitate having it come from the best and the brightest.

The Year 2000 problem is not a maintenance activity. It is a full-fledged project in itself and becomes even more of one as the number of interrelationships among components and the size of the overall system increases.

To be considered a project, an issue or problem must involve four key elements:

1. Cost
2. Schedule

0-8493-9998-X/00/$0.00+$.50
© 2000 by CRC Press LLC

3. Quality
4. People

The Year 2000 problem involves all four of these elements.

Cost. Addressing the Year 2000 problem requires large sums of money, regardless of how it is calculated. No one knows for sure the degree of impact, but estimates exist. The Gartner Group estimates a worldwide cost from $300 to $600 billion worldwide. Other experts say it will cost the United States $75 billion alone, costing a typical large company $5 to $40 million, maybe even $50 to $100 million. Some experts have estimates based on lines of code (LOC); each LOC will cost from $0.50 to $1.50. The reality is that no one really knows the exact cost. What they do know, however, is that it will cost.

Schedule. Addressing the Year 2000 problem has a defined end-date for completion. At 12:00:01 a.m. on January 1, 2000, everyone on this planet will enter a new century. Nothing can stop that deadline from approaching.

Yet, few people and organizations feel compelled to do anything. Procrastination has turned many people and organizations into IS couch potatoes regarding the issue. Some experts, like Peter de Jager, estimate that less than 35 percent of North American businesses have started working on the Year 2000 problem. Other experts take a more global perspective, saying that less than 20 percent of the firms in the world have done something.

Quality. The Year 2000 problem is not just a cost or time issue; it is a quality issue, too, that affects small, medium, and large information systems. As the world moves increasingly toward interconnected and distributed systems, quality becomes a greater concern.

The reasons are quite clear. Most systems handle dates in the MM/DD/YY format with the year hard-coded. When performing subtractions and comparisons, for instance, in the year 2000 calculations dealing with time spans, such as interest and actual calculations, can result in data manipulation problems, data loss, and system shutdowns. With the year 2000 being a leap year, the magnitude of the problem increases by affecting banks, insurance companies, and government institutions.

Many people believe that the Year 2000 problem is solely a minicomputer or mainframe issue, especially ones running COBOL-based and other third-generation applications. Wrong. Even the tiny microcomputer must face the Year 2000 problem. After all, time waits for no one or anything. Users of pre-Pentium microcomputers must face, for example, the year 2000 for applications and data.

The Year 2000 problem cannot, however, be divided conveniently into three distinct categories of problems (microcomputer, minicomputer, and mainframe) but as a big interrelated one. That is because they are typically integrated thanks to the rise of distributed computing and client/server (C/S) technology.

An integrated system can "hiccup" over the Year 2000 problem. C/S applications and mainframe databases, for example, can face problems when the former uses two-digit fields for dates and the latter uses four-digits. If one system recognizes the year 2000 as a leap year and the other one does not, the latter will reject the transaction.

People. The Year 2000 issue deals with people, especially those fixing the problem. With a rising demand for systems professionals with expertise in client/server and Internet technologies, a concomitant fall has occurred for people having knowledge of "legacy" technologies (e.g., COBOL and Assembler). Many reasons have contributed to this circumstance (e.g., the glamour of the new technologies, the higher levels of pay, career enhancement, etc.). Somehow, the people skilled in the new technology must return to address the Year 2000 problem, whether to develop a replacement system or modify an existing one. Coupled with the need and estimated hourly cost of $55 to $65 per hour for legacy expertise, the importance of managing these people will increase dramatically.

The people factor, of course, goes beyond skills expertise. It is a motivational issue, too. As noted earlier, a sense of denial exists about the foreboding impact that the Year 2000 forewarns. Coupled with denial is procrastination due to laziness, overconfidence, or belief that the Year 2000 issue is a maintenance concern. Like all maintenance issues, the backlog increases along with the accompanying costs. All this becomes important because eventually all companies must face the year 2000 and will have to pay for denial and procrastination at a higher cost and faster pace. Short of destruction of the universe, the Year 2000 issue, will turn into a perennial maintenance issue even years beyond that red-letter date, if not addressed early.

PROJECT MANAGEMENT FOR THE YEAR 2000

The Year 2000 issue then has all the makings of a project — time, cost, quality, and people — making it an excellent candidate to apply the six basic processes of project management:

1. *Leading.* Leading entails nurturing an environment that encourages people to perform their best in a manner that achieves goals and objectives.
2. *Defining.* Defining entails answering the who, what, when, where, why, and how of a project so that subsequent activities occur cost effectively.
3. *Planning.* Planning involves determining what must be done and what is required to achieve those goals and objectives.

4. *Organizing*. Organizing involves establishing a cost-effective infrastructure.
5. *Controlling*. Controlling involves ensuring the cost-effective achievement of project goals and objectives and taking appropriate action, when necessary.
6. *Closure*. Closure entails concluding a project cost effectively to ensure a smooth transition from development to implementation

How Project Management Benefits Year 2000 Efforts. These six processes offer the five following advantages:

1. They help to determine the magnitude of the effort as well as its business and technical impacts.
2. They help to identify priorities as well as assess and manage risks.
3. They help to identify the most appropriate route to pursue (e.g., reengineer or modify the application or system).
4. They help in selecting the appropriate technical and business tools and techniques.
5. They help to determine the cost of addressing the Year 2000 problem.

The following sections of this chapter further examine these processes and their benefits.

LEADING A YEAR 2000 TEAM

The importance of this process is often overlooked on projects. Yet, it is the only process that occurs concurrently with all the other processes. Leading involves creating an environment that encourages the best in people and in a way that meets project goals and objectives. It means providing a vision for the project; communicating; keeping motivation levels high; maintaining focus on the vision; being supportive; and encouraging team building.

Creating such an environment is not easy for a Year 2000 project. The Year 2000 problem has the stigma of being mainly a maintenance activity. Many managers procrastinate or operate in denial. Many developers feel the subject is not as glamorous as working on client/server and Internet projects. A tendency also exists to treat Year 2000 projects as entities unto themselves, as if they are something out of the mainstream for IS. Consequently, the "big picture" quickly fades. It is important, therefore, that the project manager keeps everyone's focus at an enterprisewide level. The best way to accomplish that is by ensuring that cross-functional representation exists on the team and at meetings.

DEFINING A YEAR 2000 PROJECT

When defining a Year 2000 project, project managers must consider several factors to determine final results. The statement of work (SOW) is the tool to do that.

Exhibit 29.1. Statement of Work Elements and Examples

Element	Examples
Introduction	General background information like the age of the relevant applications, their owners and users, their level of complexity, and maintenance history
Goals and objectives	The order of importance for the relevant applications and the desired data error rate for each one
Scope	Whether to reengineer or modify an existing application or integrate it with a commercial off-the-shelf package
Assumptions	The type and level of support from the vendors, especially if revisions are necessary to their software
Stakeholders	Senior managers, both in the IS and user arenas, responsible for the success of the project and the major tasks that they must perform
Resources	The required type and level of specific programming expertise, such as COBOL, VM, or client/server architecture
Schedule	The completion of important phases of the project, such as conducting an impact analysis or testing
Budget	The maximum direct (e.g., labor) and overhead (e.g., facilities) costs set for the project
Amendments	Changes to any of the above elements (e.g., goals and objectives)
Signatures	By the project manager, chief information officer, and system owner

Statement of Work

The SOW is an agreement between the developers and clients on just what the Year 2000 project will achieve, both from business and technical perspectives. Exhibit 29.1 shows its elements.

SOW Benefits. The importance of developing an SOW is readily apparent. It requires some forethought about the size as well as business and technical impacts. It encourages assessing and managing risks before it is too late and addressing them later becomes costlier. It also encourages advance thinking about the most appropriate approach to maximize goals and objectives attainment and minimize lost time and effort. It forces thinking about the business and technical tools, techniques, and processes to employ before taking significant action. Finally, it "irons out" the business issues before the technical activities happen uncontrolled, making it costlier and more difficult to backup and re-group later on down the life cycle.

PLANNING A YEAR 2000 PROJECT

With a complete SOW, a solid baseline exists to develop plans. These plans define in greater detail the tasks to perform and their sequence of execution. It consists of these six elements:

1. Work breakdown structure
2. Time estimates
3. Schedules
4. Resource allocation
5. Cost calculation
6. Risk management

Although these elements can exist simultaneously, they are easier to understand when discussed separately.

Work Breakdown Structure

Known also as the WBS, it is a top-down, hierarchical listing of tasks that is organized according to "deliverables" or "phases," or both.

For a Year 2000 project, it might be best to structure the WBS according to these major phases:

- Assessment
- Analysis
- Modification
- Conversion and migration
- Validation and testing
- Implementation

Assessment. The assessment phase involves acquiring a solid understanding of the existing environment and the effect Year 2000 changes will have on it. The two basic deliverables from the assessment phase are the description of the current environment and an impact analysis.

The description of the current environment includes tasks like:

- Conduct inventory at the PC, minicomputer, and mainframe levels.
- Identify source code.
- Identify run books and copy books.
- Identify databases.
- Identify reports.
- Identify screens.
- Determine existing capacity needs.

The impact analysis includes:

- Identify the most important applications affected.
- Identify which applications to reengineer or replace.
- Assess the cost and size of the changes.
- Determine the business and technical risks and their priorities.
- Evaluate the operational processes most affected.

Analysis. The analysis phase entails expanding on the details addressed in the impact study. The major deliverable is a requirements and specifications document that describes exactly what is affected and what must be done. The document includes:

- Locate date occurrences in specific source code modules.
- Determine which screen fields to change in an application.
- Determine which data files to modify.
- Identify the impact to job scheduling and report distribution procedures.
- Identify the impact to vendor products, such as storage management systems.
- Identify which source code programs and applications are and are not changeable.
- Identify which reports to modify.
- Determine which documents to update.
- Identify security issues.
- Determine tools to use.
- Coordinate with vendors.

Modification. The modification phase involves making the necessary changes. The major deliverables are the changes to the items identified in the analysis phase, which include:

- Modify source code programs.
- Update run books and copy books.
- Revise date field in screens.
- Modify data files.
- Update the outlay of reports.
- Modify source code to enable interfaces among system components.
- Modify system logic.
- Establish configuration management and change control.

Conversion and Testing for the Year 2000. The conversion and testing phases are critical. According to The Gartner Group, it may take up half the effort and cost of handling the Year 2000 problem. The major deliverables are conversion and testing. This includes:

- Convert old source code to the new or modified source code.
- Convert data into the new format for processing.
- Upgrade hardware and software.

Testing involves performing tasks like:

- Devising a testing strategy (e.g., regression and aging testing).
- Develop a test plan (e.g., test scripts and performance criteria).
- Create test data sets.
- Identify verification and validation criteria to use.
- Conduct unit testing (e.g., conversion of data and code execution).
- Conduct system testing (e.g., ensuring no corruption of data streams).

Implementation. The implementation phase involves moving the new or modified programs and data into production. The major deliverable is an implementation plan which includes:

- Assign applications and databases that go into production first, giving preference to mission-critical ones.
- Determine the best approach to re-deploy the new applications and databases (e.g., parallel implementation).
- Conduct training for the user community.

Work Breakdown Structure Components. Often the work breakdown structure is displayed graphically in a hierarchical manner (see Exhibit 29.2). The hierarchy reflects a top-down organization, from general (i.e., product or subproduct) to specific (i.e., tasks to build the product or sub-product).

Time Estimates

After tasks have been identified, the next step is to estimate the time to complete them. Estimating time requires looking at several variables (e.g., resource availability, expertise, and complexity) and using that information to calculate the total time, usually in hours and then converted to flow time, to complete it. The three-point estimating technique is the best approach to determine the amount of time to complete a task and it includes

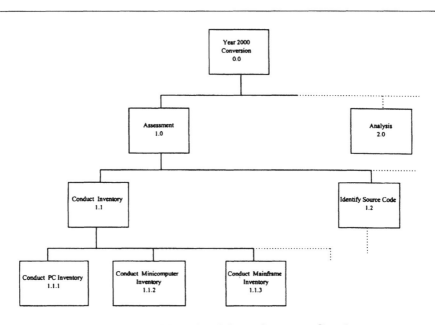

Exhibit 29.2. Work Breakdown Structure Graph

these three variables: most optimistic, most likely, and most pessimistic. The most optimistic is the ideal time it would take if everything was perfect. The most likely time is the time that it should usually take under "normal" conditions. The most pessimistic time is the amount of time it would take under the worst conditions. The figures are then calculated to determine an expected time to complete a task. The calculated time is converted into 8-hour units or whatever units are desired.

Estimating time for tasks on Year 2000 projects should be easier than under unprecedented development projects. The reason is that an understanding of the current systems to modify should exist (if well-documented and under configuration management). Other specific factors to consider when estimating are business and technical constraints (e.g., proximity to the year 2000 and complexity of legacy code, respectively), as well as the availability of expertise in legacy technology.

Risk Assessment

One of the first things prior to developing a schedule is to determine the major priorities of the project. Risk assessment enables doing that by identifying what is and is not important. It involves identifying the components of the system and its risks, and ranking both accordingly. Such information presents a better idea of the importance of tasks vis-à-vis one another. Management can then decide whether to modify, reengineer, or replace specific systems. Within applications themselves, risk assessment is just as important for identifying which data, programs, reports, documentation, and interfaces are critical, vis-à-vis one another.

Schedules

With the tasks identified, the hours and durations developed, and the priorities established, the next step is tying the tasks together into a logical framework to follow. This framework is a network diagram that shows the dependencies between tasks (see Exhibit 29.3). It also tells which tasks have float, or the time to slide, before impacting significant dates. Tasks having little or no float represent tasks on the critical path; such tasks cannot slide because it will impact the project end date. As time approaches the year 2000, the schedule must be compressed, thereby increasing the likelihood of sliding tasks and impacting the project end-date.

Resource Allocation

After developing a "straw horse" schedule, resource allocation is the next step. During this step, resources are assigned to balance the need for a realistic schedule with resource availability. Project managers can generate histograms to determine which resources will be overused and which ones will not be fully utilized. Ideally, project managers want a smooth histogram.

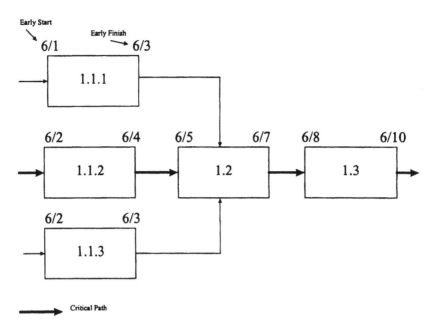

Exhibit 29.3. Schedule Framework as a Network Diagram

On a Year 2000 project, resource allocation involves sharing people on tasks requiring legacy system expertise, deciding the tools (e.g., object-oriented COBOL) to use on specific tasks, and determining the tasks to outsource, if necessary. To generate a sense of responsibility and immediacy to the Year 2000 topic, programmers and other participants should be assigned to tasks in a way that generates a sense of responsibility for replacing or updating full applications or categories of related applications (see Exhibit 29.4).

Exhibit 29.4. Task Table

Person	Lopez	Jones	Chen	Ackers
Tasks				
Conduct inventory at mainframe level	Lead	X		X
Conduct inventory at PC level	X	Lead		
Conduct inventory at minicomputer level	X		Lead	
Identify source code	Lead			X
Identify data bases	Lead		X	

Calculation

With a leveled histogram, project managers can determine project costs. The key question is: does the schedule allow accomplishing milestone dates within the available budget? If the answer is yes, no revision to the schedule or assignments are necessary. If the answer is no, changes to the schedule or resource assignments must occur. These changes may involve reassigning people, changing schedule logic, or streamlining processes.

The average cost of COBOL programmers is from $55 to $65 per hour, according to some experts. As the year 2000 approaches, this cost will likely increase. It is also likely that as tools become available (e.g., object-oriented COBOL), their tool costs will increase. It is imperative, therefore, that project managers strive to maximize productivity and minimize waste, particularly as the year 2000 gets closer.

ORGANIZING

Although planning is an essential process and a major part of project management, it is not the only process. Organizing, too, is important. It involves establishing an infrastructure to maximize efficiency and effectiveness. Three principal components entail:

- Team structure
- Documentation
- Meetings

Team Structure. Team structure involves identifying a "pecking order" that clarifies roles, responsibilities, and reporting relationships. Developing and publishing organization charts and responsibility matrices are common ways to establish and build a team structure. Because the year 2000 problem affects more than stand-alone systems, it is important that the team structure is cross-functional. This ensures that all affected parties can provide input and, consequently, obtain a sense of ownership.

Documentation. Documentation covers both technical and business materials. Some common documentation includes architecture diagrams, procedures, user manuals, source code listings, workflows, and memorandums. Some items may go into a project library, project history files, or project manual, or perhaps all three; especially applicable to year 2000 projects are process models and architecture diagrams for affected programs and databases.

Meetings. Meetings include setting up three basic types: status review, checkpoint review, and staff. Status review meetings are regularly held to collect information on tasks and major deliverables. Checkpoint review meetings are held at the completion of a major deliverable or upon reaching a milestone date in the schedule. Its objectives are to determine any lessons learned and whether to proceed. Status review meetings are held to regularly share information and experiences. Attendance at the meeting should be highly cross-functional to ensure adequate participation and coverage of the main issues. User involvement is absolutely essential to gain their acceptance of modifications.

CONTROLLING A YEAR 2000 PROJECT

Controlling involves ensuring the project proceeds cost-effectively according to plans. It entails:

- Status collection and assessment
- Change control
- Corrective action

Status Collection and Assessment. On Year 2000 projects, status collection and assessment requires looking at business and technical aspects. Regarding business aspects, for example, it requires collecting and assessing data on schedule performance. Regarding technical issues, for example, it requires collecting and assessing data about the quality of changes to data bases and applications.

Change Control. Change control involves capturing, analyzing, and evaluating changes to technical and schedule baselines. It is not only important for the schedule. Changing and recording modifications to data files and date fields in applications also require some change control or configuration management whether in staging or production.

Corrective Action. Corrective action entails taking necessary action to ensure that project goals and objectives are accomplished according to business and technical plans; if not, replanning should occur. For Year 2000 projects, corrective action is especially important when verification and validation of changes to databases and applications have negative results.

CLOSURE

Closure encompasses compiling data, converting data into information, and providing a smooth transition from product development to implementation. The idea behind closure is to develop lessons learned and to ensure that nothing is overlooked as the project concludes. Specific closure activities include identifying what did and did not go well; ensuring people and other resources were managed released efficiently; and conducting reviews to ensure that what was stated in the SOW was satisfied.

It is especially important for Year 2000 projects to capture lessons learned, particularly for the first application. Subsequent Year 2000 projects can avoid repeating mistakes. Lessons learned should address business (e.g., time availability for project completion) and technical (e.g., testing) issues. Reviews of Year 2000 projects can prove invaluable for capturing lessons learned and identifying oversights and other shortcomings that occurred, particularly to applications, source code, data bases, screens, and reports. Releasing maintenance programmers can also prove challenging because as the tasks conclude, inactivity begins, thereby losing precious time to work on another Year 2000 project.

CONCLUSION

Historically, the end of a century has often been portrayed as something negative, such as the end of the world is coming. It seems that the IS world is looking upon the Year 2000 as something even worse than that—a systems maintenance task. As long as that misconception holds, it could be the end of the world for a systems development manager's job. The year 2000 is a systems project and it should be managed as a project by using the following six basic processes:

1. Leading
2. Defining
3. Planning
4. Organizing
5. Controlling
6. Closure

By applying these six processes to the year 2000, systems development managers will be better able to tackle this massive project because they benefit it in the following ways:

- They help to determine the magnitude of the effort as well as its business and technical impacts.
- They help to identify priorities as well as assess and manage risks.
- They help to identify the most appropriate route to pursue (e.g., re-engineer or modify the application or system).
- They help in selecting the appropriate technical and business tools and techniques.
- They help to determine the cost of addressing the Year 2000 problem.

Chapter 30

Disaster Recovery Planning Tools and Management Options

Jon William Toigo

An effective disaster recovery plan can be developed either by a disaster recovery consultant or by in-house personnel. Consultants can offer considerable expertise and experience and, in some cases, help overcome internal obstacles to the plan's development. The cost of consultant-developed plans, however, is more than most small and medium-sized organizations can afford. In addition, this makes in-house disaster recovery planning an interesting option. There is an increasing body of literature to help novices understand and implement disaster recovery planning. In addition, several software packages have been developed to aid in plan development and maintenance. This chapter examines the advantages and disadvantages of both approaches to disaster recovery planning.

THE CONSULTANT OPTION

Several factors support a decision to hire a consultant. Experienced consultants bring a set of proven tools to the project, which may mean the quick development of an effective plan. A practiced consultant understands the effective construction of a disaster recovery plan, asks the right questions, and typically knows who's who in the disaster recovery products and services industry. Consultants who work in a specific industry often tailor a methodology for disaster recovery planning to that industry, which reduces the amount of time needed to learn new skills and helps speed development. Further, consultants bring a fresh perspective to the process, spotting important recovery requirements that may be overlooked by employees.

Consultants are however, expensive. Ironically, this may be an advantage in some cases. Disaster recovery planning requires the interaction of users and information systems personnel. In many large IS operations, fractious functions (e.g., programming and systems operations) must cooperate. Frequently, the only way to have all parties work together efficiently is to impress upon them the considerable cost of the consultant. Similarly, because senior management has made an investment in the consultant's plan, it may be less inclined to withdraw the support needed to implement the plan.

However, many myths surround consultant-driven plans. Many managers believe that because consultant plans are written by experts, they are more effective than those developed in-house. With the disaster recovery information and tools available to all contingency planners, however, even novice planners can develop an efficacious plan.

Another fiction is that only consultant plans are executed successfully. Although this used to be the rule, in the past few years there have been numerous instances of successful recoveries in organizations that developed their plans in-house. Along those same lines, many managers believe that auditors will accept only consultant plans; in fact, as long as the plan has been fully tested and demonstrated to be effective, auditors will accept it.

There is a common but false belief that employees of an organization using consultants do not need to be involved in developing the recovery plan. At a minimum, any organization should have at least one employee work with the consultant to develop the plan. If the consultant works entirely alone, the plan will not work because staff members will not understand their part in it.

Selecting the Right Consultant

To guard against making a contract with the wrong consultant, the data center manager should take five initial steps. They are discussed in the following paragraphs.

Obtaining Qualifications. It is important to request in advance the name and background of the consultant who will provide disaster recovery services. Which organizations has the consultant served? Were these clients satisfied with the job? An inexperienced consultant, even one that is in contact with more experienced professionals, should be avoided. The ideal consultant possesses a solid grasp of information systems, understands the specific requirements of the client's business, and has developed satisfactory disaster recovery plans for at least two other organizations.

Requesting a Plan Proposal. The consultant should submit a proposal that details the phases, tasks, and milestones of the planning project. Most consultants work from generic methodologies that they can adapt to specific client requirements. With the increasing availability of commercial products for planning and managing contingency planning and disaster recovery projects, consultants can no longer portray their work as mysterious or otherwise beyond the reach of nonpractitioners.

Validating Proposed Time and Cost Estimates. A consultant cannot develop meaningful time and cost estimates unless consulting services are packaged as a fixed-price contract. The data center manager should be particularly wary if the consultant quotes exact costs or completion times without having assessed the organization's requirements.

Estimates provided by the consultant can be of value to the data center manager in several ways. For example, valid time and cost estimates are useful benchmarks for comparing the proposals of various consultants, especially if each estimate is made on the basis of similar projects for comparable businesses. To ensure that the data presented in each proposal is as accurate as possible, the manager should verify that all predictable costs, including the consultant's travel and lodging, are reflected in the estimated cost.

Negotiating Cost. Initially, consultants often market their premium service, offering the less expensive shared-responsibility approaches only if they sense they may be pricing themselves out of a contract. Faced with the prospect of losing business, a consultant can be notably creative in finding cost-saving measures. In one case, the cost of the plan development was cut by putting corporate word processing at the consultant's disposal to take care of all documentation and by designating one of the staff members to work full time with the consultant, replacing the assistant called for. Other managers have purchased a consultant's microcomputer-based disaster recovery planning tool, contracting with the consultant only for the initial analysis and data collection. The result: substantial cost reductions.

Assessing the Consultant's Relationships with Vendors. Many consulting firms have formal and informal relationships with vendors of disaster recovery products and services. In fact, some consultants argue that it is partly their extensive knowledge of and contacts within the industry that qualify them for the rates they command. These relationships can, in some cases, benefit the client organization. The client may thereby qualify for a discount on a fire protection system, off-site storage, or the use of a hot site.

The potential for misuse of these relationships is also present. An unethical consultant may be willing to forego the objective analysis of client requirements and recommend a product or service for which the consultant receives compensation. Therefore, it is important to know with whom the consultant has marketing agreements and how these agreements may translate into cost advantages. Most vendors will openly disclose special arrangements, particularly when they profit a potential client and, in the process, improve the marketability of their service.

THE IN-HOUSE OPTION

For many organizations, the use of consulting services is a luxury, a cost over and above the already expensive disaster recovery planning project that they must undertake to satisfy legal and audit requirements. Others take the view that any reasonably intelligent employee, equipped with management support and the technical details of an organization's system and network operations, can develop a competent disaster recovery capability.

The problems faced by organizations that elect to develop a contingency plan using in-house personnel are fourfold. First, many novice planners lack fundamental knowledge about the scope of disaster recovery planning. This problem is reflected by the inordinate amount of time spent by the novice planner who creates disaster scenarios and strategies for coping with them, or by the lengthy, theoretical dissertations on disaster recovery found in many internally developed plans.

The second problem confronting many do-it-yourself planners involves procedure. Procedural difficulties arise from efforts to collect information from departmental managers and from outside agencies (e.g., fire department representatives, local civil emergency planners, and utility and telephone companies). Managers or planners who do not know the appropriate questions to ask or how to effectively manage interviews will confront major obstacles to plan development.

Vendor management is the third problem. If the planners are able to surmount the problems of scope and procedure and develop an understanding of the needs and exposures that disaster recovery planning must address, they will still be thwarted by their lack of knowledge of commercially available products and services that help reduce exposure. Even if planners have a general knowledge of products and services, they may know little or nothing about product pricing or about the contracts that govern delivery of promised commodities.

Finally, there is a problem of plan articulation. The way a planner assembles information about systems, exposures, and recovery strategies into a disaster recovery plan document determines how useful the plan will be in an actual emergency and how difficult the plan will be to maintain. A well-written plan is structured so that only pertinent sections are given to recovery teams in an emergency and so that plan procedures can be implemented readily. The plan should be structured to be updated easily as the names of vendor contacts, recovery team members, details of systems and network hardware, and software configurations change over time.

A partial solution to these difficulties is to use one of the numerous, commercially available disaster recovery planning tools: software packages typically designed for use on a microcomputer. Sometimes *irreverently* referred to as canned plans, these applications can provide scope, procedure, and format to disaster recovery planning projects.

WORD PROCESSOR-DRIVEN TOOLS VERSUS DATA BASE-DRIVEN TOOLS

Disaster recovery planning tools come in a variety of forms. Some are simply boilerplate text documents, sold on diskette in American Standard Code for Information Interchange format. The user imports this plan into a word processor, and the plan can be modified or customized using word processor editing functions. Another type of packaged plan is database driven. Both types of plans offer distinct benefits and are discussed in the following sections.

Word Processor-Driven Tools

There are several advantages of these plans, one of them being that the in-house planner can use familiar software (i.e., the word processor), which reduces the learning curve that frequently delays plan development. In addition, a text plan may be readily expanded to incorporate disaster recovery planning for user departments, for branch offices, or to account for other requirements that may not be part of the generic plan. Finally, word processor-driven plans are easy to maintain using the global search-and-replace function that is part of most business word processors.

Once customized, the word processed plan is printed as is any text document. The format and the content of the plan can be redesigned to resemble other business plans or to accommodate company standards relating to document preparation.

Data Base-Driven Tools

Another type of plan is database-driven. The generic portion of the plan is incorporated into the fields on the data entry screens, and the data requested from the user is specific and detailed. As the data is entered onto the screens, several relational databases are compiled containing information about systems, networks, and personnel. Then, through the use of vendor-supplied queries and programs, the disaster recovery plan is printed out as a series of reports.

Advantages of this approach to planning tool design are the enhanced organization and management of data derived from a database structure. For example, all data pertaining to recovery teams (e.g., the names and emergency telephone numbers of each team member) is located in a single database, making it easier to update the information regarding such matters as employee turnover or changes of telephone numbers.

Other vendors have developed planning tools that integrate enhanced data base software applications (e.g., project management software) with a generic disaster recovery plan, claiming the combination supports not only plan development and maintenance but implementation. One such package provides decision support software that can be used during a disaster to collect data on the progress of the recovery effort.

CRITERIA FOR SELECTING DISASTER RECOVERY PLANNING TOOLS

Regardless of the mode of presentation employed, the primary determinant of the microcomputer-based disaster recovery planning tool's effectiveness is the generic plan that it provides. Although this built-in plan is neither right nor wrong, it may be more or less appropriate to a specific organization and its disaster recovery planning requirements. Several planning tools should be evaluated by an in-house contingency planner before one is selected.

The in-house contingency planner should outline various criteria to aid in evaluating packages (as well as consultant-developed plans). Some criteria are suggested by the following questions, and these criteria are outlined briefly in the product evaluation checklist in Exhibit 30.1.

Does the Tool Provide the Means for Developing a Disaster Recovery Plan for the Entire Organization? If disaster recovery planning is to be comprehensive, the selected planning tool must be able to handle plans for the recovery of more than hardware, software, and electronically stored data (e.g., telecommunications recovery) and for the restoration of company operations to an acceptable level. Most planning tools do not provide this capability in their generic, noncustomized form, despite vendor claims to the contrary. The contingency planner should determine, in advance, the degree to which the plan can be modified to meet the organization's needs.

Does the Planning Tool Require Adoption of an Approach to Recovery Planning That Differs from Methodologies Used in Other Planning Activities? Effective disaster recovery planning differs little from other types of business planning. Objectives are developed, tasks are derived from objectives, and criteria are set forth to gauge task and objective fulfillment. An experienced planner can use basic project management skills to develop and maintain an effective contingency plan; novice planners, however, may need more than a generic project management software package to develop their first plans. The package that a novice planner uses should not deviate drastically from a basic project management approach. If a manual is required just to understand the plan's methodology, it is probably not the most appropriate plan.

Is the Planning Tool Comprehensive? At a minimum, the essential sections in the plan are:

Exhibit 30.1. Disaster Recovery Planning Tools Evaluation Checklist

Product Identification
Product Name: _____
Vendor: _____
Address: _____
_____
Price: _____

	Yes	No	Comments
Scope			
Data Center Only			
Companywide			
Corporationwide			
Methodology			
Project Management (if No, state other)			
Plan Description (Check Yes if feature is provided)			
Generic Plan			
Action Plan			
Plan Activities			
Recovery Team directory			
Vendor Information			
Equipment inventories			
Records and Locations			
Network Descriptions			
System Descriptions			
Company Information			
User-Friendliness (Check Yes if feature is provided)			
User Interface (menus, windows, or mouse)			
Help Screens (contextual)			
Input Methods (nonredundant data entry, batch mode)			
Output Methods (diversity of reports, query language)			

- *The action plan.* The order in which recovery activities must be undertaken to result in speedy disaster recovery.
- *Plan activities.* The tasks that must be undertaken in a recovery situation. These should be ranked in order of importance and related to an action plan.
- *Recovery teams and the notification directory.* The planning tool should have a location for recording the names of company personnel who will participate in recovery, as well as a list of telephone numbers for all personnel who must be notified in the event of a disaster.
- *Vendor information and contact directory.* The planning tool should provide a location for recording information about all vendors who will provide products or services during a disaster and the names and telephone numbers of vendor contacts.

- *Records requirements and locations.* The plan should include sections detailing the locations and types of vital records stored off site and the procedures for accessing them during recovery.
- *Equipment inventories.* An inventory of systems hardware and other equipment should be maintained in the plan, both for insurance purposes and for use as a checklist in plan testing.
- *Communications networks, line, and equipment requirements.* The plan should provide a description of network operations and communications line and equipment and of services recovery requirements.
- *Application systems software and hardware requirements.* This section should provide system descriptions and should list the hardware necessary for operations and for meeting user hardware requirements.
- *Company information.* Information regarding an organization's lawyers, insurance policies, and lines of credit should be maintained in the plan document.

Is the Package User-Friendly? An excellent disaster recovery planning application should be as user-friendly as any other software package. In fact, given the specialized work of the package, the planning tool should be even more user-friendly. Some of the factors that contribute to user friendliness are:

- *The user interface.* Complex packages should require less expertise from the user. This rule of thumb applies to nearly all applications. A well-designed package should provide menus, displays, and straightforward escape routes. Mouse controls might also be desirable, though system portability would be reduced if a fallback to cursor control is unavailable.
- *Help screens.* Contextual help screens are a definite advantage. Printed manuals are not as useful as help screens that can be invoked from anywhere in the program to explain how to avoid or repair errors and list available options.
- *Tutorials or samples.* A disaster recovery planning tool should give the user an idea of what an actual disaster recovery plan looks like. The microcomputer-based tool should come equipped with a sample that the user can modify to accommodate the organization's requirements.
- *Input.* Data input should be as simple as possible. This is a key issue in determining which type of planning package — word processor-driven or database-driven — is best for a specific environment. The plan should be organized to reduce or eliminate redundant data entry. In addition, it may be useful if the planning tool allows the importation of outside files through batch conversion or some other method, because some of the information needed for the plan may have been assembled in another form or for another purpose and importing files will reduce duplicate entry.

- *Output.* The planning tool should be able to output an actual plan. The plan should be divided into sections by subject or task, and its form should be flexible enough to accommodate documentation standards.

What Is the Pedigree of the Planning Tool? Many disaster recovery planning tools were developed by consulting firms for the consultant's use at client sites. In some cases, the package was subsequently licensed for use by the client, who then maintained the plan. Consulting firms began to customize their planning tools for disaster recovery backup facility vendors and their clients. Finally, direct sales to the client became a lucrative source of business for consulting firms. Hence, many tested, reliable planning tools were originally used to develop actual plans for specific organizations. Untested planning tools may produce inadequate plans, a fact discovered only after testing or — in the worst case — in an actual disaster. Therefore, the pedigree of the plan is extremely important.

These considerations aid in the selection of the best disaster recovery planning tool for a particular organization. In addition, the price of the planning tool, the availability of telephone support, and other factors that contribute to the selection of any software package are also important.

Exhibit 30.2 provides a list of disaster recovery planning tool vendors and their products. Most vendors offer demonstration copies of their software for evaluation.

WHAT PLANNING TOOLS DO NOT PROVIDE

Disaster recovery planning tools can aid the in-house planner in many ways. They can provide an example of the structure of a plan, which may be unavailable from other sources. From this base, the planner can build and customize. Most tools also provide emergency action plans for reacting to disasters of varying destructive potential. This helps to set limits on the endless creation of scenarios that often strangles novice planners' efforts. Planning tools underscore the information that the planner must acquire. Knowing what questions to ask and having a format for entering responses can speed project completion.

However, disaster recovery planning tools are also limited in what they can provide. For example, no planning tool can provide the in-house planner with the skills needed to obtain the cooperation of departmental managers in assessing those systems that are critical. Planning tools do not provide planners with the skills required to evaluate vendor offerings, to negotiate contracts for hot-site services, or to develop effective off-site storage plans. Nor can a planning tool convince senior management of the need for disaster recovery planning.

On the other hand, planning tools can be used to articulate a plan for business recovery, a plan that can be tested, refined, and maintained. An ef-

Exhibit 30.2. Microcomputer-Based Planning Tools

AIM/SAFE 2000
Advanced Information
  Managment, Inc.
12940 Harbor Dr.
Woodbridge, VA 22192
(703) 643-1002

Basic Recovery Computer
  Solutions, Inc.
397 Park Ave.
Orange, NJ 07050
(201) 672-6000

ComPas (Comdisco Plan
  Automation System)
Comdisco Disaster Recovery
  Services
6111 North River Rd.
Rosemont, IL 60018
(708) 518-5670

Corporate Recovery
  Executive Compumetrics,
  Inc.
P.O. Box 95
Tinley Park, IL 60477
(800) 368-3324
(708) 687-1150

Customized Disaster Survival
  Manual
Disaster Survival Planning,
  Inc.
669 Pacific Cove Dr.
Port Hueneme, CA 93041
(805) 984-9547

Disaster Recovery 2000
Disaster Recovery Services,
  Inc.
427 Pine Ave.
Suite 201
Loma Beach, CA 90802
(310) 432-0559

DP/90 Plus
SunGard Planning solutions,
  Inc.
1285 Drummers Lane
Wayne, PA 19087
(800) 247-7832
(215) 341-8700

DPS-30 Disaster Planning
  System
Arel Technologies, Inc.
1557 Coonrapids Blvd.
Suite 200
Minneapolis, MN 55433
(612) 755-6901

DRS
TAMP Computer Systems,
  Inc.
1732 Remson Ave.
Merrick, NY 11566
(516) 623-2038

RPS (Recovery Planning
  System)
Contemporary Computer
  Services, Inc.
200 Knickerbocker Ave.
Bohemia, NY 11716
(516) 563-8880

HOTSITE Recovery Plan
HOTSITE
110 MacKenan Dr.
Cary, NC 27511
(919) 460-1234

Information Security Policies
  Made Easy
Information Integrity/
  Baseline Software
P.O. Box 1219
Sausalito, CA 94966
(415) 332-7763

Living Disaster Recovery
  Planning System (LDRPS)
Strohl Systems
500 N. Gulph Rd.
Suite 500
King of Prussia, PA 19406
(215) 768-4120

NCR 911 Disaster Recovery
  Planning System
NCR Corp.
1700 South Patterson Blvd.,
  SDC-3
Dayton, OH 45479
(800) 626-3495

Recovery Architect
Dataguard Recovery
  Services, Inc.
P.O. Box 37144
Louisville, KY 40233-7144
(502) 426-3434
(800) 325-3977

Recovery/1
Computer Performance, Inc.
68 Hartford Turnpike
P.O. Box 718
Tolland, CT 06084
(203) 872-1672

Recovery PAC
Recovery PAC II
Computer Security
  Consultants, Inc.
590 Danbury Rd.
Ridgefield, CT 06877
(203) 431-8720

REXSYS
Recovery Management, Inc.
435 King St.
P.O. Box 327
Littleton, MA 10460
(508) 486-8866

Total Recovery Planning
  System (TRPS)
CHI/COR Information
  Management, Inc.
300 South Wacker Dr.
Chicago, IL 60606
(800) 448-8777
(312) 322-0150

fective tool will pay for itself in the time saved in maintaining the plan. This is arguably the greatest benefit disaster recovery planning tools can offer.

SOURCES OF INFORMATION ON PLANNING TOOLS

Generally, the best sources of information about disaster recovery planning and tools are professional contingency planning associations. The number of these organizations has increased dramatically over the past several years, and membership is booming.

Most contingency planning group members are disaster recovery or security planners from organizations within a specific geographic region. Members exchange ideas and information openly about their situations and offer advice and solutions from their own experiences. These groups can be valuable sources of new techniques and methods of plan development — from pitching the plan to management, to deciding on the best records-salvaging strategy. Many associations are self-appointed watchdogs over the essentially unpoliced disaster recovery industry. The groups invite vendors to demonstrate products and provide insight into their particular expertise. In addition, most disaster recovery groups do not allow their vendors to interfere with candid appraisals of products and services, including disaster recovery planning tools.

RECOMMENDED COURSE OF ACTION

Because of the costs associated with contracting a disaster recovery consultant, many organizations choose to develop a contingency plan in-house, either by using planning tools or by using a consultant for the initial stages of the development. Either choice is valid, but disaster recovery planning tools do not provide a comprehensive solution to an organization's disaster recovery planning needs. Only by careful study of the literature of disaster recovery planning and by interacting with other disaster recovery planners can novice planners obtain the competence to develop effective recovery capabilities for their firms. On the other hand, planning tools can be a useful adjunct in plan development activities by providing an example of plan format and by exposing the user to the plan's unique approach and method.

Chapter 31
Reengineering Methodologies and Tools

Mark M. Klein

Sometimes called process redesign or process innovation, business process reengineering (BPR) is now firmly entrenched as a buzzword, if not a concept, in the minds of U.S. managers. Yet there remain disagreements as to what BPR is and how best to accomplish it.

BPR is used in this chapter to mean the rapid and radical redesign of strategic, value-added business processes — and the systems, policies, and organizational structures that support them — to optimize workflows and productivity in an organization. Business process reengineering has these characteristics:

- BPR is process-oriented.
- BPR concurrently pursues breakthrough improvements in quality, time to market, and cost.
- BPR is holistic, both leveraging technology and empowering people.
- BPR starts with a willingness to abandon current practices.

Because of the broad scope, ambitious reach, and the profound changes BPR projects cause, they are among the most difficult that a company can undertake. Three out of four BPR projects are reported to be unsuccessful. That is why there is heightened interest in approaches to BPR that offer better odds of success. In particular, companies have sought methodologies and tools to facilitate well-disciplined and organized ways of structuring, assessing, and resolving the issues that BPR projects raise.

Methodologies refer to systematic approaches to conducting a BPR project. An effective methodology is like a road map. It helps the company select a destination and then find the best way to get there. Tools are the manual or automated aids to doing the work of the project.

METHOD VERSUS INTUITION

Not all practitioners agree that a BPR methodology is useful. Some companies rely on a more intuitive approach, shunning analysis in favor of a higher-level understanding. Some practitioners believe that overattention to current practices gets in the way of breakthrough thinking, and they would rather start with a clean slate, depending only on their imagination and experience.

Methodologists believe, on the other hand, that sitting down with a blank piece of paper and no guidance on how to begin is dismaying. Methodologists believe that people trained in intuitive approaches frequently become enthusiastic proponents of BPR at the end of their training, but they still do not know how to do it.

Difficulties Measuring BPR Effectiveness

Another distinction is that intuitives maintain that rules of thumb and general information about what has been done in other companies is useful, but that formal benchmarking is not. They say that benchmarking constrains the BPR team from finding truly innovative solutions. Methodologists, by contrast, feel that benchmarking can bring breakthrough ideas (when benchmarking outside the organization's own industry) as well as inject reality into the process.

One of the difficulties in assessing the relative value and efficacy of intuitive and methodological approaches to BPR is that most of the reported case studies are of necessity intuitive, because no methodologies existed at the time the projects were done. In fact, the projects were recognized as business process reengineering only after the fact: at the time, they were conceptualized as something else.

A second difficulty exists in assessing the relative cost and effectiveness of different BPR methodologies. Consulting firms, most of which promote a methodology, can provide references and examples of successful projects using their preferred methods (as can firms that use an intuitive approach); if they could not, they would be out of business.

Furthermore, in a survey of 500 companies, about half of them that are doing BPR projects are doing so without significant help from consultants. It is hard to define what constitutes success on some BPR projects, because the sought-after improvement goals are never quantified and BPR practitioners are reluctant to discuss their failures. Credible research on the relative merits of intuitive- versus method-based approaches, or of one methodology versus another, are difficult to find. Indeed, it is difficult to design an objective experiment to measure effectiveness in BPR.

TOOLS AND THEIR USE

BPR tools are used more frequently on methodology-based BPR projects than on intuitive ones (unless the user counts a piece of paper, a flow chart template, and a pencil as tools). In fact, some methodologies are based on the use of specific tools. For example, Gemini Consulting's Construct reengineering methodology incorporates an object-oriented toolset developed by Parc Place Systems. Similarly, Coopers & Lybrand's Break Point BPR methodology uses a proprietary process modeling and simulation tool called SPARKS.

By using tools, the BPR practitioner expects to improve productivity, finish projects faster, produce higher-quality results, and eliminate tedious housekeeping work in order to concentrate on value-added work. To produce these benefits, BPR tools should be usable by businesspeople (managers and professionals), not technicians. Tools should:

- Enhance the clarity of the BPR team's vision.
- Enforce consistency in analysis and design.
- Permit (ideally) iterative, top-down refinement from the BPR project goals to the solution. For example, if the solution includes a computer system, the refinement should end with a working system.
- Produce an acceptable return on investment.

Six Categories of BPR Tools

1. Project Management. These tools are used for planning, scheduling, budgeting, reporting, and tracking projects. Some tools, such as Texas Instruments' IEF/Project Manager, are integrated with other categories of tools, such as modeling, analysis, and systems development. Other project management tools, such as Harvard Project Manager or Microsoft Project for Windows, are stand-alone.

2. Coordination. These tools are used to distribute plans and to communicate updated details of projects. The primary subcategories are e-mail, scheduling applications, shared spreadsheets, bulletin boards, and groupware. Some of these tools, such as Microsoft Excel or Lotus 1-2-3, support a single subcategory. Others, such as Lotus Notes or WordPerfect Office, support multiple subcategories.

3. Modeling. These tools are used to make a model of something in order to understand its structure and workings. Most of the tools in this category are integrated computer-aided software engineering (ICASE) toolsets for integrated analysis, design, and development of computer systems. These include Texas Instruments' IEF, KnowledgeWare's IEW, Popkin System ARchitect, and S/Cubed DAISYS. There are also useful partial solutions, including spreadsheets.

1. Business Process Analysis. These tools are used for the systematic reduction of a business into its constituent parts and the examination of the interactions among those parts. In general, the same tools used for modeling are used for business process analysis. Indeed, analysis is necessary for modeling, although not vice versa.

2. Human Resources Analysis and Design. Tools used to design and establish the human or social part of reengineered processes are mostly standalone, partial solutions for specific, sometimes overlapping applications. One subcategory of these tools is used for requisition/candidate tracking and position history. Examples include Revelation HR-Applicant Track and Spectrum HR: AM/2000. Other subcategories include skills assessment (Performance Mentor), team building (Supersynch), compensation planning (Hi-Tech Employee Evaluation and Salary Manager), and organization charting (Corel Draw, Harvard Graphics).

3. Systems Development. These tools automate the reengineered business processes. Subcategories include the Integrated CASE tools as well as visual programming (Microsoft Visual Basic), application frameworks (Borland Application Framework, Gupta Structured Query Language Base, and SQL Windows), coding workbenches (MicroFocus Cobol/2 Workbench, IBM OS/2 Workframe 2), object reuse libraries (Digitalk Smalltalk V, Borland Object Vision), and test harnesses (McCabe & Associates Codebreaker, Software Research M-Test).

Learning, Integration, and Cost Issues

An organization must consider three important and related issues before selecting a BPR toolset: learning, integration, and cost.

Ideally, a toolset would be easy to learn and easy to use, but most are neither. Some toolsets — object-oriented ones, for example — require a new way of thinking as well as the use of a new technique. (One toolset's user manual introduces each chapter with a reference to a book with which the reader is presumed familiar.) Some tools use techniques that are arbitrary replacements for those that the user may already be using.

A toolset is easier to learn and use if each tool has the same standard look and feel. Then the user need not learn and remember several different sets of interfaces.

Anyone who uses tools on a BPR project will quickly discover the need to move the data that is output from one tool into another, as well as into more common tools such as word processing and spreadsheets. There are four basic ways of satisfying this need:

- Manually transcribing data from one tool to another. This option places the least constraint on tool selection, but is tedious and error-prone.
- Selecting one vendor's integrated toolset. Integrated tools cover several, but not all, of the potential BPR tool applications.
- Selecting nonintegrated tools from one or more vendors that support common data formats like SYLK or dBASE in order to move data from one to another.
- Selecting nonintegrated tools and using the capabilities of the operating system platform (e.g., Microsoft Windows) for cutting and pasting data among the tools.

Many tools, especially the integrated ones, are fairly expensive, and the initial purchase price is only the beginning. Experience shows that the total tool cost can easily be 10 to 15 times the initial purchase price over the first five years of use.

Understanding the Environment

To properly resolve these BPR tool issues, the organization must consider the context in which the tools are to be used.

Number of Projects Planned. If the company is considering one-time use of new tools for a single project, it may better to select only the simplest tools. Use of tools may actually reduce productivity on the first project by as much as 40 percent. It is usually not until the second or third project (for each tool user) that the more complicated tools begin to save time.

Fit with Systems Development Methodology. Will the same toolset be used from the process analysis and design phases all the way through systems development? Does the toolset support the current systems development methodology as well as the BPR methodology chosen? If the answer to either of these questions is no, then the value of the toolset is considerably reduced.

Role of Consultants. If IS selects a consulting firm's methodology and proprietary toolset, it is generally committing to heavy dependence on the consultant's personnel. IS should also consider whether it is possible to continue using the tools without using the consultant. The flip side of this issue is whether the company is using consultants with someone else's tools and thus investing in training the consultant's people. Each company contemplating a BPR project should find its own answers to these questions.

HOW TO APPLY A BPR METHODOLOGY

To illustrate some of these points, Gateway's Rapid Re methodology for BPR, which is taught in American Management Association seminars, is used as an example. The five stages of the methodology are as follows:

1. *Preparation.* The purpose is to mobilize, organize, and energize the people who will perform the reengineering project.
2. *Identification.* The purpose is to develop a customer-oriented process model of the business.
3. *Vision.* The processes to reengineer are selected and the redesign options capable of achieving breakthrough performance are formulated.
4. *Solution.* The purpose is to define the technical and social requirements for the new processes and develop detailed implementation plans.
5. *Transformation.* The reengineering plans are ready to implement.

Exhibit 31.1 is a schematic of the 54 tasks included in the five stages.

The methodology is customized to the needs of each BPR project, because that is what generally happens in practice. An individual project might skip, rearrange, or recombine tasks to meet its needs or give greater or lesser emphasis to some tasks. For example, in an ideal project, stages 1 and 2 (preparation and identification) consider all key processes within a company and conclude with a step that sets priorities for the processes to reengineer (see Exhibit 31.2). Then stages 3, 4, and 5 (vision, solution, and transformation) are executed repeatedly for each process (or group of processes) selected for reengineering.

Sometimes, depending most often on who is sponsoring the BPR project, the scope of the project is not the entire company. It may be a business unit, a division, or even a functional department. (Actually, the scope must be the processes within the department or whatever other unit is involved.) Alternatively, the specific processes to be reengineered may have been preselected. In these cases, the way in which the reengineering team is organized, and the way in which it uses the methodology, will differ from the model.

The methodology does not require a specific consulting involvement. A BPR project team should include both insiders, who have knowledge of current practices and an understanding of company culture, and outsiders who have the creative naivete to ask why things are done a certain way. Project teams also need leadership and facilitation. If they are going to use a methodology, the project team members must be trained. Rapid Re does not require that companies retain Gateway or any other consultants to work on a BPR project. The process is designed for use by managers and professionals found in all kinds of settings in U.S. companies so it is accessible to the layperson.

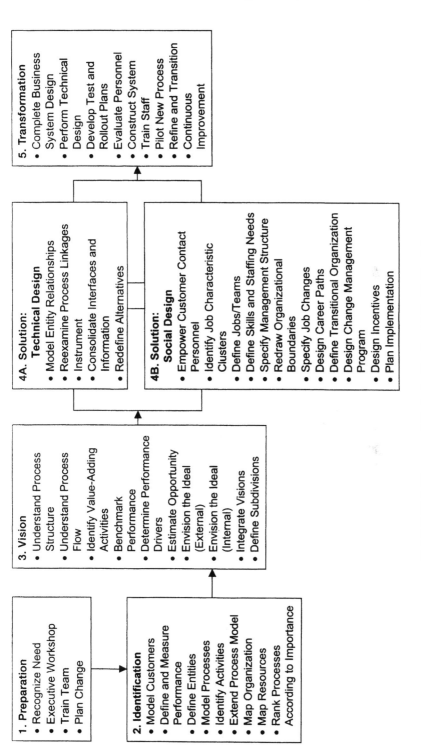

Exhibit 31.1. Stages and Tasks in the Rapid Re Methodology

1. Preparation
- Recognize Need
- Executive Workshop
- Train Team
- Plan Change

2. Identification
- Model Customers
- Define and Measure Performance
- Define Entities
- Model Processes
- Identify Activities
- Extend Process Model
- Map Organization
- Map Resources
- Rank Processes According to Importance

3. Vision
- Understand Process Structure
- Understand Process Flow
- Identify Value-Adding Activities
- Benchmark Performance
- Determine Performance Drivers
- Estimate Opportunity
- Envision the Ideal (External)
- Envision the Ideal (Internal)
- Integrate Visions
- Define Subdivisions

4A. Solution: Technical Design
- Model Entity Relationships
- Reexamine Process Linkages
- Instrument
- Consolidate Interfaces and Information
- Redefine Alternatives

4B. Solution: Social Design
- Empower Customer Contact Personnel
- Identify Job Characteristic Clusters
- Define Jobs/Teams
- Define Skills and Staffing Needs
- Specify Management Structure
- Redraw Organizational Boundaries
- Specify Job Changes
- Design Career Paths
- Define Transitional Organization
- Design Change Management Program
- Design Incentives
- Plan Implementation

5. Transformation
- Complete Business System Design
- Perform Technical Design
- Develop Test and Rollout Plans
- Evaluate Personnel
- Construct System
- Train Staff
- Pilot New Process
- Refine and Transition
- Continuous Improvement

Exhibit 31.2. Case Example: ABC Toy Company

Process	Goals				Resources				Factors		Priority
	Regain Market Share	Capture 70% Share	Maintain Gross Profit	ROI 20%	Full-Time Equivalent	Cost ($)	Time	Cost	Risk	Social	
Develop Product	0	8	5	5	15.0	2,500,000	Med.	$$	High	Easy	5
Manufacture	9	9	7	7	375.0	29,300,000	Long	$$$$	Med.	Hard	4
Fulfill Orders	8	9	9	9	22.5	2,500,000	Med.	$$	Med.	Med.	1
Service Customers Request	6	8	5	5	9.0	700,000	Short	$	Low	Easy	2
Maintain Customer Accounts	3	3	3	3	8.5	1,000,000	Short	$	Low	Easy	
Develop Human Resources	4	6	4	4	6.5	765,000	Long	$	Med.	Hard	
Compensate	3	5	3	3	11.5	1,350,000	Med.	$	High	Hard	
Fund	3	3	3	3	9.0	1,060,000	Med.	$	Med.	Easy	
Comply	1	1	1	1	7.0	825,000	Med.	$	Med.	Med.	
Acquire Customer Orders	7	7	8	8	36.0	5,000,000	Med.	$$$	High	Med.	3

KEY: 0 = No Impact; 10 = Maximum Impact.

For the same reason, the methodology requires few tools. It can be used with a pencil, paper, a flow-charting template, and a few paper forms. Spreadsheets can be used for all of the quantitative tasks, as well as for the presentation of qualitative data in tabular form. Project management systems can be used not only for planning and tracking the BPR project, but also for simple process flow diagrams. The methodology can be used with any or all of the categories of BPR tools. Flexibility is essential if the methodology is to be useful in a broad range of environments.

The overhead associated with the methodology is low and it is easy to learn, requiring only two or three days of training. The fully worked-out example in Exhibit 31.2, the ABC Toy Company, illustrates its use.

RECOMMENDED COURSE OF ACTION

BPR project teams should include various personality types and people with different functional specializations, education, experience, and levels of responsibility. A methodology may be what is needed to enable such a diverse group to work together effectively.

The BPR practitioners must select the approach and tools that best meet their needs and those of their company. In so doing, they should begin by taking the following actions:

- Defining what kind of BPR project the organization is undertaking.
  - Is it a one-time effort, a pilot, or one of a series of similar projects?
- Defining the scope of the project.
  - Is it companywide or business unit-wide, or does it have a narrower scope?
  - Who is sponsoring the project? Is it being driven from the top down or bottom up?
- Deciding who is likely to be on the BPR team.
  - How much of their time can they spend on the project? For how long?
  - What is the state of the team's readiness to do the work of the BPR project? What kind of support will the team members need?
- Determining the role, if any, for consultants.
  - What will the consultants bring to the project — methodologies? tools? experience? resources?
  - How long will the consultants be needed?
  - How will the organization ensure a transfer of know-how to its own staff? How will it wean itself from dependence on the consultants?
- Managing management's expectations of BPR.
  - Is the BPR project an experiment, or is management looking for substantive gains?
  - How long does management expect it to take? How much to cost?
  - How radical a change will the organization's management entertain?

It is only within the constraints set by the answers to these questions that an organization can realistically define a BPR project and choose the methodologies and tools that help ensure its success.

Chapter 32
Controlling Major Systems Integration Projects
Steve Mar

Most problems that arise during the design and development of major systems integration projects can be resolved without significant impact to the project budget and schedule. However, an increasing number of these projects encounter problems that are difficult to control. Such new technologies as local area networks (LANs), client/servers, and Distributed Computer Environments increase the complexity and level of challenge to the systems integrator.

An integration project can encounter control problems for a variety of reasons, including:

- Poor planning and design.
- Lack of project leadership and understanding of requirements.
- Lack of controls and standards.
- Inadequate technology.
- Inability of user, management, and developer groups to work together.
- Incorrect design of information and data structures.
- Underestimation of the time required to convert systems and provide adequate documentation.
- Cost, funding, and accounting problems.
- Change in project direction, focus or management after the project has begun.
- Unqualified or inexperienced project team members.

In one case, for example, a health care provider was forced to write off several million dollars of development costs because of a failed integration project. The project had attempted to link field office processing, claims information and other customer functions such as eligibility. The integration effort, which lasted several years, encountered problems with testing procedures, implementation of new technologies, and personnel problems.

The information security specialist plays an important role in the design and development of both project and security controls. The security specialist must be able to advise IS management on both traditional control issues and on the control problems and solutions involving LAN, client/server, UNIX, and other more advanced technologies. If security personnel are unable to contribute because of lack of in-depth knowledge of such technologies, integration projects are much more likely to be implemented without effective controls.

This chapter addresses the question of why such failures occur during large systems integration projects, discusses ways to prevent them, and provides guidelines for the information security specialist to use in assisting systems development management.

SYSTEMS INTEGRATION PROBLEMS

Problems in systems integration projects can be grouped by three kinds of factors: human, technical, and financial.

1. Human Factors. Human factors that may lead to problems in systems integration projects include:

- Lack of user group participation in the design and development process.
- Faulty coordination between users, developers, and management.
- Inadequate project leadership.
- Lack of top management focus and support.
- Lack of training.

For example, a large holding company purchased a number of different business product lines, including entertainment and publishing. The entertainment company did not have any systems experience and its users were not given adequate training. This led to major problems in converting, installing, integrating, and using the system. The publishing company, on the other hand, had an existing production system that worked extremely well. The publisher's management refused to use the integrated system, which has resulted in reporting inaccuracies at many levels.

2. Technical Factors. A number of technical problems can cause the systems integration project to run into trouble:

- Lack of reliable and accurate data files.
- Poor hardware and software capabilities.
- Misapplication of small online database systems to handle extensive transaction volumes and updates.
- Lack of experience in new technologies used to develop the system.

For example, a brokerage firm ordered and planned to install a new UNIX system that would integrate its existing customer database with a regulatory reporting database. However, after several unsuccessful attempts at integrating the applications with the UNIX platform, management cancelled the project because the technology proved to be too unreliable and was unable to process the required volume of trading system transactions.

3. Financial Factors. Financial factors that create problems in major systems integration projects may include:

- Lack of financial control over the project process.
- Funding limitations.
- Lack of financial reporting and accountability.
- Cost overruns due to poor planning, contract disputes, and other commitments by vendors.

For example, a public utility selected a specific software vendor after a review of several vendors in accordance with its request for proposal process. Unfortunately, the software company ran into cashflow problems, which resulted in a slow down in system development. The resulting delay caused the utility to lose certain competitive advantages that would have resulted from timely completion of the project.

SYSTEM INTEGRATION CONTROL REQUIREMENTS

The information security specialist should review three levels of controls:

1. *General Business Controls.* These controls include development team qualifications, business reasons for the integration, business resumption, change controls, network controls, and access controls.
2. *Application Controls.* These controls include input edit controls, communication controls, documentation controls, user controls, acceptance testing controls, processing controls, and output controls.
3. *Project Controls.* These controls include budgets, schedules, performance measures, and project management.

The information security specialist should determine the types of controls to be implemented for the integration project. The necessary controls can be identified by conducting a risk assessment.

The next two sections discuss general business and application controls in detail. Project controls are beyond the scope of this chapter.

General Business Controls

A key factor influencing the risk assessment is the business reason for the systems integration project. Management would already have considered certain economic, product, customer, and operational factors in deciding to move ahead with the systems integration project. The security specialist should evaluate why management has decided to proceed with this project and determine what general business risks may need to be addressed. Exhibit 32.1 illustrates these risks and possible control concerns.

**Exhibit 32.1. Risks and Control Concerns Associated with
Business Reasons for Systems Integration**

Business Reasons	Risk Issues	Control Concerns
Mergers and Acquisitions	• Business culture or management conflicts • Loss of experienced management and staff • Lack of long-term investment • Change in strategic direction and focus	• Inability to agree on general controls • Increased potential for operating errors and mistakes • No commitment to maintenance or upgrades • Lack of commitment to controls and direction
Corporate Downsizing	• Decrease in staff morale • Loss of loyalty • Increased workload for remaining personnel	• Employee fraud or lack of motivation • Disregard for rules and controls • Bypassing controls to get more work done
Outsourcing	• Loss of influence over development process • Inability to respond to market competition or develop new products	• Users install and create their own applications • Data integrity and reliability problems
User-Driven Integration Requirements	• Lack of technical experience • Lack of user controls awareness	• Misapplication of technical control features • Lack of support for controls by users
Improved Management Reporting	• Users create ad hoc reports without controls	• Duplication of effort • Unreliable reports
Hardware and Software Cost Reduction	• Integration of systems without a central database • Development of applications without network controls	• Data integrity problems • Network controls not implemented or given priority

Certain risks are inherent in the general business operations and information process. The information security specialist should assess the following control areas to determine the controls that should be implemented during development:

- Experience and qualifications of team members to ensure that they understand the importance of controls and can implement them correctly.
- Ability of the organization to continue processing in the event of a disaster.
- Testing of the recovery process to ensure it works as planned.

- Ensuring that updates to applications are appropriately designed, tested, and implemented.
- Ensuring that network controls are in place to route messages to the correct users.
- Maintenance of the confidentiality of messages during network transmission.
- Ensuring that the network remains stable and available to users.
- Implementing access controls to ensure that only authorized users are allowed on the system.
- Establishing procedures to determine when and how to remove users from the system.

Application Controls

When the project team begins to focus on the application controls for the system integration project, the information security specialist should assess the application risks and controls. If the new systems integration project relies on the existing mainframe system and operating environment, the information security specialist can evaluate or rely on existing mainframe controls such as the IBM Resource Access Control Facility or Computer Associates' CA-Top Secret for access control.

If open systems architectures are being implemented, a different approach to system and application control may be required. For example, workstation and LAN-based systems distribute information processing closer to the user and, in turn, require that users accept greater control responsibilities and oversight. The central data processing facility or computer center can no longer continue to provide certain application control services.

For example, when using Novell NetWare as the LAN file server and network interface, the information security specialist must know what version of NetWare will be installed for the systems integration project because different versions of NetWare provide different security features.

ASSESSING SYSTEMS INTEGRATION STRATEGIES

Organizations use a variety of integration strategies to meet their business requirements. This section describes five integration strategies and demonstrates how these strategies affect the design of controls.

Strategy 1: Full Integration

This approach takes all existing systems and integrates them into a single, unified system. In one example, a manufacturing company decided to integrate its order entry, sales, and general ledger applications. Each system ran on a different platform and required different access methods. Screens did not look the same, and function keys did not operate the same. As a result, users made many mistakes in entering and retrieving information.

A consulting firm was contracted to design and fully integrate all the procedures and products on a single system. The consulting firm developed a new sales application to manage sales units, assign accounts, report expenses, review orders, and manage territory sales data. Information was made available in a database for both general ledger and management reports.

This is the best approach for this manufacturing organization, because it allows all the applications to be installed and maintained on a single system. The information security specialist was able to assist and develop a new set of comprehensive system controls rather than update existing change procedures and controls. As noted, it is more cost-effective to design and install controls during the integration project than after the new system has been installed. However, this strategy requires a great deal of time and effort, senior management support, and a significant financial investment. Automated integration tools can make the development process more efficient and controlled, but the systems and security specialists must invest the time to learn how these tools work.

Strategy 2: Partial Integration

In the partial integration approach, only mission-critical applications are selected for integration. Noncritical applications are networked and remain outside the new system. For example, a large insurance company found it necessary to move to a larger and faster system to handle increased transaction volume. An analyst determined that the claims and provider administration systems were critical. The insurance company integrated them into a single claims and provider administration system. The system was then networked to other applications (e.g., actuarial, general ledger, and member eligibility).

This strategy permits the information security specialist to improve controls over the critical applications during integration of the new system. Older systems are often too difficult and expensive to improve. By using a partial integration strategy, the insurance company achieves a level of integration and improved control of critical applications with a reasonable investment.

Strategy 3: Surround Technology

Surround technology integrates all critical systems on an operating platform that provides significant throughput and processing capability. In this approach, the functions of the applications are not significantly changed; updates are made only to improve processing and throughput. In one example, a university research department received a used supercomputer with applications that had run on older minicomputers and an older mainframe system. These applications were moved to a networked supercomputer environment, which allowed fast access to more terminal connections. Project accounting for grants, reporting for government requirements, grant proposal tracking, and department research projects experienced increased efficiencies in processing, throughput, and information access.

A surround technology strategy improves performance and processing; the security control issues do not change. To enhance the security controls, the information security specialist should consider installing a front-end access control software package.

Strategy 4: Client/Server Processing

Creating a client/server integration strategy is an increasingly popular approach. The increased power of network management systems, routers, relational databases, and query language has given the end user effective tools to develop client/server applications. For major integration projects, the developer has the option of designing and moving information databases closer to the client. The developer can convert an application to run locally on a workstation and integrate the necessary communications and editing to the main database repository.

For example, a large California-based agricultural company relies on a network of sales representatives and customers to market and purchase its products. The company ran a batch-oriented purchase order system and separate inventory control system. The general ledger ran on another separate machine. These systems did not provide distributed online access. As a result, it might take several hours after a sales representative called in an order to receive confirmation that the order could be filled.

A technology steering group of managers, users, and systems staff decided to create a client database for the sales representatives which included purchase order and inventory update information, and another client database for the inventory storage facilities. These client databases were linked to a file server running on a minicomputer. The minicomputer-based database was updated periodically, and once a day information was downloaded to the general ledger.

A client/server strategy creates a significant challenge for the information security specialist. For example, the security specialist must determine how the client/server configuration will be structured and where information will be stored. The security specialist must thoroughly understand the client/server architecture in order to determine the relative security exposure of each of the client and file server databases. Controls are selected on the basis of this risk assessment.

Strategy 5: Back-End Processing

Integration through a back-end processor (e.g., an integrated database) can provide users with a comprehensive reporting facility. The operations and control issues regarding data input, processing, and transfer remain the same. In one case, a regional bank purchased two community banks that had different information processing systems. Converting the new systems was too expensive and time consuming; therefore, the IS conversion team decided to plug these two systems into a large back-end database processor. Operating information was routed to this processor. Management reports were developed using the query languages available with the database. Reports of activity at the two community banks could then be compared and reconciled.

In this example, the information security specialist may be able to improve the controls used to consolidate reporting, but he or she is generally unable to change controls for other major systems. There is no opportunity to improve existing applications with ineffective controls.

RECOMMENDED COURSE OF ACTION

The information security specialist can play an important role in the implementation of major systems integration projects. To ensure success, the information security specialist must have a clear understanding of the integration strategy. If such new technologies as client/server processing are used, the security specialist must take the time to learn about this technology. It is also important that the security practitioner understand the critical business reasons for the integration project.

The security specialist should consider how to advise the systems integration team. One recommended course of action includes these activities:

- Develop an information security integration work plan based on the type of integration project being implemented.
- Address the three factors — human, technical, and financial — involved in the failure of systems integration projects.
- Create an information security program focused on general controls, application controls, network controls, operating systems controls, recovery controls, and access controls.
- Determine the level of risk for the areas mentioned in the previous step and identify the controls that merit implementation and enhancement. Exhibit 32.2 rates the risks for each of the five integration strategies.
- Allocate information security resources on the basis of risk within a reasonable budgetary level.
- Work with managers, developers, business users, and auditors to ensure adequate information security coverage.

Exhibit 32.2. Ratings of Information Security Risks

	Integration Strategy				
Information Security Focus	**Full Integration**	**Partial Integration**	**Surround Technology**	**Client/ Server**	**Back-End Processing**
General Controls	High	Medium	Medium	High	Low
Application Controls	High	High	Medium	Medium	Low
System Controls	High	High	High	High	High
Communication Controls	Medium	High	High	High	Low
Backup and Recovery Controls	Medium	Medium	Medium	High	Low
Access Controls	High	High	Medium	High	Low

Integration projects represent an opportunity for the security specialist to implement and strengthen controls in a cost-effective way. The approach described in this chapter can serve as a model for improving controls given specific integration strategies and business environments.

Chapter 33

An Object-Oriented Strategy for Reintegrating IS into Mainstream Management

Richard W. Koontz

The task of the large IS shop is getting progressively more difficult as users force a multitude of quick-fix tools on top of a bewildering array of platforms and vintages, on top of legacy code that itself was a multitude of quick-fix solutions to problems. A new generation of highly trained software professionals and technical leaders views object-oriented (OO) systems development as a discipline that can bring order out of chaos and lead to the IS department becoming an agent of business change instead of its enemy.

This chapter addresses a fundamental question raised by both chief financial and chief information officers in business: Can object-oriented technology really apply to and benefit this firm? Or is the corporate IS department too big, too complex, and too burdened by the complexity to make the transition?

SURVIVAL INSTINCTS

There are times when it helps for a giant of a firm to look to small ones for help or guidance. In this case, practitioners can look to scores of small high-technology companies that chose to enter the object-oriented world. Why have they embarked on what is an expensive and slow path? Why did they risk their companies at a time when OO technology was immature?

0-8493-9998-X/00/$0.00+$.50
© 2000 by CRC Press LLC

And why are their company executives smiling today? In general, an overwhelming desire for survival dictated their actions.

What OO Technology Means to Small Companies

Small high-technology companies are fairly fast on their feet. Many of them began moving to object orientation several years ago. At that time the technology was immature, had some severe limitations, and carried an uncertain future. Today, users can buy hundreds of shrinkwrapped packages that are more or less object-oriented and run them on computers whose operating systems are also object-oriented.

These small companies went OO purely to survive in the marketplace. It was a decision forced on them by competition.

Not a Quick and Easy Path to Success. The notion that OO is a survival decision may sound contradictory to IS practitioners who have attempted to adopt object-oriented techniques. OO technology is not a quick and easy path to success. First, the IS staff must wade through a lot of research to select what tools to use. Then they must wade through a lot of indoctrination, training, learning, and assimilation. Then IS has to fight the battle of how to manage OO projects.

It has taken early adopters or so-called fast-mover companies months just to get to the point of beginning. Then they had to rethink their products. Then, being a disciplined process, the process itself even takes longer.

Furthermore, the transition to OO is expensive. Not just in dollars spent on hiring expensive outside consultants but also in the potential sales dollars lost by being later to market with that first product. The extreme possibility of missing a major market window of opportunity is that the customer buys somebody else's product.

Unexpected Market Changes Brought About by OO. The fast-movers nonetheless made the front-end investments and brought about an even more competitive market than they faced in the beginning. By making the move to object-oriented technology, their investment dollars built a foundation that was changeable, expandable, and reusable. Their investment improved their products. The product delivered was closer to the target they had been striving for.

Although these small companies gained something they had hoped for, other consequences were a bit unexpected. After shipment of a first product, when everything hangs in the balance, they found that they could make major changes quickly and inexpensively. When competitors introduced leap-frog products, those companies using object-oriented systems development discovered that their products could be adapted faster than before.

Out of their experience came a foundation of knowledge, codified in objects, that has turned the tables. These firms are now the ones setting the pace in the software marketplace, bringing out new versions that are increasingly forcing older products into obsolescence. Firms that did not go OO are at a significant disadvantage. The marketplace expects more complex packages. Do the non-OO firms throw more bodies at the problem, or do they start the shift to OO now, when the longer lead time to first product may damage their competitive stance? Or do they throw in the towel and live on the residual revenues from old products?

A Familiar Scenario. A Minneapolis company is in a similar spot. It has discovered that its leading-edge product cannot easily be adapted to enter a new and larger market. It was written in C and does many things very well, but it suffers from all of the problems of that self-same C language. Furthermore, it is now getting outdated as competition moves forward.

The management of this firm is faced with telling its shareholders that it is cheaper to write a brand-new system than it would be to reengineer the old one. As a result, the firm is faced with delaying entry into that dynamic new market by about 12 months.

Most likely, the firm will choose not to make the move to object technology because it is too expensive and takes too long. Instead of 12 months, the first OO product shipment would be 18 months out. Instead of, say, $2 million spent on the new product, it would spend $3 million.

To stay in the game, the company will ante up the $2 million and go the traditional route. It will be done in C or its chameleon twin, C++. If all goes as usual, it will still be 18 months and $3 million dollars later and the firm will be rushing the product into the market, though by that time, it will already be a slightly obsolete product. Then there will be another stockholders meeting to discuss what it is going to take to enter a bigger, larger market that has emerged.

By then it may be simply too late. The standard development cycles that were barely tolerable two years ago, and are unacceptable today, will be perceived as being disastrously long two years from now, relatively speaking (relative to the competition, that is).

WHICH OO LANGUAGE TO PICK?

Some IS practitioners ask about which object-oriented language they should pick. This is too close to the "which silver bullet" question. There is no one-size-fits-all product, and IS practitioners know that their companies are too important to treat that way.

The primary choices seem to be C++, Objective C, or Smalltalk. In general, the variations of C are viewed as being slower to develop and more difficult to maintain. The benefits have been speed of execution and smaller executable images. The single biggest complaint raised by C++ developers is that too many projects are not really following OO standards, and the results are a poor mishmash of standard C and C++. The single biggest boast is that they "can make the computer do anything."

Smalltalk was considered a pioneer's language, but by 1994 it seemed to have emerged as the large corporation's language of choice. (Anyone seriously considering PowerBuilder should first discuss it with OO technical experts at other large corporations who challenge its OO-ness and scalability.)

There are several other OO or almost-OO languages available. So far, their commercial acceptance has not approached critical mass. They may be outstanding languages, but the danger exists that their backing firms may not survive.

Both C++ and Smalltalk passed the point of critical mass some time ago. They are backed on all the major platforms. IBM Corp. seems to be positioning Smalltalk as the Common Business Oriented Language of the future. Both IBM and Hewlett-Packard Co. are pushing Smalltalk as a distributed product, part of their long-term strategies, which also fits the direction of the industry. Both C++ and Smalltalk benefit from constant advances in supporting tools. C++ has a much larger population of trained developers, but Smalltalk's growth rate is eclipsing any other language's at this time.

DOES OO HAVE A PLACE IN LARGE INFORMATION SYSTEMS DEPARTMENTS?

Within many corporate IS departments, an enormous number of day-to-day operational problems and challenges grab everyone's attention most of the time. Whereas technological gadgets generally are smuggled in by the company's leading technocrats, OO only happens as a result of concerted management direction. It will not be market competition that drives IS departments, as it would in the smaller fast-mover companies. Rather, it will be almost entirely a management-driven dictate from above that makes OO happen. This makes it an iffy equation. OO requires different styles of managing projects. Furthermore, expectations are often absurdly optimistic for the first OO project.

Larger companies are characterized as having well-developed IS staffs that rigorously handle new software development. There are standards, and projects are managed by the book. There are data administrators, technical support teams, and change control teams. There may even be specialists who spend their time sniffing out network bottlenecks and tuning environments.

Then there is that heap of legacy code. Good stuff, doing good things, written by people who have long since been promoted up, out, and sideways. Actually, there are about five, six, or seven heaps of legacy code. There is the Common Business Oriented Language pile, the dBase pile, the FoxPro pile, the PowerBuilder pile, and now the Visual Basic pile. These last two heaps are starting to resemble something from the black lagoon: slick and gooey — something people will not enjoy getting their hands into years from now.

If the management of a large corporation looks only at the discrete up-front cost of the single next new system, then it will never go OO unless the technical staff lies to management about the cost and difficulty of making the transition. OO is both more expensive and more difficult to manage the first time around. If corporate management tries to home-grow the exper-tise, the expenditure may be totally wasted. Converting a team to OO is a supremely knowledge-intensive task, and it requires bringing in a wealth of knowledge from outside.

OO Cannot Be Done on the Cheap. This expensive route is an unaccept-able path for some large corporations. Many have chosen to do it them-selves to save money, which works reasonably well for only so long. There are situations where a team of four to as many as 12 developers labored for a year trying to develop the knowledge in-house. In more than one case, a single outside mentor was employed to try to pass on knowledge to the in-house teams.

Management is, almost without exception, unhappy with the outcome — usually a year passes with nothing but wasted effort to show for it. The strongly held view is that the outside mentor was incompetent because this person was merely coding to meet deadlines instead of trying to teach and mentor and cajole and coax the in-house staff on object-oriented methods.

Even if a corporation is an exception and has management that is willing to look at the whole picture, can the improvements justify the investment?

OO Reduces Ongoing Expenses, the Single Biggest Drain on IS Investment Dol-lars. First, most of the money in IS does not go to new development, but to maintenance. Maintenance is a catchall word. A good chunk of it is un-avoidable, such as the cost of keeping the IS infrastructure operational. Much goes to keeping a support staff handy to deal with other aspects of the IS infrastructure. Yet more goes to the perpetual task of keeping the old coal-burning software systems clunking right along.

OO Develops Systems that Are More Likely to Be on Target. Maintenance includes trying to change systems that only did what they were supposed to back when they were designed. (They were obsolete by the time they were completed, and it has fallen to IS to fix them.) Maintenance includes training users to deal with systems as they are, not as they should have been. It includes workaround efforts, meetings, reviews, and approval cycles to figure out if the changes requested by, for example, the marketing department are worth the benefit.

OO Systems Are Usually Easier to Change as the Business's Market Changes. As large as the systems maintenance budget is, a firm is probably spending more, and losing more, in trying to run its business in ways that fit the restrictions forced by those same systems and in trying to live with the delays of getting modifications made. For every $1 million IS spends for development, it is spending $5 to $10 million in maintenance. The maintenance game is addictive. Every new project adds to the maintenance burden unless IS removes systems as fast as it adds new ones. Some firms may actually spend $20 million for every $1 million in new development. From many angles, it seems out of line. But there are good reasons for the ratios.

Several psychological concepts and perspectives have been applied over the years in attempts to understand why maintenance costs so much. Many of them point to the problem of communication: a story told by one person to another, down through the layers, with adaptations by each storyteller. The project initiates in the marketing department and is translated to the marketing liaison who is technically apt, to the IS liaison and the requirements team, to the team of analysts, to the design team, and finally to the coders, who then pass their version of what the project entails on to the test and implementation teams.

Every translation introduces new solutions or versions that have little to do with the original needs. Each retelling creates changes to fit the technology used at each step of the way and to fit the mind-set of the technologists. Their mind-sets are different: The people at the deepest levels of the project are almost incapable of speaking with the people at the highest levels.

The impact of this problem increases over time. Usually, much of the difficulty involved in making changes to programs stems from the language differences between the programming world and the real world of the business users. The mind-set required for successful programming is almost impossible to bring into harmony with the mind-set required for a successful marketing department, for example. This causes major and long-lasting repercussions through failed efforts at communicating both needs and possible alternative avenues. A perceived lack of vision is one of these repercussions, as is the adoption of quick fixes to get around the problem for now.

Managers should seriously question the wisdom of continuing along any path that makes this faulty communication a permanent part of the landscape. Yet that is exactly what most companies continue to do. Traditional programming languages, with data-driven tools, founded on and dedicated to the IS view of the world and its restrictions, force developers into mind-sets that are contrary to good communication.

On top of that there is the increasing complexity of the IS environment to consider. Specialization is increasing. The problems of language and conceptual incompatibilities increase.

APPLYING LESSONS LEARNED

Managers and staff members within corporate IS departments can apply some of the lessons learned from the experiences of small high-technology companies when they are studying or moving to Object Technology.

Object Technology Simplifies Many Things. The systems designers start off with real-world terms and concepts. The process keeps users in the loop, with language that users understand. It is almost mandatory that users participate and even enjoy having a say in matters they can comprehend. The excitement of brainstorming sessions transfers to the designers. The resultant systems design reflects this cooperation.

Object Technology Bends the Minds of Programmers. With languages such as C, programmers can be heard muttering incantations to linked list and recasting pointers to data structures. With object technology, they speak in an understandable language about clerk objects asking loan officer objects about loan application objects.

Developers have trained so long and to such excruciating detail that this kind of simplicity may be amazingly difficult to handle. They may not think of it as learning to think in common business English.

One thing becomes clear as object technology advances through industry. Humans, even developers, are incredibly accurate at sniffing out problems of objects with aberrant "behaviors" and characteristics. Instead of spending days trying to locate a typographical error buried in a convoluted program, they are able to see, for example, that the problem is in the loan approval object. Another thing that becomes clear is a level of understanding of business by the developers. When they work with real-world business concepts day after day, developers eventually begin to grasp what is really going on around them.

This produces an observable outcome: When enough developers think like marketing people and accountants, the systems they deliver start working as they need to work for those departments. It is not a silver bullet. It is a difficult path that requires discipline and dedication. Most of all, it requires constant and continued management backing.

OO works because it encourages people to think in real-world terms. It works because it requires a foundation of reusable objects. It works because it takes a lot of thinking to develop good objects. But it is expensive because it is front-end loaded. Developers have to have the objects before they can reuse them.

In Project Management, Flexibility Must Be Viewed as an Advantage. OO projects are difficult to manage. Because OO development reflects the real world, it is also more intuitive in nature. The design process is highly flexible. The design is reviewed against real-world needs again and again and changed to fit the real world as misfits are uncovered. There are almost no clearly identifiable stages that can be managed and reported.

The beauty of the product stems directly from its evolutionary method of growth. Within some limits, IS could change the design up to the week of the final release of the product and still expect it to work. On the other hand, IS can be coding before the first analysis is even partly finished. (Much of the system, as a result, has already been thoroughly used and tested before the start of formal systems testing.)

This flexibility might confuse someone trying to pin a precise percentage of completion on the project and would certainly irritate an orderly project manager about to report to top management. There is a real problem here: IS managers must change to fit the new situation. How can they unless top management understands what is involved?

OO is not targeted at lowering front-end costs or making life easy for a project manager. Its entire focus is on what the results are down the road: on having the technical experts become business experts able to speak the language of the business; on having a foundation of objects that do not need to be changed, but do need to be assembled in a new pattern for new systems. OO is targeted at reducing maintenance costs and the other costs of using systems that do not fit business needs.

IS departments replaced old, tolerably reliable mainframes with cheaper, more reliable ones, even though the old ones were paid for. Why? One reason is maintenance. It is actually cheaper to buy the new hardware than to keep powering and maintaining those old hogs. The same is true for software.

However, those who claim a 10:1 or even a 15:1 improvement in speed of development are only considering a narrow band of the total picture. IS will not see that kind of improvement for the entire project. Smalltalk may at most allow developers to be five times more productive than if they were using C, for instance. IS may just have to be content with better systems that are less expensive to maintain.

Learning to Accept a Four-Times Increase in Funds for New Software Development or Acquisitions. Consider what a realistically attainable improvement means. Most of the IS budget is, directly or indirectly, going to the maintenance of old systems. Many missed market opportunities stem from the IS group's inability to make those changes now, not next year. If 90 percent of IS dollars are soaked up by running in place, and IS cuts that by 30 percent, it will have quadrupled its available cash for new systems. That is worth repeating. If IS can quadruple its cash to invest in new systems, and these new systems work better and are less expensive to change, then the IS department is turbocharged.

What the expected rate of return on new investments? Does IS want the return in cash, in flexibility to handle change over time, or both? Would IS invest an extra $1 million to lower life cycle costs by $2 to $4 million? Technical experts cannot do that. Only an executive such as the CIO has the power.

CONCLUSION

This last point brings the chapter back to the beginning. The smaller fast-movers invested in OO. They risked much but are now capitalizing on that investment. Large corporations may be more secure, but actually they have much more to gain by taking the object-oriented path.

If a company decides to go the OO route, however, it must understand that it is not a technology-driven path to victory. Quite the opposite: A company cannot buy the one thing that is the most crucial element to success. That one thing is management backing, consistently and judiciously applied.

With the full backing of upper management, an IS department has the chance to become part of mainstream management. Its technical people can become business experts, able to speak with other business experts. It can focus its attention on simplifying its sphere while providing the complexity it needs to meet future challenges. It can embrace this new world of object-oriented development and keep its firm moving forward.

Chapter 34
Economic Evaluation of Data Warehouse Projects

Duncan M. Witte

Data warehouse projects have been touted as providing critical competitive advantages, rapid investment recovery, and huge financial gains. Data warehouse implementations have moved from small, back-room "skunkworks" projects into large, mainstream, strategic systems status, with a corresponding increase in project size and scope. The Meta Group estimates that the development/installation cost of data warehouse projects averages $3 million. In organizations considering a data warehouse project, management wants to know:

- What will the data warehouse cost?
- What will it cost to maintain the warehouse and keep data current?
- If unsuccessful, what is the maximum potential financial loss?
- What tangible benefits can be expected from the data warehouse?
- What intangible benefits can be expected from the data warehouse, and what are they worth?
- In an environment of scarce funding, how should a proposed data warehouse rank with other proposed information technology (IT) projects? How should it rank with other proposed non-IT projects?
- If the data warehouse project is undertaken, what are the most sensitive cost, benefit, and risk factors?

Accurately predicting the likely outcomes of a complex IT project is extremely difficult. Conventional IT projects involving well-established technologies and applications often fall short of their promised functionality. According to a Standish Group survey, more than 30 percent of projects are canceled before they are completed, and the remainder average a near doubling of both their schedules and budgets. The success of data warehousing projects is even harder to predict because the technology is newer. Five factors contribute to the riskiness of data warehousing projects:

1. Relatively new and untried (within the organization) technologies.
2. Integration of heterogeneous data sources and legacy applications.
3. Multiple vendor software sources.
4. Cross-departmental/cross-disciplinary end-user groups.
5. Introduction of a new paradigm of end-user empowerment and direct database access.

This chapter discusses a methodology for the tricky task of assessing a proposed data warehouse project.

FUNDAMENTAL PROJECT ESTIMATES

In undertaking a data warehouse, three basic areas must be estimated: costs, benefits, and risks inherent in the project. Because of the time value of money (e.g., money earned today is more valuable than the same amount of money earned a year from today), all estimates must be evaluated in the context of their timing. In addition, there is a distinct difference in the estimation and overall effect of each of these three categories during the startup phase (i.e., inception, development, and installation) compared with the ongoing economics during the remainder of the system's life cycle (i.e., rollout, useful life, and retirement).

Costs in the development of a data warehouse are divided roughly into thirds between hardware, software, and staff costs. However, as the project progresses, even though there are incremental costs for hardware and software upgrades, more of the total cost shifts toward personnel and maintenance (both software and data). The January 1996 issue of *Computer Finance* placed the overall life-cycle cost breakdown at 15 percent hardware, 13 percent software, 31 percent labor, and 41 percent maintenance.

Exhibit 34.1 summarizes some of these relationships. Because development costs are only one-third of the full life-cycle costs of the system, considerable attention should be paid to assessing the costs of maintaining and supporting the data warehouse once it is installed.

The primary tool this chapter uses to evaluate a data warehouse project is pro forma cashflow analysis. The costs and benefits realized as a result of undertaking the project are predicted for each period (i.e., year, quarter, or month) of the full life cycle.

COSTS

Cost estimates should include discrete costs incurred during the development of the warehouse as well as continuing costs that are incurred throughout the life of the project.

**Exhibit 34.1. Relationship of Cost, Benefit, and
Risk Categories to Timing**

	Startup	Ongoing
Costs	1/3 Hardware	1/6 Hardware
	1/3 Software	1/6 Software
	1/3 Personnel	2/3 Personnel and maintenance
Benefits		
Tangible	Generally none	Generally insufficient to justify project
Intangible	Generally none	Requires "indicator" metrics
Shared	Generally none	Requires management vision
Risks		
Factor	Costs	Benefits
Duration	N/A	Benefits — Usually critical

Start-up Costs

Discrete costs include the following categories:

- *Hardware purchases and periodic upgrades.* Many data warehouse implementations use a dedicated database server. Costs for this hardware, as well as periodic upgrades throughout the development and life of the warehouse, should be predicted.
- *Hardware installation.* Although hardware installation is frequently a minor cost in small warehouse projects, larger projects require considerable configuration at the customer site after delivery. An installation of large disk arrays, extended memory, and high-speed network connections, for example, requires complex configurations and significant staff effort. Heterogeneous, multivendor configurations exacerbate this problem.
- *Vendor software licensing.* Many data warehousing projects use vendor-provided software for most or all of their functionality. Software components covering the full spectrum of data warehousing needs, including data copy/replication, data modeling, data scrubbing, query generators, report generators, Decision support systems, and industry-specific analysis and modeling tools, are available from a variety of vendors. Licensing costs for those components planned for both initial and subsequent releases must be incorporated into the economic analysis.
- *Vendor software configuration and installation.* Analogous to hardware installation, complex mixes of multiple vendors' software packages are difficult to configure. Although technically compatible, inconsistent metadata needs, communications protocols, or operating system environment needs can require extensive and complex installation

377

work. In many cases, vendor support staff or external consultants are needed to perform this work on site, adding to the costs.

- *Internal software development.* Although most data warehouse projects concentrate on the use of vendor software, a considerable effort is usually expended on developing functionality not provided by the vendors, or creating interfaces between heterogeneous vendor packages. This type of development requires detailed knowledge of the development environment and the ability to handle diverse vendor software interfaces.
- *Internal software installation.* As internal software is deployed, it is difficult to configure the software to run in slightly different environments on various servers and networks throughout the enterprise.
- *Data conversion and integration.* Data conversion and integration can be complicated by legacy systems that contain irregularities and inconsistencies. Tools are available to aid in conversion, but population of the warehouse is still a labor-intensive task.
- *End-user training.* End users must be trained to use the data access tools. However, the greater challenge is training users to find information themselves. Significant time and effort can be anticipated in many companies.

Ongoing Costs

Continuing costs include the following:

- *Hardware leases.* If hardware is leased rather than purchased, lease costs will continue throughout most of the life of the project.
- *Hardware maintenance.* Hardware costs are estimated based on a maintenance cost, either through a maintenance contract with an outside vendor or anticipated expenditures to correct problems that arise. In addition, as hardware is upgraded, maintenance costs must increase to support the expanded installation.
- *Vendor software maintenance.* The cost of software maintenance is often underestimated. Vendor maintenance fees are often based on a fraction (usually 12 percent to 18 percent) of current list prices. However, most software is purchased at a discount off the list price (often 50 percent or more). Thus the maintenance costs may be double the anticipated rate. Also, vendors usually raise the "current" price of the product over time as new features are added. As a result, maintenance costs are underestimated by a factor of four or more.
- *Internal software maintenance.* Internal software maintenance is also often underestimated. Most software provides interfaces between products from multiple vendors; however, as vendors change their products, the interface software has to be updated. This is an additional expense for the organization.

- *Database administration.* A common approach to developing data warehouses is to begin with a relatively small subset of the enterprise data and then grow the warehouse by the addition of new subject areas. This approach requires an ongoing DBA effort to do tablespace definition, table creation, reorganization, backup, and tuning activities on an increasingly large and complex database.
- *Data administration.* Data warehouses, by definition, never complete their data administration phases. Although automation can assume many of data administration responsibilities, changes in applications, legacy systems, and the business itself require continuing efforts to keep the pipeline for new data flowing.
- *End-user support.* The data warehouse presents a very different approach to data access, and many users will need considerable support. This is especially true in warehouse projects involving a limited initial rollout with a long growth process to cover the entire enterprise data model.

Tangible Benefits

Just as it is important to consider all applicable costs, it is equally important to analyze the benefits of a data warehouse project. Benefits can be tangible, intangible, and shared.

Tangible, or hard, benefits include those items that can be directly attributed to the completion of the project and that can be directly measured in financial terms. Tangible benefits can result from personnel reduction and use of dedicated hardware platforms, for example.

Personnel Reduction. The main target for personnel reduction in a data warehousing project is often the staff of the information center. This staff develops and maintains data extract programs for specific groups of end users. These programs retrieve data from legacy databases and make it available to the end-user clients as printed reports, flat file, and 4GL files (such as SAS or FOCUS). Data warehouse development essentially displaces this staff. A reduction of staffing costs (i.e., salaries and overhead) is a financial benefit of data warehousing.

Other staff reductions may be realized within the IS organization. Given a stable, well-documented source for high-quality data, it may be possible to reduce the amount of labor that must be expended developing and maintaining applications for many purposes beyond the pure decision-support role of the warehouse.

Use of Dedicated Hardware Platforms. Many warehouse projects use dedicated hardware platforms, which may free up mainframe capacity and help an organization avoid costly mainframe upgrades (i.e., central processing Unit, memory, or disk storage).

INTANGIBLE BENEFITS

Few data warehouses can be justified solely on the basis of tangible benefits. In almost all cases, intangible or so-called soft benefits make or break the economic analysis of the project. Intangible benefits include shared benefits. Intangible benefits are realized indirectly through metrics assigned before the project is started.

Examples of Intangible Benefits

Increased End-User Productivity. One reason for implementing a data warehousing project is to increase end-user productivity. Employees spend an estimated 60 percent of their time looking for data, reformatting data, and transferring data to other employees. If this proportion can be reduced by providing an easy-to-navigate data warehouse, the potential increase in productivity is enormous. Because this productivity is difficult to measure, it is important to develop and consistently monitor metrics to determine the productivity of the affected employees.

Improved Customer Service. Marketing and technical support staffs can provide better customer service if they have improved access to customer information. Improved customer service is a clear benefit, but benefits such as repeat purchases and referrals are difficult to estimate. Again, consistent monitoring of predetermined metrics is essential to understand these effects.

There are two useful approaches for calculating intangible benefits. The choice between the approaches depends on the accepted practices and management culture within a specific organization.

Approach 1:

- Determine the financial worth of each soft benefit. This job is best done by the line manager rather than the technology provider.
- No matter who makes the determination, the projected incremental changes in one or more key performance indicator — preferably measures with direct impact on the compensation of the responsible manager — must be predicted and quantified.
- Calculate the project economics using all costs, as well as hard and soft benefits. Then do a calculation using only costs and hard benefits. The difference between the two cases is the "value" ascribed to the soft benefits and must be addressed in the key performance indicator in step 2.
- Establish plan to monitor these indicators and audit them to determine whether they are achieved.

Approach 2:

- Calculate project economics using all costs and only tangible benefits. Determine present worth (which in many cases will be negative) on this basis.
- Solicit line management's approval for the project, using these "tangible only" numbers.
- If line management believes that the worth of the intangibles is sufficient to justify the "tangible only" project economics, then this decision constitutes a valid proxy for the actual worth of the intangible benefits.
- If line management does not believe that the worth of the soft benefits is sufficient to justify the project, abide by that decision. Line managers have both the approval authority for the project funding and the responsibility for spending those funds wisely. Their decision should be final.

Shared Benefits

Shared benefits are sometimes difficult to pinpoint. A shared benefit is caused by some form of improved management decision making, based in part on the better or more accessible information available from the data warehouse. The challenge is to quantitatively estimate the proportion of the benefit that can be claimed as a benefit of the data warehouse. Examples of shared benefits are discussed in the following sections.

Line-of-Business Cost Savings. Data warehousing projects provide direct benefits such as decreased inventory costs, better purchasing decisions, and higher product quality. These benefits result from decisions, not the data itself. Although these benefits may be quantifiable, the proportion ascribed to the warehouse compared with the proportion ascribed to competent management is difficult to determine.

Revenue Enhancement. Increased revenues result from efficient management decision making. Improved access to high-quality information (as provided by a data warehouse) is a component of better decisions; however, it is difficult to determine how much of the improved performance can be ascribed to the data warehouse project.

RISKS

Two types of potential risks in data warehousing projects are duration and factor risks. Duration risk is the likelihood that the data warehouse will not survive its planned full life cycle. Because many of the anticipated benefits of a data warehouse accrue over its lifetime, cutting that lifetime short will likely have dramatic effects on the overall project's value. There are many reasons that a data warehouse may experience a shorter-than-anticipated life, including the following:

- The warehouse may be completed, but not work as planned.
- The warehouse may be completed and released, but end-user acceptance may never build sufficiently to justify its maintenance.
- The business may change so much that the warehouse contents are no longer relevant to high-priority information needs.
- A new toolset or technology may become available that surpasses the capabilities of the current warehouse environment.

Exhibit 34.2 shows a general curve of longevity versus probability for life-cycle duration. It is important to characterize this curve for a specific project because the cash flows (positive or negative) will be truncated at the end of the project life cycle. Long project duration is often critical to producing positive financial results. Taken to extremes, if the life cycle is interrupted before the system is released for production use (as might be the case for a project that has far exceeded its budget and schedule), only costs will have occurred, with no benefits, and the system becomes a huge liability.

Best- and Worst-Case Predictions

A "factor risk" means that individual costs and benefits may vary significantly from the values estimated for the project. Risks are greater the farther into the future estimates are projected. Therefore, it is prudent to estimate not only a planned case for the proposed project, but to also bracket the plan with best- and worst-case predictions. The key is to create cases on which the project will never be worse than the worst case and never better than the best case.

Most data warehousing plans are optimistic. Worst-case values for individual factors should deviate farther from the plan (i.e., higher costs, lower benefits) than best-case (i.e., lower costs, higher benefits) values. In addition, the chances of realizing the worst case are usually far higher than the chances of realizing the best case.

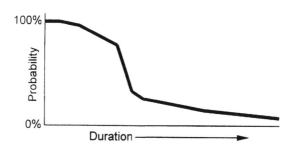

Exhibit 34.2. Duration Risk Probability Curve

Exhibit 34.3. Rules of Thumb for Relative Magnitudes and Relative Priorities of Best Case, Worst Case, and Planned Case Factor Values

	Proportions			Relative Probabilities		
	Best	Planned	Worst	Best	Planned	Worst
Costs						
Conversion	0.80	1.00	4.00	10%	60%	30%
Data Integration	0.80	1.00	5.00	10%	50%	40%
Developer Training	0.50	1.00	2.00	30%	40%	30%
End-User Training	0.75	1.00	3.00	25%	50%	25%
Hardware Costs	0.60	1.00	2.00	15%	70%	15%
Hardware Installation	0.70	1.00	2.00	20%	50%	30%
Hardware Maintenance	0.50	1.00	2.00	20%	45%	35%
Internal Software Development	0.80	1.00	4.00	20%	45%	35%
Internal Software Installation	0.80	1.00	4.00	20%	50%	30%
Internal Software Maintenance	0.80	1.00	3.00	10%	60%	30%
Network	0.80	1.00	2.50	20%	60%	20%
Ongoing Support	0.80	1.00	3.00	20%	60%	20%
Software Configuration	0.90	1.00	4.00	15%	50%	35%
Telecomm	0.60	1.00	2.00	25%	50%	25%
Vendor Software Licensing	0.90	1.00	4.00	15%	50%	35%
Vendor Software Installation	0.80	1.00	4.00	15%	50%	35%
Vendor Software Maintenance	0.90	1.00	6.00	10%	45%	45%
Benefits						
General Cost Reduction	2.00	1.00	0.00	20%	50%	30%
End-User Productivity	2.00	1.00	0.00	20%	50%	30%
Higher Product Quality	2.00	1.00	0.00	20%	50%	30%
Improved Customer Service	3.00	1.00	0.00	20%	50%	30%
Personnel Reduction	1.50	1.00	0.00	20%	50%	30%
Programming Staff Effectiveness	1.50	1.00	0.00	20%	50%	30%
Revenue Enhancement	2.00	1.00	0.00	20%	50%	30%
Competitive Advantage	2.00	1.00	0.00	20%	50%	30%

Each project will be very different, and the derivation of best, planned, and worst cases is still more of an art than a science. However, experience has led to several rules of thumb, listed in Exhibit 34.3, for assigning values and relative probabilities to best and worst cases, based on factor values in the planned case. These proportions can be used as a first approximation for poorly defined projects in their earliest stages of analysis.

CASH FLOW ANALYSIS

Once estimates have been developed for life cycle, costs, benefits, and risks, analysis of the project can proceed with construction of pro forma cash flow statements. Exhibit 34.4 illustrates a cashflow statement for the

Exhibit 34.4. *Pro Forma* Cash Flow Statement for Planned Case

Period From Period To	1/1/96 12/31/96	1/1/97 12/31/97	1/1/98 12/31/98	1/1/99 12/31/99	1/1/2000 12/31/2000	1/1/2001 12/31/2001	1/1/2002 12/31/2001	1/1/2003 12/31/2003
Benefits								
General Cost Reduction	.00	2,500.00	.00	.00	.00	.00	.00	.00
Staff Reduction	.00	450.00	450.00	450.00	525.00	525.00	600.00	600.00
Total Benefits	.00	2,950.00	450.00	450.00	525.00	525.00	600.00	600.00
Expenses								
Data Integration	60.00	25.00	.00	.00	.00	.00	.00	.00
Hardware Maintenance	.00	45.00	45.00	45.00	45.00	45.00	45.00	45.00
Software Maintenance	.00	75.00	75.00	75.00	50.00	25.00	25.00	15.00
Software Development Expenses	175.00	75.00	.00	.00	.00	.00	.00	.00
Support	.00	600.00	400.00	300.00	200.00	100.00	100.00	75.00
Vendor Software Expenses	250.00	60.00	.00	.00	.00	.00	.00	.00
Vendor Software Installation	25.00	.00	.00	.00	.00	.00	.00	.00
Vendor Software Maintenance	.00	75.00	83.00	91.00	100.00	110.00	121.00	.00
Total Expenses	510.00	955.00	603.00	511.00	395.00	280.00	291.00	135.00
Depreciation Deductions								
Hardware — Capital	80.00	138.00	92.80	55.68	91.84	92.80	41.28	23.04
Total Depreciation	80.00	138.00	92.80	55.68	91.84	92.80	41.28	23.04
Taxable Income	-590.00	1,857.00	-245.00	-116.68	38.16	152.20	267.72	441.96
Income Tax @ 39%	.00	724.23	.00	.00	14.88	59.36	104.41	172.36
Capital Costs								
Hardware-Capital	400.00	50.00	.00	.00	200.00	.00	.00	.00
Total Capital Costs	400.00	50.00	.00	.00	200.00	.00	.00	.00
Depreciation	80.00	138.00	92.80	55.68	91.84	92.80	41.28	23.04
Net CF After Tax	-910.00	1,220.77	-153.00	-61.00	-84.88	185.64	204.59	292.64
Cumulative Net CF-AFIT	-910.00	310.77	157.77	96.77	11.89	197.53	402.12	694.75

planned case of a hypothetical data warehouse project. The cash flow is calculated on an after-tax basis. Similar cashflow statements should be prepared for best and worst cases of the project. Many data warehouse projects use a phased-project methodology. The same analysis techniques are used, but the data warehouse as a whole will be the summation of all of its component subprojects.

Based on the net after-tax cash flow of the three cases, financial indicators can be calculated. Present worth (also called net present value), internal rate of return, payback, and investment efficiency (also called profitability index) are all applicable to these cash flow projections. Both present worth and investment efficiency are based on the analyst's selection of a discount rate for funds. The discount rate should represent the cost of capital, which is the interest rate that must be paid on the funding for the project, or conversely, the interest rate that could be earned with the same funds in alternative investment.

Given a project whose cases span the estimate ranges proposed in Exhibit 34.3, it is likely that the financial indicators will vary radically between best, planned, and worst cases. Exhibit 34.5 shows a typical range of financial indicator values. From this range, it is not at all clear whether this project is likely to be a tremendous success or an abysmal failure. It is likely to be somewhere in between, and history has shown that the planned case is a poor predictor of where the project will eventually end up. It is therefore important to use a method for deriving an expected outcome of the project.

Predicting Performance with Monte Carlo Simulation

Monte Carlo techniques allow users to simulate running the project many times using a series of random numbers to select project duration, and the costs and benefits for an iteration on a time-period-by-time-period and factor-by-factor basis. Although Monte Carlo simulation is a mathematically questionable technique, pragmatically it produces insights into likely project performance that are extremely valuable. Exhibits 34.6 and 34.7

Exhibit 34.5. Financial Indicators for Best, Planned, and Worst Cases

Indicator	Best Case	Planned Case	Worst Case
Present Worth @ 8%	$1,446.19	$374.42	$(5,092.81)
Internal Rate of Return	148.2%	31.9%	Undefined
Payback	2 Years	2 Years	None
Investment Efficiency	1.10	0.35	–0.74

Note: Present worth in thousands

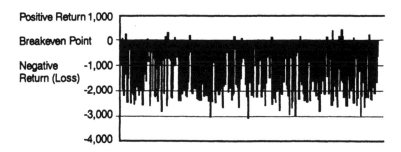

Exhibit 34.6. Plot Showing Present Worth at Eight Percent Discount Rate for 500 Iterations of a Monte Carlo Simulation

present outputs from a Monte Carlo simulation of a typical data warehouse project showing the present worth of a project. Exhibit 34.6 shows the present worth of each of the 500 individual iterations of this simulated project. Exhibit 34.7 is a histogram summarizing the overall simulation.

From these exhibits, which illustrate a case not including any soft benefits, it is apparent that:

- Without the soft benefits, the warehouse has a significant negative worth. The soft benefits may more than compensate for the negative present worth; however, this is a line management decision, not a technical decision.
- The histogram in Exhibit 34.7 shows a bimodal distribution. Further analysis should define the cause and the necessary project outcomes to ensure better project performance.

CONCLUSION

Data warehouse projects are risky. Many of the factors that contribute to poor performance in estimating schedules and budgets for conventional IT projects are particularly critical in the data warehouse environment. Economic analysis of proposed data warehouse projects should be done before the project is undertaken. This analysis consists of estimating costs and benefits in the context of their timing in the anticipated full life cycle of the project. An evaluation of risk should be done, consisting of developing best and worst cases bracketing the plan. Monte Carlo simulation of the project provides important insight into the likely financial performance of the project and the sensitivity of this outcome to changes in certain factors.

Given this approach, projects can be undertaken with an understanding of their likely outcomes, their sensitivity to various risks, and of the critical factors that demand concentrated management attention during the pursuit of the project to a successful conclusion.

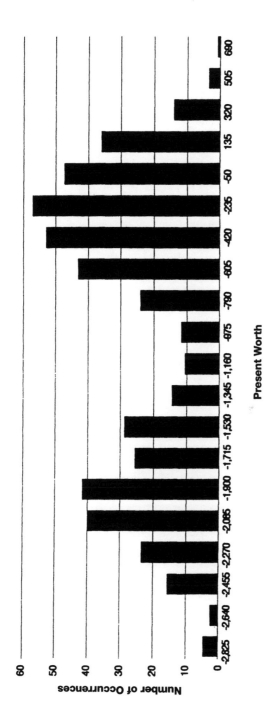

Present Worth

Exhibit 34.7. Histogram Summarizing Results of the Monte Carlo Simulation

Section V
Measuring and Improving Project Management Success

Chapter 35
Evaluating Project Performance

Ralph L. Kliem
Irwin S. Ludin

Opportunities abound for information systems (IS) projects to go awry, mostly because projects do not operate in a vacuum. A wide range of pressures are placed on them that affect quality, schedule completion, and budgetary performance. The results are often excessive costs, inadequate schedule performance, and poor quality.

A study by Standish Group International, Inc., indicates the following:

- Thirty-one percent of information technology projects are canceled before completion.
- Sixteen percent of projects finish on time and within budget.
- Fifty-two percent of projects overrun cost estimates by 189 percent.

Obviously, such a poor record affects the bottom line, costing firms thousands, even millions, of dollars. It behooves management, therefore, to assess performance before and during the project — and the earlier the better.

One approach for assessing current and future project performance is to use a ranking method adopted from basic statistical analysis and the work of Jerry FitzGerald (*Fundamentals of Systems Analysis,* New York: John Wiley & Sons, Inc., 1987). This approach, called a project assessment approach, focuses on four key fundamental elements of the project management process: people, quality, schedule, and budget. That information is used to evaluate the application of the basic processes of project management to achieve the goals of a project.

BASIC DEFINITIONS

Before describing the project assessment approach, definitions are necessary to ensure a solid understanding of what to accomplish:

- *Project Management.* The tools, techniques, and knowledge required to manage a project.
- *People.* Individuals required to ensure that a project is completed efficiently and effectively.
- *Quality.* The output from a project that meets customer requirements or standards.
- *Schedule.* The timeline required to complete a project.
- *Budget.* The money allocated to complete a project.

The project assessment approach entails four steps: Gathering background information, performing an assessment and constructing a matrix, conducting an in-depth review, and preparing the report. These steps are discussed in the subsequent sections.

GATHERING BACKGROUND INFORMATION

The person responsible for assessing a project, called an assessor, acquires a good understanding and knowledge of the project. This step involves answering the "Five Ws" and one "How" for a project:

- Why does the project exist?
- What are the major goals and objectives?
- Who are the key players?
- When are the major schedule milestones?
- Where do project activities occur?
- How are tasks executed?

Assessors acquire much of this information through interviews, surveys, documentation reviews such as project manuals and project history files, and database scanning such as archived databases.

CONSTRUCTING THE MATRIX

This step requires considerable planning to execute. Five people are key to successful execution:

1. Assessor.
2. Facilitator.
3. Subject matter experts.
4. Selected team members.
5. Scribe.

Assessors. They are responsible for the overall execution of this step and the entire project assessment approach. They usually function as the facilitator for constructing the matrix, although someone else could perform that role.

Facilitators. They facilitate, rather than run, the assessment sessions. They ensure open communications and encourage participation.

Subject Matter Experts. They are the most knowledgeable people on the project. Their knowledge may be technical or operational. The assessor selects them with the concurrence of project leadership (e.g., senior management).

Selected Team Members. They are project participants who are not necessarily subject matter experts but can provide helpful insights during this step. The assessor selects them, too, with the concurrence of project leadership.

Scribe. This person records notes during meetings for this step. He or she is neither the facilitator nor a subject matter expert. He or she may, however, be a team member.

Establishing Guidelines

To conduct an effective second step, the facilitator should remember to:

- Set up the facilities before the session.
- Have adequate supplies on hand.
- Appoint roles (e.g., that of the scribe or subject matter expert) ahead of time.
- Encourage everyone to speak.
- Be objective and noncommittal.
- Ensure everyone agrees on the process and objectives.
- Break frequently.

In addition, participants in the sessions should:

- Come prepared.
- Be tolerant of different views.
- Apply active listening skills.
- Agree on the perspective of ranking and definitions.

After identifying the participants (i.e., the team), the assessor initiates construction of a matrix for the project. The objectives are to identify and rank according to priority the project management processes and goals of the project. This ranking enables determining the existence and importance of processes and goals and how to efficiently and effectively achieve them. The assessment team, not the assessor, determines the basis for prioritization. The team does that through forced choice.

At the conclusion of this step, the assessment team produces a matrix, as shown in Exhibit 35.1. This matrix consists of rows and columns. The rows represent project management processes, ranked in descending importance. The columns represent the organization's goals, also ranked in descending order. The rows and columns are already ranked according to priority. A brief description of each follows:

Exhibit 35.1. How Measures of Success Relate to Matrix

Goal Process	Goal B	Goal C	Goal A	Goal D
Planning	Moderate	Weak	Strong	Strong
Leading	Moderate	Strong	Strong	Strong
Organizing	Strong	Strong	Weak	Weak
Closure	Weak	Strong	Weak	Weak
Controlling	Weak	Strong	Weak	Weak
Assessment	Moderate	Strong	Weak	Weak
Definition	Weak	Weak	Weak	Weak

- *Assessment.* Determining the environment in which a project occurs.
- *Definition.* Deciding in advance the goals.
- *Planning.* Determining what steps to execute, assigning who will perform those tasks, and verifying when they must start and stop.
- *Organizing.* Orchestrating project resources cost-effectively to execute plans.
- *Controlling.* Assessing how well the project manager uses plans and organization.
- *Closing.* Completing the project efficiently and effectively.
- *Leading.* Influencing people to achieve goals and objectives.

Ranking Processes

The ranking of the processes occur during a group session with the assessor, facilitator, subject matter experts, selected team members, and scribe present. Through forced choice, they rank goals according to descending order via voting. The values for each goal are tallied to determine the importance of each process. Exhibit 35.2 shows the ranking of processes and how to calculate the ranking.

When conducting the ranking, everyone must agree on the perspective. Is the ranking based on schedule? Budget? Quality? Failure to determine the perspective can quickly lead to miscommunication and misdirection.

Ranking Project Goals or Objectives

Ranking of goals or objectives is conducted the same as processes. Exhibit 35.3 shows a ranking of goals and how to calculate them.

The columns consist of the major goals or objectives for a project. The goals, ranging from one to dozens, are ranked in descending order. A goal is a broad statement of what the project will achieve; an objective is a specific, measurable benchmark that the project must achieve toward accomplishing goals.

	Assessment	Leading	Definition	Planning	Organizing	Controlling	Closure
Assessment	0 + 12 = 12						
Leading	2 / 3	2 + 15.5 = 17.5					
Definition	3 / 2	0 / 5	3 + 5.5 = 8.5				
Planning	4 / 1	2.5 / 2.5	2.5 / 2.5	9 + 11 = 20			
Organizing	3 / 2	4 / 1	4 / 1	4 / 1	12 + 5 = 17		
Controlling	1 / 4	0 / 5	5 / 0	2 / 3	5 / 0	8 + 5 = 13	
Closure	5 / 0	3 / 2	3 / 2	1 / 4	5 / 0	5 / 0	17 + 0 = 17
	12	15.5	5.5	11	5	5	0

Exhibit 35.2. Ranking of Processes (Example)

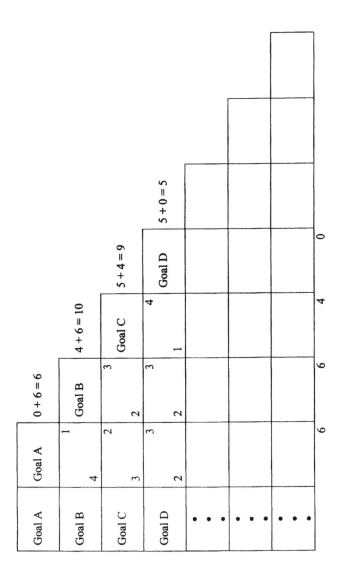

Exhibit 35.3. Ranking of Project Goals (Example)

Everyone should agree on the perspective to take when ranking. The same perspective should be used as in ranking processes.

Quadrants

The ranking of processes and goals or objectives enable determination of the importance of the cells, too, by identifying the most important quadrants or "regions" of the matrix. The first quadrant represents the most important goals and processes; the second, the next most important; the third quadrant, the next most important; and the fourth, the least important.

The importance of goals, objectives, and processes is based upon their calculated value resulting from ranking. These values play an important role in determining whether a cell (i.e., the intersection of a goal and a process in the matrix) is very important vis-à-vis other cells, as shown in Exhibit 35.4.

Each cell contains one or more measures of success. A measure of success is a set of activities, tools, expertise, and techniques necessary to complete a project management process to achieve any given goal. There are five high-level measures of success for project planning processes to achieve a goal:

1. Does a work breakdown structure exist?
2. Are reliable time and cost estimates available?
3. Has risk control been conducted?
4. Have resources been allocated?
5. Does a realistic schedule exist?

A group of internal project management experts can determine the measures of success for any given process. The assessor evaluates the degree of applying a measure of success in a methodical, consistent manner. He or she determines whether a measure for a particular cell is strong, moderate, or weak in its implementation. This judgment is based upon knowledge, experience, expertise, and research abilities. To reduce subjectivity, the assessor creates a range of values that indicate strong, moderate, or weak application of project management processes. For example, a strong application of a process falls within 100 percent to 75 percent of the total possible points, moderate application is within 74 percent to 25 percent, and weak is below 24 percent. For example, the degree of a measure of success for the first cell in Exhibit 35.1 is shown in Exhibit 35.5.

Weak measures of success in a high priority section of the matrix indicate an important area for improvement. Consequently, weaknesses in the first quadrant are serious concerns; weaknesses in the lower quadrant are of the least concern.

A wide array of tools exist for constructing the matrix. These tools include graphic, spreadsheet, and word-processing software. The keys, of

Process	Goals			
	Goal B (10)	Goal C (9)	Goal A (6)	Goal D (5)
Planning (20)	200	180 1	120	100 2,3
Leading (17.5)	175	157.5	105	87.5
Organizing (17)	170	153	102	85
Closure (17)	170	153	102	85
Controlling (13)	130	117 2,3	78	65 4
Assessment (12)	120	108	72	60
Definition (8.5)	85	76.5	51	42.5

Exhibit 35.4. Matrix Showing Quadrants

Exhibit 35.5. Cell Evaluation Scheme (Sample)

	Strong (3)	Moderate (2)	Weak (1)
___ Does a work breakdown structure exist?	X		
___ Are reliable time and cost estimates available?		X	
___ Has risk control been conducted?			X
___ Have resources been allocated?		X	
___ Does a realistic schedule exist?		X	
Total:	3	6	1

Note: Grand Total = Strong [3 * 1] + Moderate [2 * 3] + Weak [1 * 1] = 10. Maximum score = Strong [3 * 5 line items] = 15. This project's evaluation = 10/15= 66% which falls into the moderate rating.

course, in using the tool are the expertise of the person using it and the accuracy of the information coming out of it.

CONDUCTING AN IN-DEPTH REVIEW

This step verifies the contents of each cell. The assessor verifies to ensure that the contents of the matrix are thorough and accurate. The assessor does that by conducting additional interviews, reviewing documentation, and scanning databases. Good sources for documentation reviews are the project manual, project history files, and archived databases.

PREPARING THE REPORT

When the matrix is complete and its contents verified, the assessor prepares the report, which is presented either as a document or an oral presentation and contains all the basic elements of any business report, including distribution information, background, scope, findings, and recommendations. Eighty percent to 90 percent of the report, of course, should focus on the findings and recommendations, and it should answer two fundamental questions:

- What is the current state of the project?
- Where is the project going?

In the final report, certain guidelines should be followed. The writer should:

- Allow for revisions.
- Avoid spelling errors.
- Be clear and concise.

- Communicate the contents of the matrix to everyone who needs to know.
- Keep the "big picture" in focus.
- Keep the focus on the matrix.

CONCLUSION

The project assessment approach offers the IS manager many benefits. It can identify which activities are influencing the project in a positive or negative way, and which have only a moderate effect. For example, the approach can determine to what degree schedules are being developed, and how achievable they are.

This approach also provides a useful, objective assessment of project disciplines implemented. It minimizes subjectivity. This type of project assessment, for example, evaluates the effectiveness of the project leaders' styles.

The project assessment approach identifies areas to improve project management processes, increasing the opportunity for process improvement. For example, it is possible to identify aspects of updating schedules that can be improved.

The approach also provides an early warning about trouble that looms ahead for a project. Project managers and executives do not have to wait until the morning after disaster strikes. For example, managers can see what it is about the project plan that may fail to achieve a significant goal.

Finally, this method for project assessment provides a database of improvements to apply and warning signals to identify for future projects. No longer does history have to repeat itself. For example, staff can see which problems with the current project could be avoided on future projects of a similar nature.

Chapter 36
Completing Projects Successfully

James A. Ward

INTRODUCTION

Every data center manager has been involved in projects that have been less than 100 percent successful. Too many times, a project lasts longer than expected, requires greater staffing than is readily available, and strains data center resources; and sometimes a project ends in disaster. When faced with such a project, can a data center manager turn it around and achieve success? Better still, is there a way to prevent a project from becoming a problem?

The answer is yes. This chapter shows data center managers how to control projects so that they are on time, within budget, and successful.

KEYS TO GETTING STARTED

The keys that occupy a data center manager at the start of a project are planning and scheduling. These activities must also be repeated when attempting to salvage a project that is headed for disaster.

Requirements

Projects can and do fail if requirements are known, but there has never been a complete disaster when all requirements are fully defined, documented, understood, and agreed upon by all involved parties. Many projects fail when resources are devoted to the wrong things.

Project scope, objectives, and requirements must be completely defined, documented, and approved. This definition must take place before the project begins or its first activities are underway. When a project is in trouble, requirements must be revisited, restated, and reapproved.

In addition to defining project scope and objectives, a data center manager must also define the project in detail. This definition addresses the work to be done, the resources devoted to do that work, and the time that

0-8493-9998-X/00/$0.00+$.50
© 2000 by CRC Press LLC

the effort will take. Management must review and approve this project definition to ensure that resources can be applied productively. Productivity happens when the greatest amount of work is produced with the least feasible amount of resources in the shortest amount of time.

The work to be performed should be defined in such a way that when it is accomplished, the project will be successfully completed. Although it may sound elemental, this is not always the case. It is unlikely that any two project teams in an organization would perform an identical set of tasks or activities in the same manner or sequence. It is also unlikely that they would produce the same results. Each project defines its own work, and standardized work processes are essential to project success.

Resources consumed are primarily the efforts of the personnel assigned to a project, but they also include dollars, supplies, and management support and time. In a project, time can be defined as the elapsed calendar time from the inception of a project to its successful completion.

PROJECT PLAN AND SCHEDULE

Once the work to be done in the project has been defined, a data center manager can apply resources to it. Intuition says that if more resources are applied to the same amount of work, the time required should decrease. Intuition is correct, but only within certain limits. Unless a data center manager understands the dynamic interaction of these three variables — work, time, and resources — the negative effects of these dynamics during project execution will drive the project to disaster.

Resources vs. Time

Resources assigned past a certain level will not shorten project time. Beyond a point, more resources will actually lengthen the time it takes to complete a project. Brook's Law states that adding resources to a late project makes that project later. Even at project inception, this holds true.

Usually, the formula is that no more people can be productively used on a project than the square root of the total time of estimated worker months needed. If a project is estimated to take 100 worker months (i.e., eight-and-a-half years) of effort, then more than 10 people assigned to the project will not shorten the calendar time it takes to complete the project. Excess resources become wasted or counterproductive.

Law of Marginal Utility

The law of marginal utility operates in many IT projects. Accordingly, the second person assigned to a project will contribute less than the first, the third less than the second, etc. Although each new person makes a positive contribution and thereby reduces the overall calendar time it takes to complete the project, at some point the marginal utility curve turns, and the next person's contribution becomes negative.

The actual contribution of the 11th person in this project will probably not be negative, but rapidly declining marginal contribution begins at about that point. Therefore, a 100-worker-month project should take at least 10 calendar months to complete, no matter how many resources are assigned to it.

Because the productivity of each additional person added to the project will be less than the preceding person's, the average productivity of the entire project team is reduced. In allocating resources, management must achieve the optimal size of the project team that balances resources against time to achieve the most productive mix.

Overall Elapsed Time

If after estimating the total elapsed time for the project, the project will take more than one calendar year to complete, a data center manager should seriously think about redesigning the project. The project can be broken into phases or multiple projects. A 144-worker-month project (i.e., 12-year) project is about the largest discrete project that should be considered.

There are some compelling reasons not to undertake very long projects. First, an organization loses its attention span at some point. Other priorities intervene. Resources tend to disappear through either attrition or reassignment. Second, business conditions change. If a project cannot be completed within one calendar year of its inception, it risks becoming obsolete from a business standpoint. Third, the larger a project is, the greater its risk of failure. Degrees of error in planning can be overwhelming on large projects. A 50 percent overrun on a one-worker-year project is often manageable but can be disastrous on a 20-worker-year project.

Many organizations have obviously taken on very large projects. Chances of success are significantly enhanced when a project is carved up so that a major implementation occurs at least once a year. This method also provides ongoing visibility and organizational commitment to the project.

THE ROLE OF ESTIMATES

Every organization has a way of estimating projects. Whether this involves drawing lines on a Gantt chart, applying sophisticated algorithms, or just stating what the delivery dates must be, a data center manager either develops or is given an estimate of how long a project should take.

Estimates based on fact and that are accurate can be a tremendous advantage in project control. Estimates that are no more than a guess or someone's wish can be extremely detrimental. Unless estimates have a real basis in fact and are developed by those actually assigned to do the work, they are best ignored except when reporting progress to management.

The value of estimates is in productively allocating resources and in coordination of task interdependencies. Estimates should not be used as evaluation tools. A data center manager must be free to adjust plans and estimates on the basis of actual project feedback without having to explain why initial estimates were not totally accurate.

Plans are guides, and estimates are just that — best and most-educated guesses about what should happen. The reality is the actual project. If the reality does not always conform to the plan, it is likely that the plan may need to be adjusted.

TASK SPLITTING

A factor that reduces an organization's ability to use resources productively is task splitting. By assigning personnel to more than one project, management may think that more things are being accomplished or that resources are being used more productively. In fact, the opposite is true. Task splitting has a negative effect on productivity and efficiency, and this reality should not be ignored.

A person can devote 100 percent of his or her time to one project. That same individual will be productive only 40 percent of the time on each of two projects, 20 percent on each of three projects, etc. Deciding among tasks adds coordination and decision time. Time is not lost on switching from one task to another. Task splitting is a notorious resource robber. Dedicated resources are always the most productive.

PROJECT STATUS REPORTING

For a data center manager in charge of a project, project execution involves monitoring progress against the plan and schedule on a regular basis, recognizing deviations, and taking appropriate corrective action. Such a data center manager is chiefly responsible for ensuring that the work meets all quality standards and that it conforms to requirements and specifications. Providing high project visibility to users and management is also a primary project management risk.

90 Percent Done — Or Work Completed, Resources Expended, Time Used

A data center manager must invoke regular and formal status reporting. All project team members should report weekly progress against the plan and schedule. This reporting should be done at the lowest task level.

Each week, the project team members should answer the following questions about their assigned tasks:

- Is it done?
- If it is not done, when will it be done?
- If it is behind schedule, what are the reasons?

The intent of status reporting is to chart real progress and at the same time to verify the efficacy of the project plan, schedule, and estimates. Avoid any reporting of percentage of completion on any task, however, because this reporting is invariably overly optimistic and conveys no real information that a data center manager can use. In any event, the tendency to report percentage of completion usually indicates that tasks are too large to be accomplished in a time period in which they can be effectively controlled.

Providing High Visibility

When data center managers report status to management and users, they should emphasize deliverable products. Managers should report progress against major milestones and major deliverable products as defined in the project plan.

A project cannot be too visible. High visibility ensures management support. Management meddles in projects when it does not know what is going on. When a project hits rough sledding, a data center manager will need management's support to take action. This support must be nurtured through the confidence that comes from keeping management informed.

Reporting Status Frequently

Each member of a project team should have at least one task due for completion each week and on which to report. Under no circumstances should a team member ever have more than two weeks between task completion dates. If this is the case, a data center manager should go back to the plan and further break down tasks.

Management is not interested in weekly task-level reporting. Status reporting that is too detailed (or too frequent) usually obfuscates rather than clarifies project status.

A major milestone or deliverable product should be scheduled each month. Never let a project go more than two months without planning some significant event. The completion of a project phase with a formal report, including submission of the plan for the next phase, dramatizes progress most forcefully. The submission of a major deliverable product that requires management and user review and approval is also a critical event. If at least one of these events does not happen in more than two months, the project should be restructured and replanned.

Recognizing Deviations Early

Equipped with accurate project status information, a data center manager can assess progress and detect any deviations or problems at the earliest possible point. An axiom of effective project management is act early, act small. Corrective action can be instituted in small doses and in ways that will not be disruptive.

Upon receiving weekly project team status reports, a data center manager must post actual progress against the plan and note any deviations. If the project or some members of a project team are consistently ahead or behind the estimates, think about adjusting estimates accordingly. Minor adjustments in estimates, scheduled task completion dates, and task assignments should be done weekly as the project progresses. These minor adjustments do not have to be communicated beyond the project team as long as they do not affect scheduled dates for major milestones or deliverable products.

Identifying Causes of Deviations

In even the best plans, deviations happen. The first place to look for corrective action is in the plan itself.

There will be times in the course of any project when monitoring progress and making minor adjustments to the plan will not be sufficient to keep the project on schedule. This may happen for any number of reasons, and the reasons will undoubtedly influence the course of action a project may take.

The work may change because of changes in project scope. Resources may be lost to the project. Technology may be poorly understood. The project team may have problems interacting effectively. Computer time may be unavailable. When projects deviate significantly from plan and schedule, the dynamics of the key variables of work, resources, and time will determine the likelihood of success of any action that is taken to get a project back on schedule.

Leaving aside those occurrences that significantly alter the work to be done (such as changes in scope or incorrect requirements definition), the most frequently encountered problem is severe or persistent schedule slippage. The easiest course of action is to admit that estimates were overly optimistic and that the project will simply take more time to complete. However, persistent schedule slippage is more likely to be a symptom of underlying problems than the cause of the problem. Extending project time will not cure these problems and may allow a project team to dig a deeper hole for itself. It is lack of time that forces most project teams to face the reality of failure.

Instituting Corrective Measures

If a data center manager is thoroughly convinced that the problem is simply caused by overly ambitious estimates and schedules, then the schedule should be altered. Otherwise, under no circumstances will increasing resources against the same schedule be successful in and of itself.

A data center manager must subject a troubled project to detailed analysis, usually with the help of an independent party. Unless the underlying causes of problems are eliminated, the project will only experience greater problems as the data center manager and others attempt to apply corrective action. Management must be supportive of this process.

Once appropriate corrective action has been initiated, a data center manager must then go back to square one and prepare a formal project status report. Bearing in mind that the dynamics of work, resources, and time will be much different from what they were when the project was initially planned, the manager can then develop a new project plan and schedule.

CONCLUSION

A predictable pattern results when data center managers fail to understand the dynamics of work, resources, and time. First, schedules are extended, usually more than once. When this does not work, resources are added, making problems worse. Finally, in an attempt to bring a project to conclusion, the work effort is cut back, often to the point at which the resulting system no longer meets the requirements it was originally meant to address.

Heroic efforts to meet the original schedule by working large amounts of overtime for extended periods will not work. Error rates will soar, project communication will become increasingly difficult, and teamwork will be severely strained. Often, this drives a project into a never-ending sequence of test and error correction. These consequences often result because of management's inability to distinguish between effort and productivity.

By understanding and managing the interaction of the key variables of work, resources, and time, a data center manager can productively plan and control a project. Potential failures can be turned into successes. New projects can be launched with confidence in the likelihood of success — delivering systems that meet requirements on schedule and within budget — and make the most productive use of the data center's resources.

Chapter 37
Creating and Implementing a Balanced Measurement Program
Dana T. Edberg

It is still unclear why many information systems projects continue to fail, and why some succeed. Understanding the reasons for project success or failure, however, provides IS managers the information they need to form actions that enable the IS function to move forward and improve. The best way to gain this necessary knowledge is from a comprehensive IS measurement program.

Measurement is sometimes viewed as an objective in itself rather than as a way of supporting organizational goals. Much of the available advice on the application of measurement to the software development and maintenance process focuses on the intricacies and integrity of specific forms of measurement rather than on understanding the strengths and components of a comprehensive IS measurement program. This chapter focuses on the latter by describing a flexible measurement framework adaptable to specific organizational requirements. The chapter:

- Explores the concept of a measurement program.
- Uses the balanced-scorecard structure to develop a framework that serves as a guideline for the measurement procedure.[1]
- Divides the measurement procedure into manageable components.
- Provides guidelines for the development and successful implementation of a measurement program.

0-8493-9998-X/00/$0.00+$.50
© 2000 by CRC Press LLC

It has been said that the best way to understand the real behavior of software development and maintenance is to institute a measurement program that helps clarify patterns and guides decision making.[2] Measuring key attributes of software development and maintenance reveals behavior patterns that can be analyzed and interpreted to devise methods that better control and improve these functions.

WHAT IS A MEASUREMENT PROGRAM?

A measurement program is designed to help people understand and interpret an organization's processes. No company, for example, would dream of operating without a way of tracking and analyzing its financial transactions. A financial accounting system is the fundamental data collection process within an organization's financial measurement program. One measurement used by accountants in this program is the accounts-receivable turnover ratio. This ratio indicates how well assets are used by determining how many times accounts receivable is turned over each year. Calculating this ratio requires a system that collects the net credit sales and the average accounts receivable for the organization.

Although executives would not ask a credit manager to improve operations without first determining the current and potentially optimum accounts-receivable turnover ratios, they frequently ask IS managers to improve operations without any idea about important current and projected data and ratios. Whereas extensive computerized tracking systems support the financial and managerial measurement systems that underlie an organization's operations, IS managers are left with intuition and guesswork to control their part of the organization. The historical lack of systems to track and analyze key characteristics of the IS function sets the function apart from other aspects of business operations. Cutting costs or enhancing productivity is thus especially problematic in IS because it is usually accomplished without a detailed picture of expected versus current operations.

A measurement program spans the past, present, and future of a company's operations. Data from past operations are used as a historical baseline to measure present and future processes and projects. Present tasks provide current collection opportunities and data that is analyzed against the historical baseline to guide improvements in future performance. A measurement program thus consolidates data from the past and present to provide the insight that helps IS managers take action for future improvement.

A measurement program requires the formulation of specific, quantifiable metrics. Metrics are quantitative values obtained by measuring characteristics of a system or process. A metric is a piece of information that is analyzed, interpreted, and used to monitor progress toward improvement.

GOALS OF A MEASUREMENT PROGRAM

One of the most frequently asked questions about an IS measurement program is, "What are the best metrics?" A more appropriate question is, "What are the goals of IS and how can they be measured?" Understanding and defining the goals of an IS organization helps clarify the metrics that are a part of the measurement program. These goals, and the related goals of the measurement program, must be delineated before the counting begins.

Focusing on goals rather than on metrics is important for several reasons. People notice what is measured in an organization and frequently modify their behavior to make those measurements appear more favorable. Although laboriously counting the number of lines of code written per programmer per day encourages programmers to write more code and results in a lot of code, the code may not solve business problems. Tracking each computer development project and painstakingly updating visibly placed Gantt charts may prod employees to deliver systems on time, but the systems may have many defects that make them difficult to use or maintain. Surveying the satisfaction level of computer users may result in actions that produce happy users, but it could also have the effect of generating a costly and inefficient systems development and maintenance process.

Measurement helps to highlight specific areas in an organization and encourages people to focus their attention and energies on those areas. To leverage this measurement spotlight, IS managers should identify a set of combined goals that achieve the objectives of the organization. Once goals are established, managers should identify specific questions to be answered, which, in turn, leads to the metrics to be collected. This structure is termed the goal/question/metric (G/Q/M) approach.[3]

THE GOAL/QUESTION/METRIC APPROACH

The success of the G/Q/M approach is exemplified by the experience of the Motorola Corporation. Managers at Motorola identified seven goals they believed would improve their systems development organization.[4] For each goal they defined specific questions that needed to be answered to determine whether improvement had occurred. Each question was then defined in terms of an analytical equation, and the variables in the equation were divided into specific metrics that could be collected. For example, one goal was to increase defect containment. The managers defined the following two questions and related metrics to evaluate progress in this area:

1. What is the currently known effectiveness of the defect detection process before release? Total defect containment effectiveness equals:

$$\frac{\text{number of prerelease defects}}{\text{number of prerelease defects} + \text{number of postrelease defects}}$$

2. What is the currently known containment effectiveness of faults introduced during each constructive phase of software development for a particular software product? Phase containment effectiveness for phase I equals:

$$\frac{\text{number of phase I errors}}{\text{number of phase I errors} + \text{number of phase I defects}}$$

Using the G/Q/M approach gave Motorola the opportunity to clarify the semantic use of specific terms such as errors versus defects and the boundaries of given development phases while formulating questions and metrics. (For purposes of clarification, an error is a problem found during testing of the phase in which it was introduced, and a defect is a problem found later than the phase in which it was introduced.) Managers were able to use the information generated from the measurement program to pinpoint errors and defects by software development phase. This information helped them identify areas in the software development process that required changes and to make the needed changes based on information instead of intuition.

WHAT CAN A MEASUREMENT PROGRAM MEASURE?

The complexity of developing and maintaining business systems makes it difficult to isolate the activities and areas for which goals, questions, and metrics should be formed. The balanced scorecard approach to general business measures encourages managers to expand beyond traditional financial metrics and more thoroughly integrate organizational strategy with resulting performance.[5]

The balanced scorecard defines four different perspectives for performance measurement:

- *Financial* — How do we look to shareholders?
- *Internal business* — What must we excel at?
- *Innovation and learning* — Can we continue to improve and create value?
- *Customer* — How do our customers see us?

Although these perspectives were originally defined for measuring an entire organization, they can be translated to the IS world. There they respectively are the project, product, process, and performance perspectives.

PERSPECTIVES OF PERFORMANCE MEASUREMENT

Exhibit 37.1 depicts the importance of the four perspectives to IS measurement. They are discussed in-depth in the following sections.

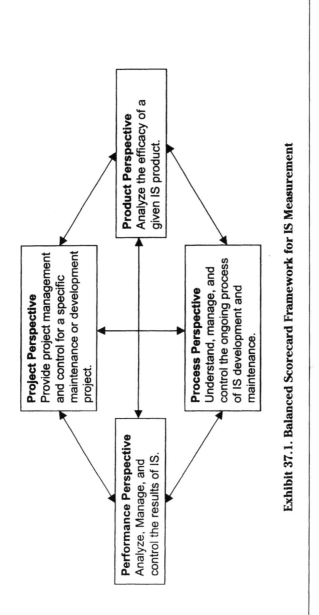

Exhibit 37.1. Balanced Scorecard Framework for IS Measurement

Project

The objective of the project perspective is to understand and measure the characteristics of a specific development or maintenance project by focusing on the attributes that make each project unique. Many organizations use a development or maintenance project as the vehicle to gather data concerning personnel effort and costs. Within the project perspective, an IS organization has the opportunity to use this data to create metrics that provide insight into how funds for software development and maintenance are used. What is measured depends on the scope of the project. The attributes of a given project provide information about such factors as personnel utilization, project estimation, and the nontechnical activities associated with a project.

Product

This perspective emphasizes the attributes that differentiate a product from others. The metrics applicable to this perspective are used to understand the growth and progression of a development and maintenance product. It is important to understand the internal scope and attributes of each specific product that composes a system. Managers can use this information to devise new testing procedures, determine individual product defects, or improve the accuracy of product estimation. Because a product frequently lives longer than the project used to create it, product data is gathered over the life of a product. Information generated from the data helps a manager better determine the life expectancy of a given product.

Process

The Software Engineering Institute (SEI) capability maturity model has brought renewed focus to the software development and maintenance process. The process perspective highlights the desire to modify the process used to develop and maintain information systems so that procedures reflect the best practices discovered in industry and within a given organization. The measures of this perspective consider organizational and human social interactions, as well as the methodological and technical implications of the development/maintenance process.

Performance

The performance perspective measures the outputs of an information system. It encompasses measurements that track both the traditional technical measures of performance as well as metrics that indicate the success of the system as defined by an organization's strategies and policies. Defining this perspective requires defining system success.

Importance of Balancing the Scorecard

Using the balanced scorecard approach helps IS managers ensure that all aspects of the IS function are appropriately represented in the measurement program. Instead of focusing on a single area, such as personnel productivity for a specific project, the balanced scorecard provides a framework from which to view each perspective of IS operations.

Using the scorecard thus helps IS managers delineate critical areas and define appropriate goals, questions, and metrics for each of them. The importance of the perspectives varies across organizations. For example, one company may be more interested in the performance of IS as a whole, whereas another might be more concerned about the productivity of project development activities. The balanced scorecard framework does not attempt to dictate the relative emphasis on each area but instead serves as a guideline for managers during development of specific measurement goals.

Sample Data for IS Metrics

Once an organization decides to implement a measurement program, the problem is usually deciding what not to measure, rather than deciding what to measure. Many organizations collect data for so many different metrics that participants in the measurement program become cynical and the effectiveness of the program is greatly reduced. In other organizations, the problem is to determine what kinds of data are available to be collected. Exhibit 37.2 lists categories of metrics for each perspective of the balanced scorecard framework, data for potential metrics in each category, and sample metrics. The exhibit is not comprehensive but rather an abbreviated list of possibilities for each perspective of the framework.

As the exhibit indicates, there are more types of data than there is time available to collect them. A measurement program would not be cost-effective if the data necessary to produce all interesting metrics was collected. The best method is to focus on basic metrics such as size, defects, effort, and user satisfaction before moving on to other metrics.

Under the goal/question/metric approach, the choice of metrics follows the definition of goals and formulation of specific, answerable questions. To achieve a balanced scorecard of measurement, IS managers must ensure that the metrics selected span each of the four perspectives. If one perspective is not measured, a distorted picture of IS may be the result of the measurement program. Because the balanced scorecard framework is used as a guideline to pinpoint areas for control and subsequent improvement, the implications of such a distortion are enormous.

WHAT MAKES AN EFFECTIVE METRIC?

It is wise to consider the criteria commonly employed to judge the usefulness of proposed metrics before selecting metrics that answer the questions deemed important to the goals of IS. A metric should be:

- *Understandable* — If a metric is difficult to define or interpret, chances are that it will not be used or it will be applied inconsistently.
- *Quantifiable* — Because metrics must be objective, IS managers should strive to reduce the amount of personal influence or judgment that must be attached to a given metric.
- *Cost-Effective* — The value of the information obtained from a measurement procedure must exceed the cost of collecting data, analyzing patterns, interpreting results, and validating correctness. A given metric should be relatively easy to capture and compute, and measurement should not interfere with the actual process of creating and delivering information systems.
- *Proven* — Many proposed metrics appear to have great worth but have not been validated or shown to have value in the drive to improve IS. IS managers should steer clear of metrics that appear overly complex or have not been tested and shown to be consistent or meaningful.
- *High Impact* — Although some metrics, such as cyclomatic complexity, offer an effective way of predicting testing time and possibly corrective maintenance time, they may not provide enough information to make their collection and calculation worthwhile in all situations. If the products being measured have relatively similar levels of complexity, it is more helpful to gather metrics with a more significant impact. For example, it is well-documented that one programmer can make a program very complex, whereas another can produce elegant, concise code. The effects of different code on actual testing and correction time, however, pale in comparison to the effects of incomplete or inaccurate design specifications. Therefore, the metric with the most impact in this case relates to the accuracy of design specifications rather than to program complexity.

IMPLEMENTING A MEASUREMENT PROGRAM

Although use of a measurement program appears to be a rational management approach backed by documented successes, some organizations find implementation a difficult undertaking. Implementing a measurement program is not a trivial task but rather a significant action requiring management commitment. The two key challenges in implementing a measurement program are time and communication.

1. Time. A measurement program is not a quick fix for a broken process with benefits that are quickly realized. Data must be gathered and analyzed over time before the program yields information that people can translate into actions that improve the development and maintenance process. It takes time to create a metric baseline, evaluate the results, and choose appropriate new actions. Then it takes additional time to compare new information about those new actions against the baseline to gauge improvements. Implementation of a measurement program is best viewed as a critical component of long-term continuous improvement.

2. Communication. Part of making a measurement program work is convincing people that it will lead to organizational improvements. If program participants are not convinced of the program's importance, chances are the effort will be abandoned before meaningful data is collected and used. If people believe that the results of the measurement program will be used to unfairly distribute blame regarding projects and products, then they will not participate in the program.

A key challenge of program implementation is thus communicating prospective benefits to the diverse audiences that will collect, analyze, interpret, and apply the information. At the same time, the proposed use of the measurement information must be made clear to all participants.

Program Activities

Although the success of a measurement program cannot be guaranteed, IS managers can increase the odds that implementation will prevail by paying attention to the individual activities composing the program. Exhibit 37.3 shows the activities necessary to implement and maintain an IS measurement program. Each activity is described in the sections that follow.

Assessment. The three primary functions of assessment are:

1. Evaluating the current position of the organization.
2. Identifying the goals of a measurement program.
3. Establishing specific measurement goals.

Since the mid-1980s, formal software process assessments such as those from the Software Engineering Institute and Software Productivity Research (SPR) have been available to evaluate the software development processes of an organization. Assessment provides a clear picture of the current organizational environment and serves as a starting point from which to gauge future improvements. For example, it would be unreasonable to state that a new development methodology provided increased programmer productivity unless the level of productivity before its implementation was known and documented.

During the assessment phase, it is also important to define the goals of the measurement procedure. Another activity performed during assessment is selling the measurement program to management and IS staff. All participants in the program must understand the relationship between measurement and improvement so that they will support the resulting program.

Formulation. A measurement program requires the formulation of specific, quantifiable questions and metrics to satisfy the program goals. The

Exhibit 37.2. Metric Categories, Data, and Samples for the Four Perspectives of IS Performance Measurement

Category	Sample Data	Sample Metrics
Project Perspective		
Financial, Type and Scope	Total estimated and actual time and estimated and actual cost per predefined project activity, type (e.g., development, maintenance), estimated and actual project function points.	• Cost per function point (FP) • Time per FP • Variance between Estimated and actual time and Cost per project activity • Variance for type of project
Personnel	Experience level, experience type and education of personnel, years using a specific development environment, number of contractor personnel, number of employees.	• Productivity ratings: time/FP For different levels of Experience and education • Cost/FP for different levels • Relative comparison of contractors to employees
Methodology	Type(s) used, level of automation, testing techniques, number of models.	The metrics for methodology are Summarized for the entire Software process rather than for a particular project.
Interface	Number of meetings, meeting type and length, number of requirements and design changes, pages of documentation, hours of customer training.	• Percent of time in meetings and by meeting type • Number of meetings/FP • Number of changes/FP • Customer training/FP
Product Perspective		
Financial, Type and Scope	The same data and metrics used for a project are also applied to a single product. One project could result in many products, or it might take many projects to produce a single product. Product measurements exist over the life of the product, whereas project metrics are closed out when the project is completed.	
Quality	Number of defects and errors, number of test cases, number of change requests, number of changes, amount of usage, complexity rating, number of reused modules, number of support calls.	• Number of defects/FP • Number of change requests/FP • Usage as related to customer training and documentation • Percent reusability
Results	Business objectives translated into quantitative goals.	• Inventory percent level • Cycle time in days • Percent of purchase order filled by a given date
Efficiency	Amount of memory, disk, processor cycles, response time, operator time.	• Average/peak response time • Average/peak disk usage

Exhibit 37.2. Metric Categories, Data, and Samples for the Four Perspectives of IS Performance Measurement *(Continued)*

Category	Sample Data	Sample Metrics
Process Perspective		
Organization	Number of general meetings, type of meetings, communication methods, hours by activity; amount of office and desk space.	• Maturity level assessment* • Percent of time in non-project-related tasks versus project-related tasks • Office space/person • Time utilization
Personnel	Data in addition to that gathered for a given project include: vacation days taken, vacation days worked, number of working days, number of employees, number of contractors, number of training days.	Metrics in addition to those Listed for a given project include: • Employee turnover • Vacation use • Training by employee level and experience • Training by activity type
Methodology	Gathered by project.	• Overall productivity by methodology • Testing productivity by methodology • Overall productivity by average number of model/FP
Performance Perspective		
Satisfaction	User satisfaction survey, number of system users, number of workstations, number of reports generated, number of reports used, number of screens, number of screens viewed, number of help requests.	• Average time to respond to help requests • Average time to fill maintenance requests • Average time to respond to development requests • Usage growth rate of workstations, reports, and screens • Customer satisfaction rating
Integrity	Number of errors discovered after delivery, number of errors Discovered within a selected period of time, error severity.	• Average number of errors (classified by severity) discovered after delivery • Average number of errors (classified by severity) discovered within a period of time

* For a summary of maturity level assessment see Jones, C., Evaluating Software Outsourcing Options. *Information Systems Management* 11, no. 4 (1994), p. 32.

previously discussed suggestions for choosing appropriate metrics and sample goals/questions/metrics provide a good starting point.

Collection. The collection of specific metrics requires a cost-accounting system aimed at gathering and storing specified attributes that act as input data for the metrics. This process should be automated so that collection takes as little time as possible and the danger of becoming mired in amassing huge amounts of data is avoided. Careful planning in assessment and formulation helps avoid the gathering of too much data.

Analysis. The physical collection of a metric does not, by itself, provide much information that helps in the decision-making process. Just as gross sales do not reveal the financial condition of an organization, the number of function points for a project does not explain how many person-months it will take to produce that project. A metric must be statistically analyzed so that patterns are uncovered, historical baselines are established, and anomalies are identified.

Interpretation. The function of interpretation is to attach meaning to the analysis; in other words, to determine the cause of the patterns that have been identified during analysis and then prescribe appropriate corrective action. For example, if analysis shows that users are consistently dissatisfied with systems that require an ever-increasing number of user and analyst meetings, then it may not be a good idea to schedule more meetings. A more effective approach is to look for other reasons behind the dissatisfaction. Perhaps the meetings are unproductive, communication skills are ineffective, or business problems are being incorrectly identified. The interpretation of metric analyses furnishes a direction in which to start looking for different problems and solutions.

Validation. As shown in Exhibit 37.3, validation occurs throughout each phase of the measurement program. It involves asking a set of questions to ensure that the goals of the measurement program are being addressed. For example, the results of the formulation phase should be validated with two key questions:

1. Are we measuring the right attribute?
2. Are we measuring that attribute correctly?

The following scenario illustrates how validation questions are applied. Let us assume that one of the overall goals of an IS organization is to improve the performance of user support. Using the G/Q/M approach, the IS organization establishes a goal of improving user satisfaction with IS support. A question that supports this goal is, What is the current level of user satisfaction with IS support? IS personnel then formulate a questionnaire they believe measures the level of user satisfaction with IS support. The questionnaire is used to collect data, which is analyzed and interpreted.

Analysis shows that there is no relationship between the type, amount, or level of IS support and user satisfaction. Why not? It could be because there is no relationship between user satisfaction and IS support, or because the questionnaire was not measuring user satisfaction with IS support. Validating the questionnaire in the formulation phase helps ensure that it is measuring what it intended to measure.

Measurement as a Passive Yet Iterative Process

Measurement is a relatively passive process; it is the actions people take based on the fact that they are being measured and the new procedures that are developed based on the information generated from the measurement program that lead to improvement. The goal of a measurement program is to provide information that can be used for continual improvement of the systems development process and its related products.

Although Exhibit 37.3 depicts the activities of assessment, formulation, collection, analysis, and interpretation as a sequential, circular process, they are interdependent and not performed sequentially. In the scenario presented in the preceding section, the IS organization found during analysis that the identified metrics were inadequate to determine any patterns. Such a result required validation of the metrics being used and a return to the formulation phase to redefine other metrics that yield information more relevant to the goals.

MANAGING A MEASUREMENT PROGRAM

A measurement program is a long-term effort requiring the cooperation and coordination of a broad set of participants. One way to support the program is to establish a metrics infrastructure. A metrics infrastructure includes the following:

- A management method.
- Data collection procedures.
- Ongoing program training.

The management method should incorporate an integrated group/committee that performs each of the measurement activities. This group is similar to a conventional project steering committee and includes representatives from general management, IS management, system users, and IS development/maintenance. It differs from a project management group primarily because it survives past the implementation of the program. As a long-term, ongoing process, measurement must have a long-term, ongoing management committee.

The management group is critical to the success of a measurement program because it keeps program participants aware of the importance of their activities and provides the broad view necessary to the program's

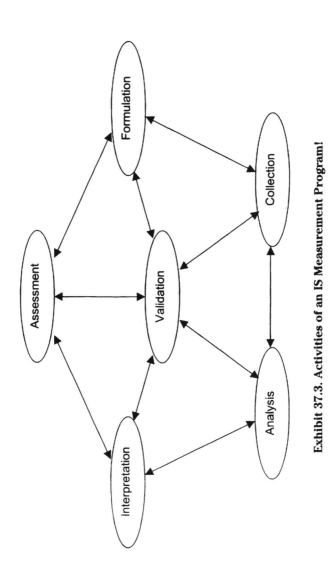

Exhibit 37.3. Activities of an IS Measurement Program!

survival. The committee determines how the program's goals evolve over time and serves as a touchstone for their achievement.

It is also beneficial to establish a metrics user group to share experiences and coordinate training. Training is a key element of the metrics infrastructure that should be periodically provided. Training programs encompass data collection, analysis, and interpretation procedures so that project participants understand not only how to collect data, but how to apply it. The infrastructure should also include tools to automate the collection and analysis phases of measurement, as well as a consolidated data base to store all metrics data.

Because the results of a measurement program are not immediately discernible, people have to perform many tasks before visible, attributable outcome is perceived. Training is one way to ensure that all project participants understand the goals and procedures that underlie what may appear, at times, to be a slow process. It also helps to alleviate employee concerns about the application of the measurement program results.

Many of the activities of measurement require the cooperation of diverse groups of people. Even though the concepts of metrics and measurement conjure up an image of required technical expertise, the most appropriate leader for the measurement program is an individual with excellent communication and negotiation skills.

Information about programs used in other companies is helpful during the process of defining program objectives and formulating metrics. The recommended reading list provides a source for gathering this information.

RECOMMENDED COURSE OF ACTION

Each day new articles describe a new practice touted to yield tremendous productivity and efficiency improvements in the IS organization. Some IS managers have discovered that it can take many years to apply the so-called best practices of other organizations recorded in the literature. A measurement program affords IS managers the opportunity to develop local proof of what really works. More important, the information produced from a measurement program helps IS managers better understand and control the process of software development and maintenance.

Creating a custom-tailored measurement program thus provides IS managers with information about the unique behavioral patterns of their organization. In doing so, it helps these managers control their professional destinies as well.

Notes

1. R.S. Kaplan and D.P. Norton, "Using the Balanced Scorecard as a Strategic Management System," *Harvard Business Review* (January–February 1996).

2. L.H. Putnam and W. Myers, Measures for Excellence (Englewood Cliffs NJ: Yourdon Press, 1992), p. 11.
3. V.R. Basili and D.M. Weiss, "A Methodology for Collecting Valid Software Engineering Data," *IEEE Transactions on Software Engineering* 10, no. 3 (1984), pp. 728–738.
4. M.K. Daskalantonakis, "A Practical View of Software Measurement and Implementation Experiences within Motorola," *IEEE Transactions on Software Engineering* 18, no. 11 (1992), pp. 998–1010.
5. R.S. Kaplan and D.P. Norton, "The Balanced Scorecard: Measures that Drive Performance," *Harvard Business Review* (January–February 1992), pp. 71–79.

Bibliography

Grady, R.B. *Practical Software Metrics for Project Management and Process Improvement.* Englewood Cliffs NJ: Prentice-Hall, 1992.
Paulish, D.J., and Carleton, A.D. "Case Studies of Software-Process-Improvement Measurement." *IEEE Computer* (September 1994), pp. 50–57.
Putnam, L.H., and Myers, W. *Measures for Excellence.* Englewood Cliffs NJ: Yourdon Press, 1992.
Roche, J., and Jackson, M. "Software Measurement Methods: Recipes for Success?" *Information and Software Technology* 36, no. 3 (1994), pp. 173–189.

Chapter 38
Negotiating Conditions for Project Success

Stanley H. Stahl

A basic principle for implementing a sustainable software productivity improvement program is to make everyone a winner. A systems project that comes in on budget and schedule and meets user requirements makes winners out of users, senior management, and the IS department. Making winners of people helps get their commitment and involvement as well as helps them overcome their natural resistance to change. It is a critical component of quality improvement in pioneer W. Edward Deming's precept of putting everyone to work to accomplish quality improvement.

Theory-W is a way to make everyone a winner. This theory was developed by Barry Boehm in the late 1980s. At the time, Boehm was chief scientist in the TRW defense systems group and a professor of computer science at the University of California, Los Angeles. In their paper, "Theory-W Software Project Management: Principles and Examples," Boehm and Rony Ross presented a unifying theory of software project management that is simultaneously simple, general, and specific. In the introduction to this paper, Boehm and Ross wrote: "The software project manager's primary problem in that a software project needs to simultaneously satisfy a variety of constituencies; the users, the customers, the development team, and management. ... Each of these constituencies has its own desires with respect to the software project. ... These desires create fundamental conflicts when taken together. ... These conflicts are at the root of most software project management difficulties — both at the strategic level (e.g., setting goals, establishing major milestones, and responsibilities) and at the tactical level (e.g., resolving day-to-day conflicts, prioritizing assignments, and adapting to changes)."[1]

Theory-W is a way to help project managers cope with the difficulty of simultaneously satisfying different constituencies. Theory-W has one sim-

0-8493-9998-X/00/$0.00+$.50
© 2000 by CRC Press LLC

ple but very far-reaching principle: make everyone a winner by setting up win–win conditions for everyone.

THEORY-W: BACKGROUND AND BASICS

Theory-W contrasts with such theories on management as Theory-X, Theory-Y, and Theory-Z. The Theory-X approach to management originated in the work of Frederick Taylor, who was active at the beginning of this century. Taylor contended that the most efficient way to accomplish work was to organize jobs into a well-orchestrated sequence of efficient and predictable tasks. Management's responsibility was to keep the system running smoothly; this task was often accomplished by coercing and intimidating workers.

For obvious reasons, Taylor's Theory-X is inappropriate for managing software projects. Theories-Y and Z, introduced in the late 1970s, were intended as alternatives to Theory-X. Theory-Y's perspective is that management must stimulate creativity and initiative, which are both important qualities for a quality software project. The difficulty with Theory-Y, however, is that is provides inadequate mechanisms for identifying and resolving conflicts.

Theory-Z seeks to improve on Theory-Y by emphasizing the development of shared values and building consensus. The problem with Theory-Z is that consensus may not always be possible or desirable; this can be the case when dealing with different constituencies that each has its own unique set of constraints and requirements.

If the Theory-X manager is an autocrat, the Theory-Y manager a coach, and the Theory-Z manager a facilitator, then the Theory-W manager is a negotiator. The manager in the Theory-W model must proactively seek out win–lose and lose–lose conflicts and negotiate them into win–win situations. Delivering software systems while making winners of all stakeholders seems, at first glance, to be hopelessly naive.

Users want systems delivered immediately and they want them with all the bells and whistles imaginable. Management not only wants systems delivered on schedule and within budget, they also want a short schedule and a low budget. Developers want technical challenges and opportunities for professional growth, and they often do not want to document their work. Maintainers want well-documented systems with few bugs and the opportunity for a promotion out of maintenance. How can a project manager expect to successfully negotiate the conflicting needs of all constituents?

IMPORTANCE OF NEGOTIATING

Although it may seem like a naive theory, there is an accumulation of evidence that Theory-W works. In fact, Theory-W is coming to be seen as fundamental to project success. The reason lies in the character of a win–win negotiation. The objective in win–win negotiating is for all parties to recognize each other's specific needs and to craft a resolution that allows all participants to share in getting their needs met. This is very different from traditional styles of negotiation, which are too often win–lose.

In the absence of an explicit commitment to foster win–win relationships, software projects have the capability of becoming win–lose. For example, building a quick but bug-laden product may represent a low-cost win for an over-pressured development organization but it is a loss for the users. Alternatively, when management and users force developers to add extra features without giving the development organization the time and resources needed to develop the extra features, the result may be a win for users and loss for developers. Software maintenance personnel often loses as management, developers, and users fail to ensure that software is well-documented and easily maintainable.

At their worst, software projects can become lose–lose situations where no one wins. It is common that management sets unreasonable schedule expectations, and as a result, the development department tries to catch up by adding more and more people to the project. The result is, all too often, a poor product that comes in over cost and over schedule. In this case, everyone loses.

THE COSTS OF NOT NEGOTIATING

The following example illustrates the effects of how ignoring Theory-W affects a project. Although this example is fictional, it is based on actual experience.

A Lose–Lose Project

A growing specialty retailer had just hired a new chief information officer. The new CIO was given the charter to modernize the company's antiquated information systems but had been explicitly told by the CEO that budgets were extremely limited and that the new systems would have to be implemented as the size of the IS staff was decreased.

The first task was to conduct a user-needs survey, which indicated that, except for the payroll systems, all of the company's existing systems were inadequate. The inventory control system was barely usable, there was no integration between different systems, and each system served, at best, only the limited needs of the department for which it had been designed. The survey also indicated that most users were unaware of the potential productivity boost that up-to-date information systems could give to the company's business.

After the survey had been analyzed, the following four recommendations were made:

1. All existing systems should be replaced by a client/server system capable of supplying timely and accurate information to both operational personnel and senior management.
2. The changeover should be implemented in stages. The first system should be a relatively simple, low-risk, stand-alone application.
3. The system should be procured from an outside contractor, preferably a software house that has a package that could be used with minimal modifications.
4. Training should be provided to middle managers to help them be better able to guide the IS department in implementing the new systems.

Basics Were Ignored. These recommendations were enthusiastically approved. A request for proposal for a new inventory distribution management control system, everyone's favorite candidate to be implemented first, was requested. However, nothing was said about budgets, schedules, or personnel needs, and in their enthusiasm, everyone seemed to forget about training.

Lack of User Input. The request for proposal (RFP) was developed with little input from distribution personnel, so it was rather open-ended and not very explicit. The result was that the IS group received from outside contractors eight responses ranging in price from $70,000 to $625,000. After lengthy negotiations, a contract was awarded to a single company that would provide both hardware and software for the new inventory control system.

Unclear RFP. The contractor was a leader in inventory management systems though their largest account was only half the size of the retail company. To land the account, the contractor promised to make any necessary modifications to the system free-of-charge. The contractor's reading of the RFP led its developers to believe that there was little technical risk in this promise.

The contractor was wrong in its interpretation of the RFP. Although the contract called for the system to be up and running in six months at a cost of $240,000, a year later the contractor was still working on change the system to meet the client's needs.

Neither was the retailer's IS department experiencing a good year. It was continually at odds with both distribution personnel and the contractor over the capabilities of the new inventory system. The users kept claiming that the system was not powerful enough to meet their needs, while the contractor argued that the system was in use by more than 200 satisfied companies.

Costly Failure. At the end of an acrimonious year, the contractor and retailer agreed to cancel the project. In the course of the year, the contractor was paid more than $150,000, and the contractor estimated that its programming staff had spent more than 10 worker-months modifying the system to meet the client's needs. The retailer estimated that it had invested the time of one senior analyst as well as several hundred hours of distribution personnel.

HOW THEORY-W WOULD HAVE HELPED

Losers and the Consequences

The most apparent source of difficulty on the project was the explicit win–lose contact established between the retailer and the contractor. By requiring the contractor to cover any expenses incurred in modifying the system, the retailer set up a situation where the contractor would only make changes reluctantly. This lessened the likelihood that distributors would get the modifications they needed and increased the likelihood that changes would be made in a slap-dash way, with too little attention paid to quality.

The IS department's relationship with senior management was also win–lose. There was little likelihood that the CIO could emerge victorious. The system had to be brought in one time and within budget, though the user community was inadequately trained to help properly identify its needs and requirements. The result was that neither the retailer nor the contractor had an adequate handle on the inventory system's requirements and were consequently unable to adequately budget or schedule the system's implementation. The IS department's situation was made worse because senior management wanted to decrease the size of the IS staff.

The users lost the most. Not only did they not receive the system they needed and had been promised, but they wasted time and money in taking time from their primary jobs to help develop the new system. Both the retailer's and the contractor's developers lost the time they invested in a failed project, the ability to grow professionally, and the opportunity to work on a successful project.

FROM A PROCESS PERSPECTIVE

Fault lies both in the contracting process and in the systems requirements management process by which the retailer and the contractor defined and managed systems requirements. These front-end processes are often the source of project management difficulties, but problems were worsened in this case by the IS department's neglect to identify the real needs of stakeholders and to negotiate an appropriate win–win package. Although the IS group was neglectful, it is not to blame — the problem lies with the process.

STEPS TO IMPROVE THE PROCESS

To improve these faulty processes, Theory-W principles of software management can be used. The following three steps, which are adapted from

"Theory-W Software Project Management," can be used to implement Theory-W software management:

- Establishing a set of win–win preconditions by performing the following:
  - Understanding what it is that people want to win.
  - Establishing an explicit set of win–win objectives based on reasonable expectations that match participants' objectives to their win conditions.
  - Providing an environment that supports win–win negotiations.
- Structuring a win–win development process by accomplishing the following:
  - The establishment of a realistic plan that highlights potential win–lose and lose–lose risk items.
  - Involvement of all affected parties.
  - Resolving win–lose and lose–lose situations
- Structuring a win–win software product that matches the following:
  - The users' and maintainers' win conditions.
  - Management's and supplier's financial and scheduling win conditions.

APPLICATION OF THEORY-W

There are several actions that the retailer's IS department could have taken to increase the project's probability of success. It could have trained distribution personnel on the key role they have in properly identifying and articulating their needs. Following this training, IS staff could have worked with these users to draft a more thorough request for proposal. After receiving RFP responses, the IS department could have involved senior management in identifying limits on resources and schedules. It could have foreseen the difficulties the contractor would have if significant program modifications were needed.

By identifying constituent win conditions, the IS department would then have been in a position to negotiate a fair contract that would have explicitly taken into account all win conditions. Having done these critical upfront tasks, the IS department would then have been in a position to structure both a win–win development process and software product. Unfortunately, the IS department never set win–win preconditions.

In the absence of an explicit philosophy to make everyone a winner and an explicit process for accomplishing this, the IS department lacked the necessary support to identify stakeholders' needs and negotiate a reasonable set of win–win objectives. Thus, it was only a matter of time until incompatible and unobtainable win conditions destroyed the project.

CONCLUSION

Boehm's work on Theory-W software project management continues. Currently, a professor of computer science at the University of Southern California and chairperson of its center for software engineering, he has a research program to develop a tool for computer-aided process engineering that has Theory-W built in. As part of this research, he is prototyping an interactive system in which constituents can enter their win conditions and all stakeholders can then simultaneously analyze and negotiate a combined set of win conditions.

Theory-W has been shown to be successful — both in terms of the paradigm it offers and in terms of its ability to help managers explicate and simultaneously manage the win conditions of all constituents and stakeholders. Theory-W is even more important for organizations embarking on a systematic program to improve productivity. Productivity improvement programs, and such similar programs as total quality management or process reengineering, require the full and complete support of all stakeholders. Theory-W offers both a theory and a process for getting and keeping this needed support.

Note

1. B. Boehm and R. Ross, "Theory-W Software Project Management: Principles and Examples," *IEEE Transactions on Software Engineering* 15, no. 7.

Chapter 39
Continuous Process Improvement in Systems Development

Robert F. Kniestedt
Pamela A. Hager

Systems development has been considered a creative effort: technological advances in systems development were closely tied to the practical use of the capabilities that were discovered. In the beginning, requirements gathering was a necessary but ill-defined process. Systems developers found it difficult coping with the unknown. With no defined techniques or method, requirements were a moving target and a great deal of recoding was needed to define them correctly. Because of their unfamiliarity with the technology, clients were at an enormous disadvantage. Data processing had no mechanism by which to educate clients; therefore, systems developers practiced their trade in a clandestine fashion. Developers were analyzing, designing, and developing while clients waited anxiously for the system.

Although the number of technological advances increased rapidly, some of the foremost development experts of the late 1960s and 1970s began efforts to assist systems developers in meeting client needs. This was the advent of structured tools and techniques. It was met with much opposition because of its threat to the creative qualities of systems development. Although developers who subscribed to the structured methods felt they were working smarter (i.e., focusing their efforts on the right areas), thousands of lines of spaghetti code continued to be written, and maintenance was an increasingly difficult problem. As the demands on the industry continued to increase, developers had little time to devote to adequately gather requirements and document systems. Although a better job was being done, the ramifications of working under the pressure posed by these legacy systems continued to be felt. These systems were under scrutiny, soon to be replaced because of their inability to adapt to change.

During the 1980s, *software engineering* became the phrase of choice to describe the formalization of the systems development process. What was previously considered an art was beginning to resemble a science. The process was being defined so that it became possible to repeat the procedure. Some developers, however, would not submit to this highly structured format, feeling it would reduce their creative pursuits to a mere set of processes and deliverables.

As much as this was considered a great advance for the systems development process, there continues to be much to be discerned. There are possibly as many approaches to the structuring of systems development as there are groups opposing structured techniques. Some of the resistance is caused by the fact that though a process has been defined, the goal of delivering systems on time, within budget, and according to client requirements has not yet been achieved. Clients expectations keep growing, allowing the developer little time to assess what is or is not effective and what would be more effective. It would probably benefit both clients and developers if time would stand still while the science was allowed to mature.

IMPROVING PAST DEVELOPMENT PROBLEMS

The information age has brought a dramatic increase in the challenges information providers must face. In this era of takeovers and buyouts, information yields power, and its users must contain this power to survive in the corporate environment. The increased dependence on information providers only heightens expectations about developers of information systems. Information systems are progressively being regarded as an asset to the business rather than an expense to be reckoned with. This increased dependence on information systems to keep a business successful is reflected in the greater value being placed on existing code.

One of the most important tasks information providers must face is assessing existing systems with regard to their longevity and adaptability to meet the increased demands. As an asset, legacy systems must be able to endure, grow, and change. Replacement of many of these systems is an enormous expense that the industry currently must bear. Organizations will not absorb those costs in the future. New systems must meet the future directly and evolve as demands dictate. There is little room for numerous defects in installed systems or systems that meet only current expectations. These expectations are reflected in demands for complex interfaces, global availability, and state-of-the-art technological capabilities. The provision of information is only the beginning — a vast array of sophisticated requirements are being placed on future information systems. The IS department must not only meet these demands but deliver systems on time that meet requirements and are affordable and maintainable.

To meet these challenges, systems developers should look to successful industries outside the information processing arena. For example, it is obvious that the critical success factor of process-specified industries (e.g., manufacturing) is their pursuit of quality. Quality is not only the natural evolutionary step that should be taken but the appropriate business strategy to face the future in information engineering.

ASPECTS OF QUALITY

Quality involves doing the right things in the right way. During the last decade, myriad tools for doing things the right way were developed; quality provides the formula for doing the right things. Doing things the right way is the role of quality control (i.e., reviewing how well the output meets established standards), whereas doing the right things is the role of quality assurance (i.e., continually improving the process).

A partnership must be formed between the client and the system provider whereby the right requirements are incorporated to produce the right system. Clients no longer entirely depend on the IS department as they often did in the past. The IS department is also not fraught with ever-changing expectations and demands. Each partner has responsibility to the other to ensure that a proper balance of requirements is achieved and that these requirements are mutually agreed on. All parties share the burden, and all parties benefit from the success of the endeavor.

Two important perspectives on quality that are most useful to IS development are quality in fact and quality in perception. It is important that both perspectives are included in the creation of the context the organization will be working within as it pursues the goal of quality; neither should be sacrificed for the other, because each is important in achieving total product quality. Quality in fact ensures that a system is fit for use and conforms to development standards. It is represented by system attributes required by the systems developers and constitutes a measure of system productivity. Some examples of systems attributes from the software developer's perspective are readability, reusability, structure, understandability, and evolvability.

Quality in perception is the set of characteristics that demonstrate value to the client. These factors measure how well the system meets user expectations. Some system attributes from the client's perspective are function, ease of use, correctness, compatibility, security, efficiency, and accuracy. Some of these characteristics overlap both the provider and the user requirements lists. Some examples of these characteristics are ease of learning, maintainability, portability, reliability, supportability, and testability. A delicate balance exists between the two sets of attributes. This balance must be achieved, however, on each systems development project.

The Cost of Quality

Information systems are expensive enough to develop and maintain without the added cost of quality. The point being missed, however, is that the cost of quality — the cost of developing a system right — is always a part of the system cost. The cost is incurred one way or another; it is merely a question of when. The most expensive time to absorb the cost of quality by reworking a system is after installation. Rewriting and retrofitting existing code has been the bane of maintenance programmer for a long time. In addition, such costs support arguments in favor of replacing systems rather than reengineering and renovating existing systems.

To reduce the cost of quality, formalized inspection and review procedures have been introduced into the systems development life cycle. There is substantial documented evidence that the earlier and more consistently these reviews occur, the more cost-effective the effort.[1] Not only is it less expensive to correct errors before system installation (where they become defects), but maintenance problems are substantially reduced.

The most effective method, however, is first-time quality — doing the right things in the right way. This is achieved by continuously improving the process and is reflected in the product. It is not enough to continually rework the product before it is released (i.e., quality control). Rather, a method is needed to ensure that the process produces the incremental pieces that satisfy the standard (i.e., quality assurance). A quality initiative encourages continued quality control while evolving the systems development methodology to include optimal quality through process improvement.

Many in the development industry fail to realize the predicament that poor tracking of the cost of quality has caused for systems development. This makes it difficult to substantiate a business case for pursuing a quality initiative. Organizations often fail to take preventive action unless they are in a financial crisis. Waiting might be unwise: there may be no time for recovery. For this reason, it seems inappropriate for organizations to stand by and let the competition overtake them.

A quality initiative requires a substantial up-front investment with additional increments during the life of the organization. This, however, is a worthwhile investment; the lack of such an investment results in lost opportunities, and the challenges will be met by those who have willingly invested in their future.

Quality and Productivity. If productivity is the goal of an organization, there is no guarantee that quality will result. When pursuing productivity, the organization often loses the quality that it expected would accompany productivity. Inevitably, however, when quality is the goal, productivity will not be far behind. Process improvement and financial results do not happen instantaneously; it takes time and effort to implement such a program. Over time, however, there will be noticeable improvements in client and employee satisfaction and eventually in the bottom line.

THE QUALITY INITIATIVE

A quality initiative comprises the first steps or actions toward implementing a program whose goal is continuous process improvement. These first steps establish the foundation and framework for a substantial change in the way an organization does business. In most cases, the initiative requires a cultural change in how clients, employees, and service or material suppliers are viewed within the context of the organization. It focuses on how the product is created rather than on the product itself. The product becomes the measure of success or failure. Systems professionals must not only develop information systems (i.e., the product) but also continually analyze how that product is developed to meet the challenges of the future.

Although a quality initiative in the IS industry typically models the quality principles outside information engineering (e.g., those in the manufacturing industry), these principles must be evaluated and molded to fit within the systems development environment. One such rule, which must be redefined, is zero defects. As developers seek to achieve a unique balance between value and productivity, it is unrealistic to require that a system be delivered defect free. In many instances, such a constraint does not allow other, higher-priority requirements to be achieved. Therefore, the real challenge is to continuously improve on how the ideal balance of requirements is achieved rather than on delivering information systems that are improved or reviewed to the point of zero defects.

Implementation of a quality initiative program has had far-reaching success in the process industries. There is certainly a place and a demand for a quality initiative in information engineering. In fact, as challenges increase and gain momentum, the need for this initiative will become increasingly evident. If an organization treats systems development as an art, however, it will be virtually impossible to adopt a quality initiative. The organization must accept systems development as a scientific endeavor, and that transition is what will enable the pursuit of quality.

THE EFFECT OF QUALITY ON METHODOLOGY

Continuous process improvement assumes that the process is already in place but must be improved. Any organization with quality as its goal must have as a fundamental requirement a structured methodology. It is not inconceivable that a methodology can be implemented as part of a quality initiative, but there is substantial risk to both when trying to do too much too fast. Each program — the quality initiative and the implementation of a structured methodology — in and of itself requires an enormous commitment and cultural change. In a sense, by introducing both simultaneously, a developer could exponentially increase the probability that either or both programs will fail.

Once an organization decides to use a methodology, it has already made a substantial commitment to producing quality systems. The methodology is a critical success factor to the quality initiative because it is within the framework of the methodology that the principles of quality can be readily integrated. The following sections briefly analyze how quality affects the basic components — the roles, processes, deliverables, tools and techniques, and project management — of an information engineering methodology.

Roles

Traditionally, roles uniquely identify who is responsible for the work effort during the information engineering life cycle. The roles identify the skills necessary to perform the prescribed activities, and the skills provide a baseline expectation against which the project director assesses available resources and determines training needs when skills are lacking.

When quality is the goal, there must be an enhanced focus on the role of the client. The client must play an integral part in defining and setting priorities for requirements and ensuring that the system requirements support the business objectives. The project team and the client must form a partnership of shared responsibility for the system under development. The task of defining system requirements cannot be left to the programmers. In addition, the project team must be able to trace the planned system requirements back so that they support the business objectives outlined by the user.

Within the project team, a more profound emphasis must be placed on teamwork and supporting efforts. Each member of the team must be seen as both a client and a supplier at each incremental step of the process during the work activities. Team members must be empowered to improve the systems development process — that is, they must be given the responsibility and authority to ensure that the right things are done the right way.

Typically, the methodology will identify individuals from both the project team and the client organization who are responsible for quality control (i.e., testing, inspections, and reviews). The quality initiative will identify individuals who will be in the quality assurance roles. The success of either the quality program or the methodology, however, is not the responsibility of the coordinators of each. These individuals are merely facilitators. Success is the responsibility of everyone in the organization — executives, middle managers, and staff.

Processes

Traditionally, a structured methodology delineates the processes to be followed in the development of a system. Typically, the information engineer iterates through analysis, design, construction, testing, and installation. This repeatable procedure provides consistency and understanding of the sequential steps to be followed to avoid omissions. When it is in place and effective, the procedure truly models an engineering endeavor.

A quality initiative forces the systems developer to evaluate the effectiveness of the processes (i.e., doing the right things). The processes are the focal point of quality assurance. Policies must be incorporated to define what elements are expected to achieve success, and procedures on how to achieve that success must be specified.

Deliverables

Traditionally, deliverables are the products developed during the information engineering life cycle to be reviewed by the client. The deliverables are documents that present a business case for proceeding to the next phase of the project or halting the effort until a better case can be developed. Generally, the supporting documentation for the business case consists of requirements specifications, design specifications, and code. Depending on the particular information engineering methodology in place, the deliverables will be broken down to finer levels of detail; the more specifically it is defined, the easier it will be to track and measure the completeness of each deliverable. The deliverables are an appropriate point at which to assess the work to date.

The greatest impact a quality initiative can have on the deliverables is that it forces developers and users to place them in proper perspective. Deliverables are a means of evaluation, not an end in themselves. When the product is more important than the process, the product is continuously reworked until it is right, which obscures the possibility that the process itself may be defective. Deliverables are vehicles by which developers can measure the success of the process. The product is important, but only in conjunction with the process by which it was produced. Clear, concise standards must be established for the evaluation of the process — the evaluation criteria must be understood and functional.

The development of standards and metrics should be the joint responsibility of all team members, including the client, so that consensus is achieved by all involved. If all team members do not participate in the determination of the measures to be used, the measurements will be meaningless.

Tools and Techniques

A methodology typically recommends particular tools and techniques to facilitate the performance of the activities defined by the process. Dozens of automated and manual tools and techniques are available. It is not so important that the right tool be chosen but that whatever set of tools and techniques is chosen is used consistently by all project participants. Traditionally, the tools and techniques outlined in standard methodologies are more project specific, aiding in the creation of the work products.

Because quality emphasizes people and process, it is appropriate to embellish the list of techniques to include those that develop the people and procedures that will ultimately improve the process. People-enrichment training should include effective team building, information gathering, and communication skills development. Procedures for process improvement should include process assessment mechanisms and configuration management.

Project Management

Central to the success of any project is the management of both the people and the project. The skills necessary to succeed in this area include leadership, facilitation, mediation, organization, planning, scheduling, tracking, and estimating.

The project director can seriously affect the success of the methodology's implementation and the quality initiative. Without the project director's relentless efforts to encourage proper use, the methodology might be neglected. Similarly, the first line of support for the quality initiative must come from project leaders. The encouragement to approach change positively and the realization that there is a learning period to be overcome when a change is implemented must all originate with management.

Quality requires a broader leadership perspective on the development of systems. All management in the organization must foster principles of the quality initiative as a way of conducting business. In particular, teamwork, partnering (i.e., shared responsibility and expectations), and empowerment of the people cannot exist in a climate that promotes the status quo. The culture of the organization must move from a rigid, traditional environment toward a more flexible, evolving one.

THE QUALITY FUNCTION

Another critical success factor for the quality initiative is the quality function. This consists of a group of individuals responsible for the orchestration, facilitation, and nurturing of quality principles throughout the organization. The quality function is instrumental in providing information and a forum for all members of the organization to participate in the initiative. The individuals chosen for this group must have the skills necessary to succeed in this capacity.

Those responsible for the quality function as a whole must:

- Be visionaries with the ability to determine the future direction of the organization and what the limitations are.
- Be knowledgeable about quality principles so that a framework specifying how to reach the future direction is defined.
- Facilitate the goal of quality.

In addition, these individuals must be given the authority to make and implement decisions without organizational politics and bureaucracy to impede their progress. They should be chosen for their evaluation expertise and effectiveness in fulfilling the role.

The quality function works with a quality council — representatives from the various departments or components of the organizations, including the quality control component (when it is distinct from quality assurance). This group makes decisions and disseminates council-related information to the remainder of the organization. Council members should be chosen for possessing many of the same qualities as the quality function.

A quality initiative will positively influence both how information systems are developed and who participates in their development. The next section defines how the quality initiative is implemented in the organization.

IMPLEMENTING A QUALITY INITIATIVE PROGRAM

Implementation of a quality initiative can be divided into a series of activities or milestones. Each milestone is dynamic and will be iterated as the process moves on. Each activity is described briefly in the following paragraphs.

Conducting an Assessment

It is important to establish a benchmark to determine how the organization ranks in terms of its implementation of structured methodologies, CASE tools, and quality programs. The areas that the assessment should focus on for each of these elements is described in the following paragraphs. This assessment should involve management, systems developers, and users. all perspectives are necessary to make an accurate, complete evaluation of the state of the organization.

Structured Methodology. In assessing the methodology, the following areas should be reviewed:

- The length of time established.
- The extent of use in terms of projects and people.
- Training available in the principles and finer details of the methodology.
- Improvement in user satisfaction.
- The level of improvement in project management.

- The degree to which the methodology can be customized to meet organizational requirements and individual project types.

This analysis should uncover the strengths and weaknesses in the methodology so that appropriate recommendations can be formulated to ensure that this critical success factor operates optimally.

CASE Tools. CASE tools, though not required, have proved beneficial to projects and to the success of the methodology. The assessment of the CASE tools should focus on:

- The tool's maturity.
- The variety of tools used and their integration quotient (i.e., measure of how well they work together and support the methodology).
- The extent of use.
- Available training on the use of the tools for project team members and clients.
- Documentation of increased productivity.

Successful implementation of CASE tools is another critical success factor of the quality initiative; ineffective use has a negative impact on both the methodology and quality.

Quality Programs. Many organizations either have quality programs in place or have tried to implement one but failed. If a quality program failed in the past, the organization should evaluate why the failure occurred to avoid the same pitfalls when introducing a new quality program. It is important to gauge the extent to which a current quality program is implemented. In many organizations, quality implies quality control exclusive of quality assurance. These quality programs may focus more on project activities than on organizationwide participation. Quality control programs are valuable to the quality initiative and must be integrated with the proposed enterprisewide quality program.

Establishing the Quality Function

To facilitate the implementation of the quality initiative, it is important that quality function members be identified early. They will need training and time to establish themselves in their new positions. Procedures for determining which tasks will be performed must be established, responsibilities defined, and the breadth of each member's authority affirmed.

Training the Staff

People must be educated regarding the principles of quality, their expectations for it, and the cultural impact the quality program will have on them. Formalized training sessions must be created and scheduled for the entire organization. This is typically an internal activity conducted through the organization. As an ongoing activity, the quality function is responsible for reviewing all internal training in quality concepts, skill enhancement, and personal development. Training is also a critical success factor for achieving quality. It is the vehicle through which people receive the message that they are vital to an organization. Perpetual training strengthens an individual's value to the organization. This is one of the most visible signs of continuing commitment to the quality process.

Influencing the Corporate Climate

Quality is a major investment and an important step for an organization. Therefore, it is important that the announcement of the quality initiative be bold and articulate. The message is best delivered consistently and continually, and organizations should let actions communicate the message. This can be accomplished through the following elements:

- Encouragement by management.
- Commitment of resources for training.
- Inclusion of clients.
- Emphasis on process rather than product.
- Expectations of incremental improvements rather than fast results.
- Rewards for both effort and success.

Creating Policies, Standards, and Procedures

A mission treatment that is not complex or contrived but simple and concise must be formulated. The executive management of the organization is responsible for creating the statement. The policies to support the mission statement are then written. These policies define how the organization intends to conduct business as well as the direction of the business. The establishment of standards or metrics will provide the measure of success or failure in complying with the policies. Finally, procedures are defined to describe in detail how the standards are to be met. All layers of the organization participate in these activities: senior managers provide the vision, middle managers establish the policies, and the systems developers create the standards and procedures.

Instilling Quality Control

Quality control measures a product against a standard; it is the measure of compliance. This is the responsibility of middle, or line, managers, not the quality function. Each phase of the life cycle should have associated quality control activities that are implemented during the phase. Control efforts consist of reviews, inspections, walkthroughs, and testing. These activities should indicate how effectively the procedures meet the standards.

Gathering Baseline Information

In order to instill control, measurements must be in place. The focus should be on two measures — one that measures the product and one that measures quality. Employees themselves should never be measured. Product measures include function points, lines of code, cost to produce, and documentation. Quality measures include number of defects, amount of rework, and attributes or characteristics (i.e., the changeable elements) of the product. Measures must be reliable (i.e., have repeatable results) and valid (i.e., measure what was intended). Many sources of measurement information are captured in the operation of the organization. The following fundamental guidelines must be met:

- The objective of the measurement should be clear.
- The measure should be acceptable (i.e., those who perform the measuring should determine what the measure is).
- Those who perform the measuring should be educated.
- The measure should be implemented, and the results should affect the process through change.

Implementation and Maintenance Issues

The program consists of reporting, recording, and assessing the measurements to identify the defect-prone products and processes. Management must then effect change in the process, taking the necessary actions to improve the process. People must work in an environment in which they can be effective. The cause of the problem must be uncovered to effectively change the way in which work is done. The program thrives in an atmosphere that fosters participation and a sense of worth. People realize they are an integral part of an organization when tools are available to improve the skills needed to perform a job, when people are given authority to determine how a job is to be performed, and when employees are provided with continuing feedback on performance.

Millions of lines of code currently exist, and this number continues to increase exponentially. The issues discussed thus far in this chapter have been concerned with improving the systems development process. It is also important to address the issue of maintenance because as much as 75 percent of the IS budget is spent on maintaining existing systems. These systems are a valuable asset to the organization. The cost to replace the thousands of lines of source code is astronomical, and the time it takes to do so is enormous. With this in mind, it is extremely critical to establish a system improvement program within an organization. The purpose of this program is to continuously improve existing systems, retrofitting systems to meet current standards and thereby extending their lives. Replacement may not be feasible or necessary in many cases if plans are established to reengineer and renovate systems to meet future challenges.

Management Issues

A quality initiative requires continuous attention to diminish the probability of its loss of momentum. Numerous impediments and obstacles exist, which must be overcome when implementing a quality initiative. Some of the common hurdles to be surmounted are:

- Lack of ongoing commitment by management.
- Lack of education or training.
- Absence of a quality function.
- Dependence on mass inspection.
- Awarding business on the basis of price alone.
- Not conducting continuous searches for problems.
- Lack of authority.
- Lack of communication.
- Lack of incentives.
- Spending excessive time in the comfort zone (i.e., in the areas people are very familiar with).
- Promotion of productivity rather than quality.
- Lack of pride in quality of work.
- Absence of mission and constancy of purpose.

Organizations must be aware of the barriers to success and strategically plan for their avoidance and dissolution should they appear.

RECOMMENDED COURSE OF ACTION

Systems developers who fail to position themselves to meet the challenges of the future cannot maintain their competitive edge. With an effective strategic plan, success is not a given but it is achievable. The effective strategic plan should be geared toward quality — the pursuit of doing the right things in the right way through continuous process improvement.

The strategic plan should start with a strong plan for implementing a structured methodology. With this foundation, the systems development department can take the first step toward achieving quality by incrementally instituting the steps of a quality initiative. First, the tone must be set — people must be chosen as standards bearers of the initiative, and all members of the organization must be trained in quality. As the momentum increases, so does the commitment to quality. This commitment is reflected through formalized procedures, policies, and standards; process improvement plans are established, and system improvement plans are eventually implemented. As the plan progresses, it incrementally changes the way systems are engineered as well as the cultural climate of the organization.

Successful implementation of quality in the IS department requires that the organization develop a positive attitude toward change. The following components will help systems development managers attain the proper mind-set to accept change with eagerness and enthusiasm:

- *Recognizing and relying on the integrity, abilities, and knowledge of employees.* People will go to great lengths to meet and exceed expectations when approached with honesty and sincerity. When support and commitment are continuously demonstrated, people will respond openly and enthusiastically with ideas and show commitment to the process.
- *Preparing to promote and support long-term training for all involved.* This provides a solid foundation for the organization as well as enhances an employee's personal competitiveness. People who feel worthwhile and valuable to the organization form a bond that is difficult to break when other job opportunities present themselves.
- *Keeping everyone informed.* Being open with the organization's operational and financial details invites engagement, commitment, and participation by the organization's most valuable asset — its people. If they are kept informed, people will pull together and maximize their contribution to make the business successful financially and functionally.
- *Involving users.* They are a source of influence and a vast resource of information. A user's presence and participation will both enhance and further the systems development process.
- *Encouraging even the slightest improvement in the process.* Everything is relative, and what appears small or insignificant to one person can be important and differentiating to another. The big breakthroughs do not usually result in success. It is the incremental steps that chip away at the barriers to success.
- *Allowing for setbacks.* Change never guarantees success; it only provides a vehicle for achieving it. If organizations discourage employees from making attempts by recognizing them only if success follows, these attempts will diminish and enthusiasm will be squelched.
- *Realizing that change must become a way of life.* Change is a critical success factor of growth and keeping an organization competitive. To manage that which has not yet occurred, businesses must be ready to adapt and evolve.

The future should not be left to chance but should be the result of choice. The challenges of the next decade present a vast array of opportunities. Those opportunities can be realized by IS departments committed to consistently delivering quality systems. A quality initiative is the first step toward this goal.

Quality is an ongoing, evolving activity that becomes part of an organization's culture and way of conducting business. It requires everyone in the organization to commit to placing quality above all else. It cannot be pursued haphazardly; a constant infusion of energy and support must surround its undertaking.

Note

1. B.W. Boehm, *Software Engineering Economcis* (Englewood Cliffs NJ: Prentice-Hall, 1981).

Chapter 40
Assessing and Improving the Software Development Process

Roger S. Pressman

The best way for software development managers to plan for the cultural changes that accompany the introduction of software engineering and CASE is to first conduct a process assessment. Such an assessment enables both managers and technical staff to better understand their software development strengths and weaknesses and to create a strategy to serve as a road map for technology transition.

Process assessment is the first step in a cycle that spans many technology transition activities. A commonsense technology transition strategy proceeds through a series of steps that enable an organization to integrate software engineering and CASE effectively. These steps form a software engineering transition cycle that includes the following.

Process Assessment. Before an organization can deal with the nuts and bolts of technology transition, it must take a close look at current software development practices. Process assessment refers to both qualitative and quantitative information gathering that enables an organization to determine the maturity with which it develops software. To do this, a series of questions must be asked, answered, and correctly interpreted.

Education. Most software development managers know relatively little about software engineering. To change this, an organization must develop an effective education strategy that is tied to the results of the process assessment and coordinates training content and timing with immediate project needs so that maximum benefits can be attained.

Selection of Procedures, Methods, and CASE Tools. Selection encompasses three activities: defining specific goals and criteria for selection of software engineering procedures, methods, and CASE tools; understanding the technology components that are available; and developing a rational mechanism for choosing, costing, justifying, and acquiring these important elements of software engineering technology. The results of the process assessment guide an organization in each of these activities.

Justification. Today's industry climate demands that all large-scale expenditures be justified quantitatively. Expenditures for software engineering procedures, methods, education, CASE tools, and associated support activities must show a return on investment before money is committed. Quantitative data collected during process assessment is a first step in the creation of a justification model that demonstrates the bottom-line benefits of new technology.

Installation. To install software engineering technologies successfully, a transition plan must be devised. The plan defines tasks, responsibilities, milestones, and deliverables and specifies a schedule for getting the work done. It identifies activities to demonstrate progress to management in a short period of time as well as long-term tasks that lead to lasting improvements in the way software is built. The findings and recommendations derived from the process assessment are key elements in the creation of a transition plan.

Evaluation. Even when a transition plan is devised and managers select and install the technology, some of them abandon their efforts and do not spend nearly enough time evaluating whether or not the technology is working. The evaluation step acts as an ongoing assessment of the software engineering installation process and answers the question, Is the technology working effectively?

These six steps define a transition strategy, and they all depend on a successful process assessment.

THE PROCESS ASSESSMENT

Managers and technical staff in most companies are all too anxious to make technical decisions — that is, to select new tools and then proceed quickly toward modern software engineering practice. The problem is that many of these same managers and technical personnel have a poor understanding of the procedures, methods, and CASE tools currently being applied within their organizations.

The term *process assessment* refers to the gathering of both qualitative and quantitative information. When process assessment is properly conducted, it satisfies the following objectives.

- Providing a framework for an objective examination of an organization's software development practices.
- Indicating technical and management strengths and weaknesses in a way that allows for comparison to industry norms.
- Establishing an indication of the relative maturity of the software development process in an organization.
- Leading to a strategy for process improvement, and indirectly, to the improvement of software quality.

To accomplish these objectives, the process assessment approach should be designed in a way that probes each of the following process attributes:

- Organizational policies that guide the use of software engineering practices.
- Training that supports the use of procedures, methods, and tools.
- The framework (i.e., a procedural model) that has been established to define a software engineering process.
- Quality assurance activities for software.
- Project management tasks that plan, control, and monitor software work.
- Software engineering methods that enable technical staff to build high-quality applications.
- CASE tools that support the methods.
- Software metrics and measurement that provide insight into the process and its product.

To probe each of these process attributes, a set of assessment questions must be asked and answered. By interpreting the answers correctly, a software development organization takes the first step toward improving its development practice.

Assessment Questions

Assessment questions enable an assessor to gather enough information to gain an understanding of the software development organization, the application of technology within it, and the relative sophistication of the project management framework for applying the technology. The assessor can be an outside consultant or staff members drawn from the organization currently undergoing the assessment.

An effective software engineering process assessment approach makes use of three types of questions: qualitative, Boolean, and quantitative. Answers to qualitative questions demand a narrative response, Boolean questions elicit a yes or no response, and quantitative questions result in a numerical response.

Qualitative Questions. Questions in this category focus on elements of software engineering practice that require a narrative explanation:

- Describe the manner in which project teams are formed. Is functional or matrix organization more common?
- Who is the customer for software within the organization?
- Describe the relationship between the customer and the people who develop software by answering the following:
  - Who initially specifies products with software content?
  - What is the customer's level of understanding of software development practices?
  - What communication problems are there between the customer and the software development organization?

Describe the role of the quality assurance, manufacturing, and service organizations with regard to software. Describe individual software development tools — available as operating system features and as stand-alone functions — used during software development.

Boolean Questions. Questions in this category elicit a yes or no response; that is, Boolean questions are used to determine whether a specific organizational policy, training approach, procedural model, quality assurance activity, project management approach, method, CASE tool, or metrics and measurement technique is present within the context of current practice. Typical questions used to assess design, programming and coding, and testing techniques include:

- Is a specific method for data design used? Is a specific method for architectural design used?
- Is procedural design constrained to the use of the structured programming constructs?
- Is a method for user interface design defined?
- Is more than 90 percent of code written in a high-order language?
- Are specific conventions for code documentation defined and used?
- Are specific methods for test-case design used?
- Are tests planned before code is written?
- Does a written test procedure define all test cases and the logistics required to execute them?
- Are the results of testing stored for historical reference?

- Is a mechanism used for routinely performing regression testing? Is a method used to determine the adequacy of regression testing?
- Is a mechanism used to ensure that testing covers all software requirements?

Quantitative Questions. Questions in this category enable an organization to obtain numerical information that can be used in conjunction with software metrics to compute costs and potential payback for new technology. The following questions are representative:

- What is the annual revenue per development organization component?
- What is the annual budget for data processing or IS?
- What is the annual budget for engineering and product-oriented software development?
- What is the annual budget for software-related training? The types of training conducted should be described.
- What is the annual budget for computer hardware? The annual budget for software tools? Hardware and software should be differentiated.
- What is the number of systems and software practitioners in all application areas?
- What is the number of IS personnel by job category?
- What is the number of software people working on engineered products and systems?
- What is the current number of outside contractors working on software in-house?
- What percentage of software personnel are working on maintenance activities?
- What is the projected growth for or reduction in these items?

The questions listed are usually presented in an assessment questionnaire. Although the size and format of assessment questionnaires vary greatly, most are organized in a way that examines specific process attributes (e.g., Software Quality Assurance or CASE tool use). Most questionnaires suggest a grading scheme for responses so that relative strengths and weaknesses can be ascertained. And most also address both management and technical topics. The structure of the questionnaire, the types of questions asked, the grading scheme proposed, and the usefulness of the results are based on the overall process assessment model.

PROCESS ASSESSMENT MODELS

A process assessment model defines the overall structure and logistics of the process assessment, the organization and application of assessment questions, the process attributes that are considered during the assessment, and the manner in which process maturity is determined. During the past few years, several assessment models have been developed and can be categorized in the following ways:

- Models developed by large companies and originally intended for internal use (e.g., Hewlett-Packard's Software Quality and Productivity Analysis [SQPA] and Bell Canada's Software Development Capability Assessment Method).
- Models developed as an adjunct to consulting services (e.g., models developed by R.S. Pressman & Associates, Inc., Rubin Associates, and Software Productivity Research, Inc.).
- Models developed by government and industry consortiums. The Software Engineering Institute (SEI) Capability Maturity Model is the most well-known of these.
- Models packaged as do-it-yourself products for use by any software development organization (e.g., Process Advisor by R.S. Pressman & Associates, Inc.).

In addition to these models, the International Standards Organization (ISO) is currently at work on a standard for software engineering process assessment. At present, no assessment model meets all the proposed requirements for the International Standards Organization assessment standard. However, there are two representative assessment models that organizations should consider reviewing.

The SEI Assessment Model

The SEI has developed a comprehensive assessment model that is predicated on a proposed set of software engineering capabilities that should be present as organizations reach different levels of process maturity. To determine an organization's current state of process maturity, the SEI uses an assessment questionnaire and a five-point grading scheme. The grading scheme provides a measure of the global effectiveness of a company's software engineering practices and establishes five process maturity levels.

Level 1: Initial. The software process is characterized as ad hoc and occasionally even chaotic. Few processes are defined, and success depends on individual effort.

Level 2: Repeatable. Basic project management processes are established to track cost, schedule, and functional capability. The necessary process discipline is in place to repeat earlier successes on projects with similar applications.

Level 3: Defined. The software process for both management and engineering activities is documented, standardized, and integrated into a corporatewide software process. All projects use a documented and approved version of the organization's process for developing and maintaining software. This level includes all characteristics defined for level 2.

Level 4: Managed. Detailed measures of the software process and product quality are collected. Both the software process and products are quantitatively understood and controlled using detailed measures. This level includes all characteristics defined for level 3.

Level 5: Optimizing. Continuous process improvement is enabled by quantitative feedback from the process and from testing innovative ideas and technologies. This level includes all characteristics defined for level 4.

Key Process Areas

The SEI has associated key process areas (KPAs) with each of the maturity levels. The KPAs describe those software engineering functions (e.g., software project planning, requirements management) that must be present to satisfy sufficient practice at a particular level. Each KPA is described by identifying the following characteristics:

- *Goals.* The overall objectives that the KPA must achieve.
- *Commitments.* The requirements imposed on the organization that must be met to achieve the goals.
- *Abilities.* Those qualities that must be in place both organizationally and technically to enable the organization to meet the commitments.
- *Activities.* The specific tasks required to achieve the KPA function.
- *Methods for monitoring implementation.* The manner in which the activities are monitored as they are put into place.
- *Methods for verifying implementation.* The manner in which proper practice for the KPA can be verified.

Eighteen KPAs are defined across the maturity model and are mapped into different levels of process maturity. Each of the KPAs is defined by a set of key practices that contribute to satisfying its goals. The key practices are policies, procedures, and activities that must occur before a KPA has been fully instituted. Key indicators are "those key practices or components of key practices that offer the greatest insight into whether the goals of a KPA have been achieved."[1] Assessment questions are designed to probe for the existence of a key indicator.

Drawbacks of the SEI Model

The SEI approach represents a significant achievement in process assessment, but it suffers from several minor drawbacks:

- Although detailed analysis of the assessment questionnaire can lead to an assessment of the efficacy of KPAs and related key practices, the maturity level alone tells little about individual KPAs.

- The manner in which the process maturity level is computed currently uses an ordering that causes a low grade if specific questions are answered negatively, even if other questions that represent reasonable sophistication are answered with a yes. (SEI is working on a new version of the questionnaire.)
- Some critics argue that the SEI questionnaire tends to under emphasize the importance of technology and over emphasize the importance of policies and standards.

These drawbacks are not as evident if a comprehensive consulting activity occurs in conjunction with the use of the questionnaire. Detailed quantitative and qualitative questions and answers (posed by trained assessors) provide the additional detail and insight that is missing with the SEI questionnaire alone.

The assessment model proposed by the SEI represents the industry's most comprehensive model, and requires broad-based organizational commitment, a five- or six-figure assessment budget, and the presence of accredited assessors to do the work. There are assessment models that enable a detailed examination of software development practice but require a lower level of commitment and a budget that is significantly less than that of the SEI approach.

The Process Advisor Assessment Model

The Process Advisor assessment model has been designed to enable self-directed assessment for those organizations that want to begin software engineering technology transition activities without incurring a substantial initial expense. Unlike the SEI assessment questionnaire, which contains only Boolean questions, the Process Advisor model incorporates qualitative, quantitative, and Boolean questions.

The general nature of Process Advisor qualitative and quantitative assessment questions follows the form discussed earlier. Responses to the qualitative and quantitative questions are assessed using a quasi-expert system built into the model. Each response to the questionnaire is compared to a set of typical responses. The quasi-expert system provides a set of inferences that helps an organization develop findings and recommendations based on the response.

Boolean questions address eight process attributes: organizational policies, training, software development process, quality assurance, project management, software engineering methods, CASE tools, and software metrics and measurement. Responses to the Boolean questionnaire portion of the Process Advisor model generate process attribute grades for each of the eight attributes. These form a process maturity footprint for a software organization.

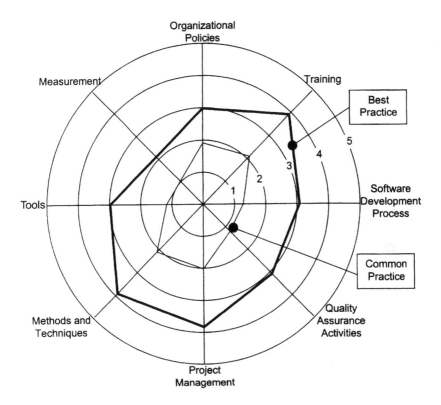

Exhibit 40.1. A Process Attribute Footprint

The process maturity footprint in Exhibit 40.1 provides an indication of relative strengths and weaknesses in the process attribute areas and enables an organization to compare itself to common practice (i.e., the level of software engineering practice commonly found in the industry) and best practice (i.e., the level of software engineering practice found in the top 10 to 15 percent of all software development organizations).

In addition to the assessment model, Process Advisor provides detailed guidance for establishing an education strategy, creating technology selection and justification models, and building an effective transition plan.

PROCESS MATURITY

The vast majority of assessment models enable an organization to compute its process maturity. But how should this number be used?

All too often, a senior manager decides that a specific process maturity level should become an organization's goal. That is, an organization that currently has a process maturity of 1.6 is chartered with becoming a 3.0 organization within 24 months. Although there is nothing inherently wrong with setting process maturity goals, solely focusing on improving the process maturity value misses the point.

The goals of every software development organization should be to improve the quality of the applications that it builds, the satisfaction of its customers and users, and the timeliness with which the work is accomplished. Improving process maturity helps to achieve these goals, but it should not become the goal.

In general, process maturity (and process attribute grades) should be used in the following ways

- To target areas of strength and weakness.
- To raise management's consciousness.
- To define areas in which further investigation (e.g., conducting assessment meetings with relevant staff) may be needed.
- To provide a comparison with industry common and best practices.
- To serve as a baseline for reassessment later in the transition life cycle.

By using process maturity in these ways, an organization can establish a foundation on which the technology transition plan is built.

RECOMMENDED COURSE OF ACTION

Findings and recommendations are derived from the results of the assessment. However, it is sometimes difficult to interpret the assessment results in a manner that leads to pragmatic recommendations for change. To assist in this activity, a solid self-directed assessment approach should provide a set of inference-based guidelines that are tied to different maturity levels for each of the process attributes under assessment. Once the assessment has been completed, the maturity grade for each process attribute (e.g., software development process or quality assurance) is determined. The grade range provides a solid indication of both findings and recommendations.

As an example of inference-based guidelines, consider the following findings and recommendations for the software development process and quality assurance process attributes. (These are taken from the Process Advisor workbook.)

The Software Development Process

Questions in the software development process section of the process assessment questionnaire explore the emphasis on the software engineering process as it is defined for an organization. The questions focus on standards as a way to determine whether an organization has codified its approach. Grades are placed in the context of the following grade ranges:

Grade Range	Identifier
Below 1.65	E
1.65 to 2.25	D
2.26 to 2.75	C
2.76 to 3.25	B
Above 3.25	A

How to interpret the results and what actions are needed to correct any inefficiencies are discussed in the following sections.

Grades E and D. It is unlikely that the organization has developed a written description of its process. In fact, it is unlikely that the organization has defined a process in any explicit manner.

Therefore, the organization should create a skeletal framework for software engineering — that is, a set of activities, deliverables, milestones, and quality assurance actions that can be applied as software is being developed. A description of the framework must be written and comments and recommendations from managers and technical staff should be solicited. Over time, the framework should be reworked and more detail added until it evolves into a standard.

Grades C and B. The organization has codified many of the activities associated with software development. It is likely that the same approach is applied across different projects and that project planning, control, and software quality assurance are easier to achieve as a result. However, just because standards exist does not mean that the process is completely effective or properly characterized.

In this situation, the organization should review each of the standards to determine whether they reflect modern software engineering practice and whether certain aspects can be streamlined or do not work well. The development staff should be asked for its input on the standards and to determine whether the standards are being used as widely as this grade range implies. Specific technical areas without standards can be determined by reviewing responses to individual questions. It may be worthwhile to develop a framework approach for a specific technical area (e.g., testing).

Quality Assurance Activities

Questions in the quality assurance activities section of the process assessment questionnaire explore the organization's emphasis on documentation, reviews, and other quality assurance functions. The grade is placed in the context of the grade ranges listed in the software development process section.

If one or more of the subsection grades is dramatically different than the overall section grade, further investigation into that area is warranted. Here is how to interpret the result for the overall grade for quality assurance activities.

Grades E and D. Software quality and the activities that help to ensure it are not a primary focus within the software development organization. Documentation is weak because there are no standard formats to guide developers. Effective reviews are not being conducted and the results of reviews are not used to improve the process. Software quality assurance is not a formally defined activity.

To address these issues, the organization must develop a plan to improve each of the following three areas: documentation, reviews, and software quality assurance. The place to begin is with documents and reviews. One or two documents should be selected and a standard format developed. Then a set of review guidelines for the documents should also be developed. Over time, these actions should be broadened until most important documents are defined, produced, and reviewed.

Grade C. The organization's approach to predictable documentation, effective reviews, and basic quality assurance activities is coming together. In this case, the organization must review responses to each of the subsections to determine which areas are in need of the most improvement. It is likely that quality assurance functions are still in need of improvement; if this is the case, the focus should be on establishing mechanisms for ensuring compliance with documentation and process standards.

The organization might also look to broaden its review approach, if this can be done in a cost-effective manner. At the same time, the organization should begin to use CASE tools to create effective documentation in a more productive manner.

Grade B. The organization is at the state of practice in the quality assurance (QA) area. It is likely, however, that it is not using quantitative data to analyze the software engineering process.

The organization should consider a fledgling program in statistical QA for software. Data should be collected on defects uncovered through other QA activities. Using the data collected, the systems development managers should work to improve methods to reduce defects and acquire tools that enable it to build quality software more effectively.

Using this inference-based approach, it is possible for software development managers to develop a set of pragmatic findings and recommendations. These results can then be used as a basis for a transition plan — the strategy that the organization needs to improve its transition to software engineering practices.

Note

1. C.V. Weber et al., *Key Practices of the Capability Maturity Model* (Pittsburgh, PA: SEI, 1991).

Chapter 41
Improving Productivity Strategically and Tactically

Stanley H. Stahl

Many software development organizations have embarked upon improvement programs designed to improve product quality or development productivity. Some programs are general, following methodologies like those of the Software Engineering Institute (SEI) or more generic Total Quality Management-based programs. Others are specific, attempting, for example, to institute upper-CASE technology or implement a software metrics program. Unfortunately, failure among both these types of improvement initiatives is common.

Although there are several reasons for failure, one of the main causes is the failure to adhere to the simple principle: "Think strategically — act tactically." All too often, in their zeal to get quick results, managers rush into action without carefully considering the strategic necessities appropriate to their cultural and environmental realties. Less frequently, but nevertheless still common, managers allow themselves to get wound around the strategy-axle, allowing their improvement programs to die from analysis paralysis.

Strategy and Tactics

Successful productivity improvement programs have both a strategic and tactical component. The strategic component, focusing on the big picture, combines a knowledge of the best practices in the industry with a deep awareness of the needs, opportunities, and constraints of the organization. The tactical component, focusing on the details, is used to translate the strategic component into the specific actions necessary for program success.

STARTING THE IMPROVEMENT PROGRAM

At the strategic level, an organization must begin its productivity improvement program by analyzing its business situation, processes, technologies, and culture. In doing this analysis, software developers must consider such strategic questions as:

- How aligned is the development organization to the business needs fo the company?
- How satisfied are users with the products of the development organization? Is product quality satisfactory?
- How satisfied are users with the development organization's time-to-deliver?
- How satisfied is senior managment with the systems development process' cost structure?
- How good are the organization's current development processes?
- How do these compare with those of other development organizations?
- How advanced is the organization's product technology? How does it compare with those of other development organizations?
- How effective is the organzition's training program?
- How is employee morale?

Asessment Progams

Because the answers to these questions form the foundation of all subsequent improvement efforts, it is vitally important that software developers objectively assess their organizaions, with respect to both current practices and best industry practices. The assessment is a thorough examination and not a public relations opportunity. Because of the importance of the initial assessment and the difficulty of getting an accurate analysis, many organizations have found it valuable to have a consultant help with it.

Following the initial assessment, the second strategic step is to identify both the organization's goals and the constraints on achieving these goals. The result of this analysis may be, for example, a conclusion that the organization needs to improve product quality and the primary constraints limiting quality are inadequate review and inspection processes and an inadequate training program. A more extreme example is where the organization needs to improve product quality and delivery time, though it has no defined process, employee morale is low, and the organization is very resistant to change.

Proceding with Caution

The next strategic step is to identify the key leverage points associated with achieving productivity improvement goals. This step requires an understanding of the organization, gathered in the initial assessment, with an understanding of the realities of productivity improductivity improvement. Organizations often err at this stage by attempting to implement a high capability method or tool without the needed infrastructure. Lots of companies, for example, have invested heavily in CASE tools only to see them underutilized. This often occurs because an organization lacked either the process discipline or the training capabilities needed to use the tools properly.

Developing an Action Plan

The final strategic step is to develop an action plan. The action plan acts as the bridge between the strategic and the tactical. Consequently, it must translate the strategic objectives and constraints into a workable plan for productivity improvement. Like any good plan, the productivity improvement action plan needs to lay out what is to be done, when it will be done, who is responsible for doing it, how it is to be tracked, and what resources are available for getting the job done. The plan should have a nominal two-year time-horizon.

Implementing the Program. After the action plan is developed, it must, of course, be implemented. There are several principles that underlie successful implementation of the productivity improvement action plan:

- Implementation improvement activities project by project.
- Providing lots of evaluative feedback for the productivity improvement process.
- Under promising and over delivering.
- Getting and maintaining the support of all stakeholders.
- Proactively managing the change process.
- Paying particular attention to employee morale.

A CASE STUDY

Hewlett-Packard Co. provides a case study of how to simultaneously think strategically and act tactically. The company needed to improve software quality, because it was finding that embedded software was becoming more and more critical to its product line. The next generation LaserJet, for example, has 1,000,000 lines of embedded code, 40 times more embedded software than the first generation LaserJet. More than 70 percent of Hewlett-Packard engineers now work, either part-time or full-time, on software. Software has become the dominant factor responsible for the company's ability to generate more than $20 billion dollars in annual sales.

Improving Productivity of Software Development

Recognizing the importance of software to their ongoing business success, Hewlett-Packard's management instituted several years ago a corporate

465

software initiative program in partnership with its business groups. The objective was to use software to a competitive advantage. The results to date have been positive. One group has reduced its time-to-market from 50 months to 10. Another group has reduced the average time needed to correct a defect from 27 hours to eight. Overall, Hewlett-Packard's management believes that the implementation of inspections has saved $20 million per year and that this amount will grow to $100 million per year as software inspections become standard throughout the company.

Management of Strategy and Tactics

There are several factors that contributed to Hewlett-Packard's success at improving its software development productivity, but an important factor is the company's explicit management of both the strategic and tactical components to process improvement. Exhibit 41.1 shows a flowchart of how Hewlett-Packard identifies and implements productivity improvement through new and revised development processes.

Strategic Component. The company starts its strategy cycle by identifying the productivity improvement efforts that are to be undertaken in support of identified business interests. This point is critical. Unless productivity improvement interests are tightly coupled to the business in-

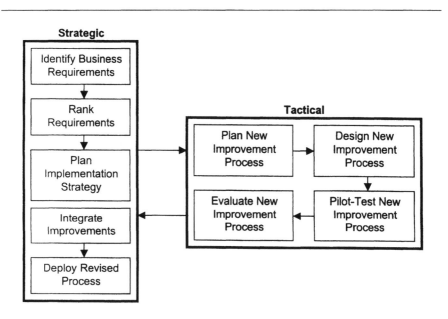

Exhibit 41.1. Flowchart of How Hewlett-Packard Identifies and Implements Productivity Improvement

terests of the organization, they are irrelevant. And if they are irrelevant, it is difficult to generate and maintain the management commitment necessary for sustainable improvement.

Tactical Component. On the tactical side, Hewlett-Packard makes a point of pilot-testing every new process before deploying it throughout the organization. Thus, early feedback on the process is available for the evaluation and fine tuning of the process before its deployment.

THE SEI PROCESS ASSESSMENT MODEL

Hewlett-Packard is not the only organization to have mapped a route to successful productivity improvement. The Software Engineering Institute (SEI) has developed a very detailed program for productivity improvement that focuses on improving the software development process. More than 100 companies in the United States are using the the SEI model to improve their software development processes.

The SEI process improvement model explicitly integrates the strategic with the tactical. It commences with an organization's taking a strtegic assessment of its current process capabilities. The output of the assessment is a set of findings, designed to capture the needs, opportunities, and constraints for process improvement. These findings are then turned into an explicit action plan that forms the bridge between the strategic and the tactical.

The Model's Framework

The foundation for the SEI model is for an organization to get basic management control over the development process. This means working on such areas as project planning, project tracking and control, requirements management, subcontractor and supplier management, quality assurance, and configuration management. After establishing basic management control, an organization is then able to work on establishing an infrastructure for standardizing effective processes for all projects. Improvement activities at this stage include introducing peer reviews, working on improving intergroup coordination, beginning an explicit process focus, and working on the organization's training program. Next, an organization focuses on establishing a quantitative understanding of both its processes and its products. Finally, it uses it quantitative understanding to improve both its processes and products in a continuous and measurable way.

The SEI model uses a set of software engineering capabilities, which are divided into five levels. Organizations are supposed to improve productivity and quality as they progress through the five levels. To determine an organization's current level, the SEI uses an assessment questionnaire and a five-point grading scheme. The grading scheme measures an organization's software development practices according to the five levels.

Level 1: Initial. The software process is characterized as ad hoc and occasionally even chaotic. Few processes are defined, and success depends on individual effort.

Level 2: Repeatable. Basic project management processes are established to track costs, schedules, and functional capabilities. The necessary process discipline is in place to repeat earlier successes on projects with similar applications.

Level 3: Defined. The software process for both management and engineering activities is documented, standardized, and integrated into a corporatewide software process. All projects use a documented and approved version of the organization's process for developing and maintaining software. This level includes all characteristics defined for level 3.

Level 4: Managed. Detailed measures of the software process and product quality are collected. Both the software process and products are quantitatively understood and controlled using detailed measures. This level includes all characteristics defined for level 3.

Level 5: Optimizing. Continuous process improvement is enabled by quantitative feedback from the process and from testing innovative ideas and technologies. This level includes all characteristics defined for level 4.

Strengths and Weaknesses of the Model

One of the most valuable features of the SEI model is that it explicitly identifies a relative time-ordering for implementing process improvement activities. This time-ordering assists a development organization strategically identify the steps it needs to take in improving its software development process capabilities. It is based on the premise that, much like building a skyscraper, it is necessary to build a strong foundation before attempting to build above ground.

A major strength of the SEI approach is that it carefully articulates a strategy model to help an organization develop a software process that is under statistical control. A limitation of the SEI model is that it explicitly focuses only on process improvement. Thus, the model provides little guidance to the organization from the perspectives of business alignment, culture, and technology. A second weakness is that it puts off peer reviews and inspections until the second stage, though these activities are among the highest leverage processes for improving product quality and shortening development time.

CONCLUSION

When senior management is pressed to provide quarterly results to shareholders, the result is, all too often, that the focus of productivity improvement is on adopting the latest and greatest whiz-bang technology. It is very important to avoid this temptation. Productivity improvement is a 26-mile marathon, not a 100-yard dash. The greatest opportunities for sustainable and meaningful productivity improvement occur by focusing on process and culture and by clearly aligning the development organization to business needs. Failure to pay proper attention to the strategic dimensions of process, culture, and business alignment too often consigns a productivity improvement program to failure.

About the Editor

Paul C. Tinnirello is chief information officer of a leading insurance information publishing organization and a consulting editor for Auerbach Publications. He is responsible for the development and support of financial software products in microcomputer and mainframe environments. He holds an M.S. in computer and information sciences, as well as a B.A. in mathematics. Tinnirello has been a graduate and undergraduate adjunct professor at state and local colleges in New Jersey and is a founding member and past director of the Software Management Association, formerly the Software Maintenance Association. He has written and published numerous articles on the development and support process and has presented his material at various computer conferences throughout the country.

Index

Printed and bound by CPI Group (UK) Ltd, Croydon, CR0 4YY

25/10/2024

01779134-0001